The Globalization of Food

D

The Globalization of Food

Edited by David Inglis and Debra Gimlin

BERG

Oxford • New York

1006572587

English edition
First published in 2009 by
Berg
Editorial offices:
First Floor, Angel Court, 81 St Clements Street, Oxford OX4 1AW, UK
175 Fifth Avenue, New York, NY 10010, USA

© David Inglis and Debra Gimlin 2009

Berg is the imprint of Oxford International Publishers Ltd.

Library of Congress Cataloging-in-Publication Data

A catalogue record for this book is available from the Library of Congress.

British Library Cataloguing-in-Publication Data

A catalogue record for this book is available from the British Library.

ISBN 978 1 84520 816 5 (Cloth)
978 1 84520 820 2 (Paper)

Typeset by Apex CoVantage, LLC, Madison, WI, USA
Printed in Great Britain by the MPG Books Group, Bodmin and King's Lynn

www.bergpublishers.com

Contents

Contributors   vii

PART I: GLOBALIZATION AND FOOD: KEY ISSUES

1 Food Globalizations: Ironies and Ambivalences of Food,
       Cuisine and Globality   3
       David Inglis and *Debra Gimlin*

PART II: FOOD GLOBALIZATIONS: PRODUCTION
AND DISTRIBUTION

2 Slow Food and the Politics of 'Virtuous Globalization'   45
       Alison Leitch

3 Standards, Science and Scale: The Case of Tasmanian
       Atlantic Salmon   65
       Marianne Elisabeth Lien

4 Virtue and Valorization: 'Local Food' in the United States
       and France   81
       Michaela DeSoucey and *Isabelle Téchoueyres*

5 Quality Conventions and Governance in the Wine Trade: A Global
       Value Chain Approach   97
       Stefano Ponte

6 Food Systems and the Local Trap   117
       Branden Born and *Mark Purcell*

7 Fairtrade Food: Connecting Producers and Consumers   139
       Caroline Wright

PART III: FOOD GLOBALIZATIONS: PREPARATION
AND CONSUMPTION

8 The National and the Cosmopolitan in Cuisine: Constructing
America through Gourmet Food Writing   161
Josée Johnston, Shyon Baumann and *Kate Cairns*

9 Difference on the Menu: Neophilia, Neophobia and Globalization   185
Richard Wilk

10 Eating Your Way to Global Citizenship   197
Danielle Gallegos

11 Exotic Restaurants and Expatriate Home Cooking: Indian
Food in Manhattan   213
Krishnendu Ray

12 Globalization and the Challenge of Variety: A Comparison
of Eating in Britain and France   227
Alan Warde

13 Hispanic Foodways in the San Luis Valley of Colorado:
The Local, Global, Hybrid and Processed Fourth of July Feast   243
Carole Counihan

14 Globalization and Obesity   255
Jeffery Sobal and *Wm. Alex McIntosh*

15 'Is It Real Food?': Who Benefits from Globalization in Tanzania
and India?   273
Pat Caplan

Index   291

Contributors

Shyon Baumann is assistant professor in sociology at the University of Toronto.

Branden Born is assistant professor of urban design and planning at the University of Washington.

Kate Cairns is a doctoral student in sociology at the University of Toronto.

Pat Caplan is emeritus professor of anthropology at Goldsmiths College, London.

Carole Counihan is professor of anthropology at Millersville University.

Michaela DeSoucey is a doctoral candidate in sociology at Northwestern University.

Danielle Gallegos is senior lecturer in public health at Queensland University of Technology.

Debra Gimlin is senior lecturer in sociology at the University of Aberdeen.

David Inglis is professor of sociology at the University of Aberdeen.

Josée Johnston is assistant professor in sociology at the University of Toronto.

Alison Leitch is lecturer in sociology at Macquarie University.

Marianne Elisabeth Lien is professor of social anthropology at the University of Oslo.

Wm. Alex McIntosh is professor of sociology at Texas A&M University.

Stefano Ponte is a senior researcher at the Danish Institute for International Studies.

Mark Purcell is associate professor in urban design and planning at the University of Washington.

Krishnendu Ray is assistant professor of nutrition and food studies at the Steinhardt School of Culture, Education and Human Development, New York University.

Jeffery Sobal is professor of nutritional sciences at Cornell University.

Isabelle Téchoueyres is a doctoral student in social and cultural anthropology at the Université Bordeaux 2.

Alan Warde is professor of sociology at the University of Manchester.

Richard Wilk is professor of anthropology at Indiana University.

Caroline Wright is an associate professor in sociology at the University of Warwick.

Part I
Globalization and Food: Key Issues

Food Globalizations: Ironies and Ambivalences of Food, Cuisine and Globality

David Inglis and *Debra Gimlin*
University of Aberdeen

Gastronomers of the year 1825, who find satiety in the lap of abundance, and dream of some newly-made dishes ... you will never see the importations which travellers yet unborn will bring to you from that half of the globe which has still to be discovered or explored. How I pity you!

—Brillat-Savarin (1825)

Introduction: Food and Globalization(s)

Food lies at the very heart of human existence. Just as the individual person must eat, so too does any form of social order have to organize the production, distribution and consumption of foodstuffs. Indeed social order makes possible the generation of food, while food makes possible social order (Simmel, 1997). The manifold ways in which food and social order can make and remake each other have led to a hugely diverse array of food-related practices throughout human history, from the localized foraging of the hunter-gatherer to the Epicureanism of the courtly aristocrat. But what happens when social order becomes globalized, that is to say, stretched and restructured to potentially planet-spanning proportions? As the realm of social order (and disorder) becomes ever more constituted by and through processes that cross political and cultural boundaries, traverse staggering physical (and mental) distances, undermine established ways of doing things and create new forms of thought and practice, how does all of this affect the realm of food, and how, in turn, do food-related processes, dynamics and activities affect globalizing and globalized social order?

These are the questions that this book seeks, to answer. The globalization of human affairs entails many fundamental changes as to how and why food is produced (or not produced), the ways in which it is distributed (or not distributed) and the manners in which it is, variously, prepared, eaten, shared, thought about, imagined, discussed and fought over in different parts of the world in the present day. As Phillips (2006:

38) puts it, 'the time seems ripe for interrogating ideas about food through the lens of globalization, and globalization through the lens of food.' Each of the authors represented here has his or her own distinctive means of focussing on and thinking through the myriad ways in which globalizing forces, phenomena, structures, networks and institutions affect food and foodways in the present day, and how, in turn, the latter can have important ramifications for the former. But a central theme that unites them all—and that the editors wholeheartedly concur with—is a commitment to teasing out the subtleties, nuances, ironies and unintended consequences attendant upon what, for convenience sake, we can refer to under the blanket-term the 'globalization of food'. In fact, given the recurring emphasis by all the authors represented here on the ambivalences, multiplicities and contradictions attendant upon food matters under conditions of advanced globalization and globality, it would perhaps be more appropriate to refer to the *globalizations of food* in the plural. This is because it is increasingly obvious, on the basis of empirical observations of food matters at the present time, that there is no singular, unequivocal globalization process, but rather there exist multifarious globalization processes in the plural, which sometimes work together, and which sometimes are wholly contradictory. Certain forces (especially those of a putatively homogenizing character) in fact often create or encourage others (especially of an apparently heterogenizing character) that stand in stark contradiction to them, or at least so it seems (James, 1994).

Thus in a world where a seemingly homogenizing, and apparently fully 'global', agro-industry generates trends towards self-conscious localizations of food production and consumption, and where the apparently unstoppable (at least, until very recently) global spread of American-style fast food leads to often visceral counterattacks in favour of 'slow food' and regional culinary authenticity, a whole series of dialectical ironies abound. Although we editors did not explicitly ask authors to take this theme as a guiding thread of their analyses, this is nonetheless a focus that comes through time and again in each of the chapters, regardless of the specific foods, places, people and cultures that are the focus of any given case study. The chapters of this book stand as eloquent testaments to what we see as the quintessential fact about contemporary food globalizations, namely that different forces, institutions and actors are related to each other in highly complex and ever-shifting ways, and that constantly changing constellations (of people, plants, animals and objects) and social networks (involving corporations, consumers, government officials, scientists, activists and so on) breed ever more ambivalences, unintended outcomes, contestations and struggles. Food globalizations are multiplicitous, multidimensional and multivalent (Nutzenadel and Trentmann, 2008). One important reason for this is the rise and spread of different forms of often highly reflexive thought and practice, coupled together with modes of action and conceptualization that seek to deal with the complexities produced by forms of reflexivity by attempting to return to cultural essentialisms and apparent forms of culinary authenticity. These issues will be returned to later. Meanwhile, we can say that for contemporary food globalizations, plurality and contradiction are the norm, not the exception. But to say this is not to say that the resulting ongoing complexity cannot be mapped and made sense of: it not only can be, as the chapters here make abundantly clear, but must be, if we—as analysts, as consumers, as activists, as citizens—are to have any chance of changing the current state of affairs, however modestly, for what we might think is the better. But a monolithic and crude analytic framework will be of little use in this regard, whereas means of analysis characterised by sensitivity to nuance, paradox and incongruity can very much aid us in this direction.

Increasing academic attention has been given to food globalizations in recent years (for reviews of the literature see Bonnano et al., 1994; Grew, 1999; Lien and Nerlich, 2004; Mintz and Du Bois, 2002; Phillips, 2006; Sobal, 1999; Watson and Caldwell, 2005), not least because the field has become a site of often great conflict and contestation between agribusiness, political activists and consumers. Indeed, nothing in the present day could be said to be quite as politicized or conflictual as the realm of food (Young, 2004), in stark contrast to the situation even just thirty years ago, when activist groups were smaller in number and less able to affect political agendas, and when consumers were generally more acquiescent than in the present day (Kjaernes et al., 2007). But writings on food matters, and how they relate to 'globalization' (however this is more specifically defined) have very much reproduced the disciplinary specialization (often over-specialisation) that characterizes the contemporary academic division of labour. On the one side, there are economists, political economists and certain kinds of historians who would regard food globalization by analyzing capitalist systems of production and distribution, where power (quite correctly) is seen as increasingly held by large-scale agribusiness, supermarkets and other kinds of corporations, in a globalizing constellation of production and trade that political bodies of both national and international hues seek to regulate and intervene in, with greater or lesser success depending on circumstances (Friedmann, 1994). On the other side are those less concerned with such macro-level economic, political and 'material' matters of production, and more oriented towards understanding the symbolic dimensions of foodstuffs and the micro-level practices of food preparation and consumption. Here anthropologists, qualitative sociologists and cultural and postcolonial studies authors are to be found (see e.g. Mintz and Du Bois, 2002). The general sense of disconnect between these two broad groups of analysts (and this is not to deny important differences *within* each grouping) certainly strikes one quite markedly if one reads through the increasingly abundant literature directly or indirectly engaging with matters of food and globalization (Phillips, 2006: 46), an issue we will return to later.

Defining Globalization and Food

The point we wish to raise here is that if we are both to make intellectual progress in studying food globalizations, and to avoid reproducing saying the same sorts of things over and over again, and to capture what we take to be the quintessential multifariousness of food globalizations in the plural, then we cannot define 'globalization' in any narrow sense, but rather we must try to understand that term in as open-minded and flexible a manner as possible, without it conversely coming to mean everything and nothing. In this regard, it helps to consider that different kinds of analysts define globalization in different ways for varying analytic purposes.

For analysts of the globalizing tendencies and structuring capacities of the contemporary capitalist economy, globalization *is* (or is primarily) the global spread of that economy. The ur-source of such theorizations is of course the work of Marx (Renton, 2001). In a famous passage from *The Communist Manifesto,* we read that

> the bourgeoisie has through its exploitation of the world market given a cosmopolitan character to production and consumption in every country ... In place of the old local and national seclusion and self-sufficiency, we have intercourse in every direction, universal inter-dependence of nations. (Marx and Engels, 1968 [1848]: 55)

Contemporary political economists, world-systems theorists and economic historians have taken their cue from these original insights to produce a range of compelling analyses of the globalization of agribusiness and the exploitative relations between developed and developing worlds fostered, reinforced and taken advantage of by Western-based transnational corporations and supermarkets (Young, 2004), which are in turn backed by the more powerful governments of the developed world and the international bodies such as the WTO and World Bank which are alleged to work in the interests of the latter (McMichael, 2005). The degree to which there is a singular, homogeneous and homogenizing global food system at the present time is an issue we will return to later.

For those, such as political scientists and international relations scholars, whose concerns are the political dimensions of globalization, in the sense of political institutions and changing forms of political practice, the focus is on processes of alleged 'de-territorialization' (Scholte, 1999) and the reconfiguring of national governments' powers over and within their sovereign territories. On this sort of view, globalization involves 'a set of processes ... which embodies a transformation in the spatial organization of social relations and transactions ... generating transcontinental or inter-regional flows and networks of activity' which problematize the sovereignty of national governments (Held et al., 1999: 16). The appearance and in some cases rapid development of phenomena such as international and regional political and economic bodies (UN, EU, WTO, GATT, etc.), trading agreements (e.g. NAFTA) and legal apparatuses and norms (Lechner and Boli, 2005), which have more or less binding powers over national states, together with the rise of a putatively global civil sphere populated by protest groups, activists, journalists and so on (Keane, 2003), can be understood as combining to create an environment far more constraining of national political elites than has ever existed before. In the case of food, the problematization—rather than, as was earlier thought, the wholesale undermining—of national states' controls over what goes on in their affairs encompasses a whole range of phenomena, from EU food safety and standardization regulations binding member states to particular modes of action, to the cross-border movement of apparently world-spanning pandemics like bird and swine flu. Moreover, at the level of trading practices and agreements, trade wars between, for example, the European Union and the United States, remain endemic, with an unfettered world global capitalist market in foodstuffs from bananas to beef being more the dream of procapitalist cheerleaders than an existent reality, as political forces of various hues—national, subnational, regional, international, transnational—create conditions of pervasive politico-economic complexity.

For analysts of social relations—notably Giddens (1990)—globalization refers primarily to the 'stretching' of social relations potentially across the whole face of the planet, and to an attendant 'disembedding' of modes of social interaction such that the latter can become radically decoupled from particular places and spaces. If we think about food matters in this light, then we are pointed towards issues to do with diasporas and mass migrations, with different sorts of foodstuffs, recipes, modes of consumption and so on both being dispersed into places far removed geographically from (what is imagined to be) their original place of origin (Zukin, 1992) and also being used to recreate feelings of 'home'—and more generally, a sense of 'ontological security'—by migrant populations living either in ethnic enclaves or in the midst of a surrounding culture they experience as alien (Law, 2001; Raviv, 2005; Ray, 2004). Deterritorialization segues into complicated modes of reterritorialization, and vice versa. Food can create powerful senses of group belonging, as well as distinguishing one group from another (Caplan, 1997). Globalizing forces can both upset, reconfigure and also re-establish such connections between food and feelings of belonging. Krishnendu Ray's chapter in this book pays testament to the senses of both rootedness and dislocation that ethnic foodways are very much bound up with, in this case of Bengalis living in the United States. And in her chapter, Carole Counihan unpacks some of the many complexities and ambivalences of 'ethnic' foodways among Hispanics and Hispanic immigrants in the United States under contemporary globalizing conditions.

For analysts of 'cultural' phenomena, there are two major ways of defining the relations of globalization and culture. The first, adopted by Marxist and other radical critics, focuses on alleged cultural *homogenization,* fostered generally by what is taken as the global spread of capitalist consumerism, and more specifically by its avatars, large Western, especially American, media corporations (Seabrook, 2004). On this view, Western-led media and consumer brands become ever more dominant in particular national and regional contexts, and the cultural specificities of the latter are thus over time 'battered out of existence' (Tunstall, 1977: 57). On this sort of reasoning, one would expect that a 'global cuisine' made up of the offerings of McDonalds, Kentucky Fried Chicken, Pizza Hut, Starbucks and other iconic American brands would eventually come to be hegemonic in most or all parts of the world, an issue we will return to later.

Alternatively, other kinds of cultural analysts—especially anthropologists and qualitative sociologists—emphasise the culturally *heterogenizing* dimensions of globalization. Indeed, while Marxist and radical critics focus on the effects of economically driven globalization forces *on* culture, these other kinds of analysts see culture as relatively autonomous of, and certainly never wholly or directly constrained by, economic forces. Thus while the former group concentrate on the capitalist economy's 'globalization of culture', the latter group focus on what could more accurately be called 'cultural globalization'. Here we encounter a number of specific theorizations of the complexifying capacities of globalization in the cultural realm: the creation of mixed 'hybrid' and 'creole' cultures depicted by postcolonial studies scholars (Bhabha, 1994) and anthropologists such as Hannerz (1996); the generation of complicated mixtures of 'glocal' cultural forms, which are simultaneously both more 'global' and more 'local' in nature, highlighted by Robertson (1992); and the ironic situation whereby when people in different parts of the world feel threatened by *what they think of* as 'globalization'—involving the loss of economic security, national political self-determination, cultural traditions and so on—they turn towards 'expressions of collective identity that challenge globalization ... on behalf of cultural singularity and [their] control over their lives and environment' (Castells, 1997: 2). Far from destroying more local and specific senses of belonging, identity and affiliation, globalization processes may actually help reinvigorate, if not in fact *create,* these. These various understandings of the cultural expressions of, and imaginative responses to, globalization—and importantly, what actors *think* is globalization—all have clear relevance for food matters: the hybrid form that is the 'English curry' (Kalra, 2004) and the imaginary, but potentially politically powerful, construction of national and regional cuisines and foodstuffs (see the chapter by Leitch) being cases in point, these sorts of issues also being returned to later.

As can be readily seen, different kinds of specialists map out the complexities of globalization that they are dealing with in their own distinctive ways. That is all to the good, because certainly we require detailed analyses of specific domains of life on the planet at the present time. But the downside of specialization is analytic narrowness. Choosing any one general approach to the study of globalization, to the systematic exclusion of the others, would mean that one would be missing vast swathes of reality, realities that point to the complexity and contradictions of present-day world conditions. The last thing that an area so vividly multifarious as contemporary food and foodways needs is an approach to globalization that *only* sees certain things and not others, because the potential complexity of those things that can be discerned may be betrayed in favour of a monological approach that only depicts those elements that are already within its purview. Openness to phenomena that are not immediately obvious, sensitivity to factors that do not quite fit one's accustomed analytic practices and political dispositions—surely these are at the roots of genuinely thoughtful social science, of human life in general and of food matters in particular?

To that end, we propose that a working definition of the processes to do with food globalizations (always understood in the plural) must necessarily draw upon all of the economic, political, social and cultural understandings and dimensions of globalization matters depicted previously. Food globalizations thus are seen to involve

> *The multiple modes of interaction (e.g. connection, penetration and mutual, although not necessarily equally weighted, influencing and restructuring) of the economic, political, social and cultural dimensions of globalization (i.e. forces, processes, institutions, structures, actors, networks, etc.) as these affect food-related matters, and as the latter in turn come to affect the former, in a series of ongoing dialectical relations characterized by the constant generation of forms of complexity.*

Seen in this regard, food globalizations can, and indeed should, continue to be construed in light of existing economic, political, social and cultural definitions and understanding of what 'globalization' is: capitalist economic—and thus cultural—hegemony, problematization and restructuring of political sovereignty, reconstitution of social relations, cultivation of cultural complexity and so on. But in addition, the analytic task is to connect these different lenses, in order to see how, at the empirical level, the phenomena viewable through each lens relate to and affect each other, in ways that may well (we believe) be more complex than standard analytic procedures might allow for. At a basic level, then, it is not enough to study food consumption in isolation from means of production and distribution mechanisms, at the same time that it is not sufficient to examine the latter without regard to how the former may be recursively affecting such fields (the case of Fairtrade food being a very good case in point, as the chapter by Caroline Wright indicates). Cutting through a whole series of unhelpful dyads that imprison thought more than encourage it, macro must be brought together with micro, structure with agency, materiality with symbolism and so on. Although there is an emphasis more on consumption than production in our selection of authors and topics (no doubt reflecting the editors' own analytic dispositions as qualitative sociologists), not only do all the chapters push in their own particular ways to broaden the horizons of globalized food inquiry, a number of them (e.g. Lien, Wright and Ponte) go quite far towards reaching the kinds of analytic syntheses we have in mind. At the very least, the proposed model we have outlined can be used to interrogate the lacunae in any given contribution to the study of food globalizations (including the remainder of this chapter) and thus to point towards how the analytical focus could be broadened and enriched with understandings of globalization taken from other disciplines and traditions. In the following sections of this chapter, we will endeavour to depict the main contours of food globalizations, as we and the contributing authors see them, in light of the multidimensional and transdisciplinary focus we have proposed.

Historically Locating Food Globalizations

As we have seen, different disciplinary dispositions think of globalization matters in different ways. This also applies to answers to questions as to when globalization 'started'. For some more economistic analysts (e.g. Friedman, 2000), it was the electronic technological revolutions of the 1970s and 1980s, plus the fall of Communism, that created the conditions for the full planetary spread of a triumphant capitalist economy. Marxist political economists, by contrast, can point to the nineteenth century—a period of both capitalist development and the spread of imperial systems that brought capitalist economic relations in their wake to many parts of the world—as the beginning of capitalist-led globalization. Other scholars (e.g. Arnason, 2003) would wish to push the starting date back to 1492 and the European conquest of the Americas, when human relations became potentially genuinely 'global' in scope for the first time. Some historians would push the date back even further, tracing out the lineaments of what they see as a 5,000-year-old world-system that has existed, sporadically and in different ways at different times, across Eurasia for almost five millennia (Frank and Gills, 1994). All of these positions have their merits, and in fact it is possible to see them as nesting within each other, the endemic (but uneven) global connectivity that starts in the 1970s being just the most recent 'phase' of much longer-term processes. Nonetheless, it is probably wise to see 1492 as a watershed period, insofar as the Americas are brought—violently—for the first time into the orbit of systems operative in Eurasia and Africa. Instances of geographically relatively wide-ranging systems of food production, distribution and consumption occurring in particular regions before that time are probably best depicted as instances of 'proto-globalization' rather than 'globalization' proper (Grew, 1999).

Whether regarded as an instance of 'proto-globalization' or not, the cultivation of grains, one of the basic foodstuffs that underpins human existence in most parts of the planet, stretches back to the start of settled agriculture in the Tigris and Euphrates valleys c. 7000 BCE. By around 5000 BCE, wheat and barley had spread into Africa and by 4000 BCE into Europe, widespread cultivation of grains leading to major deforestation between 3500 and 3000 BCE—an indication that human agricultural practices have been having major impacts on the natural environment for a very considerable period of time (Atkin, 1992). For much of human history, grains were not transported very far from their original place of production—for example, as recently as the sixteenth century CE, only 1% of the total grain produced in the Mediterranean world was transported internationally (Braudel, 1982). Internationalized, and then more fully globalized, grain production and distribution is primarily an innovation of the nineteenth century, generated at first by the repeal of the protectionist Corn Laws in Great Britain in the 1840s, with first the United States and Canada, then Australia, India and Argentina becoming major grain exporting countries to other parts of the world in the latter half of the century (Atkin, 1992: 18). The current global food crisis can be seen as being in various ways shaped by developments towards 'grain globalization' that occurred towards the end of the nineteenth century.

Going back in time again, one of the most striking instances of food proto-globalization, and a case instructive for present purposes, is that of the Roman empire. As the empire grew, basic foodstuffs were circulated around imperial terrain over quite long distances, such that Egypt, for example, became the main source of wheat for Rome and the rest of Italy. At the peak of the empire's power, the Romans had extensive trading links with southeast Africa, India, Malaysia and even far-flung China (Robertson and Inglis, 2004). There was a steady movement of goods from these places, including spices and other kinds of foodstuff that could be kept for several months (Curtin, 1998). Such trade had come about because of the appearance in Rome of foods and spices that conquering armies had brought back with them. The historian Livy (2000: 429)[1] narrated that 'the army [returning] from Asia introduced a foreign luxury to Rome; it was then the meals began to require more dishes and more expenditure ... the cook, who had up to that time been employed as a slave of low price, become dear: what had been nothing but a métier was elevated to an art'. It seems that Roman elites' appetites for exotic tastes grew increasingly over time. As the satirist Petronius (1996: 89) stated: 'Far-out and foreign win / What's out-of-bounds is in.' The Stoic philosopher Seneca (1889: 334–5) castigated those 'whose luxury transcends the bounds of an empire which is already perilously wide'. Such gourmets demanded there be brought

from all regions everything, known or unknown, to tempt their fastidious palate: food, which their stomach, worn out with delicacies, can scarcely retain, is brought from the most distant ocean ... they do not even deign to digest the banquets which they ransack the globe to obtain ... they wander through all countries, cross the seas and excite at a great cost the hunger which they might allay at a small one. (Seneca, 1889: 334–5)

The satire was directed not only at crazes for exotic tastes but also at what to the more conservative Roman palate seemed like bizarre fusions of tastes and flavours. In this regard, a certain kind of culinary cosmopolitanism is not wholly historically unprecedented before our own times, nor is the attempt by those concerned about such developments to try to promote a supposedly 'authentic' national cuisine, the allegedly virtuous plainness of old-style Roman fare being a favoured motif of conservative satirists.

The intriguing intersection in the Roman imperial case of political-economic conditions of empire, conquest and foreign trade, together with the symbolic domains of cosmopolitanism and its opposite in culinary politics, indicates that studies of present-day food globalizations might well benefit by comparing the similarities and differences between contemporary conditions and historical examples such as this, if only to avoid the presentist trap of assuming that certain forms of food globalization are wholly historically unprecedented. The same point would apply to analysis of premodern trade routes across Eurasia which sometimes stretched for thousands of miles. The cuisine of medieval European elites was heavily spice driven, and thus dependent on the spice routes from the Far East. In a medieval aristocratic feast, one might find flavours like cardamom from Africa, nutmeg from the Molucca Islands, cinnamon from Ceylon, ginger from China and pepper from south India (Colquhoun, 2007; Turner, 2005). In the thirteenth century, sugar began to appear in Europe from the Middle East and began to replace honey as a sweetener in elite diets. Such flavourings were central to the taste culture of elites, the latter involving 'a juxtaposition of the piquant with sweet fruits, nuts and sugars' (Colquhoun, 2007: 54). Although the advent of 'fusion' cuisines is sometimes understood as a development in the West of very recent times (James, 1996), medieval elite cooking stands as testament to a period prior to the construction of allegedly pure and exclusive 'national' cuisines, a time when food tastes were shared by elites across large swathes of Catholic Europe, and when the use of 'exotic' ingredients—a hallmark of elite cuisines in many times and places (Goody, 1982)—was in some ways as much the norm as it is among certain groups today (Gallegos, 2005).

If the Columbian conquests of the Americas mark the beginning of globalization proper, then it is at least plausible to argue that they also create the conditions for a series of transitions from food proto-globalizations to food globalizations as such. This not only concerned the development of the transatlantic food trade. It was also the case that the movement of foodstuffs, animals, plant-life and people between the old world and the new world involved hugely significant material and economic developments, with consequences as widely encompassing and as disruptive of hitherto-existing patterns of food cultivation, distribution and consumption as are the food regimes of the present day (Foster and Cordell, 1992; Mintz, 2008; Standage, 2009). Many of the ingredients and flavours that underpinned European food cultures over the last 500 years originated in the Americas and were wholly unknown to Europeans before the conquerors brought them back (Davidson, 1992; Messer, 1997). The expansion of the Spanish empire in the sixteenth century is at the root of the familiarity in many countries with the flavours of both chocolate and peanuts, crops now grown in various parts of the world but which once flourished only in the Americas (Coe, 2003; Rebora, 2001; Smith, 1994). The potato has come to play a great role in northern European and North American food cultures (and in parts of the world that these have been exported to), but that too is due to the unintended effects of European conquest of South America (Fernandez-Armesto, 2001; Salaman, 1949).[2] In later European history, especially from the time of the Romantic invention of the idea of 'nation' in the early nineteenth century (Anderson, 2006), supposedly authentically ancient 'national' food cultures were made possible by a collective amnesia as to the originally nonindigenous origins of certain foods. What the wider world thinks of as quintessentially 'Italian' ingredients all hail from places far outside the peninsula: tomatoes, gnocchi (made from potatoes) and polenta (made from maize) all derive from crops that originally grew in Latin America (Warman,

2003). We today generally associate chilli with the cuisines of India and some Far Eastern countries, but they too are indigenous to South America. Transatlantic movement in foodstuffs also occurred in the opposite direction: from Europe and Africa to the Americas and the Caribbean came crops like rice and bananas, and animals like beef cattle. Chilli-con-carne is sold in restaurants and supermarkets around the world today as thoroughly 'Mexican' but as it is made with beef and rice, it derives from ingredients that came to be where they are through long-term processes of empire, trade, burgeoning capitalism and a series of peculiar cultural-memory practices whereby what seems to be truly 'of' one place proves on closer examination to be nothing of the sort (Fernandez-Armesto, 2001).

Thus a key difference between early modern and late modern food globalizations is that in early modernity consciousness of novelty and exoticism in cuisine was generally replaced by processes that rendered the previously exotic into the taken-for-granted and often part of allegedly 'national' cuisines. This still continues to happen in particular ways: foodstuffs, recipes and means of preparation that were novel in one decade can be part of the everyday foodscape in the next decade (Sayid, 2004). But in advanced or late modernity, both novelty and exoticism are much more self-consciously imagined, reflected upon and utilised, as indeed are their (apparently antithetical but actually dialectically mutually constituting) corollaries, locality, region and *terroir* (Ohnuki-Tierney, 1999). Early modern people did not subject foodstuffs and their supposed social consequences to the same degree of reflexivity as can their late modern counterparts (Beck, 1992). But the post-Columbian transplantation of foodstuffs still haunts contemporary mental food landscapes (Appadurai, 1990), because characteristically late-modern endeavours to root what is rootless, and to generate stable horizons of consumption, are compelled to forget, but may uneasily start to remember, that things that are presented—fetishized might be a more appropriate word—as authentically 'local', 'regional' and 'national' are in fact the products of centuries-long processes of inter- and transcontinental mobility and exchange, driven first by colonialism (Mintz, 1986) and then by corporate agricapitalism, the latter ironically involving the very forces that advocates of locality in food regard themselves as virtuously struggling against (Leitch, 2003).

'Globalized' Food Systems

Food globalizations of the twentieth and twenty-first centuries can only be properly understood if set against the background of the development of the industrialized agricapitalist food system that has developed since the later nineteenth century (Friedmann, 1994). Over the twentieth century, this system has become ever more globe-spanning in reach, although unevenly so (Watts and Goodman, 1997). In terms of the ongoing development of this system, key features include massive and rapid urbanization in Europe and North America, leading to large urban populations needing to be fed; the diminishing social role of the peasantry; the transformation of farms into ever larger production units; the development of mass-market-oriented agricultural and livestock production systems, tending towards the factory-farm model; the application of innovative scientific knowledge, produced and utilized by new sorts of professional cadres, to both animals and crops, especially in terms of producing species that were particularly conducive to rapid and easily manipulated growth; the massification and rationalization of animal breeding techniques and slaughtering systems; the consolidation of nation-wide, and international, transportation systems, such as the development of globally standardized freight and cargo systems (Levinson, 2008); and the development of new modes of packing and preservation, such as industrial freezer systems (Shepard, 2001), and large-scale canning operations (Sorj and Wilkinson, 1985).

All of these innovations, mostly pioneered in Europe and North America, have come to have increasingly world-level ramifications and consequences (Sobal, 1999), such that agriculture worldwide, in one way or another, has come to be affected and restructured in light of the dynamics of a globalized agricapitalism (Friedmann, 1994; McMichael, 1994, 1995). One must certainly agree with political economists (e.g. Bonnano, 1998; Bonnano et al, 1994; Friedmann and McMichael, 1989; Goodman and Watts, 1997) that food production and distribution in the present day involves globalized divisions of agricultural labour and transnational, as well as national and regional, chains of production, distribution and consumption, with the effect that national agricultural systems are complexly integrated into transnational networks and that crises in one part of the world can have huge consequences for other parts (Daviron and Ponte, 2005; McMichael, 2005). The role of food-related transnational corporations (TNCs) in the creation and re-creation of these sorts of conditions has been the subject of much analysis (e.g. Bonnano, 2004; Kneen, 1999), the most recent activities of which have very much been characterized by flexible and often decentralized means of organization (Llambi, 1993), meaning that food systems are centred around both stabilized means of ongoing exploitation of producers and flexible modes of profit-making (McMichael, 1999). However, although TNCs are generally headquartered in developed world countries, how they actually operate in specific locales may vary from country to country, depending on, for example, national regulations and labour laws (Pritchard and Fagan, 1999).

It is possible to view current conditions of production and distribution as constituting various 'global food regimes' (Friedmann, 1982). Such regimes are responsible for, and are constituted out of, highly globally standardized agricultural practices such as planting and cropping (Pritchard and Burch, 2003), factory-farming and fishing (Bonnano and Constance, 2001; Boyd and Watts, 1997) and the globalized sourcing by supermarkets and other agents of agricultural products (Friedland, 1994). As such material practices have become more standardized in different countries, national agricultural economies have been sometimes radically restructured, resulting in monocultures replacing biodiversity and the undermining of food security for local populations (Murray, 2001)

However, it is important to note that this situation cannot simply be construed as constituting one single 'global food system', at least not if the latter is defined as being totally homogeneous in nature, with uniform effects in every part of the world. It is undoubtedly the case that, following the analysis of world-systems theorists, contemporary agricapitalism involves systematic exploitation of developing world producers by developed world corporations, with Fairtrade packaging and other such labelling often masking the nature of this exploitation, through creating mystified forms of connection between developed world consumers and developing world farm workers, as the chapter by Caroline Wright included here indicates. How developed world companies extract high levels of value from transnational commodity chains, thus appropriating that value from the original locations of production, can be disguised and rendered practically invisible to developed world consumers, not only by the transnational complexity of these chains, involving different sorts of actors in a series of different countries, but also by the active ideological work of corporations seeking, as it were, to cover up the trails they create through the means of re-presenting exploitative relationships between producers and buyers as spontaneously harmonious and cooperative relations between producers and consumers. Geographical distance and the economic-political complexity of commodity chains are erased through the magic of apparent connection between those who labour and those who eat the fruits of that labour. Products such as strawberries and green beans—the species of which are increasingly homogenized by the standardizing practices of large-scale agricapitalism (Rosset et al., 1999)—travel very far across the world in the present day, clocking up large amounts of 'food miles' as they go, but labelling them in certain ways can (at least attempt to) collapse that distance and the socioeconomic chasm that separates those who grew them and those who ate them (Raynolds, 2002).

But beyond this general situation of developed world/developing world inequality, we have to be sensitive to how particular types of producers are engaged with particular sorts of corporations. For example, now that Kenya has become one of the major suppliers in the world to developed world supermarkets (Dolan, 2005), it is important to know whether—as seems to be the case—the exploitation of labour and environment differs in extent and kind depending on how specific contractual relations are structured between specific producers and particular developed world supermarkets (Konefal et al., 2005), with upper-level chains such as the British Waitrose and Marks and Spencer providing a (somewhat) better deal for producers insofar as their insistence on highest-quality products produces a better living wage for farm workers (Barrett et al., 1999; see also Rosset et al., 1999, for the case of Thailand).

It is also important to note that practices of production, trading and valuation of different kinds of food commodities vary from one sector to another. Stefano Ponte's chapter indicates some of the specificities of the globalized wine trade, which marks its operations and dynamics out from other industrial sectors (Jones, 2003). How different kinds of wine are thought of and valuated very much affects how they are made in the first place, these modes of evaluative reasoning very much having been globalized in recent years. This case suggests that a political-economic approach to production always must be supplemented by attention to the specific cultural dispositions of actors within particular regimes of production (Applbaum, 2004). If these vary noticeably from one sector to another—from wine to vegetable production, for example—then that warns us against simplistic notions of a completely homogeneous global productive system in the singular. While mass market wines are evaluated in one way, middle-level and high-level wines are regarded by actors in this field in quite other ways, each subsphere of valuation and production (themselves mutually constituting) undergoing different sorts of globalization process. While mass market wines have in many countries become much more homogenized in style, taste and texture over the last twenty years (hence the ubiquity in developed world supermarket shelves of high alcohol reds and characterless whites), heterogenization and homogenization have gone hand-in-hand at higher-level production. The judgements of the pre-eminent American critic Robert Parker are often factored into how high-end wine is thought about and valued—an extraordinary case of one individual's powerful structuring role within specific sorts of globalization processes (McCoy, 2008). But just as 'Parkerization' has led to homogenization in some ways (e.g. producers making red wines in a heavier style than they had previously, in order to try to appeal to Parker's tastes), it can also lead to heterogenization, insofar as wines are supposed to 'speak of' locality, *terroir* and the unique geographical features of where they were made, and because producers often engage in self-consciously heterogenizing activities in order to augment the market appeal of their wines. One globalizing process can have variant, even contradictory, outcomes, and while this may apply to wine more than to other sectors, it is still a point very much worth attending to.

We should also attend to the fact that what is sometimes referred to polemically as the 'global food system' in fact is a highly fractured and uneven constellation of different, though complexly interrelated, systems of production, distribution and consumption (Araghi, 2003) and cannot be directly compared to other industrial sectors such as car manufacturing (Rosset et al., 1999). This is not least due to the ongoing salience of political factors and controversies in the realm of food. We noted previously the ongoing trade wars between the United States and European Union, testament to the fact that a single global, homogenous world-level market is a myth propagated by those who would like such a thing to come to pass. The actual situation is much more variegated and diverse, although strongly marked by the exploitative patterns noted already. A whole series of authors have provided rich case studies of how food production in the present day is as much characterized by non-integration of sectors and markets as by integration, by disconnections as well as by connections (e.g. Arce and Marsden, 1993; Chalfin, 2004; Cook and Harrison, 2003; Whatmore and Thorne, 1997; Watts and Goodman, 1997). This involves engaging an analytic shift, away from analysis of relatively abstract 'structures', towards more contingently organized social networks where change rather than endless repetition of standardization and homogenization is possible (Jarosz, 2000). A further reason for this, beyond the politico-economic factor of the persistence of trading blocs, is the ongoing salience of specific 'national' taste cultures, which, far from being undermined by globalization processes, may in fact either be stimulated by the latter or infact may guide them in certain ways. Mansfield's (2003) exemplary study of the Pacific fishing industry is a case in point: what may sell in Malaysia may not be acceptable to powerful intermediary actors like fish-buyers in Japan, and the transnational dynamics of the Pacific fishing industry very much reflect dispositions still rooted in national cultures. Complex interplays of the national and the transnational, the politico-economic and the cultural, characterize systems and networks of production and distribution, as much as do trends towards homogenization of both material things and the mental dispositions which regulate their creation and guide their distribution (Barndt, 2002).

Crises and Critiques

Famines have been a persistent feature of human existence for millennia (Devereux, 1993). As the economist Amartya Sen (2001) has shown, in the modern period, against the background of the industrialization of agriculture in various parts of the world, famines are often less to do with the shortage of food per se and more to do with lack of access to food by underprivileged groups. In the present day, some 848 million people around the world, the vast majority in the developing world, are undernourished according to UN criteria (Food and Agriculture Organisation of the United Nations, 2009), with the current world food crisis likely to exacerbate that number. Thus vast numbers of people currently and in the future face huge problems of food security (Pottier, 1999). In conditions characterized by multiple food globalizations, food shortages and the threat of famine have taken on new and complex contours (Chossudovsky, 2008).

'Globalization' as a term is often used—especially by certain kinds of activists—to describe contemporary conditions of flux, uncertainty and insecurity. As we wrote this chapter (mid-2008), those sorts of feelings were very much in the worldwide media, as reports of the 'global food crisis' started to flood in. This phraseology itself captures the manner in which today it seems to be impossible to understand food outside the terms set by discourses centred around notions of globalization. The crisis is depicted (for example, in *The Economist,* 2008) as generated by 'domino effects' in certain parts of the world food system having uncontrollable unintended consequences in other, often very geographically disparate, parts of the network. Thus, for example, food riots in countries all around the equator are said to be consequent on shortages in rice, cereals and other basic foodstuffs; these shortages are in part due to such factors as rising demand in the developed world for certain crops, hitherto used primarily for human food consumption, to be used in bio-fuels, which have themselves been created to ease pressure on an ever more imperilled biosphere. Thus measures intended to resolve one set of problems—in this case, carbon emissions and global warming—in turn create other serious dilemmas, here hunger, deprivation and attendant political unrest (Gregory et al., 2005).

Likewise, pressure is put on national and transnational food systems as living standards in countries such as China, India and Brazil rise because of very rapid industrialization, the latter itself being seen to contribute massively to the environmental woes of the planet (Bright, 1999). As newly economically enfranchised groups in such places demand what they think of as richer and more varied diets, further pressure is put on cereal crops, these now being diverted to the purpose of feeding intensively farmed animals, such cereals being the very crops that are now in short supply in some of the world's poorest regions. Thus as the diets of some 'improve', the access of others to basic foodstuffs goes into freefall. A further factor here is that the gases created by the intensive farming of animals such as cows and pigs are seen to contribute to global warming, such that the increased appetite for meat amongst the planet's 'new middle classes' is seen to be helping to undermine the very biosphere on which all life across the planet depends. Irony upon irony abounds, as the material conditions of globalized agriculture seem to exhibit ever more contradictory impulses and tendencies, the future outcomes of these often being represented by concerned (primarily Western) commentators in increasingly apocalyptic terms (e.g. Kimbrell, 2002). In the developing world, certain types of food globalization bring certain advantages (e.g. richer diets for some), whilst creating new problems for others. As Pat Caplan's chapter shows, the distribution of benefits and problems vis-à-vis food supply very much varies among groups according to how many resources, such as social capital, they have at their disposal: food globalizations frequently tend to advantage the advantaged and to further disadvantage the disadvantaged..

The sense of burgeoning crisis at this level is bolstered by other, though related, senses of impending or already-existent predicaments and calamities. While for most of the twentieth century, industrialized food systems operated in relatively unreported and thus uncontested ways, by the later twentieth century their crisis-prone tendencies were very much apparent, not least because these were very much reported on by the media, and the political agenda had been successfully reshaped by activist groups of various hues that had proliferated since the 1970s (Fischler, 1999). The increasing political contestation of a range of practices that had become institutionalised in industrialized food systems, from very large-scale factory farming to the development of genetically modified seeds and crops (Tulloch and Lupton, 2001), very much fits with Ulrich Beck's (1992) notion of 'risk society', which has become globe-spanning in nature and consequences. Whatever specific problems critics may have with the risk society account of late modernity (Mythen, 1999), we believe the general point holds true: the institutions of (industrialized, nation-state-centred) 'first modernity' produce consequences that they cannot themselves fully deal with, leading to a series of spiralling crises of regulation and (often failed) control.

In such conditions, not only are forms of reflexive consciousness that can no longer accept the verities of the past made possible—the gap between official claims as to food safety and security and the actualities of the situation now coming to seem so vast—but they are in fact compelled. This is, we feel, one of the major reasons for the complexity of food globalizations in the present day—reflexive modes of thought and practice have entered into food systems and networks, contesting them, reshaping them and having all sorts of consequences, mostly unintentional, on them. And while certain kinds of reflexivity (e.g. that of the bourgeois consumer who thinks she knows all about the iniquities of factory farming) may be more willed than compelled, nonetheless at all levels, from individual activities to corporate institutions, troubling uncertainties now not only threaten to undermine systems but in fact have been unavoidably incorporated into their very natures. Thus the systems and networks that constitute and are driven by food globalizations come ever more to display—and, crucially, are *perceived* by a wide range of different actors and groups as displaying—crisis tendencies, and they seem to be unable to resolve the problems generated by the nature of their own functioning.

As a consequence, while food production and consumption have never been more regulated in particular countries—and also through transnational regulatory frameworks—than in the present day (Kjaernes et al., 2007), the ways in which they are regulated are multiple, complex, overlapping and often contradictory. Various types and levels of regulation, and the bodies that produce and (try to) enforce these, accompanied the development of large-scale food systems throughout the twentieth century. These included systems of rules created by national governments, transnational economic-political bodies (the most wide-ranging to date being those of the European Union), agricapitalist organizations themselves and international agreements and treaties associated with organizations such as WTO, GATT and the United Nations' Food and Agricultural Organization (FAO), as well as the morally oriented standards promoted by nongovernmental campaigning and charitable organizations, such as Compassion in World Farming (Walls, 2002). Because of the multiplicitous, multilevelled characteristics of all these different regulative bodies, codes and norms, the world today is far from having a unitary system of food regulations and procedures, and the situation is constantly open to ongoing contestations and restructurings (Konefal et al., 2005; Raynolds and Murray, 1998), as can be seen in disputes over the *Codex Alimentarius,* the international code of food trade practice set up by the UN's FAO and WHO organizations in the early 1960s (Ilcan and Phillips, 2003).

Consequently, when crises (are seen to) arise, the lack of coordination in both diagnoses of the problems and ways of dealing with them is very marked. For example, the effects of recent outbreaks of avian flu on the worldwide chicken-rearing industry are potentially disastrous, but it is difficult to coordinate efforts to deal with the problem when, even just at the level of state-based institutions, different national governments are members of different, rival trading blocs. As Beck (1998) himself has noted, institutions of 'first modernity' such as national governments are generally ill-equipped to deal with problems that are by their very nature transnational and no respecter of national boundaries. Even institutions that are meant to be more geared towards dealing with transnational problems in food, health and related matters, such as the EU or UN, are often sclerotic and contradictory in their responses, in part because they are hamstrung by intergovernmental feuding and commercial horse-trading.

Today industrialized methods of food production and distribution are seen both as creating a whole series of problems (environmental, moral and otherwise) as well as being highly susceptible to troubles (avian flu, 'mad cow disease' and suchlike) that are themselves always potentially 'global' in reach, as the dangers they create spiral uncontrollably down the networks of the (unevenly) globalized division of labour (Fischler, 1999). It is not just the food industry which has experienced severe knocks in the developed world after such recent food-chain crises as BSE ('mad cow disease'), foot-and-mouth outbreaks and the reportedly carcinogenic nature of farmed salmon (Brown and Scott, 2004). It is also the claims to truth of scientists, both those working for governments and for private interests, that have come under attack in recent years. While the levels of public distrust in both the food industry and in food scientists varies from one national context to another (Kjaernes et al., 2007), it is certainly the case that scientific truth claims in the realm of food have never been more opened up to questioning than in the present day.

Not only has there been an erosion of scientific authority, there is also a proliferation of different sorts of authorities, each clamouring for public recognition and attention (Beck, 1992). This pluralization of food expertise can undermine scientific authority quite markedly. For example, while the advocates of genetically modified (GM) crops—such as spokespeople for the powerful global player, the Monsanto company (Kneen, 1999)—might have had in the 1970s a relatively easy time convincing public opinion as to the famine-eliminating capacities of this technology, their task in this regard is much more difficult in the present day, because increasing public scepticism towards, and uneasiness about, scientific claims, means that the views of antibiotech campaigners may well be taken as seriously, if not more so, than those of industry representatives or those seen to be in the pay of corporate vested interests (Charles, 2001; Murcott, 2001). Claims that GM foods, far from 'saving the planet' (McMichael, 2000) from the spectre of wide-spread famine in the developing world, in fact promote a corporate stranglehold over world farmers in the developing world, by compelling them to buy seeds from monopoly-holding corporations that hold lucrative patents on whole strains of plants and crops (Buctuanon, 2001; Lappé and Bailey, 2002; Shiva, 2000), may well take hold in the consciousness of diverse publics who see themselves as ethically informed 'global citizens' (see Gallegos's chapter in this regard; also Guptill and Wilkins, 2002).[3] Given the hold of these sorts of globally oriented imaginaries on economically influential middle-class groupings, the case of GM foodstuffs is exemplary, insofar as while agribusiness continues enthusiastically to embrace the 'scientization' of agriculture, such a process has now been subjected to deep contestation.

In a further ironic twist, challenges to the scientific discourses associated with industrialized food production themselves can have outcomes completely unintended by their advocates. Attempts to make systems of production and consumption both more ethical and more healthy may rebound back on their progenitors (Nestle, 2003). As Clover (2006) reports, the high praise heaped on the health-giving properties of fish by nutritional scientists and various kinds of dietary entrepreneurs simultaneously encourages developed world consumers to shun apparently health-threatening products like industrially produced hamburgers while pushing up consumption of a 'virtuous' (i.e. both health-giving and low-fat) foodstuff like fish. But increased fish consumption is made possible by environmentally damaging industrialized fishing, which damages ecosystems, threatens to wipe out certain piscine species and which increasingly is based in the waters of poorer nations (e.g. on the west coast of Africa or in Honduras) whose governments are happy to take the money offered for fishing concessions by the EU and other developed world bodies, despite the environmental havoc that is wreaked on the environment (Bonnano and Constance, 1996). As Barrett et al. (1999) point out, 'post-industrial' ideas and practices in the developed world as to consumption can have the effect of promoting further industrialization of production in the developing world, with consumers being none the wiser about such matters.[4]

In other words, one type of reflexivity (e.g. to do with 'health') can lead to forms of myopia that are the exact opposites of reflexive consciousness. If developed world consumers began to question the pleasant-sounding rhetoric of 'organic' and Fairtrade food production, they may well find that the virtuous 'food chain' they thought they were part of is in fact a much more ambivalent phenomenon than they had thought, bearing more resemblance to the mainstream agribusiness practices they had thought they were rejecting and avoiding (Dolan, 2005; Wright and Madrid, 2007). Middle-class consumers are now very much enamoured of the notion of 'organic' farming, but the actual practices of organic farmers are ambivalent, for as Guthman (2004) has shown, there are many diverse motivations among farmers who participate in organic practices, ranging from environmental philosophy through to regarding organic production purely as a money-spinning enterprise. As Born and Purcell point out in their chapter, analysts, activists and consumers would do well to avoid falling into the trap of assuming that smallness and localization of production necessarily mean virtuous practices. It is also worth remembering that the terms 'local' and 'locality'—and their apparent obverses, 'global' and 'globality'—are not only highly political and contested terms but also that their meanings vary from one context and one group of actors to another (Selfa and Qazi, 2005). Some of the complexities here are unpacked by Michaela DeSoucey and Isabelle Téchoueyres in their chapter on senses of 'locality' in both the United States and France (Norberg-Hodge et al., 2002).

Crises concerning food do not only 'happen'; they also are brought into being by new ways of thinking and evaluating, which define certain phenomena as problems that hitherto had not been defined as such. The more ways that exist of categorizing certain phenomena as problems, the more problems come to 'exist' that have to be dealt with. In the 1970s, concerns about intensive factory farming were not a major factor for agribusiness to deal with, as such practices very much occurred 'behind the scenes', out of public view. But because of the successful moral-political entrepreneurship of animal rights groups in the developed world (Lien and Nerlich, 2004), such issues are now very much in the discursive terrain that shapes perceptions of, and increasingly forms part of, globalized systems of food production, with activities previously deemed unproblematic—such as keeping vast numbers of animals in relatively small spaces—now regarded as very much open to question (Nibert, 2002). As animal rights discourses, and analogous concerns about the ethics and social and biotic consequences of genetic modification of plant and animal life, have become part of the discursive elements of globalized food production, problems have multiplied, as reality has been reconfigured in light of new morally-loaded sensibilities (Macnaghten, 2004).

Such problematizing discourses now exist in, and contribute to the structuring of, world-level discursive space (Lechner and Boli, 2005). This is the sphere of 'global civil society' (Keane, 2003). While such a sphere is certainly not globally homogenous, it being more vigorous in some locales than others, nonetheless study of it indicates that animal rights, anti-biotechnology groups and others like them have themselves become transnational in their practices and modes of organization. Lien (2004) has demonstrated how transnationally active campaign groups have successfully created new food taboos, encouraging people in different countries to reject the attempted defining by the meat industry of certain animals, such as kangaroos, as fit for human consumption. Just as food production systems have become more transnationalized, so too have certain food prohibitions and dispositions towards what is ethically unacceptable food consumption. But this is not to deny that there exist differential: national public and governmental responses to transnational campaigns, as Kurzer and Cooper's work (2007) on anti-GM food campaigns indicates (see also Benson and Saguy, 2005).

Nonetheless, contestation and contradiction rule, as the certainties of the industrialized food systems of the twentieth century recede into the past. No better example could be given of such a state of affairs than current debates over obesity. While the United States and United Kingdom are now well accustomed to debates about how a combination of fast food and industrialized commodity consumption, postindustrial work patterns and sedentary lifestyles have contributed to high levels of obesity in their populations (especially among the lower social classes), other developed world nations like France are only just beginning to engage with what they see as an emerging social problem (Willging, 2008). Likewise, recent years have witnessed the growth of obesity levels among younger people in many countries around the world.

The variety of causes of the 'globalization of obesity', and the morally loaded public debates that have accompanied them in a range of countries, are unpacked by Sobal and McIntosh in their highly instructive chapter. The recent, rather fraught attempts by McDonalds to present itself as being an enemy of childhood obesity and a friend of healthy diets was driven by increasing claims as to the company being in significant part responsible for obesity in children, not only in the developed world but also in new markets like China, forcing company executives to try to take fast remedial action (Cheng, 2004; Jing, 2000). Bad publicity about the obesity-inducing capacities of industrial food, and companies taking action to deal with public critiques, are now as much a part of globalized food systems as are advertising campaigns and customer promotions proclaiming the joys of hamburgers and coke.

Global McWorld, Re-Inventing Locality

We saw previously that the two main ways of conceptualizing the cultural dimensions (or effects) of globalization involved either regarding globalizing consumer capitalism as homogenizing cultural forms and practices in its wake, or regarding globalization as involved in the creation of cultural heterogenization, cultural differences being maintained, reinvigorated and created, rather than being destroyed. It is probably wisest to say that, rather than either broad position simply being wholly correct, different sorts of food globalizations have variously homogenizing and heterogenizing effects, sometimes simultaneously.

One of the most powerful ways to think about the homogenizing aspects of a certain kind of food globalization is to think about the new products that can be created through biotechnological means. Marianne Elisabeth Lien's chapter shows how farmed salmon is an entity that belongs to no particular place, because it has been bred in ways that make it substantially different from wild salmon whose biological characteristics root them in particular environments (see also Rosset et al., 1999, for the 'world tomato'). But publics who have been brought up on the idea that creatures which they eat are supposed to be from *somewhere* (hence the fetishization in packaging of place names to describe particular breeds—*Aberdeen* Angus beef, *Norfolk* turkey, *Gloucestershire* Old Spot pigs, etc., to name just three British examples) would probably not take kindly to facing up to the fact that this is a fish that is radically delocalized, unrooted, and in that sense 'global' because it fits everywhere—and nowhere—at the same time. The unsettling mental implications of this sort of 'radical globalization' are caught well in the Canadian novelist Timothy Taylor's (2001: 171) depiction of the horror his chef-hero has in being reduced to using farmed rather than wild salmon:

> farmed Chilean salmon finally made it into the seafood risotto. It didn't taste bad, exactly; it just didn't taste *right* ... A fish pen up the coast from Santiago might as well be up the coast from Osaka or Vladivostock or Campbell River. The fish in such a pen lived

independent of geography, food chain or ecosystem. These salmon were perfectly com-modified as a result, immune to the restrictions of place. There was no *where* that these fish were *from*.

The risotto in which the fish appears is 'homeless' because it seems to lack root-edness and proper provenance. So, as Lien indicates, it is sold to consumers as if it 'really' was rooted in a particular place's ecosystem, to circumvent fears about the health-threatening and culturally dislocating potential of a fish that has no home other than the highly artificial context of the delocalized fish-farm. If materially the salmon is a global entity—it would be just the same whether farmed in Chile or Norway—then semiotically it is recoded as quintessentially 'local' (as truly *Scottish* salmon, as really *Norwegian* fish, etc.) by a food industry all too worried about the kinds of risk mentioned previously. A certain kind of homogenization leads, through a series of complex mediations—here involving health, political protest, governmen-tal regulations and so on—to a certain kind of heterogenization, even if, in this case, the heterogenic elements are a fairly thin veil of marketing discourse (Askegaard and Kjeldgaard, 2007).

If the salmon is apparently wholly delocalized, then so too are the spaces and places of a particular kind of food globalization, involving the introduction into very many countries of the (putatively) 'global' fast food brands such as McDonalds and Kentucky Fried Chicken. We have seen already how for a certain kind of radical critique, to be found both in academic circles and in the antiglobalization movement, the increased global hegemony of such chains would amount to nothing less than the wholesale desecration, through the means of radically restructured foodways, of a whole series of particular local and national spaces and cultures. Wilkinson (2006: 69) depicts an extreme version of these sorts of fears:

> A composite nightmare of the anti-globalists might depict a world of six billion social clones all living in suburban houses, speaking Valley English, drinking coffee at Star-bucks, eating burgers at McDonald's, shopping at Wal-Mart ... in short, a universal Los Angeles filled with interchangeable Californians burning Iraqi oil in the gas tanks of Japanese cars as they drive to Ethiopian restaurants where they will drink Australian wines named after French grape-growing regions as they prepare to jet to Tokyo, perhaps to protest about globalization.

The opening up of McDonalds and similar outlets, first in the former Soviet Union in the mid-1990s, and then in China in the early 2000s, did indeed seem highly symbolically potent, an apparent portent of what was to come as this kind of food globalization came to supplant the political barriers erected by a now defunct com-munism. The important thing about McDonalds is how it has been coded—especially by radical critics and activists—as the great symbol of American-led globalization of culture, going together with other products of American 'cultural imperialism', such as Hollywood films and television, and Nike sportswear (Tomlinson, 1997).

Symptomatic of the fact that the McDonalds arch has become a truly global icon—loved by some, reviled by others—is the widespread dissemination of the idea of the political scientist Benjamin Barber (1992) that the present time is characterized by a great clash between 'jihad' (localizing religious and ethnic fundamentalisms and separatisms) on the one hand and 'McWorld' (the globalizing institutions of Western corporate capitalism) on the other. And in the almost equally well-known phraseology of the sociologist George Ritzer, McDonaldization is 'the process by which the principles of the fast-food restaurant' (namely *efficiency, calculation, predictability* and *control*) 'are coming to dominate more and more sectors of American society as well as the rest of the world' (2000: 1). In both cases, the imagery is striking, but the reality underlying it is more complicated than either analyst admits.

In a later work, Ritzer (2004) argued that globalization processes are in essence the world-wide spreading of 'culturally weightless' products like credit cards, products that have no specific cultural designations and so which are easily transported into different cultural locales. (Interestingly, the farmed salmon mentioned already is just such a product, but food taboos seem to compel its producers to code it as highly environmentally and culturally localized.) So should the products of McDonalds be seen primarily as embodiments of 'American culture' (a problematic term in its own right) or in fact devoid of any specific cultural content? If people believe the former, then they come close to a certain kind of 'anti-globalization' politics. One of the contemporary heroes of this sort of politics, possessed of a media profile now stretching far beyond the borders of his native France, is the farmer-turned-transnational activist Jose Bové, who in a well-publicized incident bulldozed a branch of McDonalds France in protest of what he saw as creeping Americanization (Bové and Dufour, 2002). But if people were to regard McDonalds food as signifying precisely (in Ritzer's terms) 'nothing', then McDonaldization would not be regarded as equivalent to Americanization (whatever that is), cultural imperialism or the destruction of allegedly 'traditional' and ancient foodways. It would instead be viewable as a rationalization process, the effects of which are contingent and fairly unpredictable.

The physical spaces of fast food chains can be understood as what the French anthropologist Marc Augé (1995) dubs 'non-places', decontextualized and deterritorialized locales like international hotels and airport departure lounges. If we were to regard such contexts as spatial embodiments of cultural imperialism, then we would regard them as sociospatial crucibles through which a globalized homogeneous cuisine usurps more localized food practices. The spread to many countries, including the People's Republic of China, of the American coffee shop chain Starbucks, could be seen in this light (Harrison et al., 2005; Plog, 2005). According to Simpson (2008), the appearance of Starbucks and other such chains in Macau in the 1990s meant that more collectivist modes of drinking and eating were significantly undermined as youth and the middle classes increasingly began to orient their daily routines around going to such places, with the result that more individualistic and consumerist modes of activity were increasingly to be found in public spaces (for other views, see Wu and Tan, 2001; see also Thompson and Tambyah, 1999, for the experiences of expatriate groups).

Nonetheless, in the last several years, the international expansion of Starbucks and similar operations seems to be in decline, the high water-mark of the early 2000s now being replaced by market stagnation, including in the United States itself (Smale, 2008). Whether the current global financial crisis will further augment 'de-globalizing' trends towards global chains reducing their operations in some countries remains to be seen. It is clear, though, that one should avoid any simple notions of the appearance of McDonalds, Starbucks or whatever chain in a particular place as *necessarily* leading to fundamental changes in modes of thought and practice. Everyday activities surely should be seen as complex webs of action and meaning constituted and reconstituted out of multiple, often contradictory, elements. As Tomlinson (1997: 87) argues:

> In everyday activities like working, eating or shopping, people are likely to be concerned with their immediate needs—their state of health, their family and personal relations, their finances and so on. In these circumstances the cultural significance of working for a multinational, eating lunch at McDonalds, shopping for Levis, is unlikely to be interpreted as a threat to national identity, but how these mesh with the meaningful realm of the private: McDonalds as convenient for the children's birthday party; jeans as a dress code for leisure-time activities [and so on].

Thus regularly going to McDonalds or Starbucks might, under particular circumstances, have large or conversely might have minimal significance on 'local' cultural practices, or may indeed calibrate these in novel, complexifying ways (Tomlinson, 1999). A lot of ethnographic work on such matters has been carried out by anthropologists and others since the 1990s, as American or Western chains started to open up in the former Communist world (e.g. Caldwell, 2004; Illouz and John, 2003, Lozado, 2005; Miller, 1998; Watson, 1997). Much of this writing was aimed at criticizing what were seen as the simplistic assumptions of claims as to cultural imperialism being manifested in and through such developments (Miller, 1998). Ethnographic studies of customers' actual practices endeavoured to show that far from fundamentally restructuring symbolic and material practices, once fast food restaurants had lost the glitter of novelty and had become part of everyday life, they were generally appropriated into the patterns of quotidian existence that had existed before their arrival on the social scene (see also Inglis, 2004, for a similar logic). One should also note the degree of reflexivity on the behalf of the managers and marketing executives of these chains in particular countries, who have often been at pains to 'glocalize' menus to make their company seem more at 'home' in what are thought of as national food cultures: thus French McDonalds has sold beer in its restaurants from their inception, making it quite unlike any other national franchise of the chain (for the place-specific practices of TNCs, see Pritchard and Fagan, 1999). This indicates that forms of reflexive consciousness are as much components of chain expansion in new markets as are obvious tendencies towards homogeneity. It remains the case, however, that ethnographic studies which stress the complexities of chain expansion may themselves be subjected to critique, insofar as they sometimes embody rather romantic assumptions about the allegedly robust and supposedly relatively homogeneous nature of 'local' and 'national' food cultures, problematic notions anyway but especially so under conditions of complex globalization.

One of the greatest ironies about food globalizations is that when actors perceive what they take to be their national and local cuisines as being under threat from 'outside' homogenizing processes, they often turn not only to the defence of such traditions, but to their actual construction. Resistance to perceived homogenization can create self-conscious modes of heterogenization—although that self-consciousness generally misrecognizes the fact that it is often inventing traditions as much as defending them. We are here dealing with the dialectics of what Rick Wilk in his chapter, on changing foodways in Belize, calls 'neophilia' and 'neophobia'—the thought of the novel in food can be intensely appealing for some, utterly threatening for others, with complicated mixtures of delight and disgust attending foodways as they are constantly unsettled and resettled through ongoing modes of appropriation and adaptation.

It would be a mistake to think that fears about culinary homogenization from 'outside' the nation or locality are wholly historically new, products of the last thirty years or so. France in that period has been the site of a whole range of denunciations of the allegedly deleterious effects of food globalization, the latter taken to range from the spread of McDonalds to the surreptitious growing of GM foods (Fantasia, 1995; Willging, 2008). But similar fears and polemics have been common since at least the 1920s, when:

> Frenchmen began to feel that the unprecedented influx of foreign tourists hurrying through the country in fast cars, Riviera or Biarritz bound, not caring what they ate or drank so long as they were not delayed on their way, was threatening the character of their cookery far more than had the shortages and privations of war. Soon, they felt, the old inns and country restaurants would disappear and there would be only modern hotels serving mass produced, impersonal food which could be put before the customers at a moment's notice, devoured, paid for, and instantly forgotten. (David, 1970 [1960]: 6)

While the French intelligentsia worry about what they regard as the apocalyptic overturning of culinary patrimony by American-inspired globalization, they tend to forget that they are reading from a script which is now almost a century old, and which has been a recurring feature of French engagements with (perceived) modernity ever since (Ross, 1996).

While the French case may be particularly pronounced, other national contexts afford us glimpses of how, paradoxically, the more the perceived threat from 'outside' forces of homogenization, the more particular groups—especially those enjoying certain types of cultural power, such as intelligentsias—are likely to engage in heterogenization projects (Wilk, 1999). For example, again in the 1920s, Greek intellectuals depicted food cultures as a key locale whereby Greek culture was 'in danger of being swept away by the onslaught of a cosmopolitan modernity' (Peckham, 1998: 173). The threats apparently posed by the appearance for the first time of American- and British-influenced canned foods galvanized certain members of the intelligentsia to write the very first pan-Hellenic cookery books, which codified for the first time what were presented as quintessentially 'Greek' ingredients, flavours and modes of preparation. In this way, a national cuisine was forged out of disparate sources—different regional cuisines, and the foods of both elites and peasantries. This involved processes of creating a certain kind of sameness (the 'national'—virtuous sameness) out of divergent materials, carried out through denunciations of globalizing homogenization (a maleficent sameness). Similar dynamics have been documented by Appadurai (1988) for another time and place, in this case the production of the first pan-Indian cookbooks in the 1980s. National culinary heritages are identified and brought into being because of perceived homogenization. In this sense, homogenization is productive of heterogenization, where the latter involves the production of a new kind of homogenization that is defined as being culturally 'pure'. But once such a heritage has been brought into being, apparent threats to it can loom ever larger in the imagination of the intelligentsia and other groups (if the former have been able to galvanize the latter in this regard), possibly provoking further and increasingly fraught attempts to freeze in time as pure essences what are in fact contingent conditions created through the dialectical interplay of homogenization and heterogenization. The convolutions of what counts as 'American' food at any given time are amply testified to in the chapter authored by Johnston, Baumann and Cairns presented here.

When culinary homogenization is alleged to take place today, its avatars are seen to be both fast food chains, large supermarket companies and large-scale agribusiness (Blythman, 2005). All of these stand charged—particularly by activists, a new type of intelligentsia—with many sins, from ethically dubious factory farming to unsustainable agricultural practices and the use of environmentally corrosive packaging (Murray, 2007). Such critiques have reached ever broader developed world publics in the last decade or so, both through mass market books (e.g. Blythman, 2005; Lang and Heasman, 2004; Patel, 2008; Pollan, 2007; Roberts, 2009; Schlosser, 2001; Tudge, 2004; Weis, 2007) and in cinema documentaries (e.g. Spurlock, 2004). What is less remarked upon, however, is that it is the large supermarkets and the agribusiness outfits which supply the latter, which have to a large extent been responsible for certain types of culinary heterogenization in the developed world (Humphery, 1998). One major feature of food globalizations in a country like the United Kingdom is the mass production of 'foreign' food (Cook and Harrison, 2003; James, 1996). In the 1950s, the food writer Elizabeth David encountered great resistance to her attempts to introduce 'Mediterranean' textures and flavours into the domestic repertoire of British cookery (Mclean, 2004). Yet now, as Danielle Gallegos illustrates in her chapter, the Mediterranean diet is understood by developed world publics as a prime location of culinary virtue, especially in health terms. In addition, what are taken to be 'typically' southern Italian, southern French, Spanish and Greek cuisines, as well as 'Indian', 'Mexican', 'Chinese' and 'Thai' ingredients and recipes are available on every high street (Warde et al., 1999). The (apparent) multiplicity of food choices in developed world countries today necessitates different ways of defining, making sense of and coping with this situation, as the chapter presented by Alan Warde amply indicates.

Many of these cuisines were introduced into developed world countries as a result of mass migrations of people from former colonies (Goody, 1998; Roberts, 2002) and by guest workers (Caglar, 1999), with often quite profound effects on the foodways of 'indigenous' populations. From the 1960s onwards, supermarkets and their suppliers exploited and further developed this state of affairs, making ever more items that had previously been regarded as queer and exotic seem indigenized and familiar (Belasco, 1987). At the present time, flavours and ingredients from Japan and North Africa are being newly pushed by supermarkets and suppliers (Cook and Harrison, 2003; Sayid, 2004). The latter are keen to promote apparent heterogenization in tastes, although the underlying material substructure of production and distribution that they have developed is best understood as primarily, although certainly not exclusively, homogenizing in nature, as we saw previously (although for recent trends in supermarkets promoting 'local' foods, see Guptill and Wilkins, 2002).

Another irony becomes apparent when we note that when fast-food chains, supermarkets and agribusiness are regarded in highly negative ways by certain groups, the threat of their apparent homogenizing influences can be very productive of modes of thought and practice which seem to be the antitheses of the latter but which are in fact their dialectically-related cousins. Thus as various 'foreign' cuisines have become part of everyday supermarket-based mass market consumption, middle-class consumers can seek to distinguish themselves from their lower-class compatriots by seeking out either new culinary terrains (locales as yet relatively uncommodified by the supermarkets, such as South African cuisine) or apparently more 'pure', more 'authentic', more 'real', versions of more familiar terrains (Boyle, 2004). Thus the parameters of what are taken to be particular 'national' and 'regional' cuisines are defined and defended. A whole section of the publishing industry is now devoted to catering for this market, purveying recipe books that say they represent the 'real Tuscany', the 'true taste of Sicily', the 'authentic Provence', and so on. Concerted efforts are made—both by those keen to show they are real 'locals' and also by expatriate authors at pains to show how much local cultural capital they have at their disposal—to capture the 'essence' of each particular cuisine and to police its boundaries. A whole series of culinary entrepreneurs, like cookbook authors, journalists and television programme hosts, are concerned to define what is 'authentic' and what is not, even though such authenticity is 'performed' (brought into being, invented, constantly created anew) rather than simply 'real', as is generally claimed by such entrepreneurs (Lu and Fine, 1995).

A particularly striking example of these trends against what is taken to be a global 'consumer monoculture' (Norberg-Hodge, 2003), is the 'Slow Food' movement (Petrini, 2003; Wilk, 2006). As Alison Leitch shows in her chapter, it was developed in northern Italy in the 1980s as a social movement of the intelligentsia, dedicated to 'saving' both local cuisine and eating habits from the perceived destructively homogenizing effects of food globalization. The movement focussed on what it took to be emblematic foods, such as particular kinds of pork fat, as the sorts of comestibles that could be 'lost' if the homogenizing forces abroad in the world today, involving not just the rise of McDonalds and so on but also the ever greater reach of EU food-safety regulations, became ever more dominant. In a further ironic twist, the success of the movement amongst middle-class audiences in Italy, France and beyond has meant that the movement is now *itself* transnational, boasting active branches across the developed world, including the greatest apparent locus of global food homogenization, the United States itself (Leitch, 2003).

This situation presents one of the most striking paradoxes of contemporary food globalization: a movement dedicated to the preservation of what it takes to be the 'national' and 'local' in food becomes itself transnational in scope, influence and means of organization. This mirrors the transnationalization of groups dedicated to other related causes such as organic food production (itself imbued with various romantic discourses concerned with locality) and Fairtrade distribution (Wright and Madrid, 2007). Thus the apparently 'local' struggles against the negatively conceived 'global' in food terms have themselves become in significant ways globalized.

Slow food represents a much broader set of tendencies involving the apparent 'defence' of locality and region in the face of what are taken as the worst kinds of food globalizations. But what advocates of food locality tend to forget—indeed, must forget, if their localizing claims are to carry resonance for audiences in the developed world—is that, as we saw already in the case of the great post-Columbian food movements, many of the cuisines that have apparently been untouched for hundreds of years are themselves hybrids, created as the result of long-term processes of migration and trade. Up until the later nineteenth century, the period of the beginnings of world-spanning systems of food production and distribution, there were relatively few compelling reasons to focus upon the 'purity' or otherwise of a given cuisine. Such matters had little reason to enter into consciousness, and they thus could not be the subject of politicization and polemic. But in the present day, characterized by the ubiquity of discourses focused around the alleged cultural degradations and health disasters attendant upon food homogenization, there exist ever more tendencies to draw demarcation lines around 'true' expressions of a food culture and to identify and condemn what are seen as mere ersatz imitations or as hybridized deviations from the alleged norm. The reclaiming of the 'local' or 'regional' in food is as much a form of food globalization as are the homogenizing practices of supermarkets, fast food chains and agribusiness. Indeed, it is when certain groups think about and endeavour to resist the latter that complex forms of food heterogenization are stimulated.

One of the central implications of this book is that today people would not put such emphasis on the virtues of locality in cuisines unless the latter were thought to be 'under threat' in various ways from what are taken as the homogenizing forces of certain kinds of food globalization. But we could not easily think of the 'local' in food matters unless there was a 'global' to contrast it against. As the latter seems—above all, through the galvanizing and often polemical efforts of different sorts of activists—to be wholly negative in nature, that negativity involving problems to do with health, with threats to cultural heritage and with the spectre of a world rendered wholly the same everywhere under the aegis of capitalist consumerism, no wonder the local seems to offer the affordance of virtue, of stability and of irreducible cultural difference.

But all of these expressions of the local—or rather, our various imaginings of them—are as much created by, and are expressions of, the complex conditions of globality that are characteristic of the planet at the present time, as are processes of homogenization and sameness. The general thematic and analytic point of this book is that food globalizations are many and manifold, not singular and uniform. The apparently homogeneous segues into the allegedly heterogeneous, and vice versa. Modes of thought related to food range from the highly reflexive to the necessarily naive, with complicated compounds of both these modes being the norm at the present time. Patterns are thrown into mess, yet mess itself is patterned and subjected to changing forms of structuring. All of the contributions to this book have paid eloquent testament to such a state of affairs. They all indicate in their own specific manners how to make sense of this state of complexity and flux. For us, one thing has also become clear: augmented understandings of how food globalizations work themselves out in all their multiplicity, nuance and abounding irony will really become possible once political economists and others like them learn to think like ethnographers and others like them, and when the latter learn to think like the former too.[5] It will be at that point—of analytic conciliation and conceptual complexification—that analysts of food of all hues will truly become refined connoisseurs of the most pungent, but also of the most delicate, of all the tastes that the many food globalizations of the future will have to offer. They will in that sense be the inheritors of the future that the great French gourmet, Brillat-Savarin, who was quoted at the start of this chapter, envisaged almost 200 years ago.

Notes

1. The original Latin reference is Book XXXIX, 6.
2. Studies of particular foodstuffs can be very useful in depicting the geographical and cross-cultural careers of particular kinds of raw ingredient. See, for

example, Salaman (1949), Mintz (1986), Kurlansky (1999), Kurlansky (2003), Allen, (2001), Hobhouse, (1999), Coe (2003) and Wild (2005).

3. For ways in which developed world consumers can attempt to operate within networks outside those created by supermarkets and agribusiness, see, for example, Barrientos (2000).

4. But for some trends towards relocalization in developing world contexts of production, see Pacione (1997).

5. An important recent development in this regard is the genre of following the tracks of a particular commodity through the various networks of production, distribution and consumption it moves through, and how these can affect—or not affect—each other. See Cook and Harrison (2007).

References

Allen, S. L. (2001), *The Devil's Cup: Coffee, the Driving Force in History,* Edinburgh: Canongate.

Anderson, B. (2006), *Imagined Communities: Reflections on the Origin and Spread of Nationalism,* London: Verso.

Appadurai, A. (1988), 'How to Make a National Cuisine: Cookbooks in Contemporary India', *Comparative Studies of Society and History,* 30/1: 3–24.

Appadurai, A. (1990), 'Disjuncture and Difference in the Global Cultural Economy', *Public Culture* 2/2: 1–24.

Applbaum, K. (2004), *The Marketing Era: From Professional Practice to Global Provisioning,* London: Routledge.

Araghi, F. (2003) 'Food Regimes and the Production of Value: Some Methodological Issues', *The Journal of Peasant Studies,* 30/2: 41–70.

Arce, A., and Marsden, T. K. (1993), 'The Social Construction of International Food: A New Research Agenda', *Economic Geography,* 69/3: 293–311.

Arnason, J. (2003), *Civilizations in Dispute,* Leiden: Brill.

Askegaard, S., and Kjeldgaard, D. (2007), 'Here, There and Everywhere: Place Branding and Gastronomical Globalization in a Macromarketing Perspective', *Journal of Macromarketing,* 27/2: 138–47.

Atkin, M. (1992), *The International Grain Trade,* Cambridge: Woodhead.

Augé, M. (1995), *Non-Places: Introduction to an Anthropology of Supermodernity,* London: Verso.

Barber, B. (1992), 'Jihad vs. McWorld', *The Atlantic Monthly,* 269/3: 53–65.

Barndt, D. (2002), *Tangled Routes: Women, Work and Globalization on the Tomato Trail,* Lanham: Rowman and Littlefield.

Barrett, H. R., Ilbery, B. W., Brown, A. W., and Binns, T.(1999), 'Globalization and the Changing Networks of Food Supply: The Importation of Fresh Horticultural Produce from Kenya into the UK', *Transactions of the Institute of British Geographers,* New Series, 24: 159–74.

Barrientos, S. (2000), 'Globalization and Ethical Trade: Assessing the Implications for Development', *Journal of International Development,* 12: 559–70.

Beck, U. (1992), *Risk Society: Towards a New Modernity,* London: Sage.

Beck, U. (1998), *World Risk Society,* Cambridge: Polity.

Bee, A. (2000), 'Globalization, Grapes and Gender: Women's Work in Traditional and Agro-Export Production in Northern Chile', *The Geographical Journal,* 166/3: 255–65.

Belasco, W. J. (1987), 'Ethnic Fast Foods: The Corporate Melting Pot', *Food and Foodways,* 2: 1–30.

Benson, R., and Saguy, A. (2005), 'Constructing Social Problems in an Age of Globalization: A French-American Comparison', *American Sociological Review,* 70/2: 233–59.

Bhabha, H. (1994), *The Location of Culture,* London: Routledge.

Blythman, J. (2005), *Shopped: The Shocking Power of British Supermarkets,* London: HarperPerennial.

Bonnano, A. (1998), 'Liberal Democracy in the Global Era: Implications for the Agro-Food Sector', *Agriculture and Human Values,* 15: 223–42.

Bonnano, A. (2004), 'Globalization, Transnational Corporations, the State and Democracy', *International Journal of Sociology of Agriculture and Food,* 12/1: 37–48.

Bonnano, A., Alessandro, A., Busch, L., Friedland, W.H., Gouveia, L., and Mingione, E. (eds.) (1994), *From Columbus to ConAgra: The Globalization of Agriculture and Food,* Lawrence: University of Kansas Press.

Bonnano, A., and Constance, D. H. (1996), *Caught in the Net: The Global Tuna Industry, Environmentalism and the State,* Lawrence: University of Kansas Press.

Bonnano, A., and Constance, D. H. (2001), 'Globalization, Fordism, and Post-Fordism in Agriculture and Food: A Critical Review of Salient Literature', *Culture & Agriculture,* 23/2: 1–18.

Bové, J., and Dufour, F. (2002), *The World Is Not for Sale: Farmers against Junk Food,* London: Verso.

Boyd, W., and Watts, M. (1997), 'Agro-Industrial Just-in-Time: The Chicken Industry and Post-War American Capitalism', in D. Goodman and M. Watts (eds.), *Globalising Food: Agrarian Questions and Global Restructuring,* London: Routledge.

Boyle, D. (2004), *Authenticity: Brands, Fakes and the Lust for Real Life,* London: HarperPerennial.

Braudel, F. (1982), *Civilization and Capitalism, 15th–18th Centuries, Volume 2, The Wheels of Commerce,* New York: Harper and Row.

Bright, C. (1999), 'Invasive Species: Pathogens of Globalization', *Foreign Policy,* 116: 50–64.

Brown, P., and Scott, K. (2004), 'Cancer Warning over Scottish Farmed Salmon', *The Guardian* (9 January 2004), <http://www.guardian.co.uk/environment/2004/jan/09/fish.food>

Buctuanon, E. M. (2001), 'Globalization of Biotechnology: The Agglomeration of Dispersed Knowledge and Information and Its Implications for the Political Economy of Technology in Developing Countries', *New Genetics and Society*, 20/1: 26–41.

Caglar, A. S. (1999), 'McDöner: *Döner Kebap* and the Social Positioning Struggle of German Turks', in C. Lentz (ed.), *Changing Food Habits: Case Studies From Africa, South America and Europe*, Amsterdam: Harwood Academic.

Caldwell, M. L. (2004), 'Domesticating the French Fry: McDonalds and Consumerism in Moscow', *Journal of Consumer Culture*, 4: 5–26.

Caplan, P. (1997), 'Approaches to the Study of Food, Health and Identity', in P. Caplan (ed.), *Food, Health and Identity*, London: Routledge.

Castells, M. (1997), *The Power of Identity, the Information Age: Economy, Society and Culture*, vol. 2., Oxford: Blackwell.

Chalfin, B. (2004), *Shea Butter Republic: State Power, Global Markets and the Making of an Indigenous Commodity*, London: Routledge.

Charles, D. (2001), *Lords of the Harvest: Biotech, Big Money and the Future of Food*, Cambridge, MA: Perseus.

Cheng, T. O. (2004), 'Childhood Obesity in China', *Health & Place*, 10/4: 395–6.

Chossudovsky, M. (2008), 'Global Famine', *Global Research* [online journal], May, <http://www.globalresearch.ca/index.php?context=va&aid=8877> accessed 30 August 2009.

Clover, C. (2006), *The End of the Line: How Overfishing Is Changing the World and What We Eat*, New York: The New Press.

Coe, S. (2003), *The True History of Chocolate*, London: Thames and Hudson.

Colquhoun, K. (2007), *Taste: The Story of Britain through Its Food*, London: Bloomsbury.

Cook, I., and Harrison, M. (2003), 'Cross over Food: Re-Materializing Postcolonial Geographies', *Transactions of the Institute of British Geographers*, 28: 297–317.

Cook, I., and Harrison, M. (2007), 'Follow the Thing: "West Indian Hot Pepper Sauce"', *Space and Culture*, 10/1: 40–63.

Curtin, P. D. (1998), *Cross-Cultural Trade in World History*, Cambridge: Cambridge University Press.

David, E. (1970 [1960]), *French Provincial Cooking*, Harmondsworth: Penguin.

Davidson, A. (1992), 'Europeans' Wary Encounter with Tomatoes, Potatoes, and Other New World Foods', in N. Foster and L. S. Cordell (eds.), *Chilies to Chocolate: Food the Americas Gave the World*, Tucson: University of Arizona Press.

Daviron, B., and Ponte, S. (2005), *The Coffee Paradox: Commodity Trade and the Elusive Promise of Development*, London: Zed Books.

Devereux, S. (1993), *Theories of Famine*, Hemel Hempstead: Harvester Wheatsheaf.

Dolan, C. S. (2005), 'Fields of Obligation: Rooting Ethical Sourcing in Kenyan Horticulture', *Journal of Consumer Culture*, 5/3: 365–89.

The Economist (2008), 'The Silent Tsunami: The Food Crisis and How to Solve It' (19–25 April, 2008).

Fantasia, R. (1995), 'Fast Food in France', *Theory and Society,* 24/2: 201–43.

Fernandez,-Armesto, F. (2001), *Food: A History,* Basingstoke: Macmillan.

Fischler, C. (1999), 'The "Mad-Cow" Crisis: A Global Perspective', in R. Grew (ed.), *Food in Global History,* Boulder: Westview Press.

Food and Agriculture Organisation of the United Nations (2009), *Number of Undernourished Persons,* <http://www.fao.org/es/ess/faostat/foodsecurity/index_en.htm>

Foster, N., and Cordell, L. S. (1992), *Chilies to Chocolate: Food the Americas Gave the World,* Tucson: University of Arizona Press.

Frank, A. G., and Gills, B. (eds.) (1994), *The World System: Five Hundred Years or Five Thousand?,* London: Routledge.

Friedland, W. H. (1994), 'The Global Fresh Fruit and Vegetable System: An Industrial Organization Analysis', in P. McMichael (ed.), *The Global Restructuring of Agro-Food Systems,* Ithaca: Cornell University Press.

Friedman, T. (2000), *The Lexus and the Olive Tree,* London: HarperCollins.

Friedmann, H. (1982), 'The Political Economy of Food: The Rise and Fall of the Postwar International Food Order', *American Journal of Sociology,* 88 (Supplement): S248–86.

Friedmann, H. (1994), 'The International Relations of Food: The Unfolding Crisis of National Regulation', in B. Harriss-White and R. Hoffenberg (eds.), *Food: Multidisciplinary Perspectives,* Cambridge: Basil Blackwell.

Friedmann, H., and McMichael, P. (1989), 'Agriculture and the State System: The Rise and Decline of National Agricultures', *Sociologia Ruralis,* 29: 93–117.

Gallegos, D. (2005), 'Pastes, Powders, and Potions: The Development of an Eclectic Australian Palate', *Food, Culture and Society,* 8/1: 39–46.

Giddens, A. (1990), *The Consequences of Modernity,* Cambridge: Polity.

Goodman, D., and Watts, M. (eds.) (1997), *Globalising Food: Agrarian Questions and Global Restructuring,* London: Routledge.

Goody, J. (1982), *Cooking, Cuisine and Class: A Study of Comparative Sociology,* Cambridge: Cambridge University Press.

Goody, J. (1998), 'The Globalization of Chinese Food' in *Food and Love: A Cultural History of East and West,* London: Verso.

Gregory, P. J., Ingram, J. S. I., and Brklacich, M. (2005), 'Climate Change and Food Security', *Philosophical Transactions: Biological Sciences,* 360/1463: 2139–48.

Grew, R. (ed.) (1999), *Food in Global History,* Boulder: Westview Press.

Guptill, A., and Wilkins, J. L. (2002), 'Buying into the Food System: Trends in Food Retailing in the US and implications for Local Foods', *Agriculture and Human Values,* 19: 39–51.

Guthman, J. (2004), *Agrarian Dreams: The Paradox of Organic Farming in California,* Berkeley: University of California Press.

Hannerz, U. (1996), *Transnational Connections: Culture, People, Places*, London: Routledge.

Harrison, J. S., Chang, E.-Y., Gauthier, C., Joerchel, T., Nevarez, J., and Wang, M. (2005), 'Exporting a North American Concept to Asia: Starbucks in China', *Cornell Hotel and Restaurant Administration Quarterly*, 46/2: 275–83.

Held, D., McGrew, A., Goldblatt, D., and Perraton, J. (1999), *Global Transformations: Politics, Economics and Culture*, Cambridge: Polity.

Hobhouse, H. (1999), *Seeds of Change*, London: Pan.

Humphery, K. (1998), *Shelf Life: Supermarkets and the Changing Cultures of Consumption*, Cambridge: Cambridge University Press.

Ilcan, S., and Phillips, L. (2003), 'Making Food Count: Expert Knowledge and Global Technologies of Government', *Canadian Review of Sociology and Anthropology*, 40/4: 441–62.

Illouz, E., and John, N. (2003), 'Global Habitus, Local Stratification, and Symbolic Struggles over Identity: The Case of McDonald's Israel', *American Behavioral Scientist*, 47: 201–29.

Inglis, D. (2004) 'Auto Couture: Thinking the Car in Post-War France', *Theory, Culture and Society*, 21/4–5: 197–219.

James, A. (1994), 'Cuisiner Des Livres: Identités Globales Ou Locales Dans Les Cultures', *Anthropologie Sociale*, 18/3: 39–56.

James, A. (1996), 'Cooking the Books: Global or Local Identities in Contemporary British Food Cultures?', in D. Howes (ed.), *Cross-Cultural Consumption: Global Markets, Local Realities*, London: Routledge.

Jarosz, L. (2000), 'Understanding Agri-Food Networks as Social Relations', *Agriculture and Human Values*, 17: 279–83.

Jing, J. (ed.) (2000), *Feeding China's Little Emperors: Food, Children and Social Change*, Stanford: Stanford University Press.

Jones, A. (2003), '"Power in Place": Viticultural Spatialities of Globalization and Community Empowerment in the Languedoc', *Transactions of the Institute of British Geographers*, 28/3: 367–82.

Kalra, V. (2004), 'The Political Economy of the Samosa', *South Asia Research*, 24/1: 21–36.

Keane, J. (2003), *Global Civil Society?*, Cambridge: Cambridge University Press.

Kimbrell, A. (ed.) (2002), *The Fatal Harvest Reader: The Tragedy of Industrial Agriculture*, Sausalito: Foundation for Deep Ecology.

Kjaernes, U., Harvey, M., and Warde, A. (2007), *Trust in Food: A Comparative and Institutional Analysis*, Basingstoke: Palgrave.

Kneen, B. (1999), 'Restructuring Food for Corporate Profit: The Corporate Genetics of Cargill and Monsanto', *Agriculture and Human Values*, 16: 161–67.

Konefal, J., Mascarenhas, M., and Hatanaka, M. (2005), 'Governance in the Global Agro-Food System: Backlighting the Role of Transnational Supermarket Chains', *Agriculture and Human Values*, 22: 291–302.

Kurlansky, M. (1999), *Cod: A Biography of the Fish That Changed the World,* New York: Vintage.

Kurlansky, M. (2003), *Salt: A World History,* New York: Vintage.

Kurzer, P., and Cooper, A. (2007), 'What's for Dinner? European Farming and Food Traditions Confront American Biotechnology', *Comparative Political Studies,* 40/9: 1035–58.

Lang, T., and Heasman, M. (2004), *Food Wars: The Global Battle for Mouths, Minds and Markets,* London: Earthscan.

Lappé, M., and Bailey, B. (2002), *Against the Grain: The Genetic Transformation of Global Agriculture,* London: Earthscan.

Law, L. (2001), 'Home Cooking: Filipino Women and Geographies of the Senses in Hong Kong', 8/3: 264–83.

Lechner, F., and Boli, J. (2005), *World Culture: Origins and Consequences,* Oxford: Blackwell.

Leitch, A. (2003), 'Slow Food and the Politics of Pork Fat: Italian Food and European Identity', *Ethnos,* 68/4: 437–62.

Levinson, M. (2008), *The Box: How the Shipping Container Made the World Smaller and the World Economy Bigger,* Princeton: Princeton University Press.

Lien, M. E. (2004), 'Dogs, Whales and Kangaroos: Transnational Activism and Food Taboos,' in M. E. Lien and B. Nerlich (eds.), *The Politics of Food,* Oxford: Berg.

Lien, M. E., and Nerlich, B. (eds.) (2004), *The Politics of Food,* Oxford: Berg.

Livy (2000), *The Dawn of the Roman Empire: Books 31–40,* trans J. C. Yardley, Oxford: Oxford University Press.

Llambi, L. (1993), 'Global Agro-Food Restructuring: The Role of Transnational Corporations and Nation-States', *International Journal of Sociology of Agriculture and Food,* 3: 19–38.

Lozado Jr, E. P., (2005), 'Globalized Childhood? Kentucky Fried Chicken in Beijing', in J. L. Watson and M. L. Caldwell (eds.), *The Cultural Politics of Food and Eating: A Reader,* Oxford: Blackwell.

Lu, S., and Fine, G. A. (1995), 'The Presentation of Ethnic Authenticity: Chinese Food as a Social Accomplishment', *The Sociological Quarterly,* 36/3: 535–53.

Macnaghten, P. (2004), 'Animals in their Nature: A Case Study on Public Attitudes to Animals, Genetic Modification and "Nature"', *Sociology,* 38/3: 533–51.

Mansfield, B. (2003), 'Spatializing Globalization: A "Geography of Quality" in the Seafood Industry', *Economic Geography,* 79/1: 1–16.

Marx, K., and Engels, F. (1968 [1848]), 'Manifesto of the Communist Party', in *Marx-Engels Selected Works,* Moscow: Progress Publishers.

McCoy, E. (2008), *The Emperor of Wine: The Story of the Remarkable Rise and Reign of Robert Parker,* London: Grub Street.

McLean, A. (2004), 'The Aesthetic Pleasures of Elizabeth David', *Food, Culture and Society: An International Journal of Multidisciplinary Research,* 7/1: 37–45.

McMichael, P. (ed.) (1994), *The Global Restructuring of Agro-Food Systems,* Ithaca: Cornell University Press.

McMichael, P. (ed.) (1995), *Food and Agrarian Orders in the World Economy,* Westport: Greenwood.

McMichael, P. (1999), 'Virtual Capitalism and Agri-Food Restructuring', in D. Burch et al. (eds.), *Restructuring Global and Regional Agricultures,* Aldershot: Ashgate.

McMichael, P. (2000), 'The Power of Food', *Agriculture and Human Values,* 17: 21–33.

McMichael, P. (2005), 'Global Development and the Corporate Food Regime', in F. H. Buttel and P. McMichael (eds.), *New Directions in the Sociology of Global Development,* Amsterdam: Elsevier.

Messer, E. (1997), 'Three Centuries of Changing European Taste for the Potato', in H. Macbeth (ed.), *Food Preferences and Taste: Continuity and Change,* Oxford: Berghahn.

Miller, D. (1998), *Material Cultures: Why Some Things Matter,* Chicago: University of Chicago Press.

Mintz, S. W. (1986), *Sweetness and Power: The Place of Sugar in Modern History,* Harmondsworth: Penguin.

Mintz, S. W. (2008), 'Food, Culture and Energy', in A. Nutzenadel and F. Trentmann (eds.), *Food and Globalization,* Oxford: Berg.

Mintz, S. W., and Du Bois, C. M. (2002), 'The Anthropology of Food and Eating', *Annual Review of Anthropology,* 31: 99–119.

Murcott, A. (2001), 'Public Beliefs about GM Foods', *Medical Anthropology Quarterly,* 15/1: 1–11.

Murray, S. (2007), *Moveable Feasts: The Incredible Journeys of the Things We Eat,* London: Aurum.

Murray, W. (2001), 'The Second Wave of Globalization and Agrarian Change in the Pacific Islands', *Journal of Rural Studies,* 17: 135–48.

Mythen, G. (1999), 'From "Goods" to "Bads"? Revisiting the Political Economy of Risk', *Sociological Research Online* [online journal], 10/3, <http://www.socresonline.org.uk/10/3/mythen.html>

Nestle, M. (2003), *Food Politics: How the Food Industry Influences Nutrition and Health,* Berkeley: University of California Press.

Nibert, D. (2002), *Animal Rights/Human Rights: Entanglements of Oppression and Liberation,* Lanham: Rowman and Littlefield.

Norberg-Hodge, H. (2003), 'The Consumer Monoculture', *International Journal of Consumer Studies,* 27/4: 258–61.

Norberg-Hodge, H., Merrifield, T., and Gorelick, S. (2002), *Bringing the Food Economy Home: Local Alternatives to Agri-Business,* London: Zed Books.

Nutzenadel, A., and Trentmann, F. (eds.) (2008), *Food and Globalization,* Oxford: Berg.

Ohnuki-Tierney, E. (1999), 'We Eat Each Other's Food to Nourish Our Body: The Local and the Local as Mutually Constituent Forces', in R. Grew (ed.), *Food in Global History,* Boulder: Westview Press.

Pacione, M. (1997), 'Local Exchange Trading Systems—a Rural Response to the Globalization of Capitalism?', *Journal of Rural Studies,* 13/4: 415–27.

Patel, R. (2008), *Stuffed and Starved: From Farm to Fork, the Hidden Battle for the World Food System,* London: Portobello.

Peckham, S. (1998), 'Consuming Nations' in S. Griffiths and J. Wallace (eds.), *Consuming Passions,* London: Times Higher Education Supplement.

Petrini, C. (2003), *Slow Food: The Case for Taste,* New York: Columbia University Press.

Petronius (1996), *Satyrica,* R. B. Branham and D. Kinney (eds. and trans.), London: Everyman / J. M. Dent.

Phillips, L. (2006), 'Food and Globalization', *Annual Review of Anthropology,* 35: 37–57.

Plog, S. C. (2005), 'Starbucks: More Than a Cup of Coffee', *Cornell Hotel and Restaurant Administration Quarterly,* 46/2: 284–7.

Pollan, M. (2007), *The Omnivore's Dilemma,* London: Bloomsbury.

Pottier, J. (1999), *Anthropology of Food: The Social Dynamics of Food Security,* Oxford: Blackwell.

Pritchard, B., and Burch, D. (2003), *Agri-Food Globalization in Perspective: International Restructuring in the Processing Tomato Industry,* Aldershot: Ashgate.

Pritchard, B., and Fagan, R. (1999), 'Circuits of Capital and Transnational Corporate Spatial Behavior: Nestlé in Southeast Asia', *International Journal of Sociology of Agriculture and Food,* 8: 3–20.

Raviv, Y. (2005), 'The Hebrew Banana: Local Food and the Performance of Israeli National Identity', *Food, Culture and Society,* 8/1: 30–5.

Ray, K. (2004), *The Migrants' Table,* Philadelphia: Temple University Press.

Raynolds, L. T. (2002), 'Consumer/Producer Links in Fair Trade Coffee Networks', *Sociologia Ruralis,* 42/4: 404–24.

Raynolds, L. T., and Murray, D. (1998), 'Yes, We Have No Bananas: Reregulating Global and Regional Trade', *International Journal of Sociology of Agriculture and Food,* 7: 7–44.

Rebora, G. (2001), *Culture of the Fork: A Brief History of Food in Europe,* New York: Columbia University Press.

Renton, D. (2001), *Marx on Globalization,* London: Verso.

Ritzer, G. (2000), *The McDonaldization of Society,* Thousand Oaks, Pine Forge.

Ritzer, G. (2004), *The Globalization of Nothing,* London: Sage.

Roberts, J. A. G. (2002), *China To Chinatown: Chinese Food in the West,* London: Reaktion Books.

Roberts, P. (2009), *The End of Food: The Coming Crisis in the World Food Industry,* London: Bloomsbury.

Robertson, R. (1992), *Globalization,* London: Sage.

Robertson, R., and Inglis, D. (2004), 'The Global *Animus:* In the Tracks of World-Consciousness', *Globalizations,* 1/1: 38–49.

Ross, K. (1996), *Fast Cars, Clean Bodies: Decolonization and the Reordering of French Culture,* Cambridge, MA: MIT Press.

Rosset, P., Rice, R., and Watts, M. (1999), 'Thailand and the World Tomato: Globalization, New Agricultural Countries (NACs) and the Agrarian Question', *International Journal of Sociology of Agriculture and Food,* 8: 71–85.

Salaman, R. N. (1949), *History and Social Influence of the Potato,* Cambridge: Cambridge University Press.

Sayid, R. (2004), 'Will Traditional British Grub Soon Be a Thing of the Pasta?', *Daily Mirror* (29 October 2004), 38.

Schlosser, E. (2001), *Fast Food Nation: The Dark Side of the All-American Meal,* New York, Houghton Mifflin.

Scholte, J. A. (2000), *Globalization: A Critical Introduction,* Basingstoke: Palgrave.

Seabrook, J. (2004), *Consuming Cultures: Globalization and Local Lives,* Oxford: New Internationalist.

Selfa, T., and Qazi, J. (2005), 'Place, Taste or Face-to-Face: Understanding Producer-Consumer Networks in "Local" Food Systems', *Agriculture and Human Values,* 22/4: 451–64.

Sen, A. (2001), *Development as Freedom,* Oxford: Oxford University Press.

Seneca (1889), 'Consolatio Ad Helvia / Addressed to His Mother Helvia: Of Consolation' in *L. Annaeus Seneca: Minor Dialogues,* A. Stewart (trans.), London: George Bell.

Shepard, S. (2001), *Pickled, Potted and Canned: The Story of Food Preserving,* London: Headline.

Shiva, V. (2000), *Stolen Harvest: The Highjacking of the Global Food Supply,* Cambridge, MA: South End.

Simmel, G. (1997), 'The Sociology of the Meal', in D. Frisby and M. Featherstone (eds.), *Simmel on Culture: Selected Writings,* London: Sage.

Simpson, T., (2008), 'The Commercialization of Macau's Cafés', *Ethnography,* 9/2: 197–234.

Smale, W. (2008). 'Why Starbucks Sales Have Gone Cold', *BBC News Online* (1 February 2008) <http://news.bbc.co.uk/2/hi/business/7219458.stm>

Smith, A. F. (1994), *The Tomato in America: Early History, Culture and Cookery,* Columbia: University of South Carolina Press.

Sobal, J. (1999), 'Food System Globalization, Eating Transformations and Nutrition Transitions', in R. Grew (ed.) *Food in Global History,* Boulder: Westview Press.

Sorj, B., and Wilkinson, J. (1985), 'Modern Food Technology: Industrialising Nature', *International Social Science Journal,* 37/3, 301–14.

Standage, T. (2009), *An Edible History of Humanity,* London: Atlantic.

Taylor, T. (2001), *Stanley Park,* Toronto: Vintage Canada.

Thompson, C. J., and Tambyah, S. K. (1999), 'Trying to Be Cosmopolitan', *Journal of Consumer Research,* 26: 214.

Tomlinson, J. (1997), *Cultural Imperialism: A Critical Introduction,* London: Pinter.

Tomlinson, J. (1999) *Globalization and Culture,* Cambridge: Polity.

Tudge, C. (2004), *So Shall We Reap: What's Gone Wrong with the World's Food— and How to Fix It,* London: Penguin.

Tulloch, J., and Lupton, D. (2001), 'Consuming Risk, Consuming Science: The Case of GM Foods', *Journal of Consumer Culture,* 2: 363–83.

Tunstall, J. (1977), *The Media Are American,* London: Constable.

Turner, J. (2005), *Spice: The History of a Temptation,* London: HarperPerennial.

Walls, J. (2002), 'The Campaign against "Live Exports" in the UK: Animal Protectionism, the Stigmatisation of Place and the Language of Moral Outrage', *Sociological Research Online* [online journal], 7/1, <http://www.socresonline.org.uk/7/1/walls.html>

Warde, A., Martens, L., and Olsen, W. (1999), 'Consumption and the Problem of Variety: Cultural Omnivorousness, Social Distinction and Dining Out', *Sociology,* 33: 105–27.

Warman, A. (2003), *Corn and Capitalism: How a Botanical Bastard Grew to Global Dominance,* Chapel Hill: University of North Carolina Press.

Watson, J. L. (1997), 'Transnationalism, Localization and Fast Foods in East Asia' in J. L. Watson (ed.), *Golden Arches East: McDonalds in East Asia,* Stanford: Stanford University Press.

Watson, J. L., and Caldwell, M. L. (2005), 'Introduction', in J. L. Watson and M. Caldwell L. (eds.), *The Cultural Politics of Food and Eating: A Reader,* Oxford, Blackwell.

Watts, M., and Goodman, D. (1997), 'Agrarian Questions: Global Appetite, Local Metabolism', in D. Goodman and M. Watts (eds.), *Globalising Food: Agrarian Questions and Global Restructuring,* London: Routledge.

Weis, T. (2007), *The Global Food Economy: The Battle for the Future of Farming,* London: Zed Books.

Whatmore, S., and Thorne, L. (1997), 'Nourishing Networks: Alternative Geographies of Food', in D. Goodman and M. Watts (eds.), *Globalising Food: Agrarian Questions and Global Restructuring,* London: Routledge.

Wild, A. (2005), *Black Gold: The Dark History of Coffee,* London: HarperPerennial.

Wilk, R. R. (1999), 'Real Belizean Food: Building Local Identity in the Transnational Caribbean', *American Anthropologist,* new series, 101/2: 244–55.

Wilk, R. (ed.) (2006), *Fast Food / Slow Food: The Cultural Economy of the Global Food System,* Lanham: AltaMira Press.

Wilkinson, D. (2006), 'Globalizations', in B. K. Gills and W. R. Thompson, eds., *Globalization and Global History,* London: Routledge.

Willging, J. (2008), 'Of GMOs, McDomination and Foreign Fat: Contemporary Franco-American Food Fights', *French Cultural Studies,* 19/2: 199–26.

Wright, C., and Madrid, G. (2007), 'Contesting Ethical Trade in Colombia's Cut-Flower Industry: A Case of Cultural and Economic Injustice', *Cultural Sociology,* 1/2: 255–75.

Wu, D. Y. H., and Tan, C. B. (eds.) (2001), *Changing Chinese Foodways in Asia,* Hong Kong: Chinese University Press.

Young, E. M. (2004), 'Globalization and Food Security: Novel Questions in a Novel Context?', *Progress in Development Studies,* 4/1: 1–21.

Zukin, S. (1992), 'The Bubbling Cauldron: Global and Local Interactions in New York City Restaurants', *Comparative and Urban Community Research,* 4: 105–32.

Part II
Food Globalizations: Production and Distribution

–2–

Slow Food and the Politics
of 'Virtuous Globalization'

Alison Leitch
Macquarie University

In 1987, a group of Italian writers and journalists produced a provocative manifesto announcing the official launch of a new movement for the defence of and the right to pleasure. Published in *Gambero Rosso,* an eight-page monthly 'lifestyle' supplement of *Il Manifesto* (which is a widely circulating national independent communist daily newspaper), the manifesto began with the assertion that 'we are enslaved by speed and have all succumbed to the same insidious virus: Fast Life, which disrupts our habits, pervades the privacy of our homes and forces us to eat Fast Foods' (Parasecoli, 2003: 39).[1] It followed with a number of statements declaring the necessity of founding a new international movement called Slow Food, which was 'the only truly progressive answer' to the 'universal folly of the Fast Life'. Defending oneself against the speed of modernity, according to the manifesto, began at the table, through the rediscovery of 'the flavours and savours of regional cooking', the banishment of 'the degrading effects of Fast Foods' and the 'development of taste' through the 'international exchange of experiences, knowledge and projects'. Not surprisingly, the manifesto immediately attracted a great deal of public attention although, initially, many commentators regarded the idea of an international organization dedicated to the sensual pleasure of slow food and the 'slow life' as something of a joke. However, only two decades later, Slow Food has emerged as a highly visible and politically influential international organization whose dedication to changing consumer attitudes towards the foods they eat has had some quite remarkable practical effects.

The founder of Slow Food—Carlo Petrini—has famously dubbed his project as a new form of 'virtuous globalization' (Petrini, 2001a; Stille, 2001). In other words, Slow Food promotes itself as providing a model for imagining alternate modes of global connectedness, in which members of minority cultures—including niche-food producers—are encouraged to network and thrive. While Slow Food has already amply demonstrated considerable organizational acumen in building an international movement around the revitalization of artisanally produced foods, its strategies and cultural politics have also been widely critiqued. This chapter traces the history of the emergence of the Slow Food movement from its origins as a lobby group engaged with the politics of food within Italy to its more recent manifestations as an international organization devoted to global biodiversity. In outlining key moments in this history, I hope to highlight some of the reasons why Slow Food politics have become so controversial.

Revolutionary Gourmets: The Origins of the 'Little Snail'

The original Slow Food manifesto demanding an end to our 'enslavement by speed' was inspired by a loose coalition of public intellectuals opposed to the introduction in Italy of American style fast food chains. Led by food and wine journalist Carlo Petrini, this relatively small, though culturally influential group, had already garnered a great deal of attention through a spirited media campaign conducted against the installation of a McDonald's franchise near the Spanish Steps in the mid-1980s. According to the *Italy Daily,* it was almost an anti-Proustian moment of the smell of French fries that first stirred Petrini into action:

> Walking in Rome one day, he [Petrini] found himself gazing at the splendid Spanish Steps when the overwhelming odor of French fries disturbed his reverie. To his horror he discovered that not twenty meters along the piazza loomed the infamous golden arches of a well-known food chain. 'Basta!' he cried. And thus began a project that would take him all over the world in order to promote and protect local culinary traditions. As a symbol for his cause he chose the snail because it was the slowest food he could think of. (*Italy Daily,* 1998)

But, if we dig a little deeper, it is clear that the origins of the Slow Food movement are located elsewhere. The organization now called Slow Food emerged out of a specific Italian cultural context: the 1970s. Popularly dubbed 'the years of lead' in reference to the activities of terrorist groups such as the Red Brigades, the decade of the 1970s was a period in which the radical ideals of the student movements of the late 1960s had ended in disillusionment. While some members of this generation had turned in frustration to the power of bullets, others abandoned revolutionary ideals for alternative forms of transformational cultural politics. The intellectual biography of Slow Food's most famous protagonist, Carlo Petrini, is forged within this milieu. Alongside his collaborators, Petrini came of age within younger leftist critiques of the Italian Communist Party, which at this time was itself in crisis (see Leitch, 2003).

The son of a teacher and an artisan, Carlo Petrini was born in 1948 in Bra, a provincial town located in the heart of the agricultural region of Piedmont, known as Le Langhe. As its name suggests, this is a landscape of rolling hills that appear as a series of elongated tongues disappearing and reappearing with mirage-like qualities across the hazy horizon, dotted here and there with the villas and castles that still belong to the descendents of the Italian aristocracy. Made famous in the luminous prose of distinguished postwar literary figures such as Cesare Pavese, as well as the detailed documentation of peasant life in the work of noted Italian oral historian Nuto Revelli (1977), the region is acclaimed for the production of some of Italy's finest agricultural produce, including truffles and prestigious wines, such as Barolo and Barbaresco. With strong connections to the aristocracy, the area is also known for its deeply entrenched working-class traditions, particularly left-Catholicism. Once a centre for the leather industry, Bra's other main industries are now the production of laminated plastics and agricultural machinery.[2]

Petrini graduated from high school in 1968, first studying to become a mechanic, but later enrolling in sociology at the University of Trento, a department which, perhaps not coincidentally, was at the epicentre of 1970s extraparliamentarian politics. After completing his studies, Petrini dedicated himself to local cultural politics, becoming a key protagonist in the foundation of a number of cooperative ventures including a bookshop, a food co-op and one of Italy's first radical-left pirate radio stations, called *Radio Bra Onde Rosse* or 'Red Waves'.[3] Like many young Italians of his generation, during these years, Petrini also immersed himself in the rediscovery of the region's rural traditions, its festivals and popular songs, as well as its food and wine culture. Indeed, according to Petrini, wine, rather than food, was the original focus of his attention. He notes, for example, that an early encounter with Italy's most well-known wine journalist and theorist of peasant life, Luigi Veronelli, had nurtured his love of gastronomy and its political potential. A self-avowed anarchist oenologist, Veronelli is famous for publishing a nine-volume work dedicated to Italian wines in the 1960s, as well as for his essays on the importance of rural and culinary traditions to the preservation of specific localities and cultural economies (Veronelli, 2004). These works subsequently became a source of inspiration to an entire generation, including the eventual founders of the Slow Food movement. As Petrini recalls:

> Once I read the texts by Renato Ratti and Gino Veronelli and learned about wine tasting, my world became one with the wine producers, vineyards and wine cellars ... we wandered though the Langhe looking for inns and new restaurants, but there was not an awful lot ... there was no wine list, and the Dolcetto was the one and only wine that the innkeeper would serve you. Hardly anyone served Barolo. So it was inevitable that we developed the gastronomic project before the environmental one, although we had the basic idea for it. (Petrini and Padovani, 2006: 61–2)

By the early 1980s, Petrini was contributing articles to *La Gola,* a magazine published in Milan by a group of young philosophers, artists and poets dedicated to epicurean philosophy. And it was out of this group that a new organization called ARCI Gola—the forerunner of the Slow Food movement—was founded in the mid 1980s.

In Italian *gola* means 'throat' as well as the 'desire for food'. Although it is commonly translated as 'gluttonous', implying a negative state of excess or greed, to be *goloso* has a more positive connotation of craving with pleasure for a particular food. As Carole Counihan (1999, 180) aptly observes, because *gola* implies both 'desire' and 'voice', it suggests that desire for food is a voice, that is, a central vehicle for self-expression in Italian social life. In turn, the Recreative Association of Italian Communists (ARCI), a national network of recreational and cultural clubs, first established in 1957 by the Italian Communist Party to counter the influence of the state recreational organization (ENAL) that supplanted the fascist one existing at the end of the Second World War. In the 1960s and 1970s, as political goals became increasingly divided within the Italian left, the ARCI network spawned a wide variety of clubs and associations dedicated to particular topical interests such as hunting, sport, women's rights, music, film and the environment. ARCI Gola was one of these groups. It emerged out of the desire to create a less hierarchical, youthful alternative to existing gourmet associations that Petrini and his collaborators viewed as linked to chauvinistic and elitist cultural politics. And although the aim of the new association was to raise the profile of regional cuisine and produce, the principle of conviviality combined with an insistence on the right to pleasure and to enjoy oneself through the consumption of good food and wine was always central to the group's philosophy.

It is worth noting that the formation of the first ARCI Gola groups also took place within the context of a number of other food scandals and environmental catastrophes that led to emerging public discussions about the fate of Italian agriculture and its oenogastronomical culture. For example, in March of 1986, there was a public outcry over the revelation of methanol-tainted wine that was eventually discovered as the cause of nineteen deaths across northern Italy. The deaths resulted from the unscrupulous practices of some bulk wine vendors who had deliberately adulterated wine with methyl alcohol in order to increase its alcoholic content, thereby ensuring higher prices. But before the public authorities were able to uncover the chain of contamination, much of this adulterated wine stock had already been sold to large supermarket chains. The consequences of this event were devastating. The scandal not only created wide scale panic among local consumers but also resulted in significant damage to the reputation of the Italian wine industry and its export markets. Later that year, yet another crisis emerged for Italian agriculture: the contamination of the aqueducts of the Po valley with a herbicide called atrazina. Residents of major cities such as Ferrara, Mantua and Bergamo were ordered to turn off their taps as health authorities investigated the damage done to local water supplies from toxic runoff caused, apparently, by the overuse of pesticides (Petrini and Padovani, 2006: 49). Finally, the Chernobyl disaster occurred in April of 1986. The meltdown of the Russian nuclear plant released a huge plume of radioactive haze over much of Europe, creating widespread panic over the consumption of leafy greens, milk and meat products, as well as wild mushrooms gathered from European forests.

The roots of the Slow Food movement are located within this political and cultural context, in the growing public outcry over future scandalous scenarios of environmental contamination and in the micro history of a particular group of left activists who were deeply engaged with transformations to their own regional cultural landscapes and the utopian possibilities of alternative cultural politics in an era of rapid social change. By the end of the 1980s, the original ARCI Gola network was consolidated into a new organization called Slow Food.

Slow Food and the 'Endangered Foods' Project: The Case of *Lardo di Colonnata**

In 1989, two years after the appearance of the first Slow Food manifesto, the International Slow Food Movement was launched at the Opéra Comique in Paris. Over the next decade, as its membership base expanded with new offices opening in France, Switzerland and Germany, Slow Food began broadening its political agenda to include discussions of the importance of food as a cultural artefact linked to the preservation of a distinctive European cultural heritage. This project became known as the 'endangered foods' campaign.

The 'endangered foods' campaign was designed as a polemical intervention into the growing circuits of a vigorous national debate concerning the potential disappearance of regional tastes and idiosyncratic products due to trends such as: the increasing drift towards farming monocultures; the disintegration of traditional rural foodways; environmental threats to national fisheries and the dearth of alternate distribution networks for small-scale agricultural enterprises. Another widely perceived threat was the rapid pace of Europeanization in the wake of the 1992 Maastricht Accord. Slow Food argued that the introduction of new EU standardizing protocols for the manufacture of cured meat products and cheeses posed particular dangers. The application of uniform European hygiene rules designed for large manufacturers would, they argued, lead inevitably to the decline of traditional production techniques, as well as diminish the economic viability of the small-scale producers of these foods. In response, Slow Food began to compile dossiers on particular products that the organization considered in special need of protection.

One example of an 'endangered food' that later became particularly noteworthy in this debate was the case of a unique type of cured pork fat: *lardo di Colonnata*. As its name suggests, *lardo di Colonnata* is produced in Colonnata, a tiny village located at the end of a windy mountain road several kilometres from the marble quarrying town of Carrara in central Italy, where I had also conducted ethnographic research on the subject of craft identity among quarry workers in the late 1980s. At that time, *lardo di Colonnata* was mainly marketed as a culinary delight—even a curiosity—to the odd bus tour and Italian tourists on weekend excursions to the quarries. Since the 1970s, it had also been celebrated at an annual pork fat festival held in the village over the late summer months. And it was certainly well known to culinary experts who reputedly made pilgrimages to eat what some gourmets referred to as 'one of the most divine foods ever produced on this earth' (Manetti, 1996: 8) at Venanzio, a local

---

* For a more extended analysis see Leitch 2000

restaurant named after its owner, a local gourmet and *lardo* purveyor. But regardless of its appreciation as a festive food or its reputation among aficionados, pork fat was not commonly eaten in any of the households I regularly visited for meals while conducting fieldwork. It was, however, almost always mentioned in the oral histories I collected detailing the conditions of work over past generations (Leitch, 1996).

In many of these narratives, the past was distinguished from the present through tales of food scarcity and physical hardship. Until quite recently, meat was a luxury item in diets that consisted predominantly of various grains, legumes and vegetables, as well as produce gathered from the woods and forests, such as chestnuts and mushrooms, wild edible roots and herbs. Many households also maintained small vegetable gardens which kept them going during periods of unemployment, and some households with access to land kept pigs. One of the by-products of these pigs, *lardo* or cured pork fat, thus constituted a kind of food safe for families in the region and was an essential source of calorific energy in the quarry worker's diet. Like sugar or coffee, *lardo* was a 'proletarian hunger killer' (Mintz, 1979: 60). Eaten with a tomato and a piece of onion on dry bread, it was a taken-for-granted element in the worker's lunch. *Lardo* was thought to quell thirst as well as hunger and was appreciated for its coolness on hot summer days. It was also adopted as a cure for a number of common health ailments, ranging from an upset stomach to a bad back. As one local *lardo* maker and restaurateur once remarked to me, 'When you went to the butcher and asked for *lardo,* everyone knew there was someone ill at home'.

Although these days *lardo* producers living in the village of Colonnata claim to have 'invented' the recipe for the product now known as *lardo di Colonnata,* in reality, cured pork fat was not unique to Colonnata. During the 1950s and 1960s, many local people cured their own batches of pork fat at home according to individual recipes that included varying proportions of raw fat, salt, herbs and spices. However, curing the pork in a basin of marble, preferably quarried from near Colonnata at Canalone, was almost always cited as an essential part of the process. Apparently, the unique crystalline structure of Canalone marble allows the pork fat to 'breathe' while at the same time containing the curing brine. If at any stage the *lardo* 'went bad' it was simply thrown out. And just like the marble workers who often reported to me that marble dust is actually beneficial to the body because it is 'pure calcium', people who made *lardo* suggested that the chemical composition of marble, calcium carbonate, was a purificatory medium that extracted harmful substances, such as cholesterol, from the raw pork fat.

Traditionally the curing process began with the raw fat—cut from the back of select pigs—and then layered in rectangular marble troughs resembling small sarcophagi called *conche*. The *conche* were placed in the cellar, always the coolest part of the house. At the time of my fieldwork, many of these cellars were quite dank and mouldy. Some still contained underground cisterns that in the past supplied water to households without plumbing. Cellars were used to store firewood and other household equipment, as laundries and, occasionally, to butcher wild boar. Once placed in the troughs, the pork fat was covered with layers of salt and herbs to start the pickling process, and six to nine months later the pork fat was ready to eat. Translucent, white, veined with pink, cool and soft to touch, the end product mimics the exact aesthetic characteristics prized in high-quality stone.

In 1996, Slow Food nominated *lardo di Colonnata* as one of Italy's ten most endangered foods. As I have detailed elsewhere (Leitch, 2000, 2003), this event resulted in some surprising, possibly unintended, consequences. Not only did Colonnata's pork fat suddenly achieve new found fame promoted as far a field as the food columns of the *New York Times* (18 February 1997) and *Bon Appétit* (Spender, 2000), the village itself was catapulted into the limelight as a major centre for international culinary tourism. There were also quite profound consequences for local producers, many of whom have now found new ways of making a livelihood out of *lardo* production. But the question remains: why did the Slow Food movement nominate *lardo di Colonnata* as a key symbol for its endangered foods campaign?

I argue that Slow Food took up the cause of pork fat for a variety of reasons. One was certainly timing. In March of 1996, the local police force had descended on what one newspaper called 'the temple of lardo' (*La Nazione,* 1 April 1996), namely Venanzio's restaurant in Colonnata. Protected by the local constabulary, regional health authority personnel proceeded to remove several samples of Venanzio's *lardo* and subsequently placed all his *conche* under quarantine. Later, samples were also taken from other small *lardo* makers in the village, but Venanzio and one other wholesaler, Fausto Guadagni, were singled out for special attention. The reasons for the quarantine were never entirely clear to the *lardo* makers involved. When I asked them later, they flatly denied it had anything to do with the spread of bovine spongiform encephalopathy (BSE), which, nevertheless, was a topic of immense anxiety at the time. Obviously, BSE has little to do with pigs, but collective hysteria over the spread of the disease had already provoked numerous articles in the local press about the benefits of vegetarianism. And, in the wake of this hysteria, it may not have been entirely coincidental that regional health authorities had decided to take a closer look at *lardo,* a product that, after all, had never undergone scientific analysis of any kind. However, local *lardo* makers simply interpreted the whole affair as a completely unreasonable attack on their autonomy to make a product that they had been producing without a single problem for many years.

This quarantine resulted in a barrage of media commentary that soon reached the national dailies. Apart from the predictable tones of conspiracy theory at the local level, the main preoccupation was the possible threat to the 1996 *lardo* festival. Nationally, the issue led to debates over the power of the European Union to impose standardized hygiene legislation regulating Italian food production, and thereby determining Italian eating habits. Writing for the national daily *La Repubblica,* Sergio Manetti responded to the quarantine with an article titled 'The European Union Ruins Italian Cuisine'. In a somewhat satirical tone he reported that:

My friend Venanzio introduced lardo di Colonnata to the world ... For centuries lardo has been preserved in marble basins and stored in cellars carved out of the rock where the natural humidity and porosity of the walls create the perfect conditions for its maturation and where it can keep for months, even years. Now all this has gone. The cave walls must be tiled up just like the floor and you need a toilet ... Lardo will probably become quite disgusting. All this has happened because some poor functionary from the health authority has to carry out their duty enforcing the bureaucratic rules of the European Union. These poor people have probably never even tasted lardo, let alone visited a cellar. Perhaps, like most city children they have never even seen a chicken, a lamb or a live pig. And so, soon, we must bid farewell to the formaggio di fossa ('ditch' cheese) and the cheeses of Castelmagno, to the mocetta valdostana (a type of fruit chutney). And then we will be forced to eat the industrial products that are made according to strict hygienic laws (but can we be sure?), but which are absolutely tasteless and with no smell ... and all of this because of the European Union. All of us are facing the end of the world. Or at least that is what Nostradamus predicted in four years time. For God's sake, just let us eat what we want over these last years! (Manetti, 1996, my translation)

According to Carlo Petrini (2001b), coinage of the term 'endangered foods' dated to the mid-1990s, just before the pork fat controversy erupted. As I have already outlined, up until then Slow Food had been perceived by the public as an association of gourmets, mostly concerned with the protection of national cuisines. But by the mid-1990s, Slow Food began to imagine itself as an international organization concerned with the global protection of food tastes. The eruption of the *lardo* quarantine controversy thus proved entirely fortuitous, providing a perfect media opportunity for the organization to promote its new international agenda of ecogastronomy, and in this regard, Petrini was certainly *not* slow to exploit *lardo*'s proletarian exoticism.

A second reason was that the case of *lardo* presented an unambiguous test case for challenging new standardized European food rules that insisted on the utilization of nonporous materials for the production of cheeses and cured meats. Although there are certainly good techniques for sterilizing the *conche,* marble is porous and its porosity is clearly essential to the curing process, to *lardo*'s claims to authenticity and its taste. Local *lardo* makers involved in this dispute thus had a vested interest in lobbying for exceptions to the generic rules designed for large food manufacturers. At this particular moment, their interests perfectly coincided with Slow Food's own political agenda, in particular its campaign to widen the debate over food rules to include cultural issues.

A third reason has to do with the discursive strategies used in Slow Food's endangered foods campaign. In the numerous publicity materials that subsequently appeared in the press, Petrini frequently likened the protection of pork fat made by local people in dank and mouldy cellars to other objects of significant national heritage, including major works of art or buildings of national architectural note. In valorizing the traditional techniques of *lardo* producers, Petrini was rhetorically distancing himself from accusations of gourmet elitism, while simultaneously challenging normalizing hierarchies of expert scientific knowledge, including, most importantly, those of the European health authorities. In this kind of strategic symbolic reversal, the food artisan is envisaged not as a backward-thinking conservative standing in the way of progress but rather as a quintessential modern subject, holder par excellence of national heritage. A food item once associated with premodern culinary otherness was reinterpreted symbolically as the culinary pinnacle of a national cuisine.

From the Ark of Taste to the Terre Madre Meetings

The campaign to protect nationally 'endangered foods' led to the 1997 compilation of the Ark of Taste, a compendium that proposed the documentation of disappearing agricultural and food products on a global scale. With its explicit biblical imagery of deluge and salvation, the Ark project thus represented a new focus for the organization that determined on making more explicit links between gourmets and environmentalists. This campaign eventually spread to include international activists working on issues of food sustainability in countries outside Europe (Kummer, 2002; Meneley, 2004). As Petrini himself was fond of repeating in numerous interviews he conducted at this time: 'An environmentalist who is not a gastronomist is sad; a gastronomist who is not an environmentalist is silly ... [to include] the environment where food is created ... has allowed us to overcome the real taboo of every gastronomist: hunger' (Petrini and Padovani, 2006: 118).

A second initiative linked to the Ark of Taste was the Presidia, a noun derived from the Italian verb *presidiare* meaning to 'garrison' or 'protect'. These were grassroots organizations of direct producers who worked in collaboration with Slow Food 'research commissions' to identify and promote local Ark foods to the public. With the launch of the Presidia, Slow Food began mixing politics with business even more explicitly, actively intervening in the promotion and distribution of Presidia products and organizing public events such as the Salone del Gusto or Hall of Tastes: giant biennial food trade fairs held in the converted ex-Fiat factory exhibition space at Lingotto in Torino. Following from this, in 2000, Slow Food sponsored its first Slow Food award for the Defense of Biodiversity—a star-studded food Oscar—honouring outstanding contributions to the defence of biodiversity. In 2003, the organization launched its own Foundation for Diversity, a nonprofit organization devoted to the defence of agricultural diversity around the world that has recently gained official recognition by the Food and Agricultural Organization (Donati, 2005: 237).

In 2004, after almost two decades of focusing on the protection of culinary diversity in Europe, Slow Food undertook an even more ambitious new project, the Terre Madre: World Meeting of Food Communities. An idea that apparently had emerged some years before in the context of discussions at the commission for the future of food in Florence, this event brought together 5,000 food producers from 131 nations around the world (Donati, 2005: 237). Its purpose was to deepen the links between communities of farmers around the globe—the so-called destiny communities—that Slow Food imagined as sharing common feelings and problems but being separated from each other and from potential global food distribution networks. Thus, according to Donati (2005), the Terre Madre initiative represented the building of a new ecogastronomic agenda for Slow Food that for the first time explicitly recognized issues of social justice within the global economy. While it was certainly not without controversy (Chrzan, 2004; Peace, 2008), the Terra Madre meeting clearly demonstrated Slow Food's remarkable organizational and financial capacities to bring together large numbers of individuals and groups from diverse cultures, as well as internationally influential figures engaged in food politics from very diverse ideological spectrums.[4]

While the majority of its members still reside in Europe, Slow Food is now represented in over 122 nations in Europe, the Americas, Asia and Oceania, as well as a small number in Africa. And while its headquarters remain in Bra—the small town in Piedmont where the movement originated—Slow Food currently has six other national associations with autonomous offices in the United States, Switzerland, Germany, France, Japan and the United Kingdom (Petrini and Padovani, 2006). Slow Food has also been active as a lobby group on food and agricultural policy within the European Union, fostering transnational alliances, such as the 2003 joint agreement with the Brazilian government to revive local food traditions using indigenous knowledge (Labelle, 2004: 88). In addition, Slow Food has successfully lobbied the Italian government to provide funding for the opening of two universities dedicated to teaching its ecogastronomic philosophy.

What accounts for Slow Food's rapid expansion and increased international visibility over the last two decades? According to Donati (2005), one explanation lies in Slow Food's organizational capacities and its extraordinary knack at securing funding for its activities through growth in membership, as well as through corporate and government sponsorship. Another key to Slow Food's success is its ingenious use of the media. From its inception, Slow Food has cultivated an ever-expanding international network of journalists and writers to promote its programs, while also developing an extremely successful commercial wing, publishing books and travel guides on cultural tourism, food and wine. And, as Julie Labelle (2004: 88) notes, Slow Food's more recent strategic merging of gastronomy with ecological issues has resulted in a further expansion of this communication network, such as the establishment in 2004 of a publishing collaboration between Slow Food and *Ecologist* magazine.

For Labelle, it is Slow Food's commitment to knowledge dissemination that is crucial. The breadth of the movement's communication networks enables individual members to connect with one another, but, perhaps more importantly, it also makes visible how all actors in the food system are linked in a network of food relations (Labelle, 2004: 90). Labelle is referring here to the shift from Slow Food's early focus on spreading knowledge to consumers about local and typical foods to the organization's new emphasis on sharing knowledge among food producers as evidenced at the Terra Madre meetings. Slow Food's official Web site (http://www.slowfood.com/about.us/eng/philsophy.lasso) makes this link explicit. It now promotes the concept of a 'co-producer', that is: 'going beyond the passive role of a consumer' to take an interest in 'those that produce our food, how they produce it and the problems they face in doing so'. As coproducers, the organization asserts, consumers become part of and partners in the production process.

However, some writers have been rather more critical of Slow Food's well-oiled publicity machine. Acknowledging the popularity of Slow Food activities among upper-middle-class professional communities in the United States, Janet Chrzan suggests, for example, that Slow Food is, in reality, an organization that relies more on rhetoric than substance. It is, she argues, little more than a 'gourmandizing fan club for celebrity food personalities and their followers' (2004: 129). Thus for Chrzan, Slow Food has become a cliché, a phrase that is repeated with 'mantra-like rhythmic repetition' to mean all that is positive to people, societies and the globe. She asks, 'Is Slow Food a movement, or is it an artfully-named organization situated at the right place and the right time ...?' (Chrzan, 2004: 122). But artful names, these days, are central to modern politics. And despite this critique of Slow Food's attention to media politics and rhetorical strategies, I argue that Slow Food has undoubtedly struck a chord because the language it adopts quite clearly taps into real concerns about the pace of modern life and its potential erasures.

Beyond Culinary Utopianism: The Critique of the Cult of Speed

One recent analysis of the Slow Food movement has argued that although the origins of Slow Food may have begun with specific campaigns devoted to the preservation of regional cuisines and traditional systems of production linked to the material cultures of local communities, mostly in Italy, its politics were never just about food. Rather, the Slow Food Movement has a much broader agenda linked to a critical re-examination of the politics of time in contemporary society. Drawing for their analysis on the texts of the Slow Food quarterly magazine and various other Slow Food manifestos, Wendy Parkins and Geoffrey Craig (2006) have highlighted the links made between Slow Food and what writers for the magazine call the 'Slow Life'. They argue that in opposing fast to slow, slow food is not just about the opposition to the idea of speed in modernity but rather is advocating its opposite, slowness. In other words, the slowness promoted by the Slow Food movement is not just a negative polemical stance towards the idea of speed and its material manifestations, such as fast food, but rather is a more positive assertion of a program for everyday living associated with valuing 'pleasure, authenticity, connectedness, tranquillity and deliberation' (Parkins and Craig, 2006: 52). Slow living, they assert, is a direct response to the processes of individualization, globalization and the 'radically uneven and heterogeneous production of space and time in post-traditional societies' (Parkins and Craig, 2006: 12).

Regardless of these debates, Slow Food's philosophical position on the ethics of food as pleasure and eating as a kind of reflective cultural politics of resistance to the role of speed in modernity have quite clearly tapped into the public nerve of current debates on the busyness of everyday life in many Western nations. Apart from the huge publishing success of popular books on this theme,[5] discussions over the organization of time, including the degree to which everyday life is increasingly colonized by work rather than leisure, are currently also hotly debated topics within academic discourse (Pocock, 2003). Moreover, these debates appear to have generated significant sociological repercussions in the growing phenomena of 'downshifting' (Schor, 1998) and sea-changing (Salter, 2001) in affluent Western nations. Indeed, in the contemporary context, there is, I suggest, an eerie mirroring of earlier, less well-remembered 'time wars', such as the late nineteenth-century international labour movement's pressing demand for the 'three eights': the division of the day into three equal eight-hour intervals of work, pleasure and rest. And just as Paul Lafargue's (1989 [1893]: 22) irreverent treatise, *The Right to Be Lazy* (critiquing the 'disastrous dogma of work' as the 'cause of all intellectual degeneracy, of all organic deformity'), captivated a new audience in the counterculture and student movements of the 1960s and 1970s, so too have Slow Food manifestos demanding an end to the 'universal folly of the Fast Life' reverberated in quite unexpected social domains.

In Australia, elements of the Slow Food programme have now entered into the realm of public policy. For example, Slow Food's campaign for the creation of so-called Slow Cities has caught the attention of local councils in key metropolitan centres. In both Australia and the United States, prominent celebrity chefs are currently fostering the expansion of other Slow Food agendas, such as its program for taste education, through the promotion of school gardens in state primary schools. In addition, the Slow Food philosophy has become something of an international brand, a marketing tool for editors of lifestyle guides to various cities, such as the recently published *Slow Guide to Sydney,* the first in a series, apparently, of guides to some of the 'fastest places on earth' (Hawkes and Keen, 2007: 3). And judging by the number of people I see wearing 'Slow Life' t-shirts walking around the coastal path where I live in Bondi Beach, the slow brand has the potential for considerable commercial success.

Revolutionary Gourmets or Culinary Luddites?

Slow Food has recently been the subject of a great deal of critical commentary. While some writers, as already mentioned, have criticized Slow Food's marketing strategies as vacuous (Chrzan, 2004; Laudan, 2004) or based on a corporate vision of food as simply a commodity (Paxson, 2006), others have accused the organization of promoting a form of 'culinary luddism' (Laudan, 2001) that deliberately obscures the democratizing benefits of modern food production over much of the twentieth century (Laudan, 2001, 2004). Thus, for Rachel Laudan, Slow Food's program for the defence of high quality local products and regional cuisines has little to say about the plight of the hungry worldwide. By following Slow Food agenda's privileging of artisanally produced foods over mass production, 'The poor' as Laudan (2004: 143) puts it, are simply 'stuck with the tyranny of the local'. Jeffrey Pilcher's (2006) detailed discussion of the history of Mexican tortilla production is a case in point. He argues that in Mexico, culinary modernism in the form of mass produced corn tortillas continues to be essential to the survival of tortillas as the daily bread of the majority of Mexican wage labourers. While middle-class Mexican elites, Slow Food activists and environmentalists are prompt to condemn factory-produced maize flour as the antithesis of traditional cooking, bags of *masa harina* have nevertheless become essential care packages for Mexican immigrants and other aficionados of Mexican food in the United States, while in Mexico, a large parastatal corporation— the *grupo Maseca*—has emerged as the unlikely champion of authentic Mexican cuisine.

At the heart of these critiques is the accusation that Slow Food is disingenuous when it comes to issues of class. For example, in her fascinating study of the marketing and production of Tuscan olive oil, Anne Meneley (2004) notes that while olive oil producers of all classes display an affective attachment to their cold pressed extra virgin olive oil and are vitally concerned with the purity of their product as well as with authenticating markers, in reality sophisticated international marketing strategies are not available to all producers. Indeed, somewhat paradoxically, Slow Food's involvement in the marketing of olive oil has mostly benefited larger consortiums. Thus, while Slow Food claims to champion small producers, it often ends up favouring elites (Meneley, 2004: 173). Other authors have raised the issue of class in respect to Slow Food's membership base in wealthy nations. Chrzan (2004), for example, questions the high cost of Slow Food activities in the North American context, and Labelle (2004) similarly observes that Slow Food fails to recognize that locally sourced high-quality foods are in reality luxuries for the privileged few. Such critiques, however, are in danger of reproducing ethnocentric accounts of Slow Food politics that are rather narrowly enmeshed within localized fields of power. While Slow Food politics does at times elide class issues especially in respect to the assumption of the buying power of consumers, it is equally true that the social and cultural contexts in which Slow Food politics now operate vary considerably.

Perhaps a more trenchant observation is that in wealthy nations the popularity of Slow Food reifies forms of 'imperialist nostalgia' (Rosaldo, 1989: 90) that sentimentalize peasant traditions within and outside Europe (Jones et al., 2003). Pilcher (2006), for example, asserts that while Slow Food has recognized some key individual Mexican contributions to agricultural biodiversity, as a whole, in Mexico the

Slow Food project bears more than a passing resemblance to the European civilizing mission of the nineteenth century. Maria Gaytån (2004) similarly observes that Californian Slow Food members often draw upon deeply essentialized notions of Italian artisanal traditions that tend to romanticize the past, a process that reflects the current mood towards what might be called 'Tuscanopia' (Leitch, 2000: 105), in which Tuscan peasant cuisines, house renovation projects and picturesque rurality all seem to have become key fantasy spaces of modern urban alienation.

These critiques not withstanding, a large part of Slow Food's success, I suggest, is due to its promotional politics, with its imaginative use of the media and discursive strategies intended to re-evaluate specific foods, not simply as economic commodities, but as cultural artefacts linked to salient notions of the past. By way of comparison, I would like to turn, briefly, to another example of a movement in Europe that similarly succeeded in reframing debates about food as a commodity—in this case genetically modified crops—to debates about taste as cultural heritage.[6]

The French Peasant's Confederation

Between 1997 and 2000 there was a public discussion in France about the future of that country's agricultural biotechnology. According to Chaia Heller (2004), during the initial phase of the debate, between 1996 and 1998, the 'risk' frame and scientific expertise played a primary role in shaping public discussion. During the second phase of the debate, between 1998 and 2000, there was a remarkable shift in which an organization of small farmers—the Confederation Paysanne or the Peasants Confederation (CP)—reframed the debate about genetically modified organisms (GMOs) in France from issues of scientific risk to questions of food quality and culture.

How did this happen? As background to this issue, Heller (2004) points out that the CP's formation in 1987 represented the culmination of a decade-long struggle to create an autonomous voice for family farmers in a milieu largely dominated by France's number-one union of industrial farmers, the National Federated Union of Agricultural Enterprises (FNSEA). Since its inception, the CP had struggled to become a contending counter-power to the FNSEA, representing a network of socialist-leaning family farmers contesting the agricultural policy that intensified during France's postwar period. During this period, the CP was engaged in a strategic campaign to reclaim the historically contested and pejorative term *paysan* or peasant, in order to align itself with an international network of peasant movements, such as the European Peasant Coordination and Via Campesina. And in 1997, the CP launched its own campaign against GMOs, presenting an antiglobalization message that defended the rights of peasant workers and indigenous peoples against agricultural biotechnology worldwide (Heller, 2004: 86).

In 1998, a radical sector of the CP, headed by Rene Reisal and the now infamous Jose Bové of anti-MacDonald's fame, organized their first major anti-GMO event that involved a group of about 100 farmers destroying three tons of Novartis transgenetic corn in a storage plant in the southern town of Nerac by spraying it with fire hoses (Heller, 2004: 87). At the subsequent trial, Bové and Reisal countered the expert scientific witnesses on the subject of GMO-related risk with their own expertise as peasant farmers and union workers, asserting that they were uniquely situated to speak about food quality, farmers' duties to protect and develop French seeds, as well as the implications of industrialized agriculture on rural peoples and cultures worldwide. According to Heller, by invoking both *paysan* expertise and the plight of the small farmer in the face of industrialized agriculture, the CP was able to appeal to a widely shared collective sense of regret felt by many French about the continued dispossession of the peasant farmer in the postwar period, a discussion that, in turn, draws upon a very long history of alternate constructions of the peasant in France (Rogers, 1987). In this most recent resuscitation of the peasant as a key symbol of French culture, the CP draws upon the trade unionist discourse of the worker, articulating not a pre-social idea of nature as wilderness but rather, a 'socialized nature whose value is not only historical, cultural or aesthetic, but also *economic,* providing *paysans* with a viable and productive way of life' (Heller, 2004: 89). This, as Heller aptly points out, is illustrated in the CP's key slogan 'To Produce, To Employ, To Preserve'. Thus in contrast to environmentalist understandings of conserving nature as wilderness, the CP promotes the idea that nature is best preserved by peasant workers whose expertise in knowing and caring for the land as a productive and meaningful landscape is of vital national importance.

In addition to advocating a view of nature as socialized, Jose Bové has also been instrumental in promoting good food as good taste, a rhetorical position quite akin to that of the Slow Food movement. For example, in many of his discussions over the negative effects of industrialized agriculture, Bové uses the symbol of *la malbouffe,* a word that is close to the idea of bad or junk food (Heller, 2004: 92). As Heller observes, *la bouffe,* or 'good food', on the other hand, brings together notions of pleasure, tradition and French cuisine, synonymous with French culture itself. To be cultured in France is to be 'cultivated' or to have 'good taste'. Taste here, of course, has a double meaning. Both people and food may be regarded as having good or bad taste. As Heller puts it, 'While a food is well cultivated when produced according to regional agricultural traditions, an individual is considered cultivated when capable of recognizing, and taking pleasure in well-cultivated, good-tasting food or *la bouffe*' (2004: 92). That which is not traditionally cultivated, foods produced without reference to cultural expertise and history, for example, fast foods and genetically modified foods, are seen as having no taste, and people who consume these foods are thus viewed as being without culture.

Conclusion

What are we to make of all these discussions of food and politics? Despite the fact that they are being conducted with reference to distinct national contexts involving particular social actors working within specific historical trajectories, one of the things that interests me in all these debates about food and identity, at least in Europe, is that they are managing to galvanize large numbers of people, and within a very short time frame have produced remarkably effective lobby groups for environmental biodiversity and the protection of both cultural landscapes and niche-food producers internationally. Slow Food has been particularly influential in this regard, partly, I believe, because the organization maintains, quite self-consciously, a strategic distance from the radical guerrilla strategies utilized by some of the more infamous actors in groups, as seen in Petrini's quite explicit response to Jose Bové's acts of sabotage against McDonald's in France: it is against 'slow style'. As he puts it, 'we prefer to concentrate our efforts on what we are losing, rather than trying to stop what we don't like' (Petrini, 2001b: 28).

This difference in style can be illustrated by Petrini's manifestos on fast food. Whereas Bové linked fast food to bad taste and an explicitly anticorporate and antiglobalization agenda, Petrini has always preferred to work in the positive, denying that Slow Food is simply anti-fast food. Rather, he suggests that Slow Food is against the homogenization of taste that fast food symbolizes. In other words, for Petrini, fast food does not necessarily represent bad taste, although he certainly argues that it is a sign of the more negative effects of modern market rationalities on cultural difference. Slowness in this formulation becomes a metaphor for a politics of place complexly concerned, like the CP, with the defence of local cultural heritage, regional landscapes and idiosyncratic material cultures of production. Whereas Bové and the CP lobbied within international networks of antiglobalization activists promoting anticorporate agendas, Slow Food has mixed business and politics from its inception. None of its public manifestos advocating slowness and the benefits of the slow life or slow cities are explicitly anticapitalist or anticorporate. Rather slowness is employed ideologically in order to promote Petrini's idiosyncratic brand of 'virtuous globalization', a new figuring of cosmopolitanism that seeks to rupture binary oppositions—rural/metropolitan, local/global—refiguring the idea of locality as a kind of 'ethical glocalism' (Parasecoli, 2003; Parkins and Craig, 2006; Tomlinson, 1999).

There are, however, significant convergences between the politics of the two movements. Both are engaged with the protection of cultural landscapes, local traditions and economies within debates about cultural homogenization in the context of Europeanization. Both are, in other words, political responses to what Nadia Seremetakis (1994: 3) has called a massive 'reorganization of public memory' accompanying the intensifications of market rationalities in European peripheries. Both utilize rhetorical strategies reframing scientific knowledge in terms of artisanal or peasant expertise, adding further weight to the thesis that political struggles in the contemporary era focus on struggles over meanings as well as political and economic conditions (McClagan, 2000). Although I have not been able to explore this in great detail, both Slow Food and CP are also caught up in a kind of generational politics in which the interpretive and cultural frames of the main protagonists are deeply influential. Both, I suggest, are intimately involved with socially productive uses of nostalgia. This is to say, following the imaginative work of literary theorist Svetlana Boym (2001), that both movements invoke a *reflective* rather than a *restorative* nostalgia, a nostalgia that 'dwells on the ambivalences of human longing and belonging, [a nostalgia] that does not avoid the contradictions of modernity' (Boym, 2001: xviii), a nostalgia that explores ways of inhabiting many places at once and imagining different time zones; a nostalgia that hopefully in the end can, as Boym suggests, 'present an ethical and creative challenge, not merely a pretext for midnight melancholias' (xviii).

Just as CP interpreted its struggle over the future of agricultural biotechnology in France in terms of the struggles for the survival of *other* farmers in *other* places, Slow Food is also deeply engaged in public debates *beyond* the politics of food in Italy, intervening in emerging discussions about the ethics and repercussions of speed in the current era. I might add here that in this sense Slow Food draws attention to some very interesting parallels between nineteenth-century rejections of machine time and current debates repudiating the orthodoxy of speed in everyday life. But this is a whole new topic. In this chapter, I have tried to indicate the ways in which food has emerged as a political topic par excellence, capable of connecting individual bodies to abstract communities, techno-scientific innovations and moral concerns. In Italy, Slow Food's campaign to protect 'endangered foods' taps into quite crucial questions about the fate of place and the taste of culture on the margins of Europe. 'Slow Life' says Petrini with typical sound-bite finesse, is not just 'Slow Food'. What I hope I have shown here is that debates about food, at least in Europe, specifically Italy and France, are debates about moral economies, not just economics. Food, in other words, is not just food.

Notes

1. All the quotes from the Slow Food Manifesto come from the official manifesto that is published on the Slow Food Web site, http://www.slowfood.com. The English version can be found at http://www.slowfood.com/about_us/eng/manifesto.lasso.

2. Bra is both a commercial centre and a working-class town with a long history of mutual aid associations launched by local craftspeople: cobblers, market vendors and tanners. In reference to Bra's main commercial activity in the immediate postwar period, Petrini and Padovani note that in the 1950s, 'the smell of tannin coming from the leather factories prevailed over the aroma of cheese' (2006: 23).

3. Petrini himself notes that his social and political upbringing did not take place in the university's sociology department but rather in a 'Catholic organization of which I had become president in 1966, at the age of seventeen' (Petrini and Padovani, 2006: 26).

4. For example, the Slow Food Terre Madre meeting attracted a wide range of prominent figures including Prince Charles, the environmental activist Vandana Shiva, ministers from the Berlusconi government and Mikhail Gorbechev (Donati, 2004: 237).

5. A recent example is Carl Honoré's (2004) *In Praise of Slow.*

6. I draw here extensively from Chaia Heller's chapter in *The Politics of Food* (2004).

References

Boym, S. (2001), *The Future of Nostalgia,* New York: Basic Books.

Chrzan, J. (2004), 'Slow Food: What, Why and to Where?', *Food, Culture and Society,* 7/2: 117–31.

Counihan, C.M. (1999), *The Anthropology of Food and the Body,* New York: Routledge.

Donati, K. (2005), 'The Pleasure of Diversity in Slow Food's Ethics of Taste', *Food Culture and Society,* 8/2: 228–40.

Gaytån, M.S. (2004), 'Globalizing Resistance: Slow Food and New Local Imaginaries', *Food Culture and Society,* 7/2: 97–116.

Hawkes, H., and Keen, L. (2007), *Slow Guide to Sydney,* Mugrave, Victoria: Affirm Press.

Heller, C. (2004), 'Risky Science and Savoir-faire: Peasant Expertise in the French Debate over Genetically Modified Crops', in M.E. Lien and B. Nerlich (eds.), *The Politics of Food,* Oxford: Berg.

Honoré, C. (2004), *In Praise of Slow,* London: Orion Books.

Italy Daily (1998), 'Slow Food an Antidote to Modern Times', (2 November).

Jones, P., Shears, P., Hillier D., Comfort D., and Lowell, J. (2003), 'Return to Traditional Values? A Case Study of Slow Food', *British Food Journal,* 105: 297–304.

Kummer, C. (2002), *'The Pleasures of Slow Food'*, San Francisco, CA: Chronicle Books.

Labelle, J. (2004), 'A Recipe for Connectedness: Bridging Production and Consumption with Slow Food', *Food, Culture and Society,* 7/2: 81–96.

Lafargue, P. (1989 [1883]), *The Right to Be Lazy,* translated by Charles H. Kerr, Chicago, IL: Charles H. Kerr Publishing Company.

La Nazione (1997), 'Bollino USL sul lardo di Colonnata Piace anche ai Gourmet Americani' (18 February).

Laudan, R. (2001), 'A Plea for Culinary Modernism. Why We Should Love New, Fast, Processed Food', *Gastronomica* 1: 36–44.

Laudan, R. (2004), 'Slow Food, the French Terroir Strategy, and Culinary Modernism', *Food, Culture and Society*, 7/2: 133–44.

Leitch, A. (1996), 'The Life of Marble: The Experience and Meaning of Work in the Marble Quarries of Carrara', *The Australian Journal of Anthropology*, 7/3: 325–57.

Leitch, A. (2000), 'The Social Life of *Lardo:* Slow Food in Fast Times', *The Asia Pacific Journal of Anthropology*, 1/1: 103–18.

Leitch, A. (2003), 'Slow Food and the Politics of Pork Fat', *Ethnos*, 68/4: 437–62.

McClagan, M. (2000), 'Spectacles of Difference: Buddhism, Media Management and Contemporary Tibet Activism', *Polygraph*, 12: 101–20.

Manetti, S. (1996), 'La Cee porta la rovina sulla tavola Italiana', *La Repubblica* (21 April).

Meneley, A. (2004), 'Extra Virgin Olive Oil and Slow Food', *Anthropologica*, 46: 165–76.

Mintz, S. (1979), 'Sugar and Sweetness', *Marxist Perspectives*, 2: 56–73.

Parasecoli, F. (2003), 'Postrevolutionary Chowhounds: Food, Globalization, and the Italian Left', *Gastronomica* 3/3: 29–39.

Parkins, W., and Craig, G. (2006), *Slow Living*, Sydney: UNSW Press.

Paxson, H. (2006), 'Artisanal Cheese and Economies of Sentiment in New England', in R. Wilk (ed.), *Fast Food/Slow Food: The Cultural Economy of the Global Food System*', Lanham: Altamira Press.

Peace, A. (2008), 'Terre Madre 2006: Political Theatre and Ritual Rhetoric in the Slow Food Movement', *Gastronomica*, 8/2: 31–39.

Petrini, C. (2001a). *Slow Food: Collected Thoughts on Taste, Tradition, and the Honest Pleasures of Food*, White River Junction: Chelsea Green.

Petrini, C. (2001b), *Slow Food: Le Ragioni del Gusto*, Roma Bari: Editori Laterza.

Petrini, C., and Padovani, G. (2006), *Slow Food Revolution*, New York: Rizzoli.

Pilcher, J. (2006), 'Taco Bell, Maseca and Slow Food: A Postmodern Apocalypse for Mexico's Peasant Cuisine?', in R. Wilk (ed.), *Fast Food/Slow Food: The Cultural Economy of the Global Food System*', Lanham: Altamira Press.

Pocock, B. (2003), *The Work/Life Collision*, Sydney: The Federation Press.

Revelli, N. (1977), *Il Mondo dei Vinti*, Turin: Einaudi.

Rogers, S.C. (1987), 'Good to Think: The "Peasant" in Contemporary France', *Anthropological Quarterly*, 60/2: 56–62.

Rosaldo, R. (1989), *Culture and Truth: The Remaking of Social Analysis*, Boston: Beacon Press.

Salter, B. (2001), *The Big Shift*, Hardie Grant Publishing.

Schor, J. (1998), *The Overspent American. Why We Want What We Don't Need*, New York: Harper Perennial.

Seremetakis, C.N. (1994), 'The Memory of the Senses, Parts 1 and 2', in C.N. Seremetakis (ed.), *The Senses Still: Perception and Memory as Material Culture in Modernity,* Boulder: Westview Press.

Spender, M. (2000), 'The Politics of Pork Fat', *Bon Appétit,* May: 54–55.

Stille, A. (2001), 'Slow Food', *The Nation* (20–27 August): 11–16.

Tomlinson, J. (1999), *Globalization and Culture,* Cambridge: Polity.

Veronelli, L. (2004), *Alla Ricerca dei Cibi Perduti,* Rome: Derive/Approdi.

–3–

Standards, Science and Scale: The Case of Tasmanian Atlantic Salmon

Marianne Elisabeth Lien

University of Oslo

If you are having fish for dinner tonight, it has quite likely been farmed. In less than thirty years, intensive aquaculture has revolutionized the way we consume marine resources, constituting what is known as the 'blue revolution'. Today, nearly half of all fish consumed globally has been raised on a fish farm, and aquaculture is among the fastest-growing food-producing sectors in the world (Food and Agriculture Organization of the United Nations [FAO], 2006). According to FAO estimates,[1] the global production of aquaculture was nearly fifty-two million tonnes in 2006, and an additional eighty million tonnes of aquatic food, or more, will be required in 2050 to maintain the current per capita consumption of fish. In order to meet this need, a continued increase in aquaculture is necessary (Food and Agriculture Organization of the United Nations, 2009). In other words, intensive fish farming has gone from being a peculiar and rare experiment to a food source we rely upon. This industrial-scale domestication of aquatic species has been spearheaded with Atlantic salmon, which is the most important species in aquaculture production in Northern Europe.

In this chapter I will tell the story of Atlantic salmon through the lens of globalization. It is not difficult to do. Farmed Atlantic salmon is an artefact that defies traditional dichotomies of the local and the global. Rather, it represents a food product which is systematically and simultaneously inscribed as a universal biogenetic artefact and a local brand commodity. The worldwide expansion of intensive aquaculture is made possible by global structures that facilitate the flow of capital, technology and science. An expanding aquaculture industry also poses challenges that require solutions on a global scale. In this way, salmon aquaculture is both shaped by, and intensifies, globalizing processes. It thus represents a case of globalization par excellence, constituting one of the most globalized fields of food production in the world today. But there are also other stories to be told. Seen through a historical lens, aquaculture represents the most recent turn in the human history of animal domestication. Like the agricultural revolution some ten thousand years ago, its importance can hardly be underestimated, yet its more specific consequences are difficult to predict.

The blue revolution has largely escaped the attention of the social sciences. As a revolution taking place literally under water, its material technicalities remain unnoticed or taken for granted by many. However, contemporary fish farming represents a unique empirical case for social sciences as it highlights current conditions in global food production in relation to transnational technologies, world trade regulations, environmental issues, technoscience and global capitalism. Furthermore, the field lends itself very well to analyses that seek to transcend the conceptual boundaries of technology and science, nature and society and humans and animals. Salmon aquaculture may be seen both as an icon of the current state of food production and as an indication of things to come.

I start with a brief account of the blue revolution as a history of domestication, and how farmed Atlantic salmon became a global artefact. In order to further problematize some paradoxes of globalizing processes, I then turn to a specific example of the implications of international trade regulations in Australian aquaculture before I conclude.

Newcomers to the Farm

This dramatic increase in aquaculture production is closely connected to the emergence of intensive systems of fish farming (Stead and Laird, 2002). While humans have shared space (*domus*) with terrestrial animals for thousands of years, salmon are still 'newcomers to the farm' (Lien, 2007a). The blue revolution thus represents a crucial moment in the history of human domestication, implying marine animal husbandry on a massive scale. It also represents a revolutionary moment in the world history of Atlantic salmon, whose genetic make-up is currently being intentionally and unintentionally modified as a result of massive salmon farming (Huntingford, 2004). But Atlantic salmon is only one among many marine species introduced to a regime of marine husbandry. A well-stocked supermarket in the UK, for example, will offer farmed trout, bram, cod, halibut, sea bass, catfish, tilapia, carp and barramundi, just to mention a few. In addition there are farmed shellfish, such as mussels, scallops and crayfish. Aquaculture thus implies the systematic enrolment of new marine species to regimes of domestication on an experimental basis. Some succeed and are subsequently produced on a commercial scale.

Parallel to this expansion towards new marine species, a geographical expansion has taken place, and salmon may again serve as an example. The domestication of salmon has underpinned a geographical movement of Atlantic salmon that reaches far beyond its native north Atlantic rim. Atlantic salmon is now produced not only in Norway, Scotland and Canada but also in the southern oceans of Chile and Australia. More tropical regions accommodate other marine species, and intensive aquaculture has spread to most parts of the world. While species' requirements differ, some basic technologies remain similar, and thus allow one domesticated marine species to pave the way for another, often at a surprisingly rapid pace.

In the case of Atlantic salmon, it is domestication that made its geographical expansion possible. In the 1860s, so-called acclimatization societies encouraged biomigration on a massive scale, for example within the British Commonwealth (Lever, 1992). Australians were particularly active, and in Tasmania,[2] for example, local angling enthusiasts, mostly of British descent, pooled their resources to try to fill the Tasmanian rivers with Atlantic salmon (which was nonexistent in this part of the world). In spite of intensive efforts to bring live salmon eggs from Europe to Tasmania,[3] the acclimatisation experiment did not succeed. For reasons that are still debated, the fry that were released into the Derwent river and then migrated to the sea never returned to reproduce, and the salmon population disappeared after some years. Consequently, it was not until the 1980s, when local aquaculture interests introduced Atlantic salmon for commercial purposes, that salmon reappeared in Tasmanian estuaries. This time broodstock was sourced from a landlocked population of salmon in New South Wales that had been brought from Nova Scotia, Canada, to the Australian mainland in the 1960s. This genetic strain constitutes the broodstock of Tasmanian salmon today (Lien, 2005). However, while the salmon that escapes from fish farms can easily survive in estuaries for quite some time, this former Canadian salmon, like its predecessor from England, seems unable to establish a self-sustaining population in the wilds. In other words, the geographical transfer of Atlantic salmon to the antipodes has come as a result of its domestication. This story of domestication as a precursor to global expansion parallels the history of many of our most familiar terrestrial farm animals, such as cows, pigs and chicken.

Beyond the Local and the Global

This book demonstrates how globalization can be understood through the topic of food, and conversely, how food may be analysed through the lens of globalization. But what exactly does that mean? Focusing on transnational movements, we may note the way food itself travels increasing distances from production to consumption, and how local commercial enterprises are upscaled through mergers and become branches of transnational business corporations. Processes of production also involve the movement of a wide range of other things: In the case of Atlantic salmon farming, we find that transnational flows involve not only the final product but also knowledge, people, technological equipment, feed, genetic strains and financial capital.[4] While some of these flows are encouraged, others are not, and the exact circuits and routes of movement that appear represent fruitful empirical entries for studies of globalizing processes.

Looking more closely at transnational flows, it appears that as food and technology travel, they also change meaning, and their usages and modes of appropriation become different (e.g. Lien and Nerlich, 2004). A similar shift may be observed in transnational corporations, as various branches take on cultural expressions that are locally appropriate (e.g. Garsten, 1994). Chilean salmon farms, for example, differ significantly from Norwegian salmon farms with regard to organizational features, even when technologies, genetic stock, investors and even corporate ownership are more or less the same (Andaur, 2006). Such local variations are often ascribed to differences in culture, but a similar role can be played by what is commonly referred to as nature. In Tasmania, for example, where salmon farming was established by Norwegian investors and operators in the 1980s, the practical challenges are often distinctly local. Such challenges include, for example, native Australian fur seals (as they break through nets), amoebic gill disease (caused by an amoebae not present in the North Atlantic) or the relatively warm ocean temperatures (Lien, 2007b). Thus, in spite of fairly successful efforts to standardize the production of Atlantic salmon worldwide, locality becomes relevant to the process in a variety of ways, from production through processing and finally to consumption. These variations are sometimes ascribed to differences in (local) culture and other times to differences in (local) nature.

A Universal Biogenetic Artefact

Such observations have inspired a broad range of analyses that seek to understand the specific interactions between 'the local' and 'the global', juxtaposing the two as opposite phenomena. In spite of criticism, dualist approaches to globalizing processes still inform social analyses in a number of ways. The persistence of such dualisms reflects an underlying epistemology in the social sciences in which culture and society are given as bounded entities, nestled in some form of locality, such as community, region or nation (Nustad, 2003). Another reason why such dichotomies are often used is that 'local' and 'global' are also often vernacular concepts that inform everyday discourse and reflect people's immediate experience of changes that they observe.[5] However, in order to better understand the processes that underlie such changes, we need to aim beyond such conceptual dualism towards a more processual understanding of what globalization entails.

First, we need to challenge what is often a rather simplistic ordering of the world through the attribution of local or global qualities to items that are in fact far more complex. Richard Wilk's excellent analysis of Caribbean cooking is a case in point (Wilk, 2006). Tasmanian Atlantic salmon is another example. Simultaneously inscribed as a universal artefact and a local brand commodity, it resists any simple categorization as either 'local' or 'global'. Instead, analyses indicate that both local and global dimensions of Tasmanian Atlantic salmon are made relevant and are purposefully incorporated at different stages of the salmon's life from production through to consumption (Lien, 2005, 2007b).

A Tasmanian Atlantic salmon that starts its life as a fertilized egg in a water tank in a Tasmanian hatchery will be treated in accordance with procedures that are highly standardized on a global scale, and there is hardly anything about this process that is highlighted as distinctly Tasmanian. Later, as it becomes smolt and is transferred to a marine grow-out site, and in this sense immersed in the microbiological and climatic features of the Tasmanian coastal waters, standardized procedures still characterize the way it is interpreted. Through inscription devices that are applied transnationally, the Tasmanian Atlantic salmon is known as 'biomass', and is compared to other instances of fish or salmon biomass produced elsewhere. As a visiting European expert once responded to a local marine farmer who speculated about the impact of specific Tasmanian challenges on salmon growth: 'A fish does what a fish does, it does not know it is living in Tasmania' (cited in Lien, 2007b: 180). However, as soon as the salmon is slaughtered, processed, packaged, and shipped to market destinations elsewhere, locality emerges for the first time as a signifying feature of the salmon itself. Through packaging, branding and marketing, the salmon becomes 'local', associated with the marine environment in which it is grown: On the Web site of Tassal, the major producer of Tasmanian Atlantic salmon, unique features of the local environment are presented as follows:

> The cool, clean waters of southern Tasmania is the perfect environment for the cultivation of Atlantic Salmon. Here the open sea rolls in from the Southern Ocean and mixes with the clear, fresh waters from the nearby snow capped mountains. These unpolluted waters have naturally high oxygen content and provide reliable current movement essential for maintaining fish health. (Tassal, 2008)[6]

Emphasized on the Web site by the marketing label 'pure Tasmania', and further underpinned by the footer 'from the great unspoiled Southern oceans of Australia', iconic features of Tasmania are inscribed in what was hitherto universal salmon biomass, making the salmon product Tasmanian. Ironically, it is not until it is literally out of the water that Atlantic salmon becomes uniquely 'Tasmanian'.

In order to attain a better understanding of globalizing processes, we need to focus not only on the movement itself but also on structures that remain stable. This requires a certain sensitivity towards the dialectic and often rather subtle relation between fixity and flow in globalizing processes (Lien and Melhuus, 2007). Simply put: in order for something to move, something else has to be kept in place. Too often in globalizing studies, the empirical attention drifts towards that which moves, at the expense of structures of immobility that, in fact, make movement possible. In relation to intensive aquaculture, natural science represents a form of knowledge which, in fact, allows the expansion and standardization of marine farming worldwide. Thus, when a foreign expert can claim that a 'fish does what a fish does', it is based, not on the observation of the specific salmon in question but on a generalized knowledge of salmon 'everywhere': a notion of salmon as a universal biogenetic entity the qualities of which may be known through a set of scientifically informed and standardized techniques. Through such techniques, a general understanding of salmon feeding behaviour, metabolism and growth may be attained, which in turn informs the interpretation of a specific problem encountered in a particular salmon pen on the southeast coast of Tasmania. If knowledge and competence in marine farming were conceived of as strictly local, and largely irrelevant for marine farmers operating elsewhere, the rapid global dissemination of aquaculture that we have witnessed during the last three decades could hardly have happened. Thus, I argue that it is precisely because it is so closely associated with science, and thus systematically standardized as a universal artefact, that intensive aquaculture has expanded so rapidly. In this way, the apparent stability of science involves a universalizing discourse that both facilitates and depends on transnational flows of concepts, people and things.

In what follows I will present a case in which science as universalizing discourse plays a particular role in directing the global flow of salmon. The case demonstrates how science as a standardizing tool, mediating between different levels of scale, is enrolled in negotiations to limit—or establish legitimate exceptions to—the overarching ideology of free trade. Yet, as we shall see, the universalizing potential of scientific discourse has its own limitations. The case also underscores how contexts are not given, but are instead conjured and made relevant through processes of social, economic and legal interaction.

Standards, Science and Scale: Australia versus the World Trade Organization (WTO)

On 19 July 1999, the Australian commonwealth quarantine authorities (AQIS), announced a dramatic change in their import policy regarding fresh salmon. Based on a new import risk analysis (IRA), they announced that the Australian ban from 1975 that had effectively prevented fresh salmon from entering the Australian continent for a quarter of a century, would be replaced by a policy which allowed the import of nonviable salmon (slaughtered but fresh) into Australia. The IRA had been conducted as a result of pressure from Canada through the WTO system and was presented as a response to the WTO decision that Australia's quarantine policies were not based on a proper scientific analysis. This change of policy marked the end of a dispute between Canada and Australia that had been going on in the WTO system for almost a decade. At the same time, it marked the beginning of an era of potentially 'free flow' of infectious salmon viruses between the rest of the world and Australia.

Partly because it is geographically remote from other salmon producing areas, Tasmania's coastline is a remarkably healthy environment for salmon. Tasmanian salmon have few of the many salmon diseases that are rampant in the North Atlantic (e.g. sea-lice, infectious salmon anaemia). Furthermore, there are no wild or native salmon that farmed salmon could spread diseases to (as is the case in Norway). The only endemic disease affecting Tasmanian Atlantic salmon is amoebic gill disease which is quite common but not as serious as many of the infectious diseases associated with salmon in the northern hemisphere and Chile. This nearly disease-free situation has been ensured through a strict regime of quarantine, both in Australia and in Tasmania.

In light of this, it hardly comes as a surprise that Tasmania strongly opposed the federal decision to allow free import of salmonids into Australia. The opposition was voiced through a number of channels, and includes sixty-six different submissions to the Federal Senate Legislation Committee regarding the importation of salmon products into Tasmania (Senate Rural and Regional Affairs and Transport Legislation Committee [SRRA] Submissions, 1999). These submissions range from marine biologists' worries about the threat that salmon impose on Tasmania's marine environment, to CEOs of the Tasmanian salmon industry who worry that fresh salmon from the North Atlantic might transfer microorganisms that would eventually destroy their businesses, to handwritten letters from trout anglers, describing the pleasure of recreational fishing and expressing fear that it may be wiped out. The submissions reveal how the imports issue stirred up a lot of political engagement in Tasmania and, to some extent, united public opinion, the industry and politicians in their shared opposition against the federal authorities and the WTO.

The opposition is not difficult to understand. A more interesting question is: why did the Australian federal government agree to open up its borders to salmon that may carry infectious salmon diseases? How could it happen? Let me briefly summarize the background for this policy change. In 1975 Australia had formalized a strict regime of quarantine, banning the import of nonviable salmonids.[7] Consequently, ten years later, when experiments with farmed marine Atlantic salmon had proved successful, broodstock for the emerging Tasmanian salmon industry had to be sourced from within Australia. A landlocked population of Atlantic salmon (brought from Nova Scotia, Canada in 1964) was found in New South Wales, and broodstock from this population was brought to Tasmania. After a few years, the industry flourished, and offspring from Canadian brood stock has formed the genetic basis of Tasmanian Atlantic salmon ever since. In 1994, Canada, another salmon exporter, requested market access to Australia, and formal bilateral WTO consultations began.[8] In 1996, AQIS presented Australia's first IRA as an attempt to justify existing quarantine regulations. The IRA was conducted at the federal level and basically supported the interests of Tasmanian salmon farmers (practically all Australian salmon farming takes place in Tasmania). The Canadians, however, were not impressed, and brought the dispute to the WTO disputes settlement panel and appellate body. WTO panellists concluded that:

1. Australia's IRA did not fulfill the requirements of the so-called sanitary phys-tosanitary (SPS) agreement.
2. Arbitrary and unjustifiable distinctions in the level of protection in relation to salmon had been applied, constituting what the WTO panellists described as a 'disguised restriction on international trade' (SRRA, 2000: 59).

In other words, Australia lost the first battle. As a consequence, a revised document had to be produced, and in July 1999 AQIS presented Australia's second IRA. This time the IRA was written in strict accordance with the outline of the SPS agreement and Office International des Epitoozies (OIE). However, as it turned out, the second IRA came up with a different conclusion, as it *no longer* provided support for the existing quarantine regulations. Consequently, and as a result of this process, AQIS had to change its import policy. The WTO endorsed the second IRA, the dispute with Canada was settled and in 2000 Canadian farmed salmon gained access to the Australian market.

What does this tell us about globalization? Is it yet another example of the power of free trade over environmental risk? On the surface, it may appear to be just that, but I want to argue that this conclusion is too simple. In the SPS agreement, it is made explicitly clear that a member state like Australia may define its own level of protection more strictly that the international standard defined by the WTO. In spite of this legal option, the second Australian IRA concluded that the risk involved in free import of nonviable salmonids was not sufficient to support existing quarantine policy. Why then did Australia produce an IRA that opened up the risk of irreversible damage to Tasmania's marine environment? I will not provide a full answer to this, but instead draw attention to the challenges of translation involved in standardization efforts on a global scale, and how these may produce outcomes that are sometimes counterintuitive and rather surprising.

Upscaling

WTO member states normally do not have to produce risk analyses. WTO defines international standards of quarantine, and when these are adopted one does not need an IRA. But for countries that set out to define their own national standard, or, according to WTO terminology, determine their own appropriate level of protection (ALOP), an IRA is needed (SRRA, 2000: 81–2). More precisely, when a country wants to depart from international standards, the IRA 'provides the technical and scientific basis for quarantine measures that determine whether or not an import may be permitted' (SRRA, 2000: 100). In such cases, the higher standard must be applied consistently across various fields of import. For instance, the principle applied for Atlantic salmon (a finfish) would have to be applied for all other finfish, including, for instance, aquarium fish.

What is a standard? Bowker and Star (2000) approach standards as sets of agreed-upon rules for the production of objects (textual or material) that have a certain spatial and temporal extension (spans communities, persists over time), and that are deployed in making things work together over distances and heterogeneous metrics (Bowker and Star, 2000: 13–14). Furthermore, standards are often enforced by some sort of legal body (state or private), have significant inertia and can be difficult to change.[9] The free trade agreement enforced by the WTO is an example of a standard that regulates trade-related transactions between member states.

The IRA has a standardizing effect as well, but unlike the international standards of quarantine it is intended to serve a broader purpose, such as to protect a particular marine environment, and to accommodate particular interests. As such, the IRA may be analysed as a boundary object, defined as 'objects that both inhabit several communities of practice and satisfy the informational requirements of each of them' (Bowker and Star, 2000: 16). Tailored to the needs of any one community, while also having common identities across different settings, boundary objects are, in principle, able to maintain some sort of coherence. Such coherence may be found, or produced, to transcend not only different communities or contexts but also different levels of scale—thus it may extend both horizontally and vertically.

The SPS agreement provides the guidelines for justifying exceptions to the international standards of quarantine and may thus be analysed as a vehicle for standardizing that which is difficult to standardize. Let us have a look at how such standardizing principles are laid down in the SPS agreement, in articles two, three and five that relate to quarantine measures (cited from SRRA, 2000: 48, emphasis added):

§2.1 Gives member the right to 'take sanitary and phytosanitary measures necessary for the protection of human, animal or plant life or health'. This is the opening up for exceptions, but not just any kind of exceptions, as §2.2 places restrictions on the exercise of that right, when it states that 'measures must be based *on scientific principles and evidence*' and must not 'arbitrarily or unjustifiably discriminate between members where identical or similar conditions prevail', or be applied 'in a manner which would constitute a disguised restriction on international trade'.[10]

§3 states that measures should be based upon *international standards,* guidelines or recommendations, but that a higher level or protection is permitted if 'there is *scientific justification*' or 'if the member considers the appropriate level or protection should be set at a higher level'. Simply put: you may define your own ALOP, but it must be justified scientifically. This is what the first IRA of 1996 failed to do.

Finally, §5 refers to the determination of the 'Appropriate level of Sanitary and phytosanitary protection' and the assessment of risk required, and states again that this assessment must be *justified scientifically* (SRRA, 2000: 49).

As this list indicates, standardization takes place at several levels. First, there are the *international standards for quarantine* laid down in the SPS agreement (not disputed in this case). Second, there are the exceptions to these standards, and the *standardization of these exceptions,* generally undertaken through the standardized format of an IRA. One important standardizing principle is the principle of consistency: you cannot be strict with salmon and lenient with trout, for example. This is why the second IRA (1999) did not only deal with salmon but had to include all other finfish, including ornamental fish for private aquariums. As a result, the second IRA became a rather complicated exercise, but what seemed to be unnecessary digressions from the sea into aquariums was significant because it helped achieve a format which complied with the standardizing principles laid down for such exceptional cases. Third, because exceptions are by definition difficult to standardize, another standardizing tool is enrolled, that of science. Science is called upon whenever the defined international standard appears insufficient to cover all possible cases. Science thus represents another level of standardization, the ultimate 'standardizer' of unstable standards. Put differently, it appears that when the WTO system cannot take responsibility for all the exceptions that could possibly be valid, the problem of standardization is delegated, so to speak, to the scientific community.[11]

Australia's change of policy may be seen as a move upwards or outwards, from the national level to the level of all WTO member states, and finally to the level of the general scientific community which, ideally, 'speaks for everything everywhere'. It is a process of upscaling through which larger and larger contexts for interpretation are evoked. The material dimension of this process consists of the production and management of the IRA that undertakes the necessary translation in an appropriate format. In this sense, the IRA is a potential boundary object, but it did not quite succeed. As the subsequent events demonstrated, the efforts failed, in so far as the first IRA (1996) failed to satisfy the standardizing principles of the WTO, while the second IRA (1999) failed to meet the needs of the Tasmanian community. What made it so difficult? Let us take a closer look at the art of assessing risk.

Downscaling

The OIE Animal Health Code provides a standard method for undertaking risk assessments, defined as 'The evaluation of the likelihood and the biological and economic consequences of entry, establishment or spread of a pathogenic agent within the territory of an importing country' (OIE agreement cited in SRRA, 2000: 106). In other words, the IRA must document in a scientific manner the likelihood of the entry of disease within a territory and the economic consequences of such an entry. In a standard IRA, members are allowed to take the following economic factors into account: the potential damage in terms of loss of sales, the cost of control or eradication, and the relative cost effectiveness of alternative approaches to limiting risk (SSRA, 2000: 106).

This is not an easy task. What would the entry of up to twenty different salmon diseases cost the Tasmanian salmon industry? How much money would they 'save' if they were avoided? Even if they could estimate such figures, they would hardly show up as big numbers in relation to Australia's national economy. Although salmon farming is important for the state economy, the state of Tasmania makes up only five per cent of the Australian population and an even smaller share of the national economy. Even a complete environmental disaster on the Tasmanian coast would have a limited impact on the national Australian economy.[12]

Risk assessments are, however, not only about economics: Not everything must be accounted for by its economic value. The SPS agreement, for example, allows an ALOP to be founded on what is called 'societal value judgment'. However, in order to be justified, such judgment must be applied to all areas of import, and standardized across different species, diseases and goods. In other words, in order to formulate unique ALOP based on 'societal value judgment', Australia must define some kind of generalized 'standard' that takes all relevant unique needs into account.

This is where confusion set in. Evaluating the hybrid mixture of Australian value judgments, potential economic losses to the industry, the economic value of a disease-free marine environment, and the scientifically calculated risk of disease, is described by AQIS as a 'judgment which somebody [else] has to make' (SRRA, 2000: 85). AQIS would certainly not make that decision; its officers were scientists and bureaucrats, not politicians. 'Somebody else' could have been the federal government, but they did not intervene. Consequently, the legal option of formulating a unique level of protection was not applied, and instead the federal authorities resorted to the more manageable IRA, in which the economic loss to the Australian nation was the only feature that was potentially relevant, but at the same time too insignificant to be taken into account.

Until 1999, Tasmanian industry and government had hoped that Tasmanian interests would be secured through the federal government, but the second IRA made it clear that this would not happen. As a result, Tasmania set its own course of action. Evoking constitutional legislation that gives Australian states the right and duty to take care of their own questions of quarantine, Tasmanian authorities simply—and very quickly—drafted, voted and passed a piece of legislation which banned the import of nonviable salmon to Tasmania. This was done by means of a new, Tasmanian IRA, which mimicked the federal one, but because the scale was now the island of Tasmania rather than the entire Australian continent, what was 'low' impact on the federal level, now became 'high' impact on the state level. Just as the salmon dispute between Australia and Canada was settled, it reappeared locally as a conflict between the Australian nation and the Tasmanian state, as Tasmania challenged Australia's federal jurisdiction over state quarantine issues. Federal authorities formally opposed Tasmania's stricter regulatory practice, but no formal sanctions were implemented.

What Tasmania did in the final run was a quick and dramatic act of downscaling: forget about the standard format for the IRAs, forget about economic impact on the national level—just consider the impact of diseases for the Tasmanian industry, marine environment and general public. The conclusion was simple and clear: import must be banned.

'The Way Things Are'

I raised the question initially of why Australia changed its policy, or more precisely: Why did the second IRA actually recommend lifting the quarantine? One way of approaching this question is through Foucault's (1991) concept of governmentality and its application to economic practices. Inspired by Foucault's work on governmentality, Miller and Rose (1993) have addressed indirect forms of political power in advanced liberal democracies, and the role of knowledge, discourse and language as technical devices that render reality amenable to particular kinds of action, calculation or intervention. According to this perspective, 'knowing' an object (such as the risk of nonviable salmon import) in such a way that it can be governed requires certain ways of representing the object that are stable enough to travel and remain stable while the object moves across continents, institutions or fields of trade (see also Bruno Latour's concept of an immutable mobile [Latour, 1987: 227]). The standard format of an IRA may be seen as an example of such a representation, and the reason why they allow mobility (and are themselves applied across continents) is that they are already thoroughly standardized.

The WTO system (and the SPS agreement) may also be seen as a complex effort towards governmentality. The stated purpose of the system is to ensure equality in international trade, and a level playing field for the actors involved. But because countries are *not equal,* the regulations must allow for exceptions. The WTO agreement thus requires that there are ways to ensure that exceptions that occur will be considered and treated fairly, hence the need for standardizing tools. As the Tasmanian example indicates, such standardizing tools also become disciplinary tools, or 'technologies of government' (Miller and Rose, 1993).

In their first attempt at trying to play the WTO game (when they submitted the first IRA in 1996), Australia failed. They temporarily kept the salmon out and thus protected Tasmanian interests, but they failed completely in rendering the object of the dispute (risk of nonviable salmon import) amenable to sympathetic evaluation within the WTO. This may be one reason why they, next time around, appear to be more eager to please the WTO than to protect Tasmanian industries. I asked one of the key participants from Tasmania, a former quarantine officer, whether the dispute was worth it. He replied:

> Yes. If we regret anything it is that we didn't know more at the beginning of the process. But again, if you were talking to people in Canberra, and they were being honest I think they would say it has been a learning process for them. I think it was a learning process in Geneva for the panelists and appellate bodies and that sort of thing, all fumbling around in the fog. And we all now know a little more about the way things are.
>
> Interview with former state quarantine officer,
> April 24, 2002

Knowing 'the way things are' refers to a process of learning in which the ability to switch your argument according to the appropriate level of scale is a key competence.

What the appropriate scale is at any given time depends, in turn, on the judgment of a few persons who struggle to compare what, in essence, remains incommensurate. Thus 'the way things are' also refers to ongoing processes of negotiation, in which contexts are systematically evoked, or discarded, in accordance with efforts to up-scale or to downscale, to standardize or to make singular.

It is significant to note that 'the way things are' has little to do with the specific features of the Tasmanian marine environment or with the propensity of, for example, infectious salmon anaemia to spread in salmon populations. These are relevant issues, but far from sufficient, to effect the kind of protection that was deemed necessary in Tasmania. In order to analyse this case, a more thorough understanding of the Tasmanian environmental context, the economy of salmon farming or Tasmanian culture would hardly be of any help. Instead, the case exemplifies how context is a product of interaction, and in a state of constant tension, interaction and conflict (Helmreich, 2005: 126). It is at this level, where contexts are systematically brought together and contested, that we, as well as my Tasmanian informant, can begin to understand 'the way things are'.

Where Economies and Ecologies Meet

Atlantic salmon farming is not only a good example of globalizing processes. It also exemplifies an arena where economies and ecologies meet; an arena where differentiating dualisms like society and nature, economy and society, or local and global, fail to keep things apart. The object which Australian authorities failed to protect was neither entirely economic, environmental or social, but all of these at once. The success or failure of AQIS had little to do with 'the way things are' under water or in annual reports, but relied instead on AQIS' ability to conjure an image of salmon through which all such potential connections were readily apparent, and even comparable, and to do so in a scientific manner. In light of these requirements, it is hardly surprising that they failed.

The Australian salmon dispute may be an extreme case. However, it indicates how foods are increasingly involved in complex processes of scale-making which render the distinction between the global and the local obsolete. Foods have travelled long distances for hundreds of years. But the various impacts of foodstuffs' potential mobilities in the present day on natural environments, legal boundaries, economic outcomes and microbiological contexts, are creating issues which we are now only beginning really to understand.

Notes

1. According to the FAO (2009), world aquaculture has grown from a production of less than 1 million tonnes in the early 1950s to 51.7 million tonnes by 2006.

2. References to Tasmanian aquaculture are informed by my ethnographic fieldwork in Tasmania in 2002, and subsequent revisits (see also Lien, 2005, 2007a, 2007b).

3. Four shiploads of fertilized salmon roe made respective three-month journeys on sailing ships from London to Melbourne, before the fourth one finally succeeded. In the three first attempts, the eggs did not survive (for a detailed account, see Lien, 2005).

4. To illustrate, a medium-sized Tasmanian hatchery sourced its oxygen from Britain, the oxygen transmitter from Canada, a recirculation filter from France, feed from Norway and Denmark, a grading machine from Italy, another grader from Germany, a high pressurizer from Scotland, an incubator from the United States, an ozone generator from Brisbane, Australia, a feeding system from Finland, counting equipment from Iceland and oxygen diffusers from Canada, while the hatchery manager himself had recently arrived from Scotland (Lien, 2007b).

5. In Tasmania, for example, this duality informs nature perceptions through the hierarchical distinction between species that are native and species that are introduced. According to this approach native is, by definition, a more valued species than the introduced. Farmed Atlantic salmon are typically introduced marine species, while Australian fur seals, for example, are native (see Lien, 2005, for details).

6. See <http://www.tassal.com.au/_aq_Aquaculture.aspx>.

7. Measures to avoid introduced species are justified, in part, by the dramatic ecological transformations that have occurred in Australia as a result of biomigration of so-called invasive species since the late eighteenth century.

8. Canada's motive seems to have little to do with market access, as Australia remained a marginal market for farmed salmon. Some Australians suggest that Canada sought WTO precedence for other issues and interests. The underlying Canadian interests are, however, not the concern of this analysis.

9. They also note that there is no natural law that the best standard shall win. Rather, there are numerous examples of standards that are installed for all kinds of social and conspiratory reasons (Bowker and Star, 2000).

10. The excerpts that follow are cited from the SRRA which in turn cites WTO, Report of the Panel 12 June 1998, p. 7.

11. To summarize, there are various tools of standardization: (1) the international standard itself, as defined by the WTO, (2) the standardized format for justifying exceptions to the WTO standard, defined as an IRA to justify exceptions, and (3) their justifications which, in turn, involves science itself.

12. A threat to Australia's reputation as a relatively disease-free continent might transfer to other primary industries and reduce what is currently often referred to in Australia as a competitive advantage. The potential economic impact of such a scenario is, however, very hard to predict.

References

Andaur, K. (2006), *Oppdrettslaks i Chile* [*Farmed Salmon in Chile*], Master thesis in Social Anthropology, Oslo: Department of Social Anthropology.

Bowker, G. C.. and Star, S. L. (2000), *Sorting Things Out. Classification and Its Consequences*, Cambridge, MA: The MIT Press.

Food and Agriculture Organization of the United Nations (2006), 'State of World Aquaculture 2006', FAO Fisheries Technical Paper, No. 500, Rome: Food and Agriculture Organization of the United Nations.

Food and Agriculture Organization of the United Nations (2009), 'State of World Aquaculture', <www.fao.org/fishery/topic/13540/en> (accessed October 7th 2009)

Foucault, M. (1991), 'Governmentality', in G. Burchell, C. Gordon and P. Miller (eds.), *The Foucault Effect: Studies in Governmentality*, Hemel Hamstead: Harvester Wheatsheaf.

Garsten, C. (1994), *Apple World: Core and Periphery in a Transnational Organizational Culture: A Study of Apple Computer Inc.*, Stockholm: Coronet Books.

Helmreich, S. (2005), 'How Scientists Think about "Natives", for Example: A Problem of Taxonomy among Biologists of Alien Species in Hawaii', *Journal of the Royal Anthropological Institute*, 11/1: 107–28.

Huntingford, F. A. (2004), 'Implications of Domestication and Rearing Conditions for the Behaviour of Cultivated Fishes', *Journal of Fish Biology*, 65: 122–42.

Latour, B. (1987), Science in Action. Cambridge, MA: Haward University Press.

Lever, C. (1992), *They Dined on Eland. The Story of Acclimatisation Societites*. London: Quiller Press.

Lien, M. (2005), ' "King of Fish" or "Feral Peril"; Tasmanian Atlantic Salmon and the Politics of Belonging', *Society and Space*, 23: 659–73.

Lien, M. (2007a), 'Domestication Downunder: Atlantic Salmon Farming in Tasmania', in R. Cassidy and M. Mullin (eds.), *Where the Wild Things Are Now: Domestication Reconsidered*, Oxford: Berg.

Lien, M. (2007b), 'Feeding Fish Efficiently: Mobilising Knowledge in Tasmanian Salmon Farming', *Social Anthropology*, 15/2: 169–85.

Lien, M., and Melhuus, M. (2007), 'Introduction', in M. Lien and M. Melhuus (eds.), *Holding Worlds Together: Ethnographies of Truth and Belonging*, Oxford: Berg.

Lien, M., and Nerlich, B. (eds.) (2004), *The Politics of Food*, Oxford: Berg.

Miller, N., and Rose, P. (1993), 'Governing Economic Life', in M. Gane and T. Johnson (eds.), *Foucault's New Domains*, New York and London: Routledge.

Nustad, K. (2003), 'Considering Global/Local Relations: Beyond Dualism', in T. H. Eriksen (ed.), *Globalization: Studies in Anthropology*, London: Polity Press.

Senate Rural and Regional Affairs and Transport Legislation Committee (1999), *Inquiry into Effectiveness of Legal and Regulatory Processes Related to the Australian Quarantine and Inspection Service and Its Decision to allow Importation of Salmon Products to Australia*. Volumes 1–5. Submissions to the Senate Rural and Regional Affairs and Transport Legislation Committee. Canberra, Australia: Parliament of the Commonwealth of Australia.

Senate Rural and Regional Affairs and Transport Legislation Committee (2000), *An Appropriate Level of Protection? The Importation of Salmon Products: A Case Study of the Administration of Australian Quarantine and the Impact of International Trade Arrangements,* Report of the Senate Rural and Regional Affairs and Transport Legislation Committee, Canberra, Australia: Parliament of the Commonwealth of Australia.

Stead, S.M., and Laird, L. (2002), *Handbook of Salmon Farming,* Berlin: Springer-Verlag.

Tassal (2008). 'About Aquaculture', <http://www.tassal.com.au/_aq_Aquaculture.aspx> accessed 10 September 2009.

Wilk, R. (2006), *Home Cooking in the Global Village,* Oxford: Berg.

—4—

Virtue and Valorization: 'Local Food' in the United States and France

Michaela DeSoucey
Northwestern University

Isabelle Téchoueyres
Université Bordeaux 2

> A society's cuisine is a language in which it unconsciously expresses its structure, unless, without knowing better, it resigns itself to revealing its contradictions there.
>
> —Claude Lévi-Strauss, 1978

The twentieth century witnessed revolutionary changes in the way food econo-mies around the Western world have become managed, promoted and controlled. Land conversion to single-crop models, corporate management of farms, technologi-cal innovations and government subsidy programs have standardized and cheapened the costs of food production, processing and distribution. For many, food is now convenient, accessible and generally inexpensive. Further, omnipresent globalizing markets have increased the availability of foods previously unseen in supermarkets. Ingredients, flavours and cuisines once considered exotic are now part of regular food repertoires, permitting Western tastes to diversify alongside the contents of their shopping carts.[1]

Developing in parallel to these processes are critical conversations regarding the scope and speed of industrial agriculture's globalization and consolidation, as well as its associated social, environmental and economic impacts. Mass-produced foods made desirable a century ago by elites' consumption are today considered objec-tionable by some in the same demographic. These critiques have given rise to the production of new market spaces for foods that are explicitly *not* produced by large-scale and global conglomerates. Those who advocate for these new market spaces seek to provide working alternatives that generally rely on production methods that advocates deem purer, safer and healthier and that serve to contrast with the work of global food conglomerates.

In this chapter, we look at the emergence of 'local food' in the United States and France as significant cases of emerging markets for alternative foods. In both countries, expanding social desire to seek out, produce and consume such alternatives derives from the general belief that the food system has taken a wrong, and unethical, turn. Yet the expansive scope of issues involved in comprehending such a belief allows for slippage and fragmentation in how virtuous foods gain definitional and categorical properties. Consequently, we ask: what makes a food local, what makes a local food virtuous and how does this cultural work in the market for local food products differ cross-nationally?

We use data from various research projects we have conducted over the last several years in order to show how local foods and their producers are identified as rooted in ideals of social and environmental virtue, assigned measures of quality and authenticity and promoted as solutions to social problems stemming from large-scale agricultural production. Broadly motivating our exploration is the notion that the people involved in creating this alternative system add as much political energy and value to local foods as the inherent qualities of the food products themselves. We thus concentrate on the rhetoric, beliefs and strategies of local foods' producers and their cultural gatekeepers in the United States and France. Additionally, we illustrate how these tactics actually denote varied qualities that assume different forms in the United States and France, to demonstrate that virtue and valorization are heavily reliant on both cultural and social structural factors.

Local Food—What Does It Mean?

The broad movement for local food encompasses diverse interests and advocates within both of our national contexts. Indeed, the term 'food', as well as 'local', has various definitions. One can talk about foods as natural resources or commodity goods (e.g. fish or fruit), foods as processed products (e.g. cheese, bread or foie gras), foods as manufactured products (e.g. soda or frozen dinners) or foods as consumption-oriented experiences (e.g. meals or snacks). Perceptions linked to local foods' origins and qualities are based on a number of different criteria (nature, the ecosystem, specific types of knowledge, health, labour, variation in types of production and distribution, and the role of 'tradition', among others).

In both the United States and France, the social worlds occupied by local food are composed of communities, social networks and individuals joined in relationships that juxtapose social movement and market-oriented domains. They additionally rely on supportive intermediary work from managers, researchers, journalists and other nodes in the systemic chain of meaning-making and cultural entrepreneurship. For such communities of advocates and eaters, it is available knowledge of the production process (including the role of producers) as much as the food itself that elicits consumer energy and enthusiasm. Interested publics are invited through the lexicon implied by local food movements to compare local products to those which may or may not be generally available from global conglomerates (e.g. Burros, 2006).

In both nations, local food is promoted as a direct challenge to the power and control of Western industrial food systems. It is the sense of active participation in this alternative market space that encourages producers and consumers alike to identify as complicit in the construction of a social world where each provides care for the other through a redefined, moralized market exchange. Foods marketed as local in both countries sometimes, but not always, imply higher costs for the consumer at the point-of-purchase, because of higher production expenses. However, several defining principles of local food in the U.S. context contrast with those of France. In the former, local food is considered especially distinct from the world of commodity food markets because of the lessened physical distance between producers and consumers. The food items themselves do not necessarily matter outside of their seasonality and smaller-scale production methods. In the latter, local food products sold throughout the country and international marketplaces are typically designated by a specific origin label, thus limiting their production and identity to bounded geographic areas.

Thus, we conceptualize local food as much more than a territorial qualification; it is a polemical and political tool that legitimizes new markets as dynamic social spaces connecting the production and consumption of culture, in addition to food. Such instruments are not only the aesthetic, sensory components of production conspicuous to the public eye; they are also assigned social virtue in order to add knowledge and value to the consumer exchange (see Martins, 2004).

Local in the United States versus France—One Virtue among Many

In the United States, the use of a 'local food' designation is associated with particular kinds of producers and distribution methods, chiefly the work of small-scale, independent farmers who actively resist practices of industrial farming, such as monocropping and long distribution chains (Norberg-Hodge et al., 2002). Many practice 'sustainable agriculture', which refers to a farm's ability to maintain productivity in both the short and long terms without causing damage to environmental properties or neighbouring communities. Additionally, such producers work to incorporate knowledge of the foods' origins and physical journey 'from farm to plate', either explicitly through documentation or implicitly through direct transactions.

Historically, local and organic food movements in the United States were conjoined. Recent corporate participation in the marketplace for organic food, however, propelled popular support for local food as a way to reclaim the virtues of alternative food production (Guthman, 2004). Indeed, agribusiness interests own and have consolidated many organic brands into several supply and distribution outlets within the global food and drink markets (Fromartz, 2007). For many U.S. advocates, local has become the new organic, valorizing it in similar manners to the way organic food was in the past. Local food producers do often use organic techniques but will call their yields 'pesticide free' or even 'beyond organic'.

Local food in France is linked to regional specialties with historic roots and includes similarly important characteristics, such as good taste, variety, the importance of personal relationships between producers and consumers, and a lack of artificial additives or preservatives. Local food designations, however, resemble some previous organic regulatory efforts in the United States or Fairtrade certifications in other countries (Raynolds et al., 2007). Institutionalized classification of food products as 'regional' began in France after World War II within the context of urbanization, modernizing food production techniques and, perhaps most importantly, the introduction of the automobile and paid vacation time, which allowed the French to travel and learn about their country's different regions (Bessiere, 1996). French cities and towns are small in geographic size in comparison to the U.S. cities, and feelings of proximity to the rural landscape are prevalent among urban populations (Mennell, 1985). In time, quality labels and certification systems demarcating products specific to different regions, originally created by producers to protect their production, became institutional phenomena, using the 1905 AOC (Appellation d'Origine Controlée) system for wines as a model (Stanziani, 2004).

Local food in the French case thus references geographic areas whose range can span from a town (such as mustard from Dijon or lentils from Le Puy) to a region (such as foie gras from the southwest). Emphasis is placed on the connectivity of particular foods' explicit narratives to their respective land, collective history and shared savoir-faire in the production and consumption of food items. Local foods are celebrated and protected through regulatory bodies and quality labelling practices specific to their places of origin, or *produits de terroir*. Food designated as local in this model is often, but need not be, produced by small-scale farmers independent of commercial or industrial interests. Food identified by a specific geographic zone cannot be legally produced elsewhere; social comprehension of its localness links production methods with historical roots and physical origins, or *terroir*, as organized promotion of traditional tastes and production methods (O'Connor, 2000).

Spaces for Local Exchange

Spaces for the market exchange of local foods, at first glance, seem remarkably similar across the United States and France. Local food products are sold in both countries through farmers' markets, cooperatives, community groups and direct-selling organizations often initiated by the producers themselves. Restaurants often serve local specialities or use ingredients from neighbouring farms, weaving together different older and newer styles of cuisine while simultaneously noting products' local origins.

Also housed in this market space are farmers' markets, public venues which allow producers to sell their products directly to consumers on selected days throughout the year. Farmers' markets in the United States are a particularly dynamic and rapidly growing organizational form for urban and suburban populations. For 2006, the U.S. Department of Agriculture's directory lists 4,385 farmers' markets around the country, an 18 per cent increase from two years prior. Within a typical market, a vendor's farm must have produced all foods sold there, skirting the formal economy of the conventional commodity value-chain (unlike in France, where vendors often sell products obtained from wholesalers). Though some regular and specialty supermarkets, particularly in urban areas, have begun to offer local food products specific to their areas, personal interaction with the farm and farmer remains key in current civic promotion of local food communities (Lyson et al., 1995).

Such exchanges demonstrate the meanings attached to U.S. local food—environmental sustainability (involved in production) and traceability (detailing the path it took to reach the consumer). Its virtues are thus defined in the negative, as noncommodity food that does not involve commercial agribusiness interests. Also currently emphasized by local food advocates in this model is its role in decreasing 'food miles', or shortening the physical distance food travels between its points of production and consumption and reducing related fossil fuel consumption. This term is utilized regularly as a modern measure of the food production's environmental impact; recent popular books such as Barbara Kingsolver's *Animal, Vegetable, Miracle: A Year of Food Life* (Kingsolver, Kingsolver, and Hopp, 2007) and Michael Pollan's *The Omnivore's Dilemma* (2006) have garnered acclaim for promoting the virtues of eating 'close to home'. The exact varieties of offerings are not crucial to their designation as local (though many local food producers do grow and market noncommercial varieties of fruits, vegetables and animal products).

In our French case, technological innovation in production methods does not necessarily affect the French definition of either local or *terroir,* as long as the item remains culturally significant to consumers and the local population. Foods characterized as local appear in supermarkets across the country and are distributed by third parties. Though open-air markets exist throughout French urban landscapes, vendors regularly sell food products from outside the local regions or even the nation.[2] It is knowledge of the product, of the historical roots of its production methods and its geographic origin, that invokes local foods pride. Additionally, local foods increasingly occupy important social spaces in promoting gastronomic tourism and economic activity in France's rural regions and departments. Culinary patrimony is thus a cultural resource as well as a popular phenomenon, aiding in both regional and national identity construction (Micoud et al., 2000).

Packaging Local Food as the Solution to Global Food Problems

In both national contexts, general perceptions of local food as a movement or community imply notions of social change. Local food movements implicate themselves by definition as providing both ideological and institutional solutions to the many currents of corresponding social problems caused by the globalizing world of food production. Our various research projects show that producers and advocates of local food in both countries frequently use culturally available rhetoric of virtue and goodness to attempt to 'trigger moral indignation' (Gamson, 1995: 105) in marketing themselves, their organizational ties and their products.

Language of trust, safety and community proliferates throughout local food marketplace exchanges, promotional materials, media outlets and the Internet. Consumers are frequently told they have the opportunity to make a political statement every time they eat and that 'eating is an agricultural act' (Berry, 1989: 125). Belief in the safety and quality of the industrial food supply throughout the twentieth century connects to food regulations developed to protect consumers against the variation in quality standards permitted by a lack of governmental or corporate oversight (exposed, for example, by Upton Sinclair's muckraking 1906 bestseller, *The Jungle*). Today, however, implicit in contemporary concerns for which local foods are positioned as alternatives are indictments of markets' and governmental bodies' permissiveness towards safety and quality risks posed by globalized agribusiness practices.

One recent example is the U.S. case of contaminated spinach in 2006, in which a virulent strain of E. coli bacteria discovered across product brands and state lines led to a massive recall, the hospitalization of almost 200 people across twenty-one states and general consumer panic about food safety (U.S. Food and Drug Administration, 2006). E. coli, in fact, thrives in the acidic stomachs of beef and dairy cattle fed with grain, the typical ration on most industrial cattle farms, where the large amounts of waste produced can contaminate groundwater and spread the bacteria to neighbouring irrigation supplies. Nearby spinach fields fell victim to cross-contamination made possible by their proximity to cattle feedlots (Plank, 2006), yet it was the profit-maximizing volume and scope of the corporate producers and distributors involved that permitted the contaminated spinach to spread across the country.

Such episodes directly implicate the need for awareness of environmental and social problems linked to the industrial food system. Solutions proposed by those reporting on the spinach outbreak ranged from improved regulation and inspection, on one hand, to increased reliance on small, local farms, on the other. A *New York Times* editorial regarding the incident closed with the statement, 'We would be appalled to find human waste on our produce. We should be equally appalled to find animal manure, if that is what happened' (Anonymous, 2006). Such rhetoric also includes messages that could be considered peripheral to the act of eating: land stewardship, social justice, pollution, species diversity and strengthening rural economies, among others. The spectrum of possible solutions implies necessary confidence in food production methods, for which local food is positioned as superior.

In France (and other European countries), problems created by globalized markets also evoke concerns about contamination, the management of risk and social fears of the centralized power of agribusiness firms. Recent fears include the bovine spongiform encephalopathy (BSE, better known as mad cow disease) crisis, European activism against the introduction of genetically modified organism (GMO) crops and cultural alarm about outsider (i.e. American) control over the food supply's homogenization.

The GMO issue, currently in the public limelight, well illustrates how these different spheres interact. The increasing ignorance faced by consumers concerning the actual content of their meals is accompanied by great anxiety (Kurzer and Cooper, 2005); GMOs, known by the general public as a cross between vegetal and animal substances, are viewed as unnatural and immoral (Pascalev, 2003). Concern also bears on the unwanted dissemination of GMO crops, which may affect the production of local food with specific labels (organic, quality or origin labels). Additionally, scientists have thus far been unable to produce conclusions concerning their impact on human health, biodiversity and the disappearance of useful organisms. Political and legal confusion add to this ambient distrust. Although a European law authorized the use of one strand of genetically modified (MON810) corn seed in 1998, a 1999 moratorium stopped its expansion until 2003. It was only in 2007 that France issued two decrees stating that farmers must report their usage of GMO seeds as well as all relevant information concerning social impacts (one wonders how they will be able to fulfil this requirement).

In the meanwhile, nobody knows exactly what has taken place; disharmony between French and European legislators enabled farmers to plant GMO fields without reporting them, resulting in discrepancies between official and nonofficial field census reports. In addition, GMO products are used in animal food, though the law does not require any indication on milk or meat products. Permission was also given to commercialize products containing GMOs, such as medication, seeds and fertilizers. In response, groups of people organized, calling themselves 'les Faucheurs Volontaires' (Volunteer Reapers), supported by Confédération Paysane (with José Bové in the lead), the Green Party and Greenpeace. Their actions have been prevalent in international media, with 4,800 people claiming to have taken part in actions of 'civil disobedience', mostly in southwest France, uprooting both experimental and commercial crops. They justify their actions by calling upon the French Constitution to protect the public's right to a healthy environment and properly taken precautions. In 2007, Reapers began organizing in Germany, Portugal and Great Britain. Such events have elevated French public consciousness of the ways local food ties into social, environmental and institutional issues.

Pastoral Visions: Valorizing the Authenticity of Local Food Production

In both national contexts, we find that local food producers market themselves alongside the food they produce as symbols of the authenticity of *themselves and their experiences,* combining their uphill struggles with the land and the economy with their foods' actual growth. These beliefs connect the availability of local foods outside of rural spaces to the idea of farming as an authentic and honourable vocation that requires not only long hours but skill and intelligence, endurance, patience and a complex knowledge of local culture and landscape. The marketization of their experiences gives local foods storied and distinctive connections to person and place within the market space.

In our U.S. research, we have found that farmers who grow and market their products as local believe that, in addition to the virtues instilled by their commitment, their growing practices improve the physical taste of the final product. Local farmers are regularly interviewed on public radio programmes about the high quality of their asparagus and tomatoes, and 'meet the grower' human-interest stories have appeared with increasing frequency in local, regional and Internet news outlets in the past decade.

One farmer in our interview sample, who sells his produce at two different farmers' markets in the Midwest, explained that he even 'used to bring pictures of the farm to the markets. People would come up, look at the photos and say "you're living our dream". These were white, middle-class types. They don't think we're crazy at all. Some people ask me, "Are you still having fun?" Fun is not a word here. Farming isn't fun. That's a very urban kind of notion, not a farmer's notion'. Another farmer at the same market spoke similarly: 'People are so romantic about farming. They think it is a wonderful life; they have pastoral visions. It's really sweat, blood and tears'. However, such narratives also work to affirm producers' own sense of morality, that they are 'doing the right thing' juxtaposed against conventional agriculture.

In our French research, we also found numerous cases of local food producers actively participating in promoting themselves alongside the qualities of the fruits of their labours. In particular, many regions around the country promote regional gastronomic tourism, including visits to the farms which make *produits de terroir,* to gain market leverage within France as well as the larger European community. Promotional work by groups such as Bienvenue à la Ferme, Gîtes Ruraux and Discovery Routes (*route des vins, des fromages,* etc.), supported by the Chambres d'Agriculture, aims to entice consumers to visit farms themselves, reducing the social distance to the producers.

Gastronomic tourism permits the valorization of local food in three ways. First, it helps in making products and the traditions surrounding them well known and appreciated by a larger public. Second, tourism allows consumers to associate the image of the product with a moment of pleasure; respondents in our French studies often discussed nostalgia for their childhoods or their vacations. Finally, it permits marketing and commercialization of these foods in their place of production, bringing money and jobs into rural communities.

Southwest France, for example, remains a very rural area with varied landscapes, and a large proportion of the population outside its cities is employed in the small-scale agricultural production of a variety of food products. Products made from fattened ducks and geese in these regions, especially *foie gras,* are considered more than just local products; they are qualified by the historical depth and local cultural mores of *terroir* (Berard and Marchenay, 1995). This area is also well-known for its decades-long orientation towards the use of labels and geographic denominations, such as Label Rouge, AOC and IGP (Indication Géographique Protégée) that serve to indicate and widen the visibility of localness.[3] Label Rouge, for instance, fashioned in 1965 by farmers in the Landes region to demarcate traditionally raised from industrially produced chickens, currently includes a repertoire of 254 products (mainly poultry, meat and dairy). Though the price today is almost double that of industrially produced chickens, those raised under Label Rouge command up to 30 per cent of French poultry sales (and therefore, this labelling is implicated in social class divisions); the work involves some 30,000 farmers and 2,500 businesses, according to industry reports. The success of such labels can be explained in part through observations of the recent evolution of French consumers' food behaviours virtues. Preoccupations with product quality become specially linked to the virtues offered by regional food products, with localized origin being the guarantor of 'good eating' (de la Pradelle, 2006; Shields-Argeles, 2004).

Across our research settings, we recognize that this cultural packaging (farm images and surroundings, the recreation of an idealized past and nostalgia), while deemed to be personally gratifying for producers and consumers alike, does not necessarily help consumers to understand and acknowledge farmers' quotidian realities. Additionally, we see the marketing techniques of gastronomic tourism as engaging cultural tensions between certain local and global economic forces. Such institutionalized moves toward normalizing localities as destinations in national and international consciousness can, on one hand, be understood as instruments serving a segmented global market, rather than local interests, with tradition and local products being marketed like any other raw material. On the other hand, such developments do enable local food producers and industries to self-manage and to act as decision makers for their own life choices. These producers, and their products, now have to become successful ambassadors of the meanings embedded in 'local food' in order for many of these foods to preserve their cultural and economic resonance.

Terroir and Globalization Processes: New Social Relations of Authenticity

Globalization and attendant changes in market scope, the '*marchandisation de la vie*' (Warnier, 1999), have deeply transformed ways of living and thinking that affect the social construction of local food as special. One response to globalization (*mondialisation* in French) is a reactive localization that stimulates aspirations towards local heritage and nostalgia, the affirmation of local identities and the production of new means of expression and uses for local heritage. However, such a market demands distortions in 'tradition'. Producers at farmers' markets across the United States sell home-grown varieties of Italian greens, Asian melons and South American hot peppers. In France, newly created village festivals and night markets increasingly take place during summer vacation months in order to suit tourist agendas. The force-feeding of ducks and geese for *foie gras,* once a fall and winter practice, now takes place year round in order to increase product availability for restaurants, tourism and consumer demand. AOC wine labelling profits well-off wine makers because the regulations cost too much for small-scale farmers to manage. French *patrimoine* is therefore a popularized cultural resource valorized through market-based social dynamics (Bessiere, 1996). The pedigree of traditional *terroir* aids in identity construction by specifying the boundaries of food stuffs' 'localness' yet shifts their temporal, as well as spatial, organization to meet market demands.

We need also take care when valorizing 'traditional' French cuisine as a historical model of food quality and availability. Until very recently, most French people ate a barely sufficient and unvaried diet: little or no meat, cabbage soup, potatoes and stale bread, and drank mediocre wine and water of questionable quality (Mennell, 1985). People generally ate somewhat better in the cities, but even so many products, such as milk and fish, were unreliably fresh until distribution chains improved, which is a historically recent phenomenon (Scholliers, 2001). Today, French agriculture and agribusiness are, similar to those in other nations, concerned with profits, marketing, modernized farming practices and responding to the French desire to consume more meat and dairy products, a variety of vegetables and fruits and pre-prepared dishes (Pitte, 2002).

Issues of Local Food in an Agri-Global Marketplace

Within local food movements, the job of consumer education and marketing typically belong to grassroots advocates. As local food becomes a more prominent choice in global markets (i.e. people want local food, even if it is not local for them), and even begins to occupy traditional commodity market spaces such as supermarkets, consumer education is increasingly enacted through labels, certifications and publicly funded marketing campaigns. Globalization, through its different dimensions of commercial logics and exchanges, interferes with personal stories that are central to what it means to be a local food producer.

In the United States, there is currently no national certification programme for local food. Rather, it is community-based organizations, cooperatives and networks that provide marketing and communication resources for those involved or interested in supporting local food systems. These groups provide and consolidate economies of scale for small producers' market viability. For example, a group called The FoodRoutes Network organizes interested parties around the country into 'chapters' dedicated to outreach and educational events. They also maintain a national list of local food providers, farmers' markets, CSAs and restaurants serving locally produced food. This group purposefully does not offer labelling or certification options for producers, instead relying upon their own message of 'Buy Fresh, Buy Local'.

In France, labelling and certification procedures have long offered local food producers sets of guidelines for production, as previously mentioned, and for inclusion into the social networks and market-based dynamics created in response to globalized food industries. For example, the founding strategies of AOC Sainte-Foy-Bordeaux as a protected wine territory near Bordeaux paradoxically illustrate the extent to which *patrimoine* can be used and manipulated by the agro-food industry. The denomination was implemented to address previously slow economic development and invisibility in the national marketplace. The region's wine producers struck compromise between modernization, innovative technology, and a stereotyped and idealised common history: 'innovation, regulation and fashion taste for the emblematic and nostalgic' (Bromberger and Chevallier, 1999: 15). While the labelling process works to build stronger social relationships and to persuade a community that its culture and interests shape a specific local identity, it engages in a type of territorialism that requires winemakers to cope simultaneously with stringent quality requirements and an evolving market.

Through this particular designation, these local winemakers exalt their 'differences', their sense of historical belonging to the contemporary place and their *terroir*. However, promotion of this wine as local masks inconsistencies such as the more industrial tools of wine-making that are used: machines, factories and finances. Many producers also see the label as negating their efforts for modernization in the region and compelling them to remain static in their methods. Patrimonialization has thus become, in the context of liberal markets, a consensual category in public space that is used to avoid analysis of the political stakes of economic and social restructuring of an industry, such as the world of local wine production, among others.

Conclusion—Choice and Reflexive Eaters

The producers of local foods simultaneously assert their legitimacy as market actors and as social stewards of food traditions acting to preserve physical and social environments. Indeed, their very viability as the former hinges strategically on the success of their claims to social responsibility and cultural virtue. Local foods are attractive to both consumers and producers because they are not commodity agriculture. However, producers must market and sell their output to maintain a livelihood, entangling them in some degree of competition and in negotiation with the very production and market practices they must oppose. Contradictions revealed within such work range from simply having agro-food industries as a foil to the possibility that local food, as a social movement, could fall victim to its own institutional success. For example, the introduction of localized foods in supermarkets may have negative consequences for their image and consumers' perception of their quality, following on the heels of what, in many ways, has already occurred within the organic food movement (Thompson, 2004).

Local foods' continued and enhanced presence depends on the cultural entrepreneurs that push for them and the avenues in which they choose to do so. One small-scale meat producer in the United States, for example, explained that he saw three choices for his locally oriented business—'get with it, find a niche, or get out'. By finding a niche in local retail meat sales, selling at farmers' markets, to restaurants and through catalogues, his enterprise occupies alternative market avenues. Such producers are at the forefront of popularized consumption patterns among those in both countries who have the knowledge, desire and income level to participate.

Small systems are not free of problems in the realms of production and processing standards. For example, small-scale farmers are more vulnerable to external conditions, such as weather; larger producers have a higher available margin for error. Further, eating only a local food diet in some geographic areas would result in nutritional deficiencies, especially in winter months. Many regions, as a result of the global food chain's development, have lost the ability to produce their own food year-round. For consumers, seeking out local food requires additional input of time and money. However, within such production and processing systems, the potential damage from a problem like contamination is less, and their transparency and traceability similarly reflect consumer concerns. Some supporters believe in supporting the ideals of local food systems at all costs, even growth. "This refusal to 'sell out' demonstrates apprehension and fear of having to compromise production methods for monetary interests."

Local food movements in the United States also face institutional challenges regarding characteristics that they do *not* possess. For example, their development remains a subordinate focus within university-based agricultural research, where agribusiness corporations frequently contribute economic and political resources. Related public subsidy programmes for commodity products, such as corn and soybeans, currently do not allow farmers to realize potential benefits of diversified crops. National and state policy reforms are necessary in order to support a decentralized system of diverse family farms, to bolster rural economies and to widen education and distribution channels (for further information, see Carolan, 2006).

Also problematic are the boundaries of the local. Consumers in the United States, for example, believe buying locally has important environmental benefits accrued from the lack of long-distance shipping. Yet urban farmers' markets regularly feature producers who drive several hours each way, from multiple states, to reach a market. As housing developments continue to grow, American urbanites (and suburbanites) physically become further away from their potential local food sources. In France, quality labels promoting local food are so numerous that they sometimes confuse consumers.[4] In fact, in southwest France, even in urban areas where *terroir* foods are readily available in retail outlets, a majority of people tend to favour buying certain local products (e.g. wine, fat duck products, poultry, eggs, seasonal fruits and vegetables) directly from producers, via local outdoor markets, directly on the farm, or via social networks. What matters within such exchanges, similar to the values expressed by producers and consumers in our U.S. research, is the importance placed on personal relationships.

In conclusion, food and food practices associated with localization play dynamic give-and-take roles in the processes of globalization (Appadurai, 2001). Local foods contribute to part of a larger conversation about the consequences of our actions as consumers and as citizens. Posing solutions to these issues allows us to explore the links between science, public policy and consumer protection. We believe that the marketplace must be utilized, in some ways, for these foods to succeed in increasing their consumer appeal because they are literally and necessarily consumable objects. Without finding stable market avenues, some local food traditions could die out. Quality labels and food tradition preservationists (such as the international Slow Food movement) alike allow for local, niche products to go beyond local boundaries. Intertwining the idea of the local with what are considered oppositional forces is an idea that may be anathema to local food purists, but it represents incremental steps toward extending 'eat local' initiatives to national or international levels.

Globalization thus reshapes categories of social distinction for producers outside the mainstream, permitting localness to be contextualized and valorised within particular spaces, while the history and evolution of how such valour manifests in each national context influences the development of meanings assigned to products themselves.

Notes

1. Importantly, this new cornucopia of choices contrasts with dwindling numbers of farmers and food producers. A typical American supermarket, for example, contains on average 30,000 food items, of which the production of about half can be traced back to ten multinational food and beverage companies.
2. See Michèle de la Pradelle's ethnography, *Market Day in Provence* (2006), for a rich and excellent description of the role of French markets in village life.
3. Instituted here were the first Label Rouge for Poulets Fermiers des Landes in 1965 and the first IGPs, with Jambon de Bayonne (1998) and Palmipèdes Gras du Sud Ouest (2000).
4. This was demonstrated through analysis of a survey conducted by one of the authors at the Bordeaux Agriculture Fair in May 2005.

References

Anonymous (2006), 'When Spinach Isn't Good for You', *New York Times* (2 October).

Appadurai, A. (ed.) (2001), *Globalization,* Durham: Duke University Press.

Berard, L., and Marchenay, P. (1995), 'Lieux, Temps et Preuves: La Construction Sociale des Produits de Terroir', *Terrain,* 24: 153–64.

Berry, W. (1989), 'The Pleasures of Eating', *Journal of Gastronomy* 5/2: 125–31.

Bessiere, J. (1996), 'Patrimoine Culinaire et Tourisme Rural', *Les Études de Ter,* Paris: Tourisme en Espace Rural.

Bromberger, C., and Chevallier, D. (1999), *Carrières d'Objets: Innovations et Relances,* Paris, Editions de la Maison des Sciences de l'Homme.

Burros, M. (2006), 'You Are What You Eat: 2006 and the Politics of Food', *New York Times* (27 December).

Carolan, M. S. (2006), 'Do You See What I See? Examining the Epistemic Barriers to Sustainable Agriculture', *Rural Sociology,* 71: 232–60.

de la Pradelle, M. (2006), *Market Day in Provence,* Chicago: University of Chicago Press.

Fromartz, S. (2007), *Organic, Inc.: Natural Foods and How They Grew,* New York: Harvest Books.

Gamson, W.A. (1995), 'Constructing Social Protest', in H. Johnston and B. Klandermans (eds.), *Social Movements and Culture.* Minneapolis: University of Minnesota Press.

Guthman, J. (2004), 'The Trouble with Organic Lite in California: A Rejoinder to the Conventionalisation Debate', *Sociologia Ruralis,* 44/3: 301.

Kingsolver, B., Kingsolver, C., and Hopp, S. L. (2007), *Animal, Vegetable, Miracle: A Year of Food Life,* New York: HarperCollins Publishers.

Kurzer, P., and Cooper, A. (2005), *What's for Dinner? Variations in European Support for Genetically Modified Food,* Pittsburgh: University of Pittsburgh Press.

Lévi-Strauss, C. (1978), *The Origin of Table Manners,* London: Jonathan Cape Limit(ed).

Lyson, T. A., Gillespie, G. W., and Hilchey, D. (1995), 'Farmers' Markets and the Local Community: Bridging the Formal and Informal Economy', *American Journal of Alternative Agriculture,* 10/3: 108.

Martins, P. (2004), 'Set That Apricot Free', *The New York Times* (24 April).

Mennell, S. (1985), *All Manners of Food: Eating and Taste in England and France from the Middle Ages to the Present,* New York: Basil Blackwell.

Micoud, A., Rautenberg, M., Bérard, L., and Marchenay, P. (eds.) (2000), *Campagne de Tous Nos Désirs: Patrimoines et Nouveaux Usages Sociaux,* Ethnologie de la France, Paris: Éditions de la Maison des Sciences de l'Homme.

Norberg-Hodge, H., Merrifield, T., and Gorelick, S. (2002), *Bringing the Food Economy Home: Local Alternatives to Global Agribusiness,* London: Zed Books Ltd.

O'Connor, M. (2000), 'The Integrity of the Terroir: An Appraisal of the State of France's Critical Natural Capital', Guyancourt Cedex: C3ED.

Pascalev, A. (2003), 'You Are What You Eat: Genetically Modified Foods, Integrity and Society', *Journal of Agricultural and Environmental Ethics,* 16/6: 583–94.

Pitte, J. R. (2002), *French Gastronomy: The History and Geography of a Passion,* New York: Columbia University Press.

Plank, N. (2006), 'Leafy Green Sewage', *New York Times* (21 September).

Pollan, M. (2006), *The Omnivore's Dilemma,* New York: Penguin.

Raynolds, L. T., Murray, D., and Heller, A. (2007), 'Regulating Sustainability in the Coffee Sector: A Comparative Analysis of Third-Party Environmental and Social Certification Initiatives', *Agriculture and Human Values,* 24/2: 147–63.

Scholliers, P. (ed.) (2001), *Food, Drink and Identity: Cooking, Eating and Drinking in Europe Since the Middle Ages,* Oxford: Berg.

Shields-Argeles, C. (2004), 'Imagining the Self and the Other: Food and Identity in France and the United States', *Food, Culture & Society,* 7/2: 14–28.

Stanziani, A. (2004), 'Wine Reputation and Quality Controls: The Origin of the AOCs in Nineteenth Century France', *European Journal of Law and Economics,* 18/2: 149–67.

Thompson, C. J. (2004), 'Marketplace Mythology and Discourses of Power', *Journal of Consumer Research,* 31: 162–80.

U.S. Department of Agriculture. (2006), 'Farmers Market Facts', Washington, DC: Agricultural Marketing Service, <http://www.ams.usda.gov/AMSv1.0/farmers markets> accessed 30 August 2009.

U.S. Food and Drug Administration (2006), 'FDA Statement on Foodborne E.coli O157:H7 Outbreak in Spinach', Press Release: 5 October 2006, Washington, DC: U.S. Department of Health and Human Services, <http://www.fda.gov/News Events/Newsroom/PressAnnouncements/2006/ucm108756.htm>

Warnier, J. P. (1999), *La Mondialisation de la Culture.* Paris: La Découverte.

–5–

Quality Conventions and Governance in the Wine Trade: A Global Value Chain Approach

Stefano Ponte
Danish Institute for International Studies

Wine production, trade and consumption have a long history. The oldest archaeological evidence of winemaking dates back to 3500–2900 BC in western Iran. Viticulture and winemaking in ancient Greece, Rome and Egypt are well documented (Unwin, 1996), and trade in wine has existed ever since. What is most relevant to this collection, however, is the fact that the proportion of wine traded internationally has almost doubled between the late 1980s and the early 2000s (Anderson, 2004a). This evolution, coupled with a dramatic increase in mergers and acquisitions and the growing use of 'flying winemakers' around the world, indicates a new phase in the globalization of the wine industry.

The general trends in the geography of wine production, trade and consumption, and the changes in the quality composition of supply and demand, have been well documented elsewhere (see, among many others, Anderson, 2004b; Spahni, 2000; Unwin, 1996). These include, in the last few decades, a dramatic fall in production volumes and per capita consumption in 'traditional' wine making and consuming countries, such as Portugal, Spain, France and Italy. This has been partly compensated for, on the one hand, by growing production and exports in New World countries (Argentina, Chile, South Africa, New Zealand, Australia and the United States) and, on the other hand, by increasing consumption in the UK and the United States. What for centuries was considered a 'cottage industry' is increasingly dominated by large multinational companies (Anderson, 2004b). At the same time, the level of concentration in production/processing in the industry is far behind other sectors in the agro-food sector such as coffee, cocoa or beer. Retail, traditionally the domain of small specialist shops, is now in the hands of supermarket chains, especially in northern Europe and the UK, but increasingly also in Southern Europe as well. Although there are fears of 'homogenization' of styles and offerings in the wine market, the industry still produces a phenomenal array of different products, which are sold under a combination of brand names, grape varieties and/or geographic indications of origin.

The purpose of this chapter is not to review these trends in detail but to examine the link between the macro and micro foundations of the putative globalization of wine. In order to do so, a combination of global value chain (GVC) analysis and convention theory will be employed.[1] These tools will allow a preliminary examination of the complex relations between corporate strategies (including in retail) and different interpretations and promotions of the concept of 'quality'.

Global Value Chain Analysis

GVC analysis has emerged since the early 1990s as a novel methodological tool for understanding the dynamics of economic globalization and international trade.[2] It postulates that the global economy can be usefully understood as a combination of discrete, product-specific 'value chains' rather than of generic 'markets'. In these value chains, firms are linked in internationally dispersed but integrated systems of input supply, trade, production and final marketing. In addition to the descriptive aspects of territoriality and input-output structure, much GVC discussion has revolved around two analytical issues: how GVCs are governed (in the context of a larger institutional framework); and how enterprise-level upgrading or downgrading takes place along GVCs. Much of this discussion has been carried out with particular attention to how power and rewards are embodied and distributed along GVCs, what entry barriers characterize GVCs and how unequal distributions of rewards can be challenged in favour of labour and/or developing countries.

The debate in the GVC literature on governance has been a rich one in the last decade or so, with evolving and sometimes conflicting views on terms, interpretations and applicability. This is not the place to rehash these debates in detail (see Bair, 2005; Gereffi et al., 2005; Gibbon and Ponte, 2005). In short, governance is interpreted here as the process of organizing activities with the purpose of achieving a certain functional division of labour along a value chain, resulting in specific allocations of resources and distributions of gains. In this approach, governance involves the definition of the terms of chain membership, incorporation/exclusion of other actors accordingly and re-allocation of value-adding activities (Gereffi, 1994; Kaplinsky, 2000; Ponte and Gibbon, 2005; Raikes et al., 2000). Within this framework, an attempt is made to identify a group of 'lead firms' that are placed in one or more functional positions along a value chain which are able to 'drive' it. Driving can be carried out in different ways and to different degrees, depending on the product under examination. Thus, GVCs can be highly driven, somewhat driven or not driven at all (in the latter case, they are akin to neoclassical 'markets').

In the GVC literature, lead firms are seen as not only dictating the terms of participation to their immediate suppliers (and/or buyers, if applicable) but also managing to transmit these demands upstream towards further layers of suppliers, sometimes all the way to primary producers. Lead firms can drive GVCs with a *hands-on* approach (vertical integration, long-term contracts, explicit control of suppliers, regular engagement with suppliers or buyers), a *hands-off* approach (use of specifications that can be transmitted in codified, objective and measurable or auditable ways; ability to set standards that are then followed along the GVCs; ability to transmit information that is not easily codifiable in other ways), or a combination of the two (Ponte and Gibbon, 2005). New research has also attempted to differentiate governance in different 'strands' of GVCs (Palpacuer et al., 2005; Ponte, 2007; Riisgaard, 2007). Strands may differ because of different product characteristics (e.g. specialty coffee vs. commercial coffee), a different institutional configuration (e.g. cut flowers sold directly to retailers vs. those sold at an auction in the Netherlands), or a different end-market/origin of production.

Convention Theory and Quality

In previous contributions to the debate on GVC governance, Daviron and Ponte (2005), Ponte (2002) and Ponte and Gibbon (2005) drew considerably on convention theory. The point of this work was to take further discussion of both the immediate normative environment within which value chain actors operate (that is, in relation to their buyers and suppliers) *and* the broader regulatory frameworks in which GVCs (and their lead firms) are found. Such contexts provide a vocabulary of prescriptions concerning, for example, which kinds of economic relation are best suited to managing specific product qualities or which corporate strategies should be employed in the interests of shareholders.

Convention theory provides an entry point to these considerations through postulating that economic action is always framed by systems of justification (Boltanski and Thévenot, 1991). These provide systematic languages for identifying the objects of economic action and the criteria for attributing functions and values to them. In Gibbon and Ponte (2005), convention theory was used to analyse the repertoires of justification that were employed to legitimize specific functional divisions of labour along GVCs, in terms of conventions on product quality and on corporate organization, and of the specific types of justification that these were tied to. It was further used to examine challenges that were raised in relation to these justifications, accommodations and/or overlaps that resulted from these challenges and the new conventions that emerged in the wake of these events. This analysis allowed an appreciation of how and why different sets of agents act in relation to external environments. Furthermore, it provided a framework for understanding social inequalities relating to specific systems of justification. This theoretical effort is continued in this chapter, with specific attention paid to how different *strands* of the global value chain can exhibit different forms of governance that are linked to specific quality conventions. In the case study of wine, distinctions will be made between three 'strands' of the value chain, based on product quality (top-quality, middle-range and basic-quality wine).

Conventions are generally defined as a broad group of mutual expectations that include—but are not limited to—institutions. While institutions are collective and intentional objects that are set up for the purpose of implementing an intention, conventions may also arise from a shared set of regularities that are unintentional (Salais, 1989). For convention theory,[3] rules are not decided prior to action but emerge *in the process* of actions aimed at solving problems of coordination. At the same time, action may be tested and thus needs to be justified by drawing on a variety of criteria of justice that are broadly accepted at a particular time. In other words, convention theory links situated action to widely accepted normative models (Borghi and Vitale, 2006). Conventions are not fixed in time and space—they include mechanisms of clarification that are themselves open to challenge. They are both guides for action and collective systems to legitimize those actions that can be submitted to testing and discussion, leading to compromises and possibly defeat (Boltanski and Thévenot, 1991; Eymard-Duvernay, 2006a, 2006b; Favereau and Lazega, 2002; Ponte and Gibbon, 2005; Wilkinson, 1997).

Boltanski and Thévenot (1991) develop six historically based 'worlds of legitimate common welfare' that draw on particular paradigms of moral philosophy (inspirational, domestic, opinion, civic, market and industrial worlds). They elaborate an account of how these worlds are embedded in the behaviour of firms on the basis of organizing principles. To these 'worlds' correspond different norms of qualification, people (e.g. employees) and objects. Depending on what justifications are employed, one can arrive at different conventions for organizing the activities of firms (see also Boltanski and Chiapello, 1999). According to Boltanski and Thévenot:

1. The *inspirational world* rests on the principle of common humanity and non-exclusion (based on Augustine), and agreement about evaluation and action refers to grace and divine inspiration (in firm parlance, creativity).
2. The *domestic world* is founded on the principle of dignity (Bossuet), and agreement is founded on the basis of tradition (firms draw on the concept of loyalty).
3. The *opinion-based world* is structured around the principle of difference (Hobbes), and objects and subjects are evaluated through the opinion of others (firms use the concept of reputation).
4. The *civic world* is based on the notion of common welfare (Rousseau), and agreement is founded on the fact that individuals are sensitive to changes in common welfare (firms are organized around the concept of representation).
5. The *market world* finds its justification in the notion that difference is justified by sacrifice, effort or investment (Smith), and agreement is founded on the basis of market principles such as price (firms organize themselves around the concept of competitiveness).

6. Finally, the *industrial world* is based on the existence of 'orders of greatness' (St Simon) and agreement is based on objective (technical and measurable) data (firms invoke the concept of productivity).

In more recent work, convention theorists and other scholars have developed further types, such as the 'green world' (Latour, 1998; Thévenot et al., 2000), the 'information world' (Thévenot, 1997) and the 'network world' (also known as 'project-oriented' or 'connectionist') (Boltanski and Chiapello, 1999; see also Thévenot, 2002). Despite the proliferation of categories, convention theory does not give a hierarchical value to these 'worlds', nor does it portray them as historical inevitabilities. Furthermore, at any particular time and locality, there may be multiple justifications of action operating at the same time. Finally, although there is an internal coherence in each world, there are also qualifications that 'bridge' different worlds.

On the basis of the Boltanski and Thévenot framework, Eymard-Duvernay (1989; see also Sylvander, 1995; Thévenot, 1995) developed a typology of quality conventions and related forms of coordination. His main point of departure is that price is the main management form of a particular market only if there is no uncertainty about quality. If this is the case, differences in price are equated with quality. This characterizes a *market* quality convention. When price alone cannot evaluate quality, economic actors adopt other conventions to solve uncertainty about quality. In a *domestic* convention, this is solved through trust (long-term relationships between actors or use of private brands which publicize the quality reputation of products). In this case, the definition of quality is resolved 'internally', and the identity of a product is guaranteed or institutionalized in the repetition of history by its region or country of origin or by a brand-name. In an *industrial* convention, uncertainty about quality is solved through the actions of an external party which determines common norms or standards and enforces them via instrument-based testing, inspection and certification. More recently, an additional category has been added—*civic* convention, where there is collective commitment to welfare, and the quality of a product is related to its impact upon society or the environment.[4]

In this chapter, to these quality conventions, two others are added to complete the original Boltanski and Thévenot framework: an *opinion* convention, where uncertainty about quality is solved through the personal judgment (rather than objective measurement) of an actor that is external to the exchange and has a 'good reputation'; and an *inspirational* convention, where the personality of one of the actors in the exchange, his/her genius, intuition, creativity, vision or downright weirdness substitutes for other means of assessing quality. Table 1, in addition to listing the modalities for assessing quality that are linked to these conventions, also specifies, in relation to wine, the actual instruments that are used to operationalize such modalities.

The consequences of such a heuristic framework for the concept of quality are far-reaching, suggesting that: (1) there is no 'universal' understanding of 'quality';

Table 5.1. An expanded framework of quality conventions

Quality convention	*Instrument of verification of 'quality' (general)*	*Instrument of verification of 'quality' (in wine)*
Inspiration	Personality	Unique wine; cult winemaker or property
Domestic	Proximity, trust and repetition	Brand/varietal, *terroir,* indication of geographic origin
Opinion	External nonobjective judgment	Endorsement by wine writer, judge, publication
Civic	Impact on society and the environment	Assessment of food safety, environmental and social impact, labels and certifications
Market	Price	Price and promotion
Industrial	External objective measurement	Laboratory tests, codification of procedures

(2) quality is cognitively evaluated in different ways depending on what 'world' is used to justify evaluation and action; and (3) there are clear links between specific understandings of quality and the social organization of production and exchange. These observations are important to avoid the overgeneralization of concepts such as the 'globalization' of taste and the 'homogenization' of production, which are often used in critical analyses of agro-food restructuring. In the next sections, the quality conventions outlined in Table 1 will be used to unpack the dynamics of governance in the GVC for wine according to different quality strands.

The GVC for Wine—a Brief Sketch

Figure 5.1 represents a simplified view of the GVC for wine, focusing on the main actor categories and product flows. The bottom part is a simplification of the configuration in producing countries (which can also be consuming countries). The middle part indicates the functional position of international producers/marketers. These operate increasingly on a global scale in order to provide retailers in consuming markets with a complete portfolio of wines from all key producing regions.

Table 2 indicates that the top five wine marketers had a global share of 11 per cent in 2006, and the top ten almost 16 per cent. In comparison, the top five breweries approach 50 per cent of the beer market, while the top five roasters control over 70 per cent of the coffee market. Among the top five wine marketers, we find companies such as Constellation and Gallo (which are U.S.-headquartered but multinational in scope), followed by Foster's of Australia and Pernod Ricard of France.

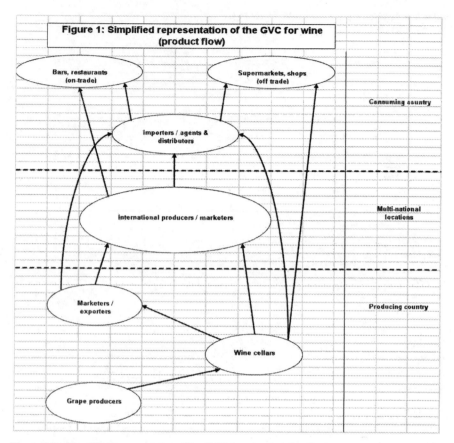

Figure 5.1 Simplified representation of the GVC for wine (product flow).

Although still fairly fragmented, this strand of the value chain is going through a process of consolidation. The last of a series of high-profile consolidation efforts was Constellation's acquisition of Vincor International in 2006 for over $1 billion US. This came after Foster's acquisition of Southcorp Ltd and Pernod Ricard's acquisition of Allied Domecq's wine portfolio. Table 3 shows the world's best-selling wine brands in 2006, which are all owned by either U.S. or Italian groups. The top two brands (and number four) are owned by the number two and three wine marketers.

The upper part of Figure 5.1 represents actors based in an importing country. Here, a distinction is made between the on-trade market (restaurants, bars) and the off-trade market (supermarket chains, other shops, Internet/mail order), although focus is placed in this chapter on the latter. Supermarket chains, of course, are also becoming internationalized, so their actual operations (and interactions with other actors) apply to more than one importing market. Between retailers and the import point,

Table 5.2.   World's top 10 wine marketers (2006)

Rank	Company	Headquarters	Volume of sales (million 9-lt cases)	World share (%)
1	Constellation Brands	United States	104.0	3.9
2	E&J Gallo Winery	United States	72.0	2.7
3	The Wine Group	United States	41.9	1.6
4	Foster's Wine Estates	Australia	39.7	1.5
5	Pernod Ricard	France	37.5	1.4
Top 5			**295.0**	**11.2**
6	Castel Freres	France	36.0	1.4
7	Bacardi	Bermuda	25.7	1.0
8	Les Grands Chais de France	France	22.0	0.8
9	Vina Concha y Toro	Chile	21.4	0.8
10	Distell	South Africa	20.5	0.8
Top 10			**420.5**	**15.9**

Source: Impact, Vol. 3, No. 11-12 and No. 15, 2007 (2007), 'Title of Article or Section', *Impact*, 37/11–12: 6.

wine can be handled by other actors (such as importers, agents and/or distributors), which may operate only in that consumption market or may be part of international producer/marketer companies.

Only product flows, but not ownership boundaries, have been drawn in Figure 5.1 because all combinations can be observed in reality—some international producers/marketers own vineyards in several countries, may have a stake in a local marketer/exporter company, often have large cellar facilities but in some cases only buy ready-made wine from other wine producers. They may also own dedicated agents in different consuming countries or deal directly with retailers. More often than not, they (as well as all other actors upstream) rely on specialist agents and distributors for the on-trade market, which needs a much more hands-on distribution effort and local knowledge of the restaurant/bar industry. In general (but not always), the on-trade market is focused more on higher quality wine and smaller volumes; the off-trade market is focused more on lower quality wine but also sells significant volumes of higher quality wine.

Evaluating quality in food and beverages and presenting quality profiles to consumers are very complex undertakings (see Daviron and Ponte, 2005). Quality means different things to different people, both geographically and along a value chain. Objectively similar products are placed and presented in different packaging and

Table 5.3. World's top 10 wine marketers (2005)

Rank	Company	Owner	Origin	Type of wine	Volume of sales (million 9-lt cases)
1	Franzia	The Wine Group	Unites States	Table	24.8
2	E&J Gallo Cellars	E&J Gallo Winery	Unites States	Table	23.7
3	Martini Vermouth	Martini & Rossi IVLAS (Bacardi)	Italy	Vermouth	14.0
4	Carlo Rossi	E&J Gallo Winery	Unites States	Table	12.5
5	Tavernello	Caviro Societa' Cooperativa	Italy	Table	12.1
Top 5					**87.0**
6	Yellow Tail	Casella Wines	Australia	Table	10.0
7	Beringer	Foster's Wine Estates	Australia	Table	8.6
8	Concha y Toro	Vina Concha y Toro	Chile	Table	7.7
9	Almaden	Constellation Brands	Unites States	Table	8.8
10	Sutter Home	Trinchero Family Estates	Unites States	Table	7.8
Top 10					**130.0**

Source: Impact, Vol. 3, No. 11-12 and No. 15, 2007 (2007), 'Title of Article or Section', *Impact,* 37/11–12: 7.

under different brands, signalling a different level of 'quality'. The skills of quality 'evaluators' (including consumers) vary widely. Quality has material, symbolic and in-person service components. Given this complexity, any discussion of how quality is evaluated, and how different tools of evaluation are wedded to different coordination mechanisms between sellers and buyers, is bound to be partial. In the following discussion, an attempt is made to link different quality conventions to the dynamics of governance in different strands of the GVC for wine.

Quality Conventions and Governance in the GVC for Wine

This section examines the 'quality pyramid' of wine as perceived in consuming countries, keeping in mind that in different countries there are different ways of approaching quality in wine, thus different configurations of quality conventions

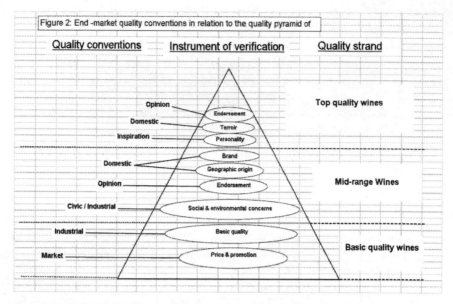

Figure 5.2   End-market quality conventions in relation to the quality pyramid of wine.

may exist. Figure 5.2 represents the quality pyramid divided into three 'ranges': top quality, mid-range and basic quality wines. This is a simplification, as wine trade publications use up to a six-tier quality pyramid. Inside the pyramid, for each quality strand, the main instruments of verification of quality are noted. To each of these correspond one or a combination of quality conventions, indicated on the left side of the pyramid. Each convention is mentioned in order of descending importance (top-to-bottom) within each quality strand. This ranking is based on an interpretation of quality perceptions in the UK wine market, based on interviews with trade operators and analysis of wine trade magazines. Thus, a different ranking may apply in other countries.

Top Quality Wines

For top quality wines, the main instrument of verification of quality is 'endorsement' by a respected (or renowned) wine writer, judge or publication (and/or sommelier in the on-trade market). This relates to an *opinion convention,* where the judgment, rather than being objectively verifiable, rests on the aesthetic approach of the endorser towards wine, the perceived independence of the endorser from industry interests and his/her own preferences. Main factors for top wines are ratings by U.S. wine writer Robert Parker, and by influential publications such as *Wine Spectator* (U.S.) and *Decanter* (UK).

Terroir, the specific combination of soils and microclimate in a particular vineyard or property, is also a factor in the quality evaluation of top wines, but less so in Anglo-Saxon markets than in continental Europe. This relates to a *domestic convention,* where intimate knowledge of the land, and long-term and repetitive fine-tuning to find the best practices and varieties that transfer the elements of *terroir* into the wine, are the main factors. Finally, other wines are reputed to be of 'top quality' because of the unique 'personality' of either the wine, its presentation, the winemaker or the property behind the wine—this includes weird, 'visionary' offerings, 'mad-winemakers', alternative labelling or a specific 'story' behind any of these. In convention theory terms, this can be related to an *inspiration convention* based on creation, innovation, vision, elements of alchemy and uniqueness.

The kinds of conventions that operate in this quality range make it difficult to 'drive' a value chain completely from one functional position: proximity, uniqueness and opinion are not elements that are easily translated and spread both functionally and territorially, although some elements can be codified. Thus, this strand of the GVC for wine exhibits a 'middle range' degree of drivenness. It is actually increasingly driven by wine critics, and specifically through Robert Parker's scores. Because the one-hundred-point Parker scale has been adopted by other influential publications, a creeping element of an industrial convention is helping to give the impression of 'objectification' of tasting, which also makes it easier to communicate information about quality, thus increasing the level of drivenness. Interestingly, Parker does not buy or sell wine, and does not have direct shareholdings in wineries or the trade. His 'empire' is based on selling his opinion (McCoy, 2005). This strand of the value chain is thus (partially) driven by an external actor. Although 'quality' in this strand is also to some extent 'producer-determined' (quality specifications do not follow a register provided by retailers, but rather are the result of tradition and/ or innovation in wineries), and it is an open secret that producers increasingly try to shadow the new aesthetics of wine that Parker and others have promoted.

Mid-Range Wines

For mid-range wines, the combination of quality conventions and of influential actors is more complex. Endorsement by wine critics (and an *opinion* convention) is still a factor, but a less determinant one than in top quality wines. Good scores from wine writers and publications do help to sell wine, as do stickers and medals awarded in international competitions (although the latter take the form of slightly more 'objective' instruments in that wines are often tasted blind by a panel of judges).

What is more determinant in this range of wines is a combination of (and sometimes a conflict between) geographic origin, brands and varieties. Indications of geographic origin are also instruments of a domestic convention, but are less precise and 'immediate' than *terroir* and can relate to fairly large and internally diverse regions;

they seek to transmit a sense of (sometimes romanticized) connection with a place, where trust is embedded in the specific geography, in the processes that are typical of that area, and by the people who carry these processes out. At the same time, there are vast differences in the wine-producing world in what an indication of geographic origin actually means and how it is operationalized. In some countries, generic indications of geographic origin actually transmit information more akin to a brand than a territory.

The 'big competition' in the wine world in the last few decades has actually taken place between two instruments of verification of quality: geographic origins/*terroir* (supported by Old World wine producers) and brand/grape variety (supported by New World wine producers), with clear indications that the latter is gaining ground on the former.[5] Brands in mid-range quality are often accompanied by the indication of one or more grape varieties. The approach here is to help the consumer recognize and appreciate the differences between varieties and to 'hook' on a specific brand to sort through myriad offerings and variations. From a convention theory point of view, brands operate as a *domestic* quality convention as well, in the sense that repetition of experience builds trust, and the brand name becomes a substitute for quality. However, as argued elsewhere (Gibbon and Ponte, 2005), the mechanisms of transmission of information are very different for brands than for repetition of interpersonal relations and intimate knowledge of places.

So, even though domestic conventions are the principal instruments of quality evaluation in mid-range wines, a reliance on branding would in theory make it easier to communicate quality information along the value chain (and in end-markets through advertising). However, there is no clear driver in this strand of the GVC because branding has not yet achieved a dominant position: wine critics, wine marketers and retailers all have influence on its governance. There is no clear locus from where explicit functional divisions of labour are imposed either. Retailers and branded wine marketers (and producer/marketers) are mutually dependent. The first need 'successful brands' to sell; the latter need a retail outlet, that is, a contact with the consumer. Both need to pay attention to wine critics' judgements.

Another element at play in quality evaluation in this wine strand is the social, environmental and food safety aspects of quality. As mentioned already, a lively debate has taken place in the literature on whether these quality aspects arise from civic conventions in agro-food trade or whether codification and certification procedures that are increasingly used to address these concerns bring these conventions closer to an industrial type. Hazard Analysis and Critical Control Points (HACCP) procedures, British Retailer Consortium (BRC) certification, and International Standards Organization (ISO) 9000-series certifications have codified and formalized food safety and quality management in ways that resemble 'industrial' convention procedures. The same is happening for environmental (ISO 14000, organic, biodynamic, biodiversity) and social (Fairtrade, Ethical Trade Initiative [ETI], SA8000) concerns. For this reason, in Figure 5.2 this convention is labelled *civic/industrial*. In all three ranges of wine quality, matching food safety procedures is considered as 'a given', so the quality description does not need specification in this regard. This characterizes an industrial convention in that procedures are formalized and tests and auditing procedures are used to verify compliance. But, in mid-range quality wines, social and environmental certifications (such as organic, or Wine Industry Ethical Trade Association [WIETA]) are still considered a 'plus', not a demand that is considered as 'a given'. Therefore, although they are operationalized through instruments that are 'industrial' in nature, they still maintain traits of a civic convention.

Basic Quality Wines

Basic wines (anything sold under £5 in the UK) are evaluated for quality in quite a different way from mid-range wines. The first and most important step is that a 'basic material quality' needs to be assured (this includes food safety as well). Three elements in delivering 'basic quality' in wine are needed: (1) intrinsics and packaging, (2) codified solutions to food safety, and (3) logistics. These are features of an *industrial* convention (see details in Ponte, 2007). UK retailers communicate very specific demands on intrinsics and packaging to their suppliers when buying basic quality wine; they tell them what to bottle, what kind of label and cork to use, the weight and shape of the bottle and the recycling possibilities. Specifications in 'intrinsics' at this level of quality can generally be measured or described easily.[6] In recent years, however, the package of 'basic quality' that needs to be provided by suppliers has become more demanding. One of the main UK retailers aims at implementing retail-ready packaging in wine, which entails unloading from the pallet to shelf in one move. Retailers are also moving towards screw-cap and synthetic closures to minimize returns for 'corked' wine. In terms of food safety, in addition to meeting EU food safety rules, suppliers are increasingly under pressure to conform to BRC certification (or the German equivalent, IFS) on food safety and quality management (which includes HACCP systems as well). In relation to logistics, UK retailers are working towards lead times of eight weeks on promotion. As a result, UK-based agents and marketers are trying to exert more direct control over logistics (previously, they sold wine FOB, or 'free-on-board' to retailers; now, some have started selling 'in-bond delivery' in the UK). This way, retailers can place a call with a lead time of three days for delivery. Retailers are seeing themselves increasingly as shelf-space providers. Suppliers can log in the retailer's supply management system, monitor movements in retail space and stocks and order replenishment themselves.

Once the 'basic quality' step is cleared, then price and promotions (instruments of a *market* convention) are the shortcuts for signalling quality. Social and environmental certifications do not play a major role in this quality strand, nor do personality, geographic origin or *terroir*. Wine in this quality strand is offered under a brand, often with the indication of a combination of varieties, but price is more important than brand recognition. External endorsements may play a role, but promotion is much more important. So domestic and opinion conventions do not play the main roles.

Because of the price wars that take place in the retail market in the UK, to be competitive a supplier needs to provide 'above the line' support, such as print and media, and 'below the line support', linked to point of sale and consumer promotion. A key feature of the UK off-trade market is that much of the volume of sales in supermarkets takes place during promotions—with some brands such as Constellation's Banrock Station and Hardy's selling upwards to 80 per cent on heavily discounted terms. It is difficult enough for a supplier to score a listing with a major retailer. Once there, listing fees are usually charged, sometimes as a fixed amount and other times as a proportion of sales. Wine companies can be asked to make payments for shelf-space, and expensive ones for end-of-aisle promotions, or for mentioning a wine in the in-store magazine. In addition, retailers have started to purchase wine through 'reverse Internet auctions', which further squeeze margins upstream in the value chain. If a wine is not selling, they will ask the supplier 'to do something about it', otherwise the supplier will be de-listed. The *industrial/market* nature of dominant quality conventions in this quality strand makes it much easier for 'lead firms' (retailers in this case) to specify quality information needs and to transmit these to their immediate suppliers and beyond. The GVC in this strand is highly driven by retailers, which also set all the elements of a quality profile.

Conclusion

Wine is at the forefront of debates on quality in the global food and beverage sector. It has provided sophisticated instruments of quality assessment and pedagogies of taste to generations of chefs, food and beverage journalists, and consumers. Techniques that were developed in the wine sector have been 'exported' to other beverages, such as beer and coffee. At the same time, increased retailing of wine via supermarket chains, corporate consolidation among marketers and producers, the growing influence of the 'Parker wine aesthetics' and the involvement of 'flying winemakers' in wine properties around four continents have raised concerns about the possible loss of diversity in wine making and the 'homogenization' of wine taste. Yet, despite claims of 'globalization', the wine trade is still relatively fragmented compared to other agro-food industries. It still offers a bewildering array of different products, styles, labels, brands and geographic indications of origin.

Through a combination of GVC analysis and convention theory, this chapter attempted to add some nuance to the 'globalization' of wine argument. The analysis suggests that, depending on the quality strand of the wine GVC, different processes are at play. At the basic quality level, wines are evaluated (by supermarket chains) on the basis of price and promotional support, once a package of 'basic material quality' is ensured. This characterizes a GVC strand that is indeed highly driven by retailers and most advanced on the road to 'globalization'. But for mid-range wines, the combination of quality conventions and influential actors is more complex. Endorsement by wine critics is a factor, but a less determinant one than in top quality wines. A combination of (and sometimes a conflict between) geographic origin, brands and varieties is also important. There is no clear 'driver' here because branding has not yet achieved a dominant position. For top quality wines, the main instrument of verification of quality is 'endorsement' by a respected wine writer, judge or publication, but other conventions also operate—for example, through the utilization of the concept of *terroir* by elite producers or the unique positioning of a wine through the cult of 'personality' of either the wine, its presentation, the winemaker or the property behind the wine. The kinds of conventions that operate in this quality range make it difficult to 'drive' a value chain completely from one functional position.

What this chapter suggests is that different instruments of discovery of quality impart different shapes to the governance of the wine value chain, depending on what quality strand is analysed. Homogenization of taste and standardization of offerings are less obvious than at first sight. In relation to GVC analysis, what these observations entail is a need to break down governance in its constituent elements and to examine them through a variety of situations even within the same value chain (e.g. by quality strand). By delineating what kind of quality conventions are used in which strand, conclusions can also be drawn on how lead firms are able to 'drive' a value chain with limited active engagement (seldom going beyond their immediate suppliers) or without a hands-on involvement at all.

Notes

1. To the author's knowledge, no attempt has been made in the literature to analyse the governance of the *global* value chain for wine. Other contributions have examined how specific wine-producing countries are inserted in the GVC for wine (for Chile and New Zealand, see Gwynne, 2006, 2007; for South Africa, see Ponte, 2007) or have used different political economy approaches (see, among others, Pritchard, 1999; Shaw, 2001).
2. The term 'GVC analysis' is used in this chapter to also include work known as global commodity chain (GCC) analysis from 1994 onwards.
3. Convention theory is also known as the economics of conventions. The term 'convention theory' is used in this chapter to avoid confusion with game-theoretical approaches (also referred to as 'economics of conventions' in France) that focus on conventions as outcomes of strategic interaction motivated by personal interest. What is meant by 'convention theory' here is thus the interpretive and normative approach to conventions (Batifoulier and de Larquier, 2001).

4. In recent Anglophone literature, convention theory has been often used as a source for typologies of various dimensions of product quality. This literature has been mainly concerned with classifying new dimensions of product quality, reflecting struggles over the content of civic conventions and judging these struggles as *for or against* a contemporary 'capitalist' project. This capitalist project is said to be striving not only to 'commodify' new product qualities but also to commodify information about them—what Freidberg (2003, 2004) terms 'double fetishism'. These dynamics are said to lead to a hollowing out of organic, fair trade and other sustainability labels (Barham, 2002; Raynolds, 2000, 2002, 2004; Renard, 2003). Alternatively, convention theory has been used to highlight the putative emergence of 'alternative food networks' based on locality and domestic conventions (Murdoch et al., 2000; Murdoch and Miele, 1999). An exception to these trends is work by Storper and Salais (1997) that builds upon the original Boltanski and Thévenot framework and focuses on forms of industrial organization.

5. A clear exception to this simplistic divide is Champagne, where both the geographic indication and brand names are important for marketing.

6. These include: levels of alcohol, total acidity, volatile acidity, sulphur dioxide content, residual sugar content, methods of protein and cold stabilization, a flavour profile, and general wooding regime (unwooded, lightly wooded, etc.).

References

Anderson, K. (2004a), 'Introduction', in K. Anderson (ed.), *The World's Wine Markets: Globalization at Work*, Cheltenham: Edward Elgar.

Anderson, K. (2004b), *The World's Wine Markets: Globalization at Work*, Cheltenham: Edward Elgar.

Bair, J. (2005), 'Global Capitalism and Commodity Chains: Looking Back, Going Forward', *Competition and Change*, 9/2: 153–80.

Barham, E. (2002), 'Towards a Theory of Values-Based Labeling', *Agriculture and Human Values*, 19: 349–60.

Batifoulier, P., and de Larquier, G. (2001), 'Introduction—De la Convention et de Ses Usages', in P. Batifoulier (ed.), *Téorie Des Conventions*, Paris: Economica.

Boltanski, L., and Chiapello, E. (1999), *Le Nouvel Esprit du Capitalisme*, Paris: Gallimard.

Boltanski, O., and Thévenot, L. (1991), *De la Justification. Les Economies de la Grandeur*, Paris: Gallimard.

Borghi, V., and Vitale, T. (2006), 'Convenzioni, Economia Morale e Analisi Sociologica', *Sociologia Del Lavoro*, 104: 7–34.

Daviron, B., and Ponte, S. (2005), *The Coffee Paradox: Global Markets, Commodity Trade and the Elusive Promise of Development,* London and New York: Zed Books.

Eymard-Duvernay, F. (1989), 'Conventions de Qualité et Formes de Coordination', *Revue Economique,* 40/2: 329–59.

Eymard-Duvernay, F. (ed.) (2006a), *L'Economie des Conventions, Methodes et Resultats. Tome 1: Debats,* Paris: La Découverte.

Eymard-Duvernay, F. (ed) (2006b), *L'Economie des Conventions, Methodes et Resultats. Tome 2: Développements.* Paris: La Découverte.

Favereau, O., and Lazega, E. (eds.) (2002), *Conventions and Structures in Economic Organization,* Cheltenham: Edward Elgar.

Freidberg, S. (2003), 'Culture, Conventions and Colonial Constructs of Rurality in South-North Horticultural Trades', *Journal of Rural Studies,* 19: 97–109.

Freidberg, S. (2004), *French Beans and Food Scares: Culture and Commerce in an Anxious Age,* Oxford: Oxford University Press.

Gereffi, G. (1994), 'The Organization of Buyer-Driven Global Commodity Chains: How US Retailers Shape Overseas Production Networks', in G. Gereffi and M. Korzeniewicz (eds.), *Commodity Chains and Global Capitalism,* Westport: Greenwood Press.

Gereffi, G., Humphrey, J., and Sturgeon, T. (2005), 'The Governance of Global Value Chains', *Review of International Political Economy,* 12/1: 78–104.

Gibbon, P., and Ponte, S. (2005), *Trading Down: Africa, Value Chains and the Global Economy,* Philadelphia: Temple University Press.

Gwynne, R. N. (2006), 'Governance in the Wine Commodity Chain: Upstream and Downstream Strategies in New Zealand and Chilean Wine Firms', *Asia Pacific Viewpoint,* 47/3: 381–95.

Gwynne, R. N. (2007), 'Tasting Wine and Consuming Places: From Chilean Valleys to British Supermarkets', mimeo, University of Birmingham.

Kaplinsky, R. (2000), 'Spreading the Gains from Globalization: What Can Be Learned from Value Chain Analysis?', *IDS Working Paper* 100, Brighton: IDS-Sussex.

Latour, B. (1998), 'To Modernise or Ecologise? That Is the Question', in B. Braun and N. Castree (eds.), *Remaking Reality: Nature at the Millennium,* London and New York: Routledge.

McCoy, E. (2005), *The Emperor of Wine: The Rile of Robert M. Parker, Jr. and the Reign of American Taste,* New York: HarperCollins.

Murdoch, J., and Miele, M. (1999), ' "Back to Nature": Changing "Worlds of Production" in the Food Sector', *Sociologia Ruralis,* 39/4: 465–83.

Murdoch, J., Marsden, T., and Banks, J. (2000), 'Quality, Nature and Embeddedness: Some Theoretical Considerations in the Context of the Food Sector', *Economic Geography,* 76: 107–25.

Palpacuer, F., Gibbon, P., and Thomsen, L. (2005), 'New Challenges for Developing Country Suppliers in Global Clothing Chains: A Comparative European Perspective', *World Development,* 33/3: 409–30.

Ponte, S. (2002), 'The "Latte Revolution"? Regulation, Markets and Consumption in the Global Coffee Chain', *World Development*, 30/7: 1099–122.

Ponte, S. (2007), 'Governance in the Value Chain for South African Wine', *TRALAC Working Paper* 2007/9, Stellenbosch: Trade Law Centre for Southern Africa.

Ponte, S., and Gibbon, P. (2005), 'Quality Standards, Conventions and the Governance of Global Value Chains', *Economy and Society*, 34/1: 1–31.

Pritchard, B. (1999), 'The Regulation of Grower-Processor Relations: A Case Study from the Australian Wine Industry', *Sociologia Ruralis*, 39/2: 185–200.

Raikes, P., Jensen, M. F., and Ponte, S. (2000), 'Global Commodity Chain Analysis and the French Filiére Approach: Comparison and Critique', *Economy and Society*, 29/3: 390–417.

Raynolds, L. T. (2000), 'Re-embedding Global Agriculture: The International Organic and Fair Trade Movements', *Agriculture and Human Values*, 17: 297–309.

Raynolds, L. T. (2002), 'Consumer/Producer Links in Fair Trade Coffee Networks', *Sociologia Ruralis*, 42/4): 404–24.

Raynolds, L. T. (2004), 'The Globalization of Organic Agro-Food Networks', *World Development*, 32/5: 725–43.

Renard, M. C. (2003), 'Fair Trade: Quality, Market and Conventions,' *Journal of Rural Studies*, 19: 87–96.

Riisgaard, L. (2007), 'What's in It for Labour? Private Social Standards in the Cut Flower Industries of Kenya and Tanzania', *DIIS Working Paper*, 2007/16, Copenhagen: Danish Institute for International Studies.

Salais, R. (1989), 'L'Analyse Economique des Conventions de Travail', *Revue Economique*, 40/2: 199–240.

Shaw, T. M. (2001), 'South Africa and the Political Economy of Wine: From Sanctions to Globalizations/Liberalizations', in S.J. MacLean, F. Quadir and T.M. Shaw (eds.), *Crises of Governance in Asia and Africa*, Aldershot: Ashgate.

Spahni, P. (2000), *The International Wine Trade*, second edition, Cambridge: Woodhead.

Storper, M., and Salais, R. (1997), *Worlds of Production: The Action Frameworks of the Economy*, Cambridge, MA: Harvard University Press.

Sylvander, B. (1995), 'Convention de Qualité, Concurrence et Coopération: Cas du Label Rouge dans la Filière Volaille', in G. Allaire and R. Boyer (eds.), *La Grande Transformation de L'Agriculture: Lectures Conventionnalistes et Regulationnistes*, Paris: INRA-Economica.

Thévenot, L. (1995), 'Des Marchés aux Normes', in G. Allaire and R. Boyer (eds.), *La Grande Transformation de L'Agriculture: Lectures Conventionnalistes et Regulationnistes*, Paris: INRA-Economica.

Thévenot, L. (1997), 'Un Gouvernement par les Norms: Pratiques et Politiques des Formats d'Information', in C. Bernard and L. Thévenot (eds.), *Cognition et Information en Societé*, Paris: Ed. de l'Ecole des Hautes Etudes en Sciences Sociales.

Thévenot, L. (2002), 'Conventions of Co-ordination and the Framing of Uncertainty', in E. Fullbrook (ed.), *Intersubjectivity in Economics,* London: Routledge.

Thévenot, L., Moody, M., and Lafaye, C. (2000), 'Forms of Valuing Nature: Arguments and Modes of Justification in French and American Environmental Disputes', in M. Lamont and L. Thévenot (eds.), *Rethinking Comparative Cultural Sociology: Repertoires of Evaluation in France and the United States,* Cambridge: Cambridge University Press.

Unwin, T. (1996), *Wine and the Vine: An Historical Geography or Viticulture and the Wine Trade,* London: Routledge.

Wilkinson, J. (1997), 'A New Paradigm for Economic Analysis?' *Economy and Society,* 26/3: 305–39.

–6–

Food Systems and the Local Trap
Branden Born and *Mark Purcell*
University of Washington

Along with many others, scholars of food systems have become increasingly inter-ested in the multiple processes of globalization that are currently transforming po-litical, economic, and cultural relations. Food systems, of course, have been deeply affected by acute mechanization, industrialization and globalization. We fully sup-port the growing attention to globalization in food systems research. However, this chapter offers a strong caution as this work moves forward. Food systems research and advocacy, we argue, contains a widespread and important problem that future research should avoid. Following work by Brown and Purcell (2005), we call this problem 'the local trap' (see also Purcell and Brown, 2005). The local trap refers to the tendency of food activists and researchers to assume something inherently good about the local scale. The local is assumed to be desirable, and it is preferred a priori over larger scales. What is desired varies and can include ecological sustainability, social justice, democracy, better nutrition and food security, freshness and quality. For example, the local trap assumes that a local-scale food system will be inherently more socially just than a national-scale or global-scale food system. This chapter argues that the local trap is misguided and poses significant intellectual and political dangers to food systems research. To be clear, our argument against the local trap is not an argument against the local *scale*. We are not suggesting that the local scale is inherently *un*desirable. Rather, we are arguing against the local *trap:* the assumption that local is inherently good. Far from claiming that the local is inherently bad, we argue that there is nothing inherent about any scale. Local-scale food systems are equally likely to be just or unjust, sustainable or unsustainable, secure or insecure. No matter what its scale, the outcomes produced by a food system are contextual; they depend on the actors and agendas that are empowered by the particular social relations in a given food system.

 The food systems literature is broad and diverse. It includes academics, advo-cates, and activists. Some in the literature fall prey to the local trap more fully than others. The question of scale has been examined in the literature, and some are sensi-tive to the possibility that the local scale does not always result in desirable outcomes (see, for example, Hinrichs, 2000; Hinrichs et al., 1998). Nevertheless, our argument is that in the literature one can find numerous examples of locally trapped thinking, and in general there is a pervasive predilection for the local scale. In order to avoid such thinking, we offer a way to theorize geographical scale that entirely precludes the local trap.

The Local Trap: Problems

There are several problems with the local trap that we contend should give pause to those interested in food systems. The first is the most basic: the assumption that the local is desirable does not always hold. Mounting case study evidence suggests that in some cases local-scale food systems produce one outcome (e.g. greater democracy) and in other cases they produce very different outcomes (e.g. oligarchy). The local trap can therefore seduce with an incorrect assumption. Second, the local trap conflates the scale of a food system with a desired outcome. It treats localization as an end in itself, rather than as a means to an end such as justice or sustainability and so forth. We can therefore become sidetracked pursuing localization and become distracted from pursuing our real goal, whatever that might be. At the very least this dynamic will cause us to lose sight of our goal. In the worst case, it will subvert the goal, as when someone who desires greater food democracy pursues localization that results in more oligarchical decision making. Third, the local trap obscures other scalar options that might be more effective in achieving a desired outcome. For example, an activist who assumes that localization necessarily leads to more sustainable agriculture will fail to pursue the option of, say, a European Union-wide law that mandates more sustainable agricultural practices in member countries (Goodman, 2003). The local trap can thus blind us to the most effective strategy for achieving desired ends.

Among some scholars in rural studies there has been growing concern over the assumption that local is inherently good (Hinrichs, 2003; Weatherell et al., 2003; Winter, 2003). That concern has not been theoretical; rather it is largely borne of the growing body of empirical evidence that local-scale food systems often result in undesirable outcomes, such as environmental degradation or exacerbated inequality. One exception is Bellows and Hamm's test of the theory of import substitution, in which they propose measures by which one could understand the 'shifting and integrated balance between more local and more global food systems' (Bellows and Hamm, 2001: 271). A more common narrative, however, is that researchers were surprised to find that a local food system resulted in negative outcomes, and they conclude that we should be cautious about advocating local solutions. While these empirical cautions are a promising opening, we argue that they do not go far enough because they do not yet offer a theoretical solution to the local trap. Each empirical case where local-scale systems result in undesirable outcomes demonstrates that the local is not always better, but it still leaves open the fall back position that the local *tends* to be more desirable, even if it is not always so. The empirical findings of Winter (2003), for example, have not yet moved them beyond the local trap. For them,

> it is *open to question* whether we can equate ... the turn to localism as the first steps towards an alternative food economy which will challenge the dominance of globalized networks and systems of provision and herald a more ecologically sound agricultural sector (2001: 31, emphasis added).

We contend that one cannot equate a scalar strategy ('turn to localism') with a particular outcome ('an alternative food economy'). Therefore, it should not be 'open to question' as Winter has it. Their position leaves essentially unchanged the dangers of the local trap, because they leave open the possibility that localization will tend to lead to desirable outcomes. If we retain the a priori assumption that the local scale tends to be more desirable, all the problems mentioned already—deflection of attention, unintentional exacerbation of problems, and blindness to better alternatives—still apply. What we need, therefore, is to *close* the question of whether the local is inherently more desirable. Because empirical cautions have so far left that question open, this chapter offers a theoretical rejection of the local trap. We draw on recent work in political and economic geography to construct a theoretical approach to scale that stresses the social construction of scale. That is, it maintains that scale is not ontologically given but socially constructed. Therefore, there can be nothing inherent about any scale. No scale can have an inherent extent, function or quality. In this view, scale is not an end goal itself; rather, it is better seen as a *strategy*. Scale is a means that may help achieve any of many different ends. Which end is achieved will depend not on the inherent properties of the scale itself but on the agenda(s) of those who are empowered by the scalar strategy. Localizing food systems, therefore, does not lead inherently to greater sustainability or to any other goal. It leads wherever those it empowers want it to lead.

For those interested in food systems, this theoretical approach to scale encourages a very different research agenda that the one currently being pursued. Accepting that there is nothing inherent about scale makes it unnecessary to carry out extensive empirical work to investigate if localization is inherently desirable. Rather, the research agenda must be to examine the agendas of those who pursue scalar strategies. The question is not whether we should pursue localization in food systems. The question is whether we want to advance the agendas of those who will be empowered by a given localization, or whether other scalar strategies (e.g. globalization) would produce better results. And because there is nothing inherent about scale, the question of who is empowered by localization (or globalization) will vary by case. The particular social and ecological outcomes of each strategic rescaling must never be assumed but always subjected to critical analysis. The next section lays out our theoretical argument about scale and develops why it solves the problems of the local trap.

Scale Research in Geography

For about the last fifteen years, there has been a proliferation of research on geographical scale. Much of this new work has been undertaken by political and economic geographers concerned with understanding the recent rapid changes in the world economy that were touched off by the crises of the early 1970s. As capital extended its operations beyond the national scale, effectively globalizing economic production, and as the nation-state's regulatory mechanisms struggled to respond, it seemed clear that the global political economy was being remade by a massive and important process of rescaling. As part of the effort to understand that rescaling, geographers undertook a new theoretical engagement with scale. While this work is diverse and constantly developing, we argue there is widespread agreement on at least three key principles about scale: scale is socially produced, scale is both fluid and fixed and scale is a fundamentally relational concept.

Social Construction: Scale Is a Strategy

Perhaps the most important theoretical claim is that geographical scale is socially produced. That is, any given scale—for example, the local, the regional, the national or the global—is socially produced through political struggle (Delaney and Leitner, 1997; Kelly, 1997). Therefore, the particular qualities of a given scale, such as its extent, its function and its relations with other scales, are never eternal or ontologically given (Smith, 1992, 1993). Instead they are contingent: they will grow out of particular political struggles among particular actors in particular times and places (Marston, 2000). While the principle of social construction is fairly common to the social sciences, what flows from it is, we argue, significantly destabilizing for the local trap. If we take this principle seriously, we cannot assume a priori anything about the characteristics of a particular scale or scalar arrangement. For example, we cannot assume that local food systems are inherently more ecologically sustainable than global ones, that locally grown produce is healthier than produce grown elsewhere, or that local control over agricultural decision making is inherently more democratic than, say, national-scale control.

In each case, the outcome of the scalar arrangement is dependent not on the inherent qualities of a particular scale but on the particular agendas that are empowered by the arrangement. Thus local food systems can be sustainable or not, depending on the particular practices that agents pursue. The same is true of global food systems. Just because the current global food system is capitalist and industrial and unsustainable does not mean that *all* global systems exhibit those failings. This principle of social construction means that the best way to think about scale is not as an ontological entity with particular properties, but as a strategy to achieve a particular end. As we seek to re-imagine the current structure of food systems, we must be careful to distinguish scalar strategies (localization, globalization, etc.) from socio-environmental ends (social justice, sustainability, etc.)

Scale Is Both Fluid and Fixed

If scales are not ontologically stable but are produced through social struggle, it follows that they are not permanent. Rather, scales and scalar relationships are constantly in the process of being made and remade. Erik Swyngedouw (1997), for example, is particularly insistent on this point. He argues that geographers and others have tended to think of scales as fixed and given, and that the current extent and function of a particular scale is somehow natural and eternal. The classic example of this thinking is the association of the state with the national scale. John Agnew (1994) argues that the national-scale state is a socially produced and therefore temporary arrangement. The state was not always predominantly national and will almost certainly not be predominantly national in the future. In fact, a wealth of research suggests that the dominance of the national-scale state is waning as part of the political aspect of global restructuring. On the one hand, many governing functions are being transferred to larger-scale bodies such as the European Union, the United Nations, the World Trade Organization, the World Court and so forth (e.g. Balibar, 1999; Brenner, 1999; Leitner, 1997; Wallace, 1999). On the other hand, numerous state functions are being devolved to more local scales as a way to both deflect discontent associated with restructuring and to better tailor competitiveness strategies to specific local areas (Raco, 2003; Rodriquez-Pose and Gill, 2003; Staeheli et al., 1997). In short, scalar arrangements, such as the national-scale character of the state, are constantly in flux; they are constantly being produced and reproduced, defended and resisted.

At the same time, many have stressed that scale is not only fluid, but that scalar arrangements, once produced, can become routinized into enduring and hegemonic structures for certain periods of time. Although a given scale has no inherent or eternal characteristics, it can still become tied to a given social process. Again, the national state provides an excellent example. Although there is no inherent link between the national scale and the state, in the post-Westphalian era that link was forged through political struggle. While the link has to be continually reproduced, it has endured for an extended period and has real effects. To take just one example, state sovereignty at the national scale has been critical for shaping geopolitics. The geopolitical definition of internal and external, its 'us versus them', has long been defined at the national scale. Thus for a long time geopolitics has predominantly involved relations among national-scale groups, rather than relations among, say, groups at the imperial, urban or continental scale. Those who stress the fixity of scale thus argue for the importance of path dependence: the current globalization and localization of state practices is occurring in the context of a hegemonic national-scale state, and that context has a deep influence on how state rescaling is playing out. While that fact can produce some observable regularities, they are never *necessary* regularities.

Neil Smith (1993) is particularly clear on the idea of fixity. He uses the phrase 'jumping scales' to signify a political strategy that circumvents and challenges the present entrenched structure of scale. Groups that are at a disadvantage at one scale can jump scales to pursue their agenda at a different scale in an effort to shift the balance of power in their favour (Born, 2003). That strategy is often used by marginalized groups who are disadvantaged by present scalar arrangements. Smith asserts that the present structure is not natural or eternal, but it is nevertheless *real* and it does favour certain groups over others. Along these lines we might speak of the 'structuration of scale'. Giddens's (1984) idea of structuration is that social agents both reproduce and are constrained by social structures. In the context of scale, structuration involves the continual process of agents fixing, unfixing and refixing scalar structures. Scale, then, is simultaneously fluid and fixed.

Scale Is Relational

The last insight of this literature is that geographical scale is a fundamentally relational concept (Agnew, 1997; Howitt, 1998; Kelly, 1999). That is, the idea of scale necessarily implies a set of interscalar relationships. The meaning of a 'local' scale, for example, only comes alive in relation to other, larger scales. And those relationships are contingent: they are the product of social production. The hegemony of the national-scale state, to take our earlier example, established the national scale as the dominant scale of state sovereignty and the local as a subordinate scale. As a result, decisions made by local-scale state bodies can be overturned by national-scale bodies. However, governing bodies at scales larger than the national are not empowered to overturn national-state decisions. The rescaling that is currently unfolding seems to be altering those interscalar relations of sovereignty, both by localizing greater authority and by internationalizing it, such that the national scale is no longer so unquestionably the dominant seat of sovereignty. Neil Brenner (2001) is particularly insistent on the relational qualities of scale. For Brenner, analyses that focus on only one scale—what he calls the 'singular connotation' of scale—are not really about scale per se, since examining only one scale misses the relationships among scales. He argues that such singular analyses are really about a region, a territory, a place or a space rather than a scale. Brenner argues instead for what he calls the 'plural connotation' of scale, in which the analysis focuses on the 'shifting organizational, strategic, discursive, and symbolic relationships between a range of intertwined geographical scales' (Brenner, 2001: 20). Therefore, analyses that are specifically analyses of *scale*—rather than of territory or place or space—must examine a range of scales at once (rather than focusing on a single scale alone) and they should specifically interrogate the changing interrelationships among the various scales.

If we were to tie the three preceding theoretical principles together into a coherent methodological directive, we might say that descriptive research on scale should examine how the interrelationships among scales are fixed, unfixed and refixed by particular social actors pursuing specific political, social, economic and ecological goals. Normative research should analyse why a particular rescaling (e.g. localization) is better than other scalar strategies (global/national/regionalization) for achieving specific *goals* (e.g. democratization, sustainability, quality, etc.), and these goals should be clearly articulated and distinguished from the scalar *strategy* used to pursue them.

If we adhere to these theoretical principles, the local trap becomes untenable. If there is nothing inherent about any particular scale, then we cannot associate a particular scale with a particular goal, as when the local scale is conflated with sustainability, democracy or justice. We can no longer assume essential qualities for particular scalar arrangements, as when a globalized food system is conflated with a capitalist, industrial and ecologically destructive food system. And we need not engage in extensive empirical research to undermine the local trap. We need not build a case file of instances where localization failed to produce justice or sustainability or democracy. Instead we have a theoretical starting position that averts the local trap. If we start from these principles, localization raises no a priori assumptions; instead it evokes an ongoing struggle among competing interests. It invites inquiry to discover what actors and agendas achieved localization and who was empowered by it. It is those actors and agendas that produce outcomes, not the scales through which the agendas were realized.

The Local Trap in Food Systems Activism and Research

In this section we make the claim that debates about food systems, both in the academy and in civil society, are marked by the local trap. We do not mean that all arguments are equally trapped; the degree to which the local trap is present varies significantly. Some simplistically and uncritically equate local and good. Others are beginning to become uneasy about that equation but still retain an assumption that local tends to be good. Others have discarded the equation but have not yet developed an explicit theoretical approach to scale in food systems. We try to do justice to that variation, but we also want to make clear that the local trap remains a pervasive problem and that there is a real danger that it will continue to cloud our evolving understanding of food systems and globalization.

The Roots of the Local Trap

To avoid the local trap it is helpful to understand why it has come to be. There are certainly many reasons, but we want to highlight one we think is particularly powerful: the contextual power of the current historical moment. Over the last fifty or sixty years, especially in developed economies, agricultural production has undergone profound and much-discussed changes. The primary changes have been to intensify the industrial capitalist nature of food production. Food is increasingly grown on large corporate farms. More and more, crops are commodities to be sold on the open market. Farm labour is being commoditized or eliminated through mechanization. Fields are being increasingly irrigated and treated by chemicals to ward off pests and disease. More seeds are being produced in corporate research and development labs rather than being managed by farmers in the field. As so much research has shown, while in the aggregate those trends have increased crop yields, they have also increased injustice, environmental degradation, food insecurity and oligarchical decision-making structures (Magdoff et al., 2000; Norberg-Hodge et al., 2002; Shiva, 2000). Certainly those changes have been uneven and they have been resisted in different places and at different times. But it is hard to ignore this tendential process of what we will call the 'capitalistization' of food production.[1]

One important scalar *strategy* through which firms have pursued the capitalistization of agriculture has been globalization. Food production, supply chains and food markets have become increasingly global as a means to achieve capitalistization. We suggest that because capitalistization has been so closely associated with globalization in this (very brief) historical era, many have conflated the two, assuming global agriculture is somehow the same thing as capitalist agriculture, that globalization necessarily equals capitalistization. We frequently see terms like 'global agro-food complex' (Winter, 2003: 24) or the 'global industrialized food system' (Campbell, 2004: 342) or 'free (global) market' (Henderson, 1998: 1) that equate a global food system with a capitalist one. What follows logically from this assumption is that resistance to capitalist agriculture, what are termed 'alternative agro-food networks' (Goodman, 2003: 1), must be necessarily local. Thus we see representations of a 'tension' between 'the global industrialized food system and the alternative community food system' (Kaufman, 2004: 338; see also Campbell, 2004). Here 'community' is used synonymously with 'local community' (Peters, 1997). That conflation is another manifestation of the local trap. It ignores the fact that communities exist at all scales, as when we speak of an 'international community'. Lacy (2000: 20) heralds the 'numerous scholars and practitioners ... trying to redress the imbalances in the global food system through the development of locally based alternatives'. Henderson (1998: 1) notes Wendell Berry's

> fierce critique of the irresponsibility of the impersonal relations of the industrialized, corporate, global food system, while lifting up the homely values of stewardship of the land and respect for the local people, their farms, businesses, and living web of interdependencies.

Allen et al. (2003, 61–2) find that most alternative food movements 'frame their engagement as opposing the global by reconstructing the local ... The alternative to globalized agriculture many advocate is "localization"'. In arguing for more attention to food systems among urban planners, Clancy (2004: 435, italics added) suggests that 'food system advocates engage planners on specific, well-targeted issues *at the local or regional level*'. Thus a powerful historical narrative of simultaneous globalization and capitalistization has led many food activists to advocate 'a return to the local' and 'relocalization' as the only alternatives to capitalist agriculture (Pacione, 1997; Pothukuchi, 2004). They speak of 'resisting globalization' when they actually mean resisting the corporate capitalist food system (McMahon, 2002). Such visions seek in part to regain an imagined past of the idyllic localized and noncapitalist food systems that were dismantled by capitalistization.

The Manifestations of the Local Trap

Certainly the local trap has other sources, among them rural sociology's 'long devotion to local community research' (Goodman, 2003: 1), a devotion very similar to that of geography's subdisciplinary analogue, cultural ecology. Also important has been the influence of poststructural approaches such as that of Arturo Escobar (e.g. Escobar, 2001) that contend locally based social movements are they key to resisting the hegemony of global capitalism. Despite the numerous benefits of such poststructural critique, one ironic drawback is that many in that tradition offer an essentialized view of scale that sees the global as hegemonic and oppressive and the local as radical and subversive. Within urban planning, the local trap advocates local over regional or national planning, or the push for devolved authority from central bodies to ostensibly more democratic local ones (Born, 2003). Such devolution of governmental authority is a good example of how scale is a malleable strategy: it is a cornerstone of the agenda of both advocates of alternative food systems and advocates of neoliberal free-market policies (Herbert, 2005; Raco, 2003; Rodriguez-Pose and Gill, 2003; Staeheli et al., 1997).

In addition to having many sources, there are also diverse manifestations of the local trap. Many arise outside academia and have built concrete resistance movements to the capitalist food system. The Slow Food movement, for example, 'advocates a return to traditional recipes, locally grown food and wines, and eating as a social event' (Petrini, 2004, front flap). The movement is a loose confederation of thousands of local chapters, each of which link local production and consumption to resistance to the dominant agro-food system. A related set of initiatives is associated with famous chef and writer Alice Waters. She advocates that restaurants buy and serve only locally produced food (e.g. a recent menu offered 'Hoffman Farm chicken breast' or 'local Halibut poached in oil'). This notion has deeply affected menus in higher-priced restaurants all over the United States. Another of her projects is the Edible Schoolyard, which conflates local food with a whole range of other goals:

Now if every school had a lunch program that served its students only local products that had been sustainably farmed, imagine what it would mean for agriculture. Today, twenty percent of the population of the United States is in school. If all these students were eating lunch together, consuming local, organic food, agriculture would change overnight to meet the demand. Our domestic food culture would change as well, as people again grew up learning how to cook affordable, wholesome, and delicious food (Waters, 2004).

Similar ideas include the hundred-mile diet (Ketcham, 2007), countless exhortations to consume only food grown in one's metaphorical backyard (Kingsolver et al., 2007), and 'buy local' campaigns. In the last, local produce is commonly conflated with organic produce (Center for Sustainable Environments, 2005; Grady, 2002–3; Hutchings, 1994; Peters, 1997; Weatherell et al., 2003). Figures 6.1 and 6.2 show outreach material for 'buy local' campaigns that conflates local with a whole range of goals, including organic produce, better taste, increased health, avoiding genetically modified organisms (GMOs), saving family farms, preserving open space, creating stronger communities, and even lowering taxes.

But in fact buying local guarantees no particular end. Consider the hypothetical example of a 'buy local' campaign in Arizona. Any ecological benefit from using less fuel for transport would clearly be outweighed by the need for massive water inputs. While the use of petrochemicals for transportation are a valid concern, it does not by itself determine ecological sustainability. There is no necessary linkage between local food and ecological sustainability. While 'buy local' campaigns are perhaps an extreme example of the local trap, since they uncritically conflate so much with localization, they are quite common and accepted among food activists.

As we have suggested already, some in academia have begun to be more cautious about the assumption that local equals desirable (Allen et al., 2003; Campbell, 2004; Hinrichs, 2003; Winter, 2003). Nevertheless, the local trap is also present in research among academics who study food. Here again the work is diverse, but we contend that it can be broadly grouped into three concerns: *ecological sustainability* (including the minimization of food miles, the use of organic or other sustainable production methods and the organization of contemporary food marketing/retailing structures); *social and economic justice* (including the [re]development of local economies, community stability, democracy, local empowerment and food security); and *food quality and human health* (a typical argument being fresh is best, or local foods are healthier).

Ecological Sustainability

The broadest claim against the capitalist food system concerns environmental sustainability. The simplest version of this claim is that local production is more ecologically sustainable. The argument is that conventional agriculture and the global networks that it uses for marketing, distribution and waste disposal are too dependent

10 Reasons to Buy Local Food

1. Locally grown food tastes better.
Food grown in your own community was probably picked within the past day or two. It's crisp, sweet and loaded with flavor. Produce flown or trucked in from California, Florida, Chile or Holland is, quite understandably, much older. Several studies have shown that the average distance food travels from farm to plate is 1,500 miles. In a week-long (or more) delay from harvest to dinner table, sugars turn to starches, plant cells shrink, and produce loses its vitality.

2. Local produce is better for you.
A recent study showed that fresh produce loses nutrients quickly. Food that is frozen or canned soon after harvest is actually more nutritious than some "fresh" produce that has been on the truck or supermarket shelf for a week. Locally grown food, purchased soon after harvest, retains its nutrients.

3. Local food preserves genetic diversity.
In the modern industrial agricultural system, varieties are chosen for their ability to ripen simultaneously and withstand harvesting equipment; for a tough skin that can survive packing and shipping; and for an ability to have a long shelf life in the store. Only a handful of hybrid varieties of each fruit and vegetable meet those rigorous demands, so there is little genetic diversity in the plants grown. Local farms, in contrast, grow a huge number of varieties to provide a long season of harvest, an array of eye-catching colors, and the best flavors. Many varieties are heirlooms, passed down from generation to generation, because they taste good. These old varieties contain genetic material from hundreds or even thousands of years of human selection; they may someday provide the genes needed to create varieties that will thrive in a changing climate.

4. Local food is GMO-free.
Although biotechnology companies have been trying to commercialize genetically modified fruits and vegetables, they are currently licensing them only to large factory-style farms. Local farmers don't have access to genetically modified seed, and most of them wouldn't use it even if they could. A June 2001 survey by ABC News showed that 93% of Americans want labels on genetically modified food - most so that they can avoid it. If you are opposed to eating bioengineered food, you can rest assured that locally grown produce was bred the old-fashioned way, as nature intended.

5. Local food supports local farm families.
With fewer than 1 million Americans now claiming farming as their primary occupation, farmers are a vanishing breed. And no wonder - commodity prices are at historic lows, often below the cost of production. The farmer now gets less than 10 cents of the retail food dollar. Local farmers who sell direct to consumers cut out the middleman and get full retail price for their food - which means farm families can afford to stay on the farm, doing the work they love.

6. Local food builds community.
When you buy direct from the farmer, you are re-establishing a time-honored connection between the eater and the grower. Knowing the farmers gives you insight into the seasons, the weather, and the miracle of raising food. In many cases, it gives you access to a farm where your children and grandchildren can go to learn about nature and agriculture. Relationships built on understanding and trust can thrive.

7. Local food preserves open space.
As the value of direct-marketed fruits and vegetables increases, selling farmland for development becomes less likely. You have probably enjoyed driving out into the country and appreciated the lush fields of crops, the meadows full of wildflowers, the picturesque red barns. That landscape will survive only as long as farms are financially viable. When you buy locally grown food, you are doing something proactive about preserving the agricultural landscape.

8. Local food keeps your taxes in check.
Farms contribute more in taxes than they require in services, whereas suburban development costs more than it generates in taxes, according to several studies. On average, for every $1 in revenue raised by residential development, governments must spend $1.17 on services, thus requiring higher taxes of all taxpayers. For each dollar of revenue raised by farm, forest, or open space, governments spend 34 cents on services.

9. Local food supports a clean environment and benefits wildlife.
A well-managed family farm is a place where the resources of fertile soil and clean water are valued. Good stewards of the land grow cover crops to prevent erosion and replace nutrients used by their crops. Cover crops also capture carbon emissions and help combat global warming. According to some estimates, farmers who practice conservation tillage could sequester 12-14% of the carbon emitted by vehicles and industry. In addition, the habitat of a farm - the patchwork of fields, meadows, woods, ponds and buildings - is the perfect environment for many beloved species of wildlife, including bluebirds, killdeer, herons, bats, and rabbits.

10. Local food is about the future.
By supporting local farmers today, you can help ensure that there will be farms in your community tomorrow, and that future generations will have access to nourishing, flavorful, and abundant food.

Buy local food. Sustain local farms.

Figure 6.1 'Buy local' promotional material.

Figure 6.2   'Buy local' campaign in Washington State.

on petroleum, petrochemicals, greenfield land and pavement in the form of trans-portation networks to be sustainable in the long term (see for example, Norberg-Hodge et al., 2002; Pirog et al., 2001; Shiva, 2000). Extensive and excessive food transport, often spoken about in terms of 'food miles', uses large amounts of fuel and contributes to greenhouse gases and thus global warming (Norberg-Hodge et al., 2002: 19–33; Pirog et al., 2001). Alternatively, chemical inputs in the form of pes-ticides, herbicides and fertilizers pollute surface and groundwater supplies and call into question the safety of our food supply. These are all major concerns, and we agree with those who have identified them as such. However, the solutions should not be assumed to be necessarily local. There is nothing inherently good about local methods of production, which can easily be as unsustainable as those in conventional agribusiness. In fact, if the 'local' in question is corn or hog country, Iowa, wheat farms in eastern Washington or the Central Valley of California, then consuming local food means consuming conventional capitalist agriculture.

Social and Economic Justice

Another set of arguments for localism is based in social or economic justice. Here the assumption is that localizing the food system, in terms of production, consumption or both, will improve the social and economic fortunes of the community (Center for Sustainable Environments, 2005; Feenstra, 1997; Norberg-Hodge et al., 2002; Pa-cione, 1997). Feenstra's (1997: 28) argument is representative: 'the development of a local sustainable food system provides not only economic gains for a community but also fosters civic involvement, cooperation, and healthy social relations'. Figure 6.2 shows a poster published by the King-Pierce County Farm Bureau in Washington State. It argues that buying local is a matter of 'homeland security'. The phrase 'homeland security' is clearly used playfully to refer to preserving local economies. The poster is not explicitly saying that the stakes are so high that not buying local is equivalent to treason or that nonlocal consumption leaves us open to a fate as awful as the World Trade Center attacks. Nevertheless, the use of that particular term seems to suggest that the bureau believes the stakes are equally high.

In fact, buying locally can just as easily produce economic losses for the com-munity if it is missing an opportunity to benefit from another region's comparative or absolute advantage. Even when local consumption does produce economic gains, existing inequalities within the local community can allocate those gains in a way that exacerbates rather than alleviates social injustice, as Hinrichs (2000) suggests. Moreover, if the local community is relatively rich, its economic gains will worsen injustice at wider scales. There is certainly no social justice in Beverly Hills captur-ing more of its own wealth for local investment. Those problems suggest that the key is to concentrate on the end goals, not on the scalar strategy itself. Local as an end, *for its own sake,* is merely nativism, a defensive localism that is frequently not allied with social justice goals. Those same problems would apply more generally to all local economic development projects. Local economic development should not be thought of as an end in itself. It should be thought of as a scalar strategy to produce ends like poverty reduction or greater social justice. Where it is the best strategy to achieve the desired end, it should be used; where it is not, as in the Beverly Hills example, other scalar strategies should be pursued.

The work on 'embeddedness' is another, more nuanced example of the emphasis on local exchange systems. That work argues that face-to-face interaction helps strengthen community, justice and security; it therefore tends to privilege locally organized food systems (Murdoch et al., 2000). 'Good food', for Sage (2003: 50), should include among other characteristics 'socially embedded features that are established by its scale of production and by its generally localized distribution through short food supply chains'. But while local systems can lead to greater face-to-face interaction which can lead to more trust and 'regard' between producers and consumers, that causal chain does not necessarily result in either better information for the customer or more sustainable or just food systems (Sage, 2003). It is possible, for example, that food produced far away could be labelled 'sustainable' by a trade organization (analogous to 'Fairtrade' labels, see Renard, 2003). That label is just as likely to provide reliable information as a farmer/merchant at a local farmers' market, who wants to sell and has an incentive to misinform. There is also no reason why distant producers are not more sustainable or abide by more just social relations than ones whom the consumer knows personally.

In addition to being misleading, the local trap also occludes scalar strategies that may be essential for achieving justice. In a given context, there is no way to know a priori which scalar strategy will be most effective. It is critical to consider strategies at a range of scales. Large-scale strategies might include: changing national agricultural policy to move away from monocultural methods; federal policies for more integrated food quality/access/nutrition; assisting organizations like the national Second Harvest food bank in collaborating with local food pantries and reforming food-related bills such as the U.S. national Farm Bill. Such national strategies may or may not be the right approach. It is critical to choose the scalar strategy that is most likely to produce the desired outcomes. To narrow the scope of action to the local level alone, while ignoring other scales, is dangerous for both practice and theory.

Food Quality and Human Health

As with the other two concerns, the local trap assumes that localized food systems will lead to higher quality, fresher, healthier foods (Center for Sustainable Environments, 2005; Peters, 1997). Holloway and Kneafsey's (2000) examination of farmers' markets, for example, found among participants a pervasive conflation of local food with high-quality food. With regard to food quality, some focus on the question of transportation and the time spent after harvest in shipping and handling (Nygard and Storstad, 1998). Clearly a farmer fifty miles from a local farmers' market might have a faster and easier trip to make than grocery store produce from California's Central Valley (much less another continent entirely). However, to make the leap that this is always the case is, practically speaking, incorrect. Large-scale organic farming operations can afford, and must use, rapid shipment methods and quick refrigeration to keep produce fresh. In some cases it might be fresher and better for consumption than the local choice. One can imagine a local farmer picking produce in the afternoon one day, loading it into a nonrefrigerated truck, and driving it to market the following morning. By noon that produce has spent almost twenty-four hours in the truck and during several of those hours the truck is exposed to the hot sun. That produce is not necessarily fresher or healthier than the same product, produced using the same methods, immediately placed into a refrigerated truck and shipped 1,000 miles to the same market. While the local option may be the better choice for some foods—difficult-to-ship products like heirloom tomatoes, for example—it cannot be said that local food is always better or delivers healthier products.

Recall the argument about food miles (Marin, 2003). The distance food travels from field to table has grown tremendously in the last three decades. An estimate by the U.S. Department of Defense in 1969 suggested that the average American meal had travelled 1,300 miles from farm to plate. A more recent estimate suggested 1,500–2,500 miles (Halweil, 2002) and another 5,000 miles in the UK (Pretty et al., 2005). The resources expended for this transportation are argued to be unnecessary and unsustainable. Certainly minimizing the unnecessary transportation of goods (see Norberg-Hodge et al., 2002: 18) is desirable. But the blanket assumption that the reduction of food miles that local production provides always trumps other considerations can be harmful environmentally and economically. In some cases it may be environmentally desirable to transport products instead of degrade local resources. We need to critically compare the environmental costs of local production of, for example, rice in California or Texas, with all of its water requirements, with the transport of rice from places in the world in which rice production makes more ecological sense. Which is more, the environmental costs of transport or of water pumping and groundwater depletion? The question is more complex than a localist argument suggests. Pretty et al. (2005) suggest it is better for environmental sustainability to buy local conventionally grown produce instead of buying nonlocal organic produce. But the balance sheet is complex, and the most sustainable strategy is likely to vary from case to case. That complexity, and responses to it, have been recognized by some food system researchers. Hassanein (2003) suggests that in cases like these in which values conflict and outcomes are uncertain that democracy becomes the appropriate method for decision making. She does not assume the primacy of the local. The local trap, though, assumes localness trumps other considerations. In the case of food miles, we contend that they must be one of many considerations in deciding which option is the most desirable.

Patrick Martins (2004), director of Slow Food USA, notes in his *New York Times* editorial that while local farms are important, we need to move beyond 'buy local' campaigns to support the alternative agricultural system. Martins' thinking is clearly about ends—diversity and safety in our food system and sustainable agricultural economies—while his means are adaptable to individual circumstances. A good example of this type of approach is Urban Organic, a home-delivery company for organic products in the New York–New Jersey–Connecticut region. They purchase from a network that not only includes local farmers but also co-operatives and distributors. That network is important for keeping small farms in business because when farmers are involved in sales either directly or through co-operative arrangements they receive more profit on their product than if they are forced to go through multiple middle tiers of distribution to reach consumers. We could extend this type of model to larger regions. Red Tomato, and its close relation, Equal Exchange, support fair trade and small, noncorporate family farms, but they coordinate on more than just a local level. Equal Exchange coordinates fair-trade coffee markets internationally and Red Tomato brokers U.S.-grown foods across New England. These organizations have used the Internet and other networking tactics to think beyond local, utilizing the powers typically associated with capitalist agribusiness for more sustainable, socially just agriculture. In some cases, the local is the appropriate scale for action. But it is never necessarily so. Rather a variety of scalar strategies can be effective in preserving family farms and accomplishing many other goals of food systems practitioners.

Network Theory

We should mention one other literature relevant to the problem of the local trap. Some have begun to explore how network theory can inform research on agro-food systems (Murdoch, 2000; Murdoch et al., 2000; Whatmore and Thorne, 1997). Kneafsey et al. (2001) begin to suggest some ways network theory can transcend the local trap. They set out the concepts of endogenous and exogenous development, arguing that research is increasingly advocating the former, in which local areas pursue self-sufficiency through 'economic activities which are explicitly based on locally embedded resources, skills and knowledge' (Kneafsey et al., 2001: 296). They argue that endogenous development is increasingly seen as mutually exclusive with exogenous development, in which local areas are linked economically to outside systems, which are regularly assumed to be capitalist, industrial and destructive. They reject this dualism and argue that local places must forge a combination of what they call 'vertical and horizontal' networks. Vertical networks refer to a local agricultural economy's links to a 'broader set of processes which exist beyond rural areas', while horizontal networks refer to links to nonagricultural interests in or near the local area (Kneafsey et al., 2001: 299). For network theorists, local food sectors must establish linkages (and interdependencies) with *both* local networks and networks that transcend the local. Thus, for example, in order to thrive, a sustainable hog farming cooperative in northern Iowa might need a much larger market than the sparse local population in Iowa is able to provide (Grey, 2000). In a different way, then, the network approach can offer an alternative theoretical solution to the local trap.

That said, we wish to defend the need for our *scalar* solution to the local trap. First, those working with networks have not clearly identified the preference for the local scale as a specific problem. While their approach offers promise, that promise is not yet fully realized because they have not articulated the problem of the local trap and how network theory might avoid it. Second, the local trap, in general, is a particularly *scalar* trap. While it is true that the work on local embeddedness is celebrating local *networks* in particular, most locally trapped work favours the local *as a scale* in opposition to larger scales that are believed to be inherently less just, sustainable and so forth. As such, a theoretical solution that is specifically scalar provides the most appropriate solution to the problem of the local trap. So both scale and network approaches offer value. Both are helpful for thinking clearly about urban food systems. Recent debates in geography have made clear that scale and network are different concepts, and each has particular strengths and weaknesses in how they illuminate contemporary society (Amin and Thrift, 2002; Brenner, 2001; Whatmore and Thorne, 1997). Ultimately, a theoretical solution to the local trap must include a skilful weaving of both scale theory and network theory. While such a feat is beyond the scope of this chapter, it is certainly an important imperative for future research.

Conclusion

Our hope is that our theoretical approach to scale can help food systems research systematically avoid the local trap. Moreover, beyond just avoiding the trap, we hope thinking about scale in this way encourages scholars and activists to pursue a very different research agenda than the one currently developing in the food systems literature. They need not carry out extensive empirical studies to determine whether or not the local is inherently desirable. Rather they can see scale as a strategy that can have a range of outcomes, both good and bad. Since the outcomes depend on the agendas of those empowered by a scalar strategy, research can make those agendas the subject of critical inquiry by asking questions like: who will benefit from localization (or nationalization, etc.)? What is their agenda? What outcomes are most likely to result from a given scalar strategy? For those pursuing a particular normative goal, scale theory encourages them to use scalar strategies shrewdly rather than unconsciously. It leads them to take very seriously the question of which scalar strategy is most likely to produce the outcome they desire. Of course this chapter is largely a theoretical argument, and so what is needed in future work is empirical explorations of the preceding questions. The theoretical and methodological implications of our argument need to be grounded in and learn from particular food struggles.

While this chapter has been largely a cautionary tale, we want to sound a note of excitement for what scale theory has to offer food systems research more broadly. We suggest that thinking more consciously about scale by drawing on the insights of geographers can help researchers better distinguish strategies from goals. In that way, scale theory provides us with a powerful tool to more effectively resist the destructive capitalist agro-food system and more creatively imagine more sustainable, just and democratic alternatives.

Note

The previous version of the Purcell/Born chapter appeared as: B. Born and M. Purcell, 'Avoiding the Local Trap: Scale and Food Systems in Planning Research', *Journal of Planning Education and Research,* 26/2: 195–207.

1. This is admittedly an ugly word, but we want to be very specific about the process. The terms 'industrialization' and 'globalization' are misleading, since those can be capitalist or not, and we want to stress that it is specifically the *capitalist* logics of industrialization (and its globalization strategy) that result in the negative effects cited by the research.

References

Agnew, J. (1994), 'The Territorial Trap: The Geographical Assumptions of International Relations Theory', *Review of International Political Economy,* 1/1: 53–80.

Agnew, J. (1997), 'The Dramaturgy of Horizons: Geographical Scale in the "Reconstruction of Italy" by the New Italian Political Parties, 1992–95', *Political Geography,* 16/2: 99–121.

Allen, P., FitzSimmons, M., Goodman, M., and Warner, K. (2003), 'Shifting Plates in the Agrifood Landscape: The Tectonics of Alternative Agrifood Initiatives in California', *Journal of Rural Studies,* 19/1: 61–75.

Amin, A., and Thrift, N. (2002), *Cities: Reimagining the Urban,* Cambridge: Polity Press.

Balibar, E. (1999), 'Is European Citizenship Possible?', in J. Holston (ed.), *Cities and Citizenship,* Durham: Duke University Press.

Bellows, A., and Hamm, M. (2001), 'Local Autonomy and Sustainable Development: Testing Import Substitution in Localizing Food Systems', *Agriculture and Human Values,* 18: 271–84.

Born, B. (2003), *'Evaluation of State-Based and Civil Society-Based Collaborative Planning in the Context of Urban Social Justice',* Madison: University of Wisconsin.

Brenner, N. (1999), 'Globalisation as Reterritorialization: The Re-Scaling of Urban Governance in the European Union', *Urban Studies*, 36/3: 431–51.

Brenner, N. (2001), 'The Limits to Scale? Methodological Reflections on Scalar Structuration', *Progress in Human Geography*, 25/4: 591–614.

Brown, J. C., and Purcell, M. (2005), 'There's Nothing Inherent About Scale: Political Ecology, the Local Trap, and the Politics of Development in the Brazilian Amazon', *Geoforum*, 36: 607–24.

Campbell, M. (2004), 'Building a Common table: The Role for Planning in Community Food Systems', *Journal of Planning Education and Research*, 23/4: 341–55.

Center for Sustainable Environments (2001), '10 Reasons to Buy Local Foods', <http://home.nau.edu/environment/>.

Clancy, K. (2004), 'Potential Contributions of Planning to Community Food Systems', *Journal of Planning Education and Research*, 22: 435–8.

Delaney, D., and H. Leitner (1997), 'The Political Construction of Scale', *Political Geography*, 16/2: 93–7.

Escobar, A. (2001), 'Culture Sits in Places: Reflections on Globalism and Subaltern Strategies of Localization', *Political Geography*, 20: 139–74.

Feenstra, G. (1997), 'Local Food Systems and Sustainable Communities', *American Journal of Alternative Agriculture*, 12/1: 28–37.

Giddens, A. (1984), *The Constitution of Society*, Berkeley: University of California Press.

Goodman, D. (2003), 'The Quality "Turn" and Alternative Food Practices: Reflections and Agenda', *Journal of Rural Studies*, 19/1: 1–7.

Grady, M. (2002–3), 'A Preference for Local Food', *Conservation Matters*, Winter: 31–36.

Grey, M. (2000), ' "Those Bastards Can Go to Hell!" Small-Farmer Resistance to Vertical Integration and Concentration in the Pork Industry', *Human Organization*, 59/2: 169–76.

Halweil, B. (2002), *Homegrown*, Washington, DC: Worldwatch Institute.

Hassanein, N. (2003), 'Practicing Food Democracy: A Pragmatic Politics of Transformation', *Journal of Rural Studies*, 19/1: 77–86.

Henderson, E. (1998), 'Rebuilding Local Food Systems from the Grassroots Up', *Monthly Review*, 50/3: 112–25.

Herbert, S. (2005), 'The Trapdoor of Community', *Annals of the Association of American Geographers*, 95/4: 850–65.

Hinrichs, C. (2000), 'Embeddedness and Local Food Systems: Notes on Two Types of Direct Agricultural Market', *Journal of Rural Studies*, 16: 295–303.

Hinrichs, C. (2003), 'The Practice and Politics of Food System Localization', *Journal of Rural Studies*, 19/1: 33–45.

Hinrichs, C., Kloppenburg, J., Stevenson, S., Lezberg, S., Hendrickson, J., and De-Master, K. (1998), 'Moving Beyond Global and Local', NE-185 Working Statement, 2 October, <http://www.ces.ncsu.edu/depts/sociology/ne185/global.html>.

Holloway, L., and Kneafsey, M. (2000), 'Reading the Space of the Farmers' Market: A Preliminary Investigation from the UK', *Sociologia Ruralis,* 40 (3): 285–99.

Howitt, R. (1998), 'Scale as Relation: Musical Metaphors of Geographical Scale', *Area,* 30/1: 49–58.

Hutchings, C. (1994), 'Food Miles Mount Up', *Geographical Magazine,* 66/11: 5.

Kaufman, J. (2004), 'Introduction to a Special Issue on Planning for Community Food Systems', *Journal of Planning Education and Research,* 23/4: 335–40.

Kelly, P. (1997), 'Globalization, Power and the Politics of Scale in the Philippines', *Geoforum,* 28/2: 151–71.

Kelly, P. (1999), 'The Geographies and Politics of Globalization', *Progress in Human Geography,* 23/3: 379–400.

Ketcham, C. (2007), 'The Hundred-Mile Diet', *The Nation* (10 September).

Kingsolver, B., Kingsolver, C., and Hopp, S. (2007), *Animal, Vegetable, Miracle: A Year of Food Life,* New York: Harper Collins.

Kneafsey, M., Ilbery, B., and Jenkins, T. (2001), 'Exploring the Dimensions of Culture: Economies in Rural West Wales', *Sociologia Ruralis,* 41/3: 296–310.

Lacy, W. (2000), 'Empowering Communities through Public Work, Science, and Local Food Systems: Revisiting Democracy and Globalization', *Rural Sociology,* 65/1: 3–26.

Leitner, H. (1997), 'Reconfiguring the Spatiality of Power: The Construction of a Supernational Migration Framework for the European Union', *Political Geography,* 16/2: 123–44.

Magdoff, F., Foster, J., and Buttel, F. (2000), *Hungry for Profit: The Agribusiness Threat to Farmers, Food, and the Environment,* New York: New York University Press.

Marin, M. (2003), 'Time for Topia', *New Internationalist,* 357: 16–17.

Marston, S. (2000), 'The Social Construction of Scale', *Progress in Human Geography,* 24/2: 219–42.

Martins, P. (2004), 'Editorial', *New York Times* (24 April): A25.

McMahon, M. (2002), 'Resisting Globalization: Women Organic Farmers and Local Food Systems', *Canadian Woman Studies,* 21/3: 203–6.

Murdoch, J. (2000), 'Networks—a New Paradigm of Rural Development?', *Journal of Rural Studies,* 16: 407–19.

Murdoch, J., Marsden, T., and Banks, J. (2000), 'Quality, Nature, and Embeddedness: Some Theoretical Considerations in the Context of the Food Sector', *Economic Geography,* 76/2: 107–25.

Norberg-Hodge, H., Merrifield, T., and Gorelick, S. (2002), *Bringing the Food Economy Home: Local Alternatives to Global Agribusiness,* London: Zed Books.

Nygard, B., and Storstad, O. (1998), 'De-Globalization of Food Markets? Consumer Perceptions of Safe Food: The Case of Norway', *Sociologia Ruralis,* 38/1: 35–53.

Pacione, M. (1997), 'Local Exchange Trading Systems—a Rural Response to the Globalization of Capitalism?', *Journal of Rural Studies,* 13/4: 415–27.

Peters, J. (1997), 'Community Food Systems: Working toward a Sustainable Future', *Journal of the American Dietetic Association,* 97/9: 955–7.

Petrini, C. (2004), *Slow Food: The Case for Taste,* New York: Columbia University Press.

Pirog, R., Van Pelt, T., Enshayan, K., and Cook, E. (2001), *Food, Fuel, and Freeways: An Iowa Perspective on How Far Food Travels, Fuel Usage, and Greenhouse Gas Emissions,* Ames: Leopold Center for Sustainable Agriculture, Iowa State University.

Pothukuchi, K. (2004), 'Community Food Assessment: A First Step in Planning for Community Food Security', *Journal of Planning Education and Research,* 23/4: 356–77.

Pretty, J., Ball, A., Lang, T., and Morison, J. (2005), 'Farm Costs and Food Miles: An Assessment of the Full Cost of the UK Weekly Food Basket', *Food Policy,* 30/1: 1–20.

Purcell, M., and Brown, J. C. (2005), 'Against the Local Trap: Scale and the Study of Environment and Development', *Progress in Development Studies,* 5/4: 279–97.

Raco, M. (2003), 'Governmentality, Subject Building, and the Discourses and Practices of Devolution in the UK', *Transactions of the Institute of British Geographers,* 28: 75–95.

Renard, M. (2003), 'Fair Trade: Quality, Market and Conventions', *Journal of Rural Studies,* 19/1: 87–96.

Rodriguez-Pose, A., and Gill, N. (2003), 'The Global Trend toward Devolution and Its Implications', *Environment and Planning,* 21: 333–51.

Sage, C. (2003), 'Social Embeddedness and Relations of Regard: Alternative "Good Food" Networks in South-West Ireland', *Journal of Rural Studies,* 19/1: 47–60.

Shiva, V. (2000), *Stolen Harvest: The Hijacking of the Global Food Supply,* Cambridge, MA: South End Press.

Smith, N. (1992), 'Geography, Difference and the Politics of Scale', in J. Doherty, E. Graham and M. Malek (eds.), *Postmodernism and the Social Sciences,* London, Macmillian.

Smith, N. (1993), 'Homeless/Global: Scaling Places', in J. Bird (ed.), *Mapping the Futures: Local Cultures Global Change,* New York: Routledge.

Staeheli, L., Kodras, J., and Flint, C (eds.) (1997), *State Devolution in America: Implications for a Diverse Society,* Thousand Oaks: Sage.

Swyngedouw, E. (1997), 'Neither Global nor Local: "Glocalization" and the Politics of Scale', in K. Cox (ed.), *Spaces of Globalization,* New York: Guilford Press.

Wallace, W. (1999), 'The Sharing of Sovereignty: The European Paradox', *Political Studies,* 47/3: 503–4.

Waters, A. (2004), 'Slow Food, Slow Schools: Transforming Education through a School Lunch Curriculum', <http://www.edibleschoolyard.org/alice_message.html>

Weatherell, C., Tregear, A., and Allinson, J. (2003), 'In Search of the Concerned Consumer: UK Public Perceptions of Food, Farming and Buying Local', *Journal of Rural Studies,* 19: 233–44.

Whatmore, S., and Thorne, L. (1997), 'Networks: Alternative Geographies of Food', in M. Goodman and M. Watts (eds.), *Globalising Food: Agrarian Questions and Global Restructuring,* New York: Routledge.

Winter, M. (2003), 'Embeddedness, the New Food Economy and Defensive Localism', *Journal of Rural Studies,* 19/1: 23–32.

Fairtrade Food: Connecting Producers and Consumers

Caroline Wright
University of Warwick

Fairtrade food is increasingly common on the shelves of northern hemisphere supermarkets: tea, coffee, rice, avocados, chocolate, wine, black pepper and fruit juice are just some of the fifty-eight food and beverage product categories available with a label guaranteeing a better deal for their producers in the southern hemisphere (Fairtrade Foundation, 2007a). The UK certified Fairtrade sector grew 49 per cent between 2005 and 2006 in terms of retail value, with over 3,000 products now available (Fairtrade Foundation, 2007b). Fairtrade has a longer history in other European countries, notably the Netherlands and Switzerland, but the UK has grown rapidly to become the second biggest Fairtrade market in the world after the United States by retail value (Fairtrade Labelling Organization [FLO], 2007: 11).[1] Food products dominate the sector, with coffee, tea, chocolate/cocoa and bananas constituting 78 per cent of the retail value of all UK Fairtrade certified products in 2005 (Fairtrade Foundation, n.d.). This chapter addresses this growth in the production and consumption of Fairtrade food both in the context of globalization and within a tradition of theorizing food as both material and symbolic good. It charts the specific development of Fairtrade-labelled food in the UK economy as it goes from niche outlets to mainstream supermarkets, drawing on coffee for purposes of illustration. Particular attention is then paid to Fairtrade's mission to reconnect southern producers and northern consumers in a globalized world, using the concept of commodity fetishism.

The chapter begins by introducing Fairtrade, its central assumptions and characteristics, and by introducing food, a very special commodity. It then seeks to embed Fairtrade food in the context of globalization. Thereafter the specific development of the UK's Fairtrade food sector is addressed, charting the origins of fair-trade labelling among nongovernmental organizations (NGOs), the rise of specific Fairtrade brands and the subsequent arrival of mainstream food retailing capital in the Fairtrade sector. The spectacular growth of Fairtrade food purchases is argued to lie not only in consumers' concern with 'fairness' for producers but also in their concerns about the safety and quality of globalized food. There then follows an analysis of the degree and content of the connectivities between producers and consumers that

Fairtrade food promotes. It is argued that while Fairtrade seeks to educate consumers about producers and hails them to make a difference to their lives, its embedding in a capitalist market sees a simultaneous commodification of producers' lives and landscapes as well as commodification of the ethics and politics of Fairtrade itself.

What Is Fairtrade and What Is Food?

Fairtrade began as an initiative to improve market access and trading conditions for small scale producers in the south who were considered 'disadvantaged'. Originally focussed on handicrafts, Fairtrade certification from the 1990s concentrated mainly on food. Labelling initiatives developed to signal to consumers that all or part of the commodity being purchased conforms to the following principles:

1. Trade at agreed minimum prices, usually above the market price, to enable producers to generate a living wage.
2. Promotion of producer capacity and community development through the payment of an additional social premium which producer groups decide how to spend.
3. Direct trade (cutting out middlemen) to increase the value returned to the producer and long run contracts to enhance producer security.
4. Up to 60 per cent pre-financing to secure producer cash flow and enhancements of producers' knowledge of the market.
5. Democratic organization of producers, who must produce sustainably and without abuse of other labourers (Nicholls and Opal, 2005: 6–7).

Early Fairtrade certification was nationally organized and NGO led. Max Havelaar was the first Fairtrade label, launched in the Netherlands in 1988 for Mexican Fairtrade coffee; the UK's Fairtrade Foundation label first appeared in 1994 on Green and Black's Maya Gold chocolate and Cafédirect coffee; and the U.S. Transfair label was launched in 1999. In 1997 FLO International was founded as an umbrella organization to harmonize national labelling bodies; it now sets the criteria for Fairtrade on a commodity by commodity basis. The certification of tea and sugar, largely plantation grown, has seen the remit of Fairtrade expanded to encompass southern agricultural wage labour as well as own-account producers. As part of a wider Fairtrade movement, it is important to note that certified Fairtrade has ambitions beyond what is codified to transform all international trade, by informing and mobilizing consumer purchasing power, setting a good example and lobbying for changes to the international trading system (Murray and Raynolds, 2007: 5).

According to Madeley (2000: 25), food is a special commodity that differs from any other. Food is a basic need, providing the nutrients we require to stay alive, and it is a human right under the UN Charter; lack of food or lack of the right combinations of food mean (often serious) illness at best, starvation and death at worst. Data from the Food and Agriculture Organization of the United Nations (FAO) show that one seventh of the world's population faces severe food insecurity (FAO, 2007). While the ingestion of food helps govern both our quantity of life and its quality in terms of health, it also shapes and is shaped by broader qualities of life. Food and how we process and eat it are central to our identities, our sense of place, our history, our social interaction, our rituals and our sense of belonging (or exclusion) (Korthals, 2001: 206–9). In short, food is both a material and cultural good par excellence.

What does this mean for Fairtrade food? Small producers in Africa, Asia and South and Central America have a long history of producing food crops for export to the north, along trade routes shaped by colonial and postcolonial links. Central to the global food economy, it is more than ironic that many earn insufficient funds from food cash-crops to achieve food security for themselves and their families. It is in this context that Fairtrade seeks to enhance producer livelihoods and security by transforming the terms of trade. Moreover, the production and marketing of Fairtrade foods brings new symbolic values to the field and the table. For producers, these include preoccupations with food quality to satisfy consumer tastes, and for consumers, it includes stories of places and producers far away and moral norms about consumer responsibilities to them; both are addressed later in the chapter.

Globalization and Fairtrade Food

Globalization is a much invoked but highly contested concept: what it is, when it began, whether its impact is positive or negative, the extent to which it can be governed, how it is resisted and reshaped (Held, 2004). Often when globalization is cited, what is being referred to is economic globalization, the idea of an increasingly global economy for the production of goods and services, dominated by multinationals. At the same time, political globalization (i.e. the idea that power to shape nation-states' destiny is shifting from national to regional, transnational and supra-state organizations) has also received considerable attention. Cultural globalization (i.e. the idea that cultural practices and cultural goods are increasingly global as we eat the same food brands, watch the same films and use Google all around the world) is also part of the debate. A fourth element, social globalization—the idea that our social relations and identities are less attached to particular places and may be virtual as well as transnational—is sometimes added to this trio (Munck, 2007: 8). What does seem clear is that globalization is an uneven and partial process, variously resisted; it is precisely not as all-encompassing as the metaphoric ink stain Whatmore and Thorne set against their more nuanced account (1997: 287).

Murray and Raynolds understand Fairtrade as a response to (economic) globalization's adverse impact on the livelihoods of small agricultural producers (2007: 6). Certainly trade liberalization has generally worsened primary commodity prices

(Scholte, 2000: 215). In the case of coffee, following the collapse of the International Coffee Agreement in 1989, the average price on world markets almost halved from US $1.34 (1984–8) to US $0.77 (1990–4) (Daviron and Ponte, 2005: 88) and has dipped below US $0.50 since. Fairtrade sees conventional trade as the problem and a new, alternative system of trading partnerships with particular producers as the solution. Fairtrade can also be understood as a response to political globalization. It has emerged from the NGO sector and has sought to mobilize consumers to effect change through a new Fairtrade market, in the face of ineffective state power vis-à-vis global commodity markets and social justice. For example, during the 2005 'Make Poverty History' movement, Fairtrade food purchases were highlighted as an immediate and tangible way consumers could make a difference as they waited (somewhat in vain) on world leaders. Where Fairtrade governs the conditions of wage labour it also speaks to state failure to implement ratified International Labour Organization (ILO) Conventions and ILO impotence in terms of sanctions. Cultural globalization is also addressed by Fairtrade food, in that it seeks to counter the delocalization of food production that began with industrialization and has accelerated through economic globalization, emphasizing instead the places (and people) of production.

According to Robertson (1992: 10), 'anti-global gestures [are] encapsulated within the discourse of globality'. Certainly Fairtrade operates both within and against globalization, seeking to influence multinationals rather than eradicate them; increasingly relying on conventional capital as importers, processors and retailers of Fairtrade commodities (Raynolds and Long, 2007: 19) and premised on mono-crop production for export. Moreover, FLO's work to harmonize Fairtrade labels and increase brand recognition for the Fairtrade Mark contributes (modestly) to cultural globalization, just as their advocacy relies on the space-transcending technology of the Internet and the quest to shorten the social distance between producers and consumers speaks to social globalization.

The Rise and Rise of Fairtrade Food

The growth of certified Fairtrade food can be attributed to a range of overlapping factors categorized here in terms of producer demand, advocacy, market characteristics, consumer demand, institutionalization, marketing strategies and corporate participation. First, the plight of producers facing rock-bottom prices was the stimulus for Fairtrade food certification. Since then the queue of producer groups seeking participation, as well as the reality that most can only sell a fraction of their total output Fairtrade, maintains the pressure to grow the market. Second, the NGO-led initiatives that first developed Fairtrade food successfully mobilized their supporters to buy the products in niche outlets and, when mainstream distribution began, to lobby their local supermarkets to list them. Third, the market for food provides opportunities for scaling up Fairtrade, in terms of branding, packaging and level of demand (Nicholls,

2004: 106); in terms of differentiation, Fairtrade situates itself in the growing high-value food niche (Hendrickson and Heffernan, 2002: 360–1). Fourth, Fairtrade food speaks not only to consumer concerns for social justice but also to wider concerns about food safety and sustainable production (Low and Davenport, 2005: 147; Nicholls, 2004: 106). These trends, together with a mistrust of the global food system and unease that 'experiential knots of connection' with agriculture have been lost (Korthals, 2001: 209), foster an appetite for knowledge about the places and conditions of food production that Fairtrade food can meet.[2] Fifth, the institutionalization of Fairtrade commodities under FLO has enhanced the product range,[3] bananas being particularly successful, and raised the profile of Fairtrade food. Sixth, the marketing of Fairtrade foods emphasizes premium quality as much (if not more than) ethical criteria and opens up distribution through supermarkets, enabling them to reach into the mainstream (Nicholls and Opal, 2005: 24). Finally, having been persuaded to stock independent Fairtrade food brands and seeing their success, supermarkets have developed 'own brand' Fairtrade goods (Barrientos and Smith, 2007).

Setting aside definitional questions as to whether coffee is food, it provides an excellent example of the rapid growth of Fairtrade food in line with the previously mentioned factors. The first UK Fairtrade coffee initiative, Cafédirect, was founded in 1991 by four alternative trade organizations, Oxfam Trading, Traidcraft, Equal Exchange and Twin Trading, and their coffee was labelled Fairtrade certified from 1994.[4] Cafédirect relied on Alternative Trading Organization (ATO) supporters to promote and buy the new coffee, initially through Oxfam and Traidcraft and then in all major supermarkets from the mid-1990s. Fairtrade coffee has mass market potential, coffee being the second most traded commodity in the world, and relatively standardized production making it amenable to branding via a Fairtrade label (Nicholls and Opal, 2005: 24). It has taken advantage of product niches, emphasizing origin, strength, quality and flavour, to both position itself and diversify (Hendrickson and Heffernan, 2002: 360–1; Renard, 1999: 495). Cafédirect launched Teadirect in 1998, and four new organic coffees in 1999. It started supplying a Fairtrade coffee to Costa Coffee from 2000 and launched Cocodirect in 2003. Cafédirect is now the fifth-largest UK coffee brand and the third largest Fairtrade importer in Europe (Krier, 2005: 28). Recently, it has faced competition from supermarket 'own label' Fairtrade coffee. Sainsburys first initiative in 2002 has been widely emulated. For example, The Co-op switched all its 'own label' coffee to Fairtrade certified in 2003, and Marks and Spencer followed with both tea and coffee in 2005. Other mainstream brands have also introduced a Fairtrade offer to their range—for example, Percol as early as 1996 and Nescafe in 2005.

Supermarket distribution may be central to the growth and mainstreaming of Fairtrade food, but involvement of the corporate sector is not without its critics. There is concern that supermarkets are opportunistically cashing in on the work ATOs have done to develop the Fairtrade brand, that consumers cannot easily tell how far Fairtrade extends across a product range, that the supply side imperatives of going mass

market will favour plantation production rather than small producers and that the capacity of FLO and other NGOs may be insufficient to negotiate effectively with large
enterprises such as supermarkets chains (Barrientos et al., 2007: 58). At the same time,
research shows that supermarket approaches to Fairtrade are differentiated, some
showing more commitment to Fairtrade than others and being more likely to foster
long-term relationships with producers based on dialogue and respect (Smith, 2008).

Connecting Producers and Consumers

The Fairtrade Mark includes as its fifth guarantee 'a closer link between consumers and producers', a quest that features in Cafédirect's original mission statement
(1991–2008): 'To be the leading brand which strengthens the influence, income and
security of producer partners in the south and links them directly to the consumer'
(Cafédirect, 2008: 2). Raynolds (2002: 420) is optimistic about the prospects of success: 'The case of Fairtrade demonstrates that it is possible to "shorten" the social
distance between consumers and producers'. However, my earlier work on Cafédirect advertising left me troubled in that the (virtual) proximity of consumer and
producer relied on tropes of difference as it 'rendered the lives and landscapes of
the majority world as consumables in their own right, alongside cash crops' (Wright,
2004: 678). Goodman (2004: 902) has also highlighted how integral 'the commoditization of people and place' is to the development of Fairtrade, seeing it as the 'commodification of difference [that] can make a difference'.

Here I seek to unpack the connectivities between producers and consumers in
more detail,[5] focusing where possible on Cafédirect as a case study. The term 'connectivities' is borrowed from Whatmore and Thorne (1997: 295), who use the phrase
'mode of ordering of connectivity' to refer to the discourse of 'partnership, alliance,
responsibility and fairness' that characterizes the alternative commodity network.
Connectivity privileges fairness to producers on the part of consumers, being distinct
from an 'enterprise mode of ordering' that privileges cost minimization by consumers. I'm interested to look in more depth at the degree, quality and maintenance
of connectivities between producers and consumers, both material and discursive.
For analytic convenience I've distinguished social, ethical, political, economic and
cultural connectivities; they are, of course, intermeshed. Conceptually, I draw on the
concept of commodity fetishism, widely used in analyses of Fairtrade (Bryant and
Goodman, 2004; Goodman, 2004; Hudson and Hudson, 2003; Lyon, 2006a; Watson,
2006; Wright, 2004).

In the first volume of *Capital*, Marx (1961) expounded his theory of the fetishism
of commodities. This is the illusion at the heart of capitalism whereby our relationship to goods becomes a relationship with money rather than the producers of the
goods, and the value of the commodity is understood in terms of its exchange value

and not the value of the labour that produced it (Marx, 1961: 73). Where money represents the value of the product then as long as the market price is paid there is no further obligation between buyer and seller. From a neo-Marxist perspective the commodity fetish is actually two-fold, both an obscuring of the relations of production and an imbuing of the commodity with symbolic value, that is, with aesthetic qualities beyond its use value. This generates both economic surpluses for capital, in the form of rent (Guthman, 2002: 305), and cultural surpluses for consumers, in the form of satisfaction and identity. According to Hudson and Hudson (2003: 416) this latter commodity fetishism is intrinsic to modern capitalism as consumers alienated from their own labour seek creativity or satisfaction in consumer goods rather than in productive work.

Who Are the Producers and Consumers?

The producers in this case are own-account coffee farmers mainly in Latin America, producing 83 per cent of certified Fairtrade coffee (Raynolds and Long, 2007: 25), and Africa. Although Fairtrade is aimed at poor, disadvantaged producers, those participating are not generally the poorest in their communities, as access to land and capacity to meet production and quality standards are required (Goodman, 2004: 909). Nonetheless, research with Latin American coffee growers supplying Fairtrade markets confirmed their relative socioeconomic inequality; most had under five acres of land and less than four years of education (Raynolds et al., 2004: 1115). Although women may make crucial contributions to production, where land ownership is vested in men they may also be denied official co-op membership, as Tallontire (2000: 170) found in Tanzania. Cafédirect buys coffee from the 3,000 growers of Gumutindo coffee co-op in Uganda, 8,500 growers of COCLA in Peru and 2,300 growers of PRODECOOP in Nicaragua, among others (Cafédirect, n.d.).

Consumers are not organized into groups that make them readily distinguishable in the same way, although institutions such as churches, schools and universities may be pivotal in recruiting Fairtrade consumers. Nonetheless, the price premium of Fairtrade foods and the cultural capital its marketing draws may be assumed to leave middle-class consumers with the greatest capacity for purchase. The UK's Fairtrade Foundation has funded regular sampling to test recognition of the Fairtrade mark; this indicates that half the UK population recognizes the mark, and that recognition is highest in the twenty-five to thirty-four age-group and among social class ABs (professional and managerial occupations) but is increasing in C1s (nonmanual skilled occupations). More than three-quarters recognizing the mark report having purchased a certified Fairtrade product in the last year, and one-third say they do so at least monthly; of course reported and actual purchases may diverge (Fairtrade Foundation, 2005).

Social Connectivities

What are the social interactions between producers and consumers and their associated social positions and social roles? Producers and consumers are in an indirect trading relationship; they do not exchange goods and money directly but instead do so across considerable space and time. Their transactions are also mediated by other actors in the Fairtrade network. Face-to-face meetings are very rare; Cafédirect and other Fairtrade brands typically bring producer group representatives to the UK for Fairtrade Fortnight, and some consumers may visit producer co-ops in the south. In contrast, virtual meetings of producers by consumers are ubiquitous, facilitated by Fairtrade marketing and labels. As I have argued elsewhere, 'Fairtrade vignettes' are a commonplace feature of marketing and product packaging; these short descriptions of producers' lives stress the hardships of the 'free' market and the benefits that Fairtrade brings (Wright, 2004: 671). So, for example, Cafédirect's Web site has a moving panoramic banner across the top through which one can 'meet' several producers, co-op officials and staff. These include Elfazu Nandala, a Ugandan coffee farmer whose household comprises eighteen people and who earned 250,000 Ugandan shillings (seventy pounds sterling) in Fairtrade premiums for his coffee last year, and Cecilia Mwambebule, tea co-op member from Tanzania, who says, 'Fairtrade is helping us improve our lives' (Cafédirect, n.d.).

Such 'meetings' and producer stories are clearly intended to persuade consumers that buying Fairtrade makes a difference; it can transform a 'once upon a time' narrative of arduousness and inequality for producers into a 'happily ever after'. While no such representation could ever be fully referential, these are rather simplistic; one would need to know much more about Uganda to judge what difference an extra seventy pounds sterling per year might make to Elfazu and family. Nonetheless, these vignettes reflect Fairtrade's quest to make our relationship with coffee also a relationship with those who produced it, thereby undermining commodity fetishism in Marx's original sense. However, the way the story about the 'labour behind the label' is told makes it but a partial defetishization, still a far cry from realizing the 'mutual relations' Marx envisaged (1961: 72). Moreover, there is a simultaneous refetishization in terms of symbolic value, as the story of production is itself commodified.

First, the virtual 'meetings' between consumer and producer are one-way and necessarily partial. I may 'know' Elfazu's face from the Cafédirect Web site but I can't know him as a person. Moreover, it's highly unlikely that he grew the coffee I buy; rather, his face represents an imagined community of producers. Second, he knows nothing of me as an individual; he can't see my picture and has little opportunity to know me or other consumers more generally. Cafédirect's former CEO, Penny Newman, may insist that producers do know about consumers, 'Because we tell them … and they desperately want to know … Our role is very much to paint the picture back to them about people like ourselves and our habits, our consumption habits, our shopping habits, the way that we think … the things that we demand' (Newman, 2001: 25).

However, the quote itself highlights producers' lack of knowledge and that what they might glean is both mediated by Cafédirect and premised around market growth. Meanwhile, research with Guatemalan Fairtrade coffee producers holds that 'members of the researched co-operative had little knowledge of the consumers who bought their coffee' (Lyon, 2006a: 458). Third, and crucially, this limited defetishization simultaneously refetishizes the commodity, as the lives of producers become commodified, rendered items of consumption in themselves as images and text on the product packaging. In short, Fairtrade may reduce the anonymity of the trading relationship between consumer and producers but in a form that typically renders producers the known about object, rather than the knowing subject.

Ethical Connectivities

What principles or values should govern the reciprocal conduct of producers and consumers? Following Nicholls and Opal (2005), it is helpful to distinguish the principles surrounding action (the deontological) from those concerned with the outcome of actions (the consequential). It is also useful to contrast the ethical imperatives of the conventional liberal and Fairtrade markets. In the liberal market model, the principles of action are voluntary trade and the honouring of contracts and property rights, backed up by law and state power. Consequentially, consumers and producers have a duty to pursue their own wealth and utility so as to simultaneously promote the greater good; the 'invisible hand' will bring prices into equilibrium, optimizing utility and the division of labour. On the other hand, the Fairtrade model begins from the premise that the liberal market is distorted against producers. It isn't free, and many producers lack price information and market access, having to rely on unscrupulous middlemen, as well as capital or credit to switch to other sectors of production if prices fall below costs (Nicholls and Opal, 2005: 32–8). Moreover, there are negative externalities that undermine the greater good, for example, unsustainable use of environmental resources and human capital. The Fairtrade model seeks redress by adjusting the terms of trade in producers' favour. The principle of action for consumers is treating producers as an end in themselves rather than as a means to an end, thus according them dignity and respect. In terms of the consequential, consumers are to be concerned with the impact of their purchase on the well-being of producers, their families and communities. Since consumers do not trade directly, they rely on the Fairtrade system and its certification regimes to put these ethical principles into practice.

The ethical dispositions of Fairtrade consumers are under-researched. One study of Fairtrade coffee purchasers in France finds that their leading motives are socially oriented around the 'wish to attain the value "equality between humans"' (de Ferran and Grunert, 2007: 226). However, the second most frequent motives were individually oriented, around the satisfaction of 'a good product with a good taste' and a wish to maximize health (de Ferran and Grunert, 2007: 226). Moreover, those purchasing in a supermarket favoured individual values while those purchasing in specialist stores favoured social values (de Ferran and Grunert, 2007: 227). This latter finding has surely not been lost on Fairtrade marketers. My analysis of Cafédirect's print advertising from 1999 to 2002 argued that interpellation through the pleasures of consumption and distinction was privileged over interpellation through an appeal to ethics: 'whenever the ethical dimensions of Fairtrade come to the fore the attention of the potential consumers is quickly returned to the theme of self-reward: … this is the coffee that tastes so good to those who have good taste' (Wright, 2004: 668–9). Putting quality before ethics was a strategy the Cafédirect CEO was very conscious of: 'We've really made ourselves look as good, taste as good and be as good at marketing as the biggest brands such as Nescafe or Kenco … [long pause], and by the way, it's Fairtrade' (Newman, 2001: 6).

A more recent advert for Cafédirect shifts back to the ethical imperative. The tagline 'There's only half an inch between poverty and paradise' denotes the distance between Cafédirect and non-Fairtrade coffees on supermarket shelves and the difference that choosing the 'right' coffee will make for producers. Here ethics become the unique selling point lighting up Cafédirect in contrast to its dismal competitors. The impact of Fairtrade is obviously exaggerated and, of course, it is not only the producers who apparently reach paradise but consumers too, both immediately in the 'aromatic, delicate fragrance and floral acidity' of the gourmet coffee and in the future from having done the right thing by others. As Watson argues, 'consumers are able to express solidarity for distant strangers through the purchase of fairly traded products, but on the other [hand] they also buy for themselves additional feelings of self-worth for knowing that they have acted in this way' (2006: 436). Here the fetishism of the commodity in terms of symbolic value includes commodification of the 'ethic of care' itself, as consumers 'pay to enact such displays of conscience' (Watson, 2006: 444).

It would be easy to forget that the Fairtrade certification model also imposes ethical norms on producers. Principles of solidarity, democracy and participation are encoded, requiring producers to associate and practise one-farmer, one-vote. Principles of environmental sustainability are also codified, pesticide management being required and some pesticides banned. So within a Fairtrade system, producers owe it to consumers to organize themselves democratically and to safeguard the environment. However, we know very little about how producers experience these ethical norms; in fact, existing research suggests that many producers don't understand the system beyond the higher and more stable commodity price (Camp et al., 2005; Lyon, 2006a).

Political Connectivities

How are producers and consumers connected politically? Most attention has been paid to Fairtrade consumers, understood to combine consumption (the satisfaction of needs and wants through the purchase and use of goods and services) with citizenship (making a positive contribution to the solving of public problems) (McGregor, 2002: 1). In this case the responsibilities of the citizen-consumer are extended beyond other nationals to a global level, attuned to a feature of globalization Robertson (1992: 8) calls an 'intensification of consciousness of the world as a whole'. So, as argued already, the Cafédirect consumer is simultaneously purchasing a high quality cup of coffee and the opportunity to make a (modest) difference to remote coffee producers' lives. Goodman characterizes Fairtrade purchase as the 'grocery-line activism' of the 'morally reflexive consumer' (2004: 907–8) and Grimes emphasizes the collective power of consumers by describing Fairtrade as a 'decentralized, grassroots citizen movement' (2005: 237). Certainly while the terrain of political action is everyday consumption choices, the political ripples may be wider. Fairtrade consumers can be understood to contribute to a new form of civil regulation, whereby business standards are increasingly set and regulated by civil society organizations such as NGOs, rather than by state or supranational bodies (Harrison, 2005: 65–6). Consumers are also expressing 'economic votes' through their Fairtrade purchases. Indeed the indirect effect of increasing Cafédirect sales on multinational coffee retailers, nudging them towards a Fairtrade offer (or at least to pay more attention to producers in their commodity chain), arguably has more transformatory potential than its direct impact (Harrison, 2005: 63). However, others are more sceptical about the extent to which consumers are sovereign and how far and how fast market choices can be transformatory (Shaw et al., 2008).

It is rather less clear how producers link politically with consumers; as argued above, they have little opportunity to know them concretely or imaginatively except perhaps as demanding high quality coffee. According to Watson (2007), this has important repercussions for the type of political act that a Fairtrade purchase constitutes. Generally assumed to be an act of (re)distributive justice, whereby the rights-based claims of producers are recognized and the injustices of the conventional market are corrected, Watson argues from a Smithian perspective that Fairtrade purchasing is better understood as an act of beneficence. This is both because producers know so little of consumers that the relationship between them inevitably lacks the mutual sympathy that justice requires and because Fairtrade addresses a generalized absence of good (to southern producers) rather than a specific harm (to a specific producer) (Watson, 2007: 281–3).

Where consumers and producers may be more equivalent politically is that both are largely excluded from the governance of Fairtrade, the setting of standards, their monitoring and verification. According to Reed (2008), FLO has a legitimacy deficit in that it is not democratically organized and it is not sufficiently accountable to producers or consumers. This exclusion has also been expressed by producer groups themselves and is beginning to be taken seriously; FLO is currently reviewing its governance, and the representation of producers is on the agenda. For its part, Cafédirect has two producer representatives on its board of directors and, following a public issue in 2005, producer groups own 5 per cent of its shares.

Economic Connectivities

What resources flow between producers and consumers? The producer is paid a 'fair' price, that is, a guaranteed minimum price together with a social premium. For coffee this means a Fairtrade price of 125 cents/lb for washed Arabica beans from 1 June 2008, together with a 10 cents/lb premium, against a market price as low as 45 cents/lb in 2001 and 116 cents/lb in February 2007. In return, the consumer is offered a high quality product, both intrinsically in terms of use value and extrinsically in terms of virtue. Most research indicates at least a doubling of earnings for producers selling in Fairtrade rather than conventional markets (Raynolds et al., 2004; Utting-Chamarro, 2005: 591), and in 2003 coffee producers supplying Cafédirect realized an additional £2.8 million from so doing (Nicholls and Opal, 2005: 25). FLO estimates that upwards of seven million producers and their families in the south now benefit from Fairtrade sales (Fairtrade Foundation, 2007b). However, Fairtrade's redistribution is not as straightforward as it might at first appear.

First, most Fairtrade coffee producers fail to sell their entire crop on a Fairtrade basis, mainly because of a lack of demand at the consumption end. Second, while Fairtrade coffee prices are always higher than conventional prices, the monetary benefit of Fairtrade to the producer varies, being greatest in a low-priced coffee market. Third, what the producer has to sell (raw coffee beans) is not what the consumer buys (a latte on the high street; roast and ground coffee for the cafétiere; a jar of instant), and the majority of value added accrues in the north. The gap between the extra the consumer pays for Fairtrade coffee and what the producer receives varies depending on the mark-up of intermediaries. In one estimate the producer gets 11 per cent of the coffee's retail value (compared with 7% in the conventional market), with the co-op taking 6 per cent, the roaster 38 per cent, the coffee company 14 per cent and the retailer 30 per cent (Nicholls and Opal, 2005, 83). Certainly consumers who imagine a direct transfer from their pocket to that of producers face disillusion. Yet Fairtrade marketing may well perpetuate this myth, promising the romance of a full and transparent social relationship with named coffee producers. One leading supermarket was said to be reaping a 160 per cent gross margin on 'own label' Fairtrade coffee (Oppenheim, 2005) and the charge that some retailers are cashing in on the popularity of Fairtrade may damage its prospects.

In the meantime, Fairtrade organizations draw consumers' attention to other economic benefits for producers than price, notably stable trading relationships and the Fairtrade premium. Producer co-operatives typically choose to invest premiums in community infrastructure (schools, clinics, roads) as well as product infrastructure (technical training, new warehouses, quality control) and income diversification. Raynolds et al. (2004) argue that in the long term this capacity building is more important for producers than are higher prices. Modest stakes by producers in Fairtrade brands offer further potential for income redistribution. While Cafédirect producers own a 5 per cent stake, the co-operative supplying Divine Fairtrade chocolate enjoys 45 per cent, yielding almost £50,000 when the first dividend was paid in 2005.

Fairtrade may promote modest redistribution from northern consumers to southern producers. However, critics question the levels of redistribution, its sustainability if consumer preferences change and the appropriateness of recruiting affluent consumers to 'redeem' poor producers through their consumption choices (Goodman, 2004; Hudson and Hudson, 2003; Lyon, 2006a; Utting-Chamorro, 2005). Maldistribution, they argue, needs to be understood structurally and tackled politically, not reduced to individualized projects of consumer choice. Instead, Fairtrade may perpetuate historical inequalities in promoting 'monocultural production for export' and 'dependent development in which third world producers are whipped by the whims of first world colonial-style luxury consumption' (Starr and Adams, 2003: 23).

Cultural Connectivities

How are producers and consumers represented by Fairtrade and what do they know of each other? As argued already, Fairtrade marketing has laudable aims—to promote redistribution—but produces 'voyeuristic knowledge' for consumers (Goodman, 2004: 900). It commodifies producers' lives, reducing them to one-dimensional stories of poverty and exploitation before Fairtrade and a better life afterwards, to what Bryant and Goodman (2004: 359) call a 'spectacle' for northern consumers. Producers may well be aware of their role—coffee co-op leaders in Mexico expressed a dislike of coffee marketing because of its depersonalization and promotion of stereotypes (Taylor, 2002: 28)—but have little chance to represent themselves. They also have limited opportunities for a 'reverse gaze'. What producers know about consumers is under-researched, but it is feasible that producers 'know' consumers mainly through their 'good taste', a taste that has to be satisfied to safeguard market access (Goodman, 2004: 910). They may know little else of them, including how they consume the coffee itself.

Fairtrade marketing commodifies not only producers' lives but also their landscapes, as it indulges in what Bryant and Goodman (2004: 350) call 'Edenic myth-making', the invoking of beautiful, fecund and untouched places. I argued in an earlier analysis of Cafédirect's advertising that it positioned its coffee to promise 'an escape from the trials of a post-industrial world via an imaginary location ... circulating as an image empty of the meanings its inhabitants might provide (Wright, 2004: 678). We might consider today the moveable panoramic banner on Cafédirect's Web site, a collage of verdant sunny landscapes and happy, laughing producers, with birds flying overhead. Meanwhile, Lyon (2006b: 378) concluded that the market for shade-grown coffee was 'shaped by North American fantasies of pure untouched nature and romantic portrayals of small coffee farmers as natural conservationists, eager to protect birds, biodiversity and natural resources'. As well as colonizing the production of meaning, such myth-making belies the material realities of the places of coffee production.

In essence, then, Fairtrade accomplishes only a partial commodity defetishization (Wright, 2004). It accomplishes 'a removal of the commodity veil, but also a replacing of the fetish in the images of indigenous producers, tropes of productive tropical nature, and meanings of alternative development' (Goodman, 2004: 902), all cultural surpluses for the consumer to enjoy. According to Castree (2001: 1520), the unveiling of commodity fetishism is inevitably constrained by categories of thought prone to the essentializing of places and cultures. Moreover, selling in capitalist markets subordinates Fairtrade to consumer preference for goods 'pre-packaged with lifestyle signifiers' (Raynolds, 2002: 413).

As for consumers, Fairtrade marketing assumes and affirms their entitlement to high quality products alongside their 'good taste', thus conferring distinction. Cafédirect coffee is not only enchanted with imaginative stories of escape, authenticity, leisure and luxury for the consumer, offering a break from the stresses and strains of late modernity; it also offers them 'temporary peace of mind' that they have done the right thing by faraway producers, and can be seen to have done so (Watson, 2006: 445). Over-simplistic narratives make consumers agents of justice and development. As Dolan (2005: 365) concludes, writing about Fairtrade flower and vegetable production in Kenya, 'a consuming public (re)constitute[s] the African worker as an object of their duty and obligation'. Thus consumers are represented as redeeming both themselves and producers.

Conclusion

The spectacular growth of Fairtrade food is usefully understood as both a response to the negative features of globalization and simultaneously embedded within its trends. It perpetuates global economy and global brands just as it seeks to reform them; its attempts to relocalize food contribute to one-way social globalization; it offers a politics from below that is largely unaccountable. Part of its success story lies in Fairtrade food's capacity to capitalize on wider trends in food retailing, such as consumer concerns for food safety and provenance and the growth of high value foods in an increasingly differentiated sector.

Now selling in a mainstream capitalist market, it should not surprise us that the Cafédirect brand needs to keep promising the consumer more than coffee itself. Moreover, the Fairtrade project means that these cultural surpluses go well beyond the invocations of luxury, status, entitlement and authenticity that characterize other medium- to high-priced coffees. Product labels and marketing invite consumers to 'meet' the producers who they are invoked to take some responsibility for. This process simultaneously defetishizes the commodity, (partially) revealing the social relations of production, and refetishizes it, as new cultural surpluses of appropriation and redemption of distant lives and landscapes are generated.

While consumers may claim various connections to producers through Fairtrade, producers remain barely connected to consumers except in terms of benefiting economically from modest redistribution. Of course one must ask if this matters given that the original purpose of Fairtrade is to offer direct market access to producers at a fairer price. On the one hand, it could be argued that the means justify the ends; the more Fairtrade food takes off the better for small farmers in the south. On the other hand, it could be argued that the means contradict the ends. If the recognition of producers embodied in a fair price and a fairer trading relationship is undercut by the one-way commodification and 'othering' of their lives, and by their lack of ownership and control of a system designed for them but not by them, then Fairtrade's transformatory potential is compromised.

Hendrickson and Heffernan (2002) conceive alternative systems of food production and consumption as attempts to wrest food from what Habermas called the systems world, governed by power and money, and (re)place it in the life world, the sphere of social relations. Fairtrade might declare itself to have similar aims, to reconnect producers and consumers and reduce the social distance between them. Ultimately, however, I would argue that in going mainstream Fairtrade has been unable to resist the colonization of and encroachment of the systems world. It remains to be seen whether Fairtrade's failure to put producers at the heart of the movement will be addressed in the future and how far new research will examine how producers conceive of consumers: what Fairtrade means to them and how they would wish to be represented. In the end these lacunae have a long history; as Frank (2003) concluded of earlier mobilizations of consumers on behalf of working people, such as the nineteenth-century union-label movement, 'Where Are the Workers?'

Notes

1. The U.S. population is five times the UK population; its Fairtrade sector is 25 per cent bigger than the UK's.
2. This factor has also fuelled the growth of the organic food sector. While Fairtrade food may sometimes be organic, the two are not synonymous. As Golding and Peattie (2005: 157–8) explain, both types of food make a virtue out of how they are produced, but the Fairtrade project is also about solidarity with producers, about altering market structures and relations in their favour.
3. FLO certification has concentrated on food products, but cotton, cut flowers, ornamental plants and sports balls are also covered.
4. In fact, Cafédirect's so-called Gold Standard exceeds FLO's Fairtrade standards for coffee.
5. Producers and consumers are of course part of a wider commodity network of roasters, importers, buyers, labelling organizations, retailers and so forth.

References

Barrientos, S., and Smith, S. (2007), 'Mainstreaming Fairtrade in Global Production: Own Brand Fruit and Chocolate in UK Supermarkets', in L. T. Raynolds,

D. Murray and J. Wilkinson (eds.), *Fairtrade: The Challenges of Transforming Globalization,* London: Routledge.

Barrientos, S., Conroy, M. E., and Jones, E. (2007), 'Northern Social Movements and Fairtrade', in L. T. Raynolds, D. Murray and J. Wilkinson (eds.), *Fairtrade: The Challenges of Transforming Globalization,* London: Routledge.

Bryant, R. L., and Goodman, M. K. (2004), 'Consuming Narratives: The Political Ecology of "Alternative" Consumption', *Transactions of the Institute of British Geographers,* NS, 29: 344–66.

Cafédirect (2008), *The Gold Standard: Cafedirect Annual Report 2007/8,* <http://www.cafe direct.co.uk/our_business/investorrelations/annualreports/> accessed 1 September 2009

Cafédirect (n.d.), 'Home Page', <http://www.Cafedirect.co.uk/> accessed 1 June 2008.

Camp, M., Flynn, S., Portalewska, A., and Cullen, T. T. (2005), 'A Cup of Truth', *Cultural Survival Quarterly* [online journal], 29/3: <http://209.200.101.189/ publications/ csq/csq-article.cfm?id+1846> accessed 1 June 2008.

Castree, N. (2001), 'Commodity Fetishism, Geographical Imaginations and Imaginative Geographies', *Environment and Planning A,* 33: 1519–25.

Daviron, B., and Ponte, S. (2005), *The Coffee Paradox: Global Markets, Commodity Trade and the Elusive Promise of Development,* London: Zed Books.

de Ferran, F., and Grunert, K. G. (2007), 'French Fairtrade Coffee Buyers' Purchasing Motives: An Exploratory Study Using Means-End Chains Analysis', *Food Quality and Preference,* 18/2: 218–29.

Dolan, C. S. (2005), 'Fields of Obligation: Rooting Ethical Sourcing in Kenyan Agriculture', *Journal of Consumer Culture,* 5/3: 365–89.

Fairtrade Foundation (n.d.), 'Sales of Fairtrade Products in the UK', <http://www. Fairtrade.org.uk/about_sales.htm> accessed 1 June 2008.

Fairtrade Foundation (2005), 'Press Release', May 2005, <http://www.Fairtrade.org. uk/pr270505.htm> accessed 1 June 2008.

Fairtrade Foundation (2007a), 'Press Release', 26 February, <http://www.Fairtrade. org.uk/pr260207.htm> accessed 1 June 2008.

Fairtrade Foundation (2007b), 'Press Release', July, <http://www.Fairtrade.org.uk/ pr100807.htm> accessed 1 June 2008.

Fairtrade Labelling Organizations International (2007), *Shaping Global Partnerships: Fairtrade Labelling Organizations International Annual Report 2006/07,* <http://www.Fairtrade.net/fileadmin/ user_upload/content/FLO_AR_2007.pdf> accessed 1 June 2008.

Fair Trade Organization (2007), 'The Right to Food News', <http://www.fao.org/ righttofood/news4_en.htm> accessed 1 June 2008.

Frank, D. (2003), 'Where Are the Workers in Consumer-Worker Alliances? Class Dynamics and the History of Consumer-Labor Campaigns', *Politics and Society,* 31/3: 363–79.

Golding, K., and Peattie, K. (2005), 'In Search of a Golden Blend: Perspectives on the Marketing of Fairtrade Coffee', *Sustainable Development,* 13: 154–65.

Goodman, M. K. (2004), 'Reading Fairtrade: Political Ecological Imaginary and the Moral Economy of Fairtrade Goods', *Political Geography*, 23: 891–915.

Grimes, K. M. (2005), 'Changing the Rules of Trade with Global Partnerships: The Fair Trade Movement', in J. Nash, ed., *Social Movements: An Anthropological Reader*, Oxford: Blackwell.

Guthman, J. (2002), 'Commodified Meanings, Meaningful Commodities: Re-thinking Production-Consumption Links through the Organic System of Provision', *Sociologica Ruralis*, 42/4: 295–311.

Harrison, R. (2005), 'Pressure Groups, Campaigns and Consumers', in R. Harrison, T. Newholm and D. Shaw, eds., *The Ethical Consumer*, London: Sage.

Held, D. (ed.), (2004), *A Globalizing World? Culture, Economics, Politics*, London: Routledge/Open University.

Hendrickson, M. K., and Heffernan, W. D. (2002), 'Opening Spaces through Relocalization: Locating Potential Resistance in the Weaknesses of the Global Food System', *Sociologia Ruralis*, 43/4: 347–69.

Hudson, I., and Hudson, M. (2003), 'Removing the Veil? Commodity Fetishism, Fairtrade and the Environment', *Organization and Environment*, 16/4: 413–30.

Korthals, M. (2001), 'Taking Consumers Seriously: Two Concepts of Consumer Sovereignty', *Journal of Agricultural and Environmental Ethics*, 14: 201–15.

Krier, J. M. (2005), *Fairtrade in Europe 2005: Facts and Figures on Fairtrade in 25 European Countries*, Brussels: FINE/ Fairtrade Advocacy Office.

Low, W., and Davenport, E. (2005), 'Postcards from the Edge: Maintaining the "Alternative" Character of Fairtrade', *Sustainable Development*, 13: 143–53.

Lyon, S. (2006a), 'Evaluating Fairtrade Consumption: Politics, Defetishization and Producer Participation', *International Journal of Consumer Studies*, 30/5: 452–64.

Lyon, S. (2006b), 'Migratory Imaginations: The Commodification and Contradictions of Shade Grown Coffee', *Social Anthropology*, 14/3: 377–90.

Madeley, J. (2000), *Hungry for Trade: How the Poor Pay for Free Trade*, London: Zed Books.

Marx, K. (1961), *Capital: A Critical Analysis of Capitalist Production*, vol. 1, Moscow: Foreign Languages Publishing House.

McGregor, S. (2002), 'Consumer Citizenship: A Pathway to Sustainable Development?', Keynote at International Conference on Developing Consumer Citizenship, April, Hamar, Norway.

Munck, R. (2007), *Globalization and Contestation*, London: Routledge.

Murray, D. L., and Raynolds, L. T. (2007), 'Globalization and Its Antimonies: Negotiating a Fairtrade Movement', in L. T. Raynolds, D. Murray and J. Wilkinson (eds.), *Fairtrade: The Challenges of Transforming Globalization*, London: Routledge.

Newman, P. (2001), Transcript of interview at Cafédirect's London office, 14 December.

Nicholls, A. (2004), 'Fairtrade New Product Development', *The Service Industries Journal,* 24/2: 102–17.

Nicholls, A., and Opal, C. (2005), *Fairtrade: Market-driven Ethical Consumption,* London: Sage.

Oppenheim, P. (2005), 'Fairtrade Fat Cats', *The Spectator,* November, <http://www.igreens.org.uk/Fairtrade_fat_cats.htm> accessed 1 June 2008.

Raynolds, L. T. (2002), 'Consumer/Producer Links in Fairtrade Coffee Networks', *Sociologia Ruralis,* 42/4: 404–24.

Raynolds, L. T., and Long, M. A. (2007), 'Fair/Alternative Trade: Historical and Empirical Dimensions', in L. T. Raynolds, D. Murray and J. Wilkinson (eds.), *Fairtrade: The Challenges of Transforming Globalization,* London: Routledge.

Raynolds, L. T., Murray, D., and Taylor, P. L. (2004), 'Fairtrade Coffee: Building Producer Capacity via Global Networks', *Journal of International Development,* 16: 1109–21.

Reed, D. (2008), 'The Legitimacy of Fairtrade Certifying Bodies', Plenary paper presented at the 3rd Fairtrade International Symposium, FTIS, Montpellier, France, 14–16 May 2008.

Renard, M. R. (1999), 'The Interstices of Globalization: The Example of Fair Coffee', *Sociologia Ruralis,* 39/4: 484–500.

Robertson, R. (1992), *Globalization: Social Theory and Global Culture,* London: Sage

Scholte, J. A. (2000), *Globalization: A Critical Introduction,* Houndmills: Palgrave.

Shaw, D., McMaster, R., and Özcaglar-Toulouse, N. (2008), 'Voting for a Fairer World? The Myth of Ethical Consumption', paper presented at the 3rd Fairtrade International Symposium, FTIS, Montpellier, France, 14–16 May 2008.

Smith, S. (2008), 'For Love or Money? Fairtrade Business Models in the UK Supermarket Sector', paper presented at the 3rd Fairtrade International Symposium, FTIS, Montpellier, France, 14–16 May 2008.

Starr, A., and Adams, J. (2003), 'Anti-Globalization: The Global Fight for Local Autonomy', *New Political Science,* 25/1: 19–42.

Tallontire, A. (2000), 'Partnerships in Fairtrade: Reflections from a Case Study of Cafédirect', *Development in Practice,* 10/2: 166–77.

Taylor, P. L. (2002), *Poverty Alleviation through Participation in Fairtrade Coffee Networks: Synthesis of Case Study Research Question Findings,* New York: The Ford Foundation.

Utting-Chamorro, K. (2005), 'Does Fairtrade Make a Difference? The Case of Small Coffee Producers in Nicaragua', *Development in Practice,* 15/3–4: 584–99.

Watson, M. (2006), 'Towards a Polanyian Perspective on Fairtrade: Market-based Relationships and the Act of Ethical Consumption', *Global Society,* 20/4: 435–51.

Watson, M. (2007), 'Trade Justice and Individual Consumption Choices: Adam Smith's Spectator Theory and the Moral Constitution of the Fair Trade Consumer', *European Journal of International Relations,* 13/2: 263–88.

Whatmore, S., and Thorne, L. (1997), 'Nourishing Networks: Alternative Geographies of Food', in D. Goodman and M.J. Watts (eds.), *Globalising Food: Agrarian Questions and Global Restructuring,* London: Routledge.

Wright, C. (2004), 'Consuming Lives, Consuming Landscapes: Interpreting Advertisements for Cafédirect Coffees', *Journal of International Development,* 16: 665 80.

Part III
Food Globalizations:
Preparation and Consumption

The National and the Cosmopolitan in Cuisine: Constructing America through Gourmet Food Writing

Josée Johnston, Shyon Baumann
and *Kate Cairns*
University of Toronto

Introduction: Wither the Nation?

American gourmet culture is frequently described as being obsessed with the exotic other, much like a culinary version of *National Geographic* (Heldke, 2003: 18). Clearly, the exotic is a key element of the American foodscape. Recent research on gourmet food writing in the United States finds that exoticism is highly valued in food, not only serving as a status marker, but also working to broaden the culinary canon to include the food of non-Western cultures (Johnston and Baumann, 2007). Indeed, part of the food writer's job is to present new and unusual foods to his or her readership. With globalization processes accelerating processes of cultural and commodity exchange, once-exotic items like sushi are transformed into banalities for many Americans. The search for new, more exotic fare often necessitates travel to specific locations in order to delight readers keen on culinary adventure.

While the exotic is ubiquitous in American food writing, does this mean that a sense of the American nation constructed through food is absent? The analytic unit of the nation state may appear an archaic focus in an age of globalization, when commodities and cultures move fluidly across state borders, forming culinary diasporas in their wake. Scholars have not completely overlooked the relationship between food and the nation,[1] however, in the U.S. context, more attention is often paid to localized, subnational culinary traditions and the influence of exotic cuisines on domestic tastes. For example, renowned food scholar and anthropologist Sidney Mintz argues against the idea of a nationally defined American cuisine, suggesting that the term 'cuisine' more properly refers to ethnic and regional culinary traditions existing within the United States, like Cajun cuisine (Mintz, 1996: 94). Philosopher Lisa Heldke (2003) begins from a different starting point but similarly denies the idea that there is a strong culinary sense of a nation in the United States. Heldke's work on food adventurers critiques a neocolonial impulse to consume the other, and argues that an obsession with the exotic Other makes food adventurers blind to their own culinary traditions (Heldke, 2003: 58). Although we appreciate Mintz's point about the significance of regional American cooking and greatly admire Heldke's philosophical unpacking of food adventuring, we question whether the role of the nation in the American foodscape has been underestimated and whether a sense of nationhood is in part constructed, rather than obscured, by a culinary quest for the exotic.

In this chapter we take the question of the nation as an analytic jumping off point and investigate the construction of a national imaginary in American gourmet food writing. More specifically, we ask whether there is a dialectical and mutually constitutive relationship between the local–national imaginary and the global–cosmopolitan in the American foodscape. As Said (1978) demonstrated in his classic writing on the historic colonial relationship between East and West, European cultural constructions of the Orient produced a set of understandings and institutions that not only rendered the East 'primitive' and inferior but simultaneously built a sense of the colonial centre as rational and superior. Put differently, constructing the Other is also an identity project for the (neo)colonial core. The dialectic nature of this process leads us to ask whether contemporary culinary Othering occurs in tandem with the cultural construction of America as a nation—not simply in the sense of an explicitly articulated political philosophy but also in the more mundane, quotidian sense of communicating what it means to be American and eat American food.

With this question in mind, we approached the empirical topic of American gourmet food writing in magazines. In this data, we found both explicit and implicit illustrations of an American nation constructed through culinary discourse. This is not the unitary, 'container' version of nationhood associated with the Westphalian state system, but nationhood in a transnational era that enables a rapid flow of people, ideas and capital across national contexts—even as this era continues to rely on national imaginaries and state boundaries to regulate flows of labour and capital (Basch et al., 1994; Faist, 2004; Mahler, 1998; Portes et al., 1999). We argue that the relationship between the nation and exoticism in American gourmet cuisine is highly complex and represents a dialectic between the national and the cosmopolitan. The exotic Other helps frame a purified, rural white image of America as 'home' and simultaneously works to construct a cosmopolitan image of a sophisticated, worldly eater. Our investigation illustrates one way in which discourse is central to the social construction of an American nation and helps flesh out a national imaginary within the culinary field, where often none is thought to exist. It also sheds light on a common usage of the neutral, white, nonethnic 'we'—a subject position that presumes universal access and perpetuates the colonial notion that the culture of exotic Others exists to be explored and consumed (Heldke, 2003: 53).

The chapter proceeds as follows. First, we briefly review the literature on nations, nationalism and cosmopolitanism, drawing out its implications for the study of gourmet cuisine. We affirm the idea of nationalism not simply as a formal political ideology, but as a set of ideas that structure everyday lives, identities and cultural practices. We argue that ideas about the nation don't exist in isolation, but co-exist and intermingle with cosmopolitan aspirations to transcend the confines of the nation-state. Second, we explore nationalism and cosmopolitanism in the case of gourmet food writing found in four of the most popular American gourmet food magazines: *Bon Appétit, Saveur, Gourmet* and *Food & Wine*. Our sample is based on a close reading of all issues from 2004. We concentrate not only on the text of these magazines, but the messages implicit in the visual content as well. It is important to qualify that these magazines are written for a particularly affluent and educated audience (see Johnston and Baumann, 2007), and we acknowledge that the nation will be discursively constructed in varying ways for different audiences. From these sources, we suggest that American gourmet food culture implicitly and explicitly constitutes an image of the American nation, even as it draws from cosmopolitan norms, ideals and practices.

Context: Nations, Cosmopolitanism and American Cuisine

Flagging the Nation through Food

Anthropologists have long argued that an understanding of food and foodways provides a unique way of understanding belonging (Douglas, 1966; Levi-Strauss, 1963). More recent scholarship has emphasized how food represents not just cultural belonging but can play a role communicating exclusion and domination in national communities (e.g., Dupuis, 2002; Pilcher, 1998; Pillsbury, 1988). Just as most searches for identity involve an assertion of self as well as a differentiation of oneself from another (Benhabib, 1996: 3), our food tastes establish both what we will eat and what we will not eat (Belasco, 2002: 2). As Dupuis writes, 'eating mirrors the general racial politics of exclusion and inequality', and our understanding of the ideal diet 'mirrors the exclusions and dominations of white middle-class American society' (2006: 4). This chapter builds on food scholarship that connects food to the construction of national belonging and Otherness (e.g. Dupuis, 2002; Gabaccia, 1998; Parkhurst-Ferguson, 2004; Penfold, 2002; Pilcher, 1998; Wilk, 2002) but also seeks to engage with debates on the meanings of nationalism and cosmopolitanism in an era of globalization.

To understand how American food writing relates to America as a nation, we must begin by clarifying our use of the terms 'nation' and 'nationalism'—a difficult endeavour since minimal consensus exists on the origins of national sentiment (Anderson, 1991 [1983]; Brubaker, 1996; Hall, 1993; Hechter, 2000; McCrone, 1998). Just as the idea of a national cuisine is a modern notion (Belasco, 2002: 12), the idea of a national community is also understood as a modern notion that originated sometime in the late eighteenth century in the wake of the French revolution and that ascribed a universalistic sense of belonging to communities based on a shared sense of culture, language and identity (Calhoun, 1997; Smith, 1998). Anderson's (1991 [1983]) seminal work describes nations not as fixed identities rooted in essential characteristics but as socially constructed 'imagined communities', arguing that their rise was strongly linked to the development of print media that facilitated the construction of a national social imaginary. This perspective abandons concern about which national constructions are more or less 'real' and authentic (Renan, 1882) and directs scholarly attention towards the social processes that construct a sense of national belonging, as well as towards the idea that nation-building has an essential discursive dimension (Hall, 1996: 612; Wodak et al., 1999). Calhoun (1997: 3), for example, suggests that we understand the nation as a dynamic discursive formation—'a way of speaking that shapes our consciousness, but also is problematic enough that it keeps generating more issues and questions, keeps propelling us into further talk, keeps producing debates over how to think about it'.

In short, the nation can be understood as a socially constructed sense of belonging to national communities. The related concept of nationalism refers to the ideology and movements for defending the autonomy and identity of the national community (Smith, 2005).[2] Because it is not self-evident in the definitions of nation and nationalism, we emphasize here that the nation and nationalism are experienced and constituted through the mundane routines of everyday life. In common usage, the term 'nationalism' frequently evokes extreme examples like Nazi Germany or the ethnic nationalist warfare of war-torn Yugoslavia. Against the idea that nationalism is an idea confined to such extreme examples, or the formal political realm of states, Calhoun argues that 'to limit nationalism simply to a political doctrine ... is to narrow our understanding of it too much. It doesn't do justice to the extent to which nationalism and national identities shape our lives outside of explicitly political concerns' (1997: 11). Similarly, Billig (1995) suggests that traditional understandings of nationalism have tended to ignore the everyday symbols of nationalism that are often overlooked in the West. Billig introduces the useful concept of 'banal nationalism' to describe 'the ideological habits which enable the established nations of the West to be reproduced' (1995: 6). He argues that 'these habits are not removed from everyday life', but rather, on a daily basis 'the nation is indicated, or "flagged", in the lives of its citizenry. Nationalism, far from being an intermittent mood in established nations, is the endemic condition' (1995: 6). While banal nationalism often goes unnoticed, both in everyday life and in scholarly settings, Billig argues that it is essential to constructing a sense of national belonging, as well as creating a sense of where the nation fits within the larger global community of nations. While many globalization scholars have suggested that the significance of the nation state is on the decline (e.g., Featherstone and Lash, 1995: 2; Soysal, 2000), Billig insists that nations are still being reproduced on a daily basis, although often in ways that seem ordinary and commonsensical (Billig, 1995: 8–9).[3]

Relating Billig's conceptualization of banal nationalism to cuisine, food scholars from various disciplines have drawn a connection between food and constructions of national identity. Penfold (2002) argues, for instance, that the mass-produced Tim Horton's donut connotes an important, albeit ironic, sense of Canadian national identity. What emerges from studies of national cuisines is not the excavation of a pure or authentic sense of national cuisine that has existed for time immemorial. Instead, we learn that foods are labelled as 'national' through contestation and effort, just like nation-building more generally. Today, national culinary projects occur in a context shaped by numerous facets of globalization processes—like the multinational corporation that currently owns Tim Horton's, a key symbol of Canadian national identity, or the transnational tourist trade and Belizean diasporas that are key to understanding the construction of national cuisine in Belize (Wilk, 2002). Understanding the interplay between food and the nation requires not an insular approach but an appreciation of larger processes at work, and this brings us to the topic of cosmopolitanism.

Cosmopolitanism: An Openness to Eating the Other

Following Billig, we contend that the idea of the nation and national identity are structured by the banalities of everyday lives in advanced industrialized states like the United States. This argument can be taken one step further and extended to cosmopolitanism. This means that cosmopolitanism, like nationalism, can be understood not simply as an abstract political philosophy but as a social construction that is shaped through the banality of everyday acts and interactions, including dining, cooking and eating.[4] While cosmopolitanism is a fundamentally contested concept, like nationalism, we can begin our discussion by understanding it in rudimentary terms as a way of thinking and acting that emphasizes global belonging, global identities and globalized moral commitments.[5] Interest in cosmopolitanism is not historically new, but the space-time compression of globalization processes has brought heightened concern and attention for its normative ideals and empirical possibilities at the global scale, such as global human rights, global warming and global civil society. As Featherstone (1993: 169) writes, 'The flows of information, knowledge, money, commodities, people and images have intensified to the extent that the sense of spatial distance which separated and insulated people from the need to take into account all the other people which make up what has become known as humanity has become eroded'.

It might first appear that nationalism and cosmopolitanism are polar opposites and that the presence of one precludes the existence of the other. Indeed, contemporary theories of cosmopolitanism are frequently understood as anti-nationalist or anti-nation, posing a vision of power, social structures and normative ideals that are deterritorialized and that supersede state boundaries. However, Calhoun reminds us of the historic interpenetration of nationalism and cosmopolitanism that is instructive for contemporary scholarship. Calhoun writes: '[i]t may be hard to remember today, when we associate nationalism with "backward" claims to ethnic localism, but from the 1780s to the 1870s [nationalism] flourished as a liberal, cosmopolitan discourse emphasizing the freedom of all peoples' (1997: 86). In fact, in eighteenth-century Europe, the question of how to make concrete enlightenment ideals was frequently answered through the ideology of nations and nationalism (Calhoun, 1997: 89). The cosmopolitan ideal was connected to an emerging sense of nation as a political polity, now understood as civic nationalism, and was challenged by those who saw nations in more primordial, ethnic terms (Calhoun, 1997: 89)

The historic interpenetration of nationalism and cosmopolitanism is relevant to contemporary debates for at least two reasons. First, postcolonial scholarship emphasizes that understandings of the Other are inextricably linked to understandings of the self (hooks, 1992; Longley, 2000; Mohanty, 1997; Muppidi, 2004; Narayan, 1997; Said, 1978). Put differently, social constructions of national belonging are not formed in isolation but are constructed through an idea of who is excluded and who is Other. Recent work on nationalism and cosmopolitanism has not necessarily drawn from these postcolonial viewpoints but has argued for an interpenetration of nationalism and cosmopolitanism (Beck and Sznaider, 2006: 8).[6] Kwame Anthony Appiah claims that nationalism and cosmopolitanism are inextricably intertwined and argues for a rooted cosmopolitanism, or cosmopolitan patriotism which recognizes that people are rooted in specific places, at the same time they may interact with a cosmopolitan world of 'migration, nomadism, diaspora' (1998: 91).

Second and from a more materialist perspective, we argue that gourmet food culture serves to construct the nation through processes of banal nationalism, while simultaneously displaying cosmopolitan traits. Put simply, contemporary gourmet food culture in the United States is both local and national, as well as global and cosmopolitan, and to deny either end of this spectrum would be empirically erroneous. At least since the late 1960s, as well as in earlier periods (Gabaccia, 1998), American gourmet food culture has been profoundly interested in eating and cooking the food of the exotic Other. In this specific context, we can understand cosmopolitanism as representing the desire for global cultural and culinary exchange, as well as the reality that food (like most commodities) flows rapidly across national borders through heightened processes of global trade and cultural exchange that characterize the globalization period. In terms of gourmet food culture and cosmopolitanism, we emphasize that the neocolonial dimensions of culinary adventuring are not simply dissolved in the face of cultural fluidity and commodity mobility. Even though culinary cosmopolitans may consume exotic cuisines with greater consciousness about the relative race and class privilege they enjoy, this reflexivity is not guaranteed and awareness alone does not dissolve privilege or power inequalities.[7] Narayan emphasizes 'the fact that mainstream eaters ... remain privileged consumers, benefiting from the structural inequalities and unpleasant material realities that often form the contexts in which 'ethnic food' is produced and consumed' (1997: 182). Narayan's words remind us that nationalism and cosmopolitanism are not only shaped by ideas and traditions but by material structures and power relations that exist within and across the state boundaries of the United States. The United States's geopolitical and economic power in the world system facilitates access for its gourmet citizens to the world's culinary delicacies.

In sum, the nation is not snuffed out by globalization processes and the associated space given to cosmopolitan practices and ideals. Instead, the nation retains its viability by linking local lives to global processes (Calhoun, 1997: 94). We suggest that a sense of the American nation need not be seen as antithetical to a cosmopolitan culinary terrain. Instead, we contend that there is a dialectical relationship between the national and the cosmopolitan in the construction of gourmet food identities. These identities are flagged not simply through overt political statements but through the banality and material realities of everyday life, including food practices. We now turn to the subject of food writing to see how these themes operate in practice.

The National and the Cosmopolitan in Gourmet Food Writing

To investigate American nationalism and cosmopolitanism in food writing, we approached U.S. gourmet magazines with the following questions: First, what does American gourmet writing say about the American nation and cosmopolitanism—especially in light of racial, ethnic and class divides at the national and global scale? Second, how does gourmet food writing help construct a sense of who is a citizen of the imagined community and who is an Other?

By addressing these questions, this analysis details several ways in which gourmet food writing contributes to America's national imaginary. We explore the explicit rhetoric used to characterize a sense of national holiday cuisine and American 'classics', as well as the implicit constructions of the nation that are cultivated through portraits of rural America. We then demonstrate how discursive boundaries are reinforced by depictions of various Others who, while residing within the geographical borders of the United States, are projected outside of the imagined nation. Finally, we consider how the American nation is complicated by discourses of cosmopolitanism, which produce the American citizen as sophisticated and open-minded through the savouring of foreign delicacies in their authentic contexts.

Emerging from these overlapping discourses, we find that there are five themes contributing to the national/cosmopolitan dialectic in gourmet food writing; two of these themes are explicit presentations of American cuisine, whereas three of the themes operate at a more implicit level. The two explicit themes—holiday food and American classics—are supported by three implicit themes: portraits of rural America, portraits of Others in America and portraits of American cosmopolitans. By tracing the discursive interplay among these distinct but interdependent themes in food writing, we demonstrate how notions of cosmopolitanism intermingle with constructions of the American nation in gourmet food writing.

Holiday Food

In gourmet food writing, national holidays mark distinct occasions on which food is explicitly tied to celebrations—and therefore definitions—of the American nation. Unsurprisingly, nationalist imagery and rhetoric is most explicitly presented surrounding Independence Day festivities. The July issues of gourmet food magazines present an array of patriotic images—vintage Fourth of July postcards show rosy-cheeked children waving the American flag (*Bon Appétit*, July 2004: 64) and a fair-haired family sitting at picnic tables enjoy a festive barbeque amidst the stars-and-stripes pinwheels that speckle their lush green lawn (*Food & Wine*, July 2004: 184). While such nationalist symbols are embedded within a well-defined ritual, they are not rigidly confined to one day. Indeed, the suggestion that a set of red, white and blue patterned napkins are 'perfect for July 4th—and every summer barbeque after that' (*Bon Appétit*, July 2004: 64), effectively normalizes this patriotic imagery within the daily routines of gourmet cooking.

According to gourmet food writing, the July 4th holiday extends an opportunity, or perhaps an obligation, for gourmands to honour American cuisine. Readers are encouraged to 'let the sparks fly with a menu that celebrates regional flavors from across the U.S.A' (*Bon Appétit*, July 2004, 68). We are told of 'a former farm boy turned world-class chef', who 'returns every summer to spend the Fourth of July with his parents' (*Food & Wine*, July 2004: 184). Within this sentimental article, patriotic duty is discursively articulated through narratives of coming 'home', as even a well-travelled world-class chef is depicted as honouring the roots of his American heritage. The July 4th barbeque is not just the fare of local patriots; with this ritualized meal, cosmopolitan citizens are reminded that they too have a responsibility to wave the American flag, if America is the place they call 'home'. However, these festivities are not uniformly inclusive. Visual representations of the Independence Day feast in our sample of gourmet food writing repeatedly feature the white, nuclear family. The range of people featured is drastically narrower in terms of race and ethnicity than the range of actual Americans. The reason for this lack of diversity is probably related to the tailoring of stories to particular audiences. However, the message created by a consistent link between the celebration of a national holiday and an ethnically narrow range of American people is independent of any intent on the part of the producers of gourmet discourse. The lack of an association between minorities and national self-definition in gourmet discourse creates a type of 'symbolic annihilation' (Tuchman, 1978) where visible minorities are excluded from the national imaginary.

While lacking the patriotic imagery of a July 4th barbeque, representations of American Thanksgiving rival those of Independence Day in overt articulations of the American nation and U.S. nationalism. The dominant discourse conveys a shared culinary experience in which one's membership within the imagined nation is reflected through one's relationship to food. The traditional Thanksgiving feast is represented as a universal feature in the lives of citizens, for 'common wisdom has it that Thanksgiving is the one day on which all Americans sit down to essentially the same meal' (*Gourmet,* November 2004: 103). As one well-known chef states matter-of-factly, 'there comes a time in every adult's life when he or she must cook a Thanksgiving turkey … If it hasn't happened to you yet, it's coming' (*Bon Appétit,* November 2004: 112). This directive assures readers of their inevitable participation within this ritual, thus naturalizing a practice that is culturally specific. Excluded are citizens who do not identify with the culinary duty of cooking a turkey, a possibility so foreign that it is not even acknowledged within the magazines. As 'our most American holiday' (*Gourmet,* November 2004: 192), Thanksgiving is presented as a natural fact of (American) life.

While the custom of cooking a Thanksgiving turkey is preserved as a sacred rite, there is flexibility regarding the other components of this holiday meal. Here, we see the national imaginary inscribed with cosmopolitan elements. Gourmet food magazines actively encourage readers to incorporate 'an innovative side dish' that strays from the old standards of corn and mashed potatoes, as 'flavors from around the world will bring new life to [the] holiday table' (*Gourmet,* November 2004: 103). While the canonical elements of the Thanksgiving meal remain unchanged, ethnic ingredients are added as spices to diversify and add cosmopolitan sophistication to the palate. Americans' eagerness to incorporate such 'contemporary' additions into their most traditional feast is framed as a reflection of the nation's embrace of diversity. Readers are asked to ponder, 'what could be more appropriate on this uniquely American holiday than borrowing from the traditions of others?' (*Gourmet,* November 2004: 103). Rather than acknowledging that many Americans *are* the 'others' referred to, a distinction between Americans and Others is reinforced through the foods identified with each group. However, Americans are also free to cross this divide. Thus, the understanding of the quintessential American Thanksgiving is refined within discourses of cosmopolitanism. As one food writer explains, 'The traditional Thanksgiving meal in our family remains a work in progress. It is surely all-American: Chinese water chestnuts and sesame oil, Hungarian paprika, Jewish challah, wine from Madeira, a California turkey and, once in a while, a French truffle. What a fitting way to give thanks for this melting pot of a country' (*Saveur,* November 2004: 86)

Gourmet food writing honours the American melting pot through a Thanksgiving feast that incorporates diverse culinary influences; a recipe for 'multicultural stuffing' lies alongside a full-page image of a steaming golden turkey. This discursive move is a complex one, for the cosmopolitan Thanksgiving does not replace the nationalist sentiment that defines this tradition, but rather, it is embedded within the national imaginary. An additional article exemplifies this dialectic. Titled 'Pilgrims

Progress', it begins as follows: 'New England is steeped in culinary tradition. After all, the region is the home of the original Thanksgiving feast. But America is the land of reinvention and that impulse shapes even this most traditional of dinners' (*Bon Appétit*, November 2004: 158). This article incorporates the colonial history of the feast even as it celebrates is reinvention. The multicultural Thanksgiving is situated within a linear progression from the original colonial encounter, but this effect is contradictory because its reinvention is prompted by a cosmopolitan embrace of multicultural cuisine. The contradictory features of this multicultural feast are born of the national/cosmopolitan dialectic, as genuine efforts to incorporate diverse influences within a core American tradition have the unintended effect of legitimizing colonial processes in the nation's narrative.

Within gourmet food writing, explicit expressions of nationalism are not limited to festive occasions. In the next section, we describe how the nation is constituted through everyday American cuisine. These foods lack the distinctive appeal of a special holiday occasion; in fact, their significance derives from their quotidian qualities, which allows them to function as symbols of a shared American experience.

American Classics

Within the mundane rituals of daily living, Americans perform their membership in the imagined community by consuming classic foods, which are inscribed as normal ways of eating. Gourmet food writing contributes to the discursive construction of belonging by including the reader within references to familiar 'classics'. We take pride in 'our country of great steak' (*Saveur*, October 2004: 112) and agree that 'chicken potpie is the kind of comfort food most of us crave but rarely have the time to make' (*Saveur*, January/February 2004: 38). We are familiar with 'America's quintessential summer menu ... [of] burgers, corn on the cob, ripe tomatoes and berries' (*Food & Wine*, August 2004: 19) and can appreciate the pressures of growing up in a town where 'pie-baking mastery was practically a prerequisite for entry into heaven' (*Gourmet*, October 2004: 219). Well versed in American discourses of egalitarianism, the culinary discourse frames a nation free of inequality and social boundaries, a world where 'truckers, cowboys and Los Angeles socialites converge at [an] unpretentious roadside steak house' (*Food & Wine*, May 2004: 152). In gourmet food writing, the appeal of a classic American dish such as steak is presented as residing 'deep in the American psyche' (*Gourmet*, November 2004: 50) and thus is naturalized as though it were innate, rather than a cultural practice.

Visual components of the text reinforce a sense of community built around common foods, as representations of 'classic' American cuisine are steeped in patriotic imagery. In an article titled 'Our Daily Bread', a photo from the National Cornbread Festival depicts the fair's regal welcome banner, which hangs on a streetlight above an American flag. The caption reads: 'A festival in Tennessee celebrates the ultimate (and original) American loaf' (*Saveur,* April 2004: 31). Photos sprinkled throughout this American tale depict a happy community of white residents honouring their heritage by participating in the festivities of cornbread. In one image, a plump woman with permed hair, hoop earrings, heavy blush and wearing an American flag t-shirt shows a fierce competitive spirit within the cornbread-eating contest. Although readers may never attend such an occasion, as members of the national community they are invited to identify with this scene and various others, as each 'serves up a big slice of American life' (*Saveur,* December 2004: 24). Whether celebrated through boisterous festivities, or idealized as a source of comfort, 'normal' foods are constructed as symbols of the American essence and are integral to the social practices through which citizens identify themselves as members of the national community.

Sometimes the status of American 'classic' is justified because of a food's historical location within national narratives. For example, the growing popularity of pork in gourmet food circles is viewed through a historical lens, as 'pork kept America well fed when we were still a country of farmers' (*Food & Wine,* November 2004: 189). Similarly, the appeal of ranch dressing, 'the most popular salad dressing in America', is explained as a result of its authentic origins, for it was 'first concocted—it is perhaps surprising to learn, in this day of made-up brand legends—at an actual ranch' (*Saveur,* June/July 2004: 36). In this way, gourmet food writing secures particular foods within the national imaginary by narrating them into American history.

Because this rhetoric incorporates a sense of nostalgia, these accounts may erase histories of violence that mark America's past. Within the 'storied history of cornbread in America', for example, this classic dish is mythologized as the product of congenial colonial relations: 'American Indians taught European settlers to make corn pone, the predecessor of these breads, by mixing meal ground from corn ... with salt and water, wrapping it in leaves or corn husks and baking it over an open fire' (*Saveur,* April 2004: 31). Stories like this one portray an imperial encounter as a friendly social and culinary exchange between two cultures with equal social, economic and political power. As these narratives circulate within America's public memory, they obscure the histories of conquest that continue to structure unequal power relations within the United States. One indicator of this discursive effect is the virtual absence of current representations of aboriginals within gourmet food magazines. Within the national imaginary, aboriginal peoples are relegated to the realm of history, where they perform a crucial role in the narrative of national progress. Positioned at the heart of these legends, classic American foods provide citizens access to their shared heritage, just as 'every batch of corn bread made in whatever fashion ... connects to the past and honors tradition' (*Saveur,* April 2004: 33). Readers are invited to pay tribute to the nation by consuming the foods of their collective history—a history that sends subtle messages to communicate who is and is not a member of the national community.

From classic historic dishes to current culinary trends, gourmet food magazines produce detailed accounts of America's eating habits and do so within a discursive frame that takes for granted the existence of a national community. Writers map the 'contours of the American food landscape' (*Gourmet,* July 2004: 16) through consumer surveys, restaurant profiles and national awards. While this knowledge is disseminated through a variety of strategies, the discourse is frequently and consistently framed at the level of the nation (rather than more universally). What is celebrated is not simply the best food on offer, but the best food *in America.* Features such as 'Ten Years of Food in America' (*Saveur,* October 2004: 82) catalogue the country's recent food history, while the annual 'How America Eats' survey invites readers to 'savor America's revealing epicurean diary' (*Bon Appétit,* February 2004: 69). The 'American Food and Entertaining Awards' honour the 'best and brightest members of the culinary community'—a community that is defined at the national level (*Bon Appétit,* October 2004: 29). These discursive mappings not only mark the nation as referent but also produce portraits that communicate national ideals. For example, *Food & Wine*'s list of 'America's best new chefs' in 2004 included nine men and one woman, all light-skinned and all dressed in expensive-looking clothing (July, 2004). Contrary to claims that the nation is irrelevant within a globalized world, gourmet food magazines consistently frame culinary trends within the state-bound imagined community, and in doing so reproduce an ideal member who reflects the prevailing raced, classed and gendered relations of power that organize American society.

Of course, American classics are not untouched by global cuisine and here too discourses of nationalism and cosmopolitanism intermingle. Even the beloved American steak is enhanced with a series of 'global rubs' inspired by seasonings from India, Jamaica, Mexico, Morocco and Thailand (*Food & Wine,* June 2004: 66). As a food writer reflects upon one chef's expertise in merging 'different inspirations on one plate', he concludes that, in fact, 'there's nothing more American than that' (*Food & Wine,* June 2004: 56). Much like the multicultural Thanksgiving, classic American dishes are infused with cosmopolitan sophistication. Sometimes this transformation is named outright, such as when 'all-American sweets from layer cake to apple pie meet very cosmopolitan ingredients like lemongrass, quince and crème fraiche' (*Bon Appétit,* January 2004: 102). As these enticing flavours revive American classics with contemporary flare, they make a complicated entry into nationalist discourses; here, the cosmopolitan sophistication of American eaters becomes the defining mark of inclusion within the imagined community.

To this point, the analysis has described the explicit constructions of nationalism that permeate gourmet food writing. Within the categories of holiday cuisine and American 'classics', the nation is explicitly constituted through foods, both extraordinary and ordinary in kind. We now explore *implied* meanings that are embedded within stories and images of American cuisine. Three implicit themes within food writing contribute to understandings of the nation: portraits of rural America, portraits of others in America and portraits of American cosmopolitans. Many of the examples in these categories do not name the nation outright, but each uses food to communicate something about what it means to be American.

Portraits of Rural America

While gourmet food tends to be associated with the sophisticated, urban palate, epicurean tales are not reserved for the fast life of the metropolis. In fact, gourmet magazines take frequent forays into the country, a discursive move which integrates the rural imaginary into the larger construction of the national state. Through romanticized portraits of rural America, readers discover remote eateries 'where the welcome is warm and the flavor is regional' (*Gourmet,* October 2004: 103). We are invited to reflect upon the 'simple pleasures' of farm life, such as 'picking fresh greens from the garden [and] gathering eggs from the henhouse' (*Saveur,* June/July 2004: 28). Accompanying these narratives are images of green fields, roaming livestock and happy, peaceful people who are tough enough to live the rustic life but sheltered from the harsh realities of the city. This purified white image of rural America invites readers to come 'home' and experience the goodness of 'Mama's cooking' (*Saveur,* June/July 2004: 28).

These countryside portraits often feature rural festivities where locals congregate around classic American foods. In one story, we venture to Ole Miss campus, 'the site of the most famous tailgating party in America', where 'Southern picnic staples like fried chicken and potato salad' are laid out upon red, white and blue tablecloths alongside 'good old American layer cakes' (*Saveur,* October 2004: 109). In another, we are introduced to the 2003 National Cherry Queen, a young blonde woman who is crowned with a sparkling tiara and who sits atop a red float and smiles broadly to crowds of supporters. On the next page, we relive the personal transformation of a scantily clad teenage girl, who reconnects with her youthful innocence after winning the National Cherry Festival's pie-eating contest: 'All of a sudden she looks much less like Britney Spears and much more like a happy young girl … a living illustration … of what cherry eating can bring about in all of us' (*Saveur,* June/July 2004: 61). Through narratives such as this one, rural living is depicted as a haven of wholesome American values. Even as it sometimes seems to poke fun at 'simple' folks and country living, gourmet food writing idealizes this lifestyle as the heart of the American nation.

As a safe haven for national values, the American countryside is a fountain of nostalgia for the days and eats of yesteryear. Similar to the way in which 'classic' American foods are embedded within narratives of the nation's past, rural America is idealized as a pristine space of preserved history where 'rampant success and expansion have not obliterated the joys of this rambling, vine-clad country idyll' (*Gourmet,* April 2004: 162). Laughing children sit atop a tractor as their wind-blown hair catches rays of sunlight; a middle-aged woman leans her back against the soft surface of a sturdy haystack, while her faithful dog sniffs the ground nearby. Portrayed in black and white, these images project rural inhabitants into the past. Some visions of country living provoke a sense of loss, as when 'the potent smoke flavor, woodsy and sharply sweet, of the pepper-rubbed beef … tastes of campfires, cattle drives and the state's vanishing rural past' (*Gourmet,* October 2004: 108). Just as 'classic' American dishes are discursively located within a shared psyche, this longing for the rural idyll is attributed to 'a primal hunger deep in all of us' (*Gourmet,* October 2005: 108).

As country cooking is framed within memories of true American living, it evokes nostalgic visions of conquering the frontier. Beside the worn image of a Colorado log cabin, we are assured that 'it's the sour cream apple pie that you'll remember, along with the quiet splendour of a frontier fireside' (*Gourmet,* October 2004: 126). A Kansas rancher who 'keeps it small, local and organic', works her farm on the very site 'where the beginning of the final westward trek began'; now, however, 'only a wind-beaten covered wagon and picnic table mark the spot' (*Gourmet,* July 2004: 86). These memories of 'no-frills eating' remind readers of their modest origins; this is 'food that creates a bridge between the eaters and the land, food that tells you where you are' (*Gourmet,* June 2004: 126). Through these romantic visions, readers are invited to form an authentic bond with the vast rural landscape and to cultivate their own citizenship identities on the nation's soil.

Memories of the frontier are cast with predictable characters in the national narrative, and cowboys perform a starring role within portrayals of the rural foodscape. Readers journey to remote getaways, where 'congregants in cowboy hats and shirtsleeves gather for unaffected Texas fare at mismatched wooden tables in a former barn' (*Gourmet,* October 2004: 108). At the 'self-proclaimed cowboy capital of the world', customers indulge in 'legendary' cuisine while perched upon 'barstools [that] are literally a row saddles' (*Food & Wine,* May 2004: 152). As if these enchanting descriptions are not enough, the visual imagery provided through photography makes a vivid impression for the reader: a man in chaps and a cowboy hat, leather reins in callused hands, leans his back against a rustic log cabin; a pale girl smiles from beneath the brim of a straw hat; her dark hair falls upon the shoulders of her denim shirt; the warm glow of a cobblestone fireplace casts light upon a deer head that is mounted on the wall of a country diner (*Food & Wine,* August 2004: 113). As readers consume the country cooking within each charming tale and nostalgic image, they actively reproduce America's collective memory.

Lest readers worry that the rural idyll is reserved for the rustic adventurer, increasingly popular are country experiences that are framed as catering to more sophisticated gourmet sensibilities. Again, the cosmopolitan sensibility is not located externally to the national imaginary but is intricately interwoven within the story of a rural homeland. The upscale rural getaway is 'all about saddle leather and feather beds, fly-fishing and fine dining', and promises epicureans a 'stylish Wild West fantasy' with a 'different kind of cowboy cuisine' (*Food & Wine,* August 2004: 112). At one Texas ranch where 'blissful seclusion is guaranteed', a husband and wife team treat their guests to 'haute-cowboy dishes' made with local ingredients, like 'Davis Mountain venison stuffed with jackrabbit' (*Food & Wine,* January 2004: 81). These extravagant retreats unite the rural romantic with the cosmopolitan sophistication of urban elites, a fusion that satisfies the appetite for 'city chic and small-town charm' (*Bon Appétit,* August 2004: 95). The food itself reflects this urban/rural synthesis, as 'country tart meets city topping; the streusel is revved up with nutty-tasting brown butter' (*Bon Appétit,* January 2004: 106). As the appeal catches on, this transformation works both ways: while classic country cooking undergoes a cosmopolitan makeover, urban chefs re-imagine their 'most sophisticated dishes in their equally delicious and rustic incarnations' (*Food & Wine,* May 2004: 158). The sophisticated rural dining experience is yet another site in which nationalist imagery engages with cosmopolitan discourses, preserving America's rustic ideal even as its citizens assume a sophisticated self-image.

Portraits of Others in America

In addition to depicting national rituals, shared habits and collective histories, gourmet food writing contributes to the construction of the American nation through representations of various others. Co-existing within the same geographical spaces, yet positioned with varying degrees of access to the imagined boundaries of the nation, these groups help to define the identity of national citizens through their very *difference* from the American ideal. Within detailed descriptions of 'foreign' culinary customs, ethnic populations within the United States are essentialized as homogeneous groupings with stable, fixed identities. Readers learn that 'the Polish would be lost without Polish sausage' and that 'in Louisiana, you can't be a Cajun if you don't eat boudin' (*Gourmet,* September 2004: 132). Within these essentialized representations, ethnicity is often overlaid with classed connotations, such as when an Italian family ritual is fuelled by a 'trunkful of cheap jug wine' (*Saveur,* January/ February 2004: 29). In contrast, when a young Indian couple throws a party for a few friends, the 'exotic food' sits atop a 'gorgeous table' that is covered with jewels and elegant candles—photography and language that evokes Orientalist imagery of enchanting people eating exotic foreign dishes (*Bon Appétit,* October 2004, 140). In further contrast, a writer reflects upon the good old days in New York's lower east side and suggests that it 'may be cleaner and safer now, but everything was a lot simpler when the Jews and Puerto Ricans lived there' (*Bon Appétit,* September 2004: 97). With this framing, racialized groups are constructed as an implicit but external counterpoint to white America. This is reproduced in a filmmaker's account of his first experience in a Cajun dance hall, where 'no one spoke any English and the waiters wore revolvers' (*Gourmet,* September 2004: 130). In the description of how this filmmaker 'uses cuisine as a backstage pass to other ethnic worlds', the article consigns racialized citizens to distant communities. By delineating the contours of these other 'worlds', gourmet food writing reproduces the imagined boundaries of the white, 'nonethnic' American nation.

Food stories of ethnic Others also operate as a source of national pride within romantic narratives of the immigrant experience. For example, there is an emotional tale of one family's journey from humble beginnings to the top of a 'Mexican food empire'; happily, they 'never had to worry about money again' (*Saveur*, March 2004: 82). We are encouraged to read the memoirs of kitchen philosopher Angelo Pellegrini, 'a vibrant, curious family man and educator who was forever a food-loving Italian immigrant and an embodiment of the American Dream' (*Gourmet*, July 2004: 103). We learn that 'in immigrant settlements, it is always food that defines the community' (*Gourmet*, December 2004: 193) and are invited to taste the creations of our poor but resourceful new neighbours. The fact that the Chinese condiment *chow-chow* was brought to America by Chinese railroad workers is presented as a happy story of shared cultural traditions, while the brutal exploitation of these immigrant workers is left unmentioned (*Saveur*, December 2004: 91). Through these narratives of newfound prosperity, the white American citizen is constructed as the generous host who willingly shares the nation's wealth and who in turn is given access to the other's culinary treasures. In the words of one gourmand: 'I was seated at a table so small, in a room so tightly packed that I felt a kinship to all who had journeyed to America in steerage, seeking a new life' (*Bon Appétit*, September 2004: 84). These narratives, each centring upon food, define the immigrant experience as one of prosperity, shared customs and companionship and work to frame a proud image of the American nation.

As gourmet food writing discursively maps the contours of the nation, it also delineates the divisions between the white American reader and the ethnic Other. This process often operates through subtle differences in pronouns, addressing *you*, the reader (assumed to be the white, neutral Archimedean vantage point) and referring to *them*, the Other. Consider the discussion of popular 'ethnic' cuisines within *Bon Appétit*'s annual survey on American eating habits: 'Variety is not only the spice of life, it's also the key to your dining habits. Italian and French may be perennial faves, but these other cuisines draw you out and into their restaurants' (*Bon Appétit*, February 2004: 70). Statements like this one define 'you', the (white) reader, by your appetite for 'their' food. In extreme cases, tantalizing descriptions of foreign cuisines present racialized individuals as just another tempting dish. One article describes how 'local Japanese families gather over bubbling copper pots of *shabu-shabu*', and invites readers to 'join them at one of the long, diagonal tables and use your chopsticks to pick at oily-sweet tuna cheeks or creamy, smoky pumpkin' (*Bon Appétit*, August 2004: 52). Once again, 'you' are invited to eat alongside 'them' for an authentic dining experience.

For the most part, these distinctions are implicit within the text; rarely are race-based patterns of social organization named outright. The one exception within our sample is the Ole Miss tailgating party. After characterizing the attendees as 'a big, fun-loving, hearty-eating family', the author notes that this picnic remains an exclusively white affair. As one alumnus explains, 'White folks wouldn't mind Groving with black folks … But it's hard to be the first black family to go into the Grove and set up your tent. So far, few black folks are doing it and no white folks are going out to invite black folks in' (*Saveur,* October 2004: 106). The author shrugs off this segregation as the result of social awkwardness that will be remedied with time, suggesting that 'as blacks become part of the history of the university, Groving will become a more integrated event'. So even in those rare cases where race is named, divisions are normalized and the possibility of rac*ism* is excluded from the discussion. Yet, as exoticized depictions of 'ethnic' cuisines promise to reveal the 'margins of American societies' (*Gourmet,* September 2004: 131), the position of the white 'nonethnic' citizen is secured within the nation's core.

Portraits of American Cosmopolitans

While a notion of the American nation is both constructed and celebrated throughout these texts, we emphasize that gourmet food magazines remain geared toward the cosmopolitan eater. Not surprisingly, national constructions are overlaid with cosmopolitan connotations and these magazines devote much attention to the sophisticated palate of the American citizenry. The country's urban centres are consistently imbued with a high degree of global refinement, such as in a glowing restaurant review of the Zuni Cafe, which states that 'idiosyncrasy and diversity are hallmarks of Zuni—and of San Francisco' (*Saveur,* August 2004: 76). As 'a globe-trotting cooking teacher serves up delicious new pastas at his New England retreat', readers scrutinize the blend of international flavours that inspire each tantalizing dish (*Bon Appétit,* March 2004: 100). We take pride in the impeccable performance of the White House head chef, who welcomed 'counterparts from 30 nations' to feast at the world leaders' favourite food festival (*Saveur,* November 2004: 14). And we admire the elegant dinner prepared by two young professionals who exhibit stunning 'international flair' and are the very embodiment of cosmopolitanism: 'Florencia is from Argentina, Brian is from Michigan and they met at a wedding in Mexico' (*Bon Appétit,* February 2004: 94). This analysis does not deny the importance of a cosmopolitan respect for cultural diversity. We argue, however, that discourses of diversity as they appear in gourmet food writing also trade on the value of multiculturalism to bolster the cosmopolitan character of American identity for the white mainstream. Inclusivity, then, serves not just to include but also to define a sophisticated version of the nation.

While honouring multicultural values, gourmet food magazines imagine and naturalize a cosmopolitan American reader who possesses considerable economic and cultural capital. In a tribute to a famed Manhattan dining establishment that offered 'glorious food and impeccable hospitality to the most famous people in the world', the reader is invited to imagine the area one century ago: 'You might spend the afternoon here shopping at Tiffany's ... [and] in the evening, you could take in an opera at the Academy of Music' (*Saveur,* 74 2004: 87). These highly exclusive practices are naturalized through an assumption of the reader's affluence. The article goes on to describe the area as 'a neighbourhood where the classes mixed—a single example of the wondrous diversity upon which New York thrives' (88). As the article crafts a romantic vision of a community that transcended class divisions, gourmet readers are framed at the top of this supposedly fluid social hierarchy, while their own positive self-image is upheld through the nation's imagined egalitarianism.

American gourmands do not limit their spending to local cuisine, for even greater amounts of wealth are normalized through the assumed transnational mobility of the reader. In addition to the innumerable stories that depict American cosmopolitans overseas, this assumption is also conveyed through memories of global culinary adventures. Consider this leading caption: 'If you're the sort of traveler who remembers Paris for its profiteroles, Rome for its bucatini and Bangkok for its meek rob, these food-focused trips to culinary hot spots around the world will suit your summer travel plans' (*Bon Appétit,* June 2004: 28). The suggestion is that gourmet readers can freely recall first-hand experiences with an assortment of distant cuisines and have the economic capital to comfortably imagine future global culinary escapades. One editor journeys through the tastes that have imprinted upon her own travel memoirs, including 'tender little crabs marinated in chile-spiked rice wine that I ate in a tin-roofed shack in Bangkok with the rain thundering against the metal like music' (*Gourmet,* May 2004: 24). She characterizes the magazine's followers as 'the most adventurous eaters in the world' and acknowledges that while 'you', the reader, may have 'already been everywhere on earth', she hopes to 'have found a few new flavors you have yet to discover'. While this assumed mobility has obvious class implications, the depiction of the unfettered cosmopolitan traveller also involves whiteness as an unmarked referent, particularly since racialized groups are especially vulnerable to surveillance regimes (Lyon, 2003; Walby, 2005). Thus, an examination of the national/cosmopolitan dialectic in the context of culinary tourism makes visible the privileged position of a particular kind of American citizen within the system of global capitalism.

Conclusion

Although a large amount of scholarly attention has been paid to food in the United States, there has been scant attention given to the construction of national identity through food and culinary discourse. Our reading of a broad sample of gourmet food writing, however, reveals a strongly defined portrait of the American nation. Among many other cultural resonances present in this discourse, themes of the nation and nationalism are salient.

This finding has several important implications. First, scholars of food and nationalism should be in closer dialogue with respect to the American case. The American culinary field appears to us to be an important site for the construction of nationalist ideals, and at the same time long-standing nationalist ideals, interwoven as they are with cosmopolitanism, appear to play a role in shaping American culinary trends and traditions. The culinary field and the nation are mutually constitutive.

Second, the picture that emerges through gourmet discourse of the American nation and its ideal members is an idealized and traditional version of America. The United States is a highly urban country with a large proportion of its population composed of racial and ethnic minorities. However, gourmet discourse often links American identity to the people and culinary traditions of the country's rural and Anglo-Saxon past. In other words, the national imaginary as it appears in this discourse is out of step with the demographic realities of the contemporary United States. We speculate that similar nationalist ideals appear across many discursive realms and within the media more broadly and that the themes we identify here are linked to broadly held 'master frames' (Snow and Benford, 1992) concerning the issue of American identity.

Third, rather than contradict our assertions about the portrait of the nation, the cosmopolitan aspects of gourmet discourse both refine and reinforce our argument. We find that Others and their respective foods are not framed as full members of the national imaginary, yet they are integral to its construction in these sources. The presence of Others and their foods suggests that full Americans are inclusive, privileged and sophisticated cultural consumers—at least in the particular discursive realm we examine, a realm which is clearly influenced by the socioeconomic privilege of its readership.

Cosmopolitanism is a key ideal woven into the American nation, but only to the extent that a core, traditional identity is not significantly decentred. In this vision of America, 'we' eat the food of the Other; this process both solidifies the cultural construction of the nation and raises questions about the limits of cosmopolitan inclusivity. Theorists of cosmopolitanism are frequently interpreted as having a relatively optimistic outlook in regards to cosmopolitan political projects. We don't engage here with debates about the merits of idealism in relation to cosmopolitanism, particularly since cosmopolitan theorists offer highly sophisticated and complex theories of cosmopolitanism (see Appiah, 1998; Beck, 2006). However, we would emphasize the importance of the insight, inspired from postcolonial scholarship, that cosmopolitanism can be used as a way of defining the self as sophisticated and worldly, an iteration that can obscure the relative class, geopolitical and racial privileges of its subjects.

Notes

1. See Wilk (2002), Penfold (2002), Parkhurst Ferguson (2004), Mennell (1996), Gabaccia (1998).

2. Smith (2005) argues that the concept of nation and nationalism are analytically distinct. While a useful analytic distinction, it remains important to acknowledge empirical slippage between the terms. For instance, a sense of the nation as libratory lends greater credence to movements and ideologies of nationalism. This chapter focuses on the construction of the American national community, while exploring the possibility that national constructions affect and help constitute nationalist movements and ideologies.

3. See also Smith (2005) and Johnston and Laxer (2003) for arguments contesting the decline of the nation.

4. Beck argues that globally scaled phenomena, like climate change, terrorism and trade, increase ecological, sociocultural and economic interdependence; as a result, cosmopolitanism 'cross[es] frontiers as a stowaway' in everyday life, as reflected in a 'passion for ... "Indian" food', or an 'attempt to evade global risks through a particular diet' (2004: 132–4).

5. This is not to argue that cosmopolitanism is a universal normative perspective, or to deny that cosmopolitanism as a normative philosophy has been associated with upper-middle-class and upper-class lifestyles (Hannerz, 1996; Lamont, 1992: 107). However, transnational scholars increasingly contend that cosmopolitanism also includes the cross-borders flows of the underprivileged and coerced (Parry, 1991; Rabinow, 1996; Robbins, 1998).

6. Understanding the comingling of the national and the cosmopolitanism can be clarified by drawing on Beck's distinction between philosophical cosmopolitanism (the often unsubstantiated normative desire to be a citizen of the world), and 'really existing' cosmopolitanism (which takes shape, often as an unanticipated outcome of acts that have no normative cosmopolitan intent) (Beck, 2004, 2006). Beck contends that 'really existing cosmopolitanism is deformed cosmopolitanism' (2006: 20) where local allegiances, national parochialism and cosmopolitan cultures 'interpenetrate, interconnect, and intermingle' under the mélange principle (2006: 5, 7).

7. Reflexivity, understood as greater self-confrontation towards the logic of modernity (Beck 1992: 153) is critical to the cosmopolitan outlook theorized by Beck (2006: 21).

References

Anderson, B. (1991 [1983]), *Imagined Communities: Reflections on the Origin and Spread of Nationalism,* London: Verso.

Appiah, K.A. (1998), 'Cosmopolitan Patriotism', in P. Cheah and B. Robbins (eds.), *Cosmopolitics.* Minneapolis: Minnesota University Press.

Basch, L, Glick Schiller, N., and Szanton Blanc, C. (1994), *Nations Unbound: Transnational Projects, Postcolonial Predicaments and Deterritorialized Nation States,* Basel: Gordon and Breach.

Beck, U. (1992), *Risk Society: Towards a New Modernity,* London: Sage.

Beck, U. (2004), 'Cosmopolitical Realism: The Distinction between Cosmopolitanism in Philosophy and the Social Sciences', *Global Networks,* 4/2: 131–56.

Beck, U. (2006), *Cosmopolitan Vision,* Cambridge: Polity Press.

Beck, U., and Sznaider, N. (2006), 'Unpacking Cosmopolitanism for the Social Sciences: A Research Agency', *British Journal of Sociology,* 57/1: 1–23.

Belasco, W. (2002), 'Food Matters: Perspectives on an Emerging Field', in W. Belasco and P. Scranton (eds.), *Food Nations: Selling Taste in Consumer Society,* New York: Routledge.

Benhabib, S. (1996), *Democracy and Difference,* Princeton: Princeton University Press.

Billig, M. (1995), *Banal Nationalism,* London: Sage Publications.

Brubaker, R. (1996), *Nationalism Reframed: Nationhood and the National Question in the New Europe,* New York: Cambridge University Press.

Calhoun, C. (1997), *Nationalism,* Minneapolis: University of Minnesota Press.

Douglas, M. (1966), *Purity and Danger. An Analysis of Concepts of Pollution and Taboo,* London: Routledge & Kegan Paul.

Dupuis, M. (2002), *Nature's Perfect Food,* New York: New York University Press.

Dupuis, M. (2006), 'White Food: Milk, Race and the History of Nutrition', unpublished paper presented at ASA meetings, August.

Faist, T. (2004), 'Towards a Political Sociology of Transnationalization: The State of the Art in Migration Research', *European Journal of Sociology,* 45/3: 331–6.

Featherstone, M. (1993), 'Global and Local Cultures', in J. Bird et al. (eds.), *Mapping the Futures: Local Cultures, Global Change,* London: Sage.

Featherstone, M., and Lash, S. (1995), 'Introduction', in M. Featherstone, S. Lash and R. Roberston (eds.), *Global Modernities,* London: Sage.

Gabaccia, D. (1998), *We Are What We Eat: Ethnic Food and the Making of Americans.* Cambridge, MA: Harvard University Press.

Hall, J. (1993), *The State,* New York: Routledge.

Hall, S. (1996), 'The Question of Cultural Identity', in S. Hall and D. Hubert (eds.), *Modernity: An Introduction to Modern Societies,* London: Blackwell.

Hannerz, U. (1996), *Transnational Connections: Culture, People, Places,* New York: Routledge.

Hechter, M. (2000), 'Nationalist Puzzles' in M. Hechter (ed.), *Containing Nationalism,* Oxford: Oxford University Press.

Heldke, L. (2003), *Exotic Appetites: Ruminations of a Food Adventurer,* New York: Routledge.

hooks, b. (1992), *Black Looks: Race and Representation,* Boston: South End Press.

Johnston, J., and Baumann, S. (2007), 'Democracy versus Distinction: A Study of Omnivorousness in Gourmet Food Writing', *American Journal of Sociology,* 113: 165–204.

Johnston, J., and Laxer, G. (2003), 'Solidarity in the Age of Globalization: Lessons from the Anti-MAI and Zapatista Struggles', *Theory and Society,* 32/1: 39–91.

Lamont, M. (1992), *Money, Morals, and Manners: The Culture of the French and American Upper Middle Class,* Chicago: University of Chicago Press.

Lévi-Strauss, C. (1963), *Totemism,* Boston: Beacon Press.

Longley, K. O. (2000), 'Fabricating Otherness: Dimidenko and Exoticism', in I. Santaolalla (ed.), *New Exoticisms: Changing Patterns in the Construction of Otherness,* Amsterdam: Rodopi.

Lyon, D. (2003), *Surveillance after September 11th,* Malden: Polity.

Mahler, S. (1998), 'Theoretical and Empirical Contributions Towards a Research Agenda for Transnationalism', in M. P. Smith and L. E. Guarnizo (eds.), *Transnationalism from Below,* New Brunswick: Transaction Publishers.

McCrone, D. (1998), *The Sociology of Nationalism,* London: Routledge.

Mennell, S. (1996), *All Manners of Food: Eating and Taste in England and France from the Middle Ages to the Present,* New York: Blackwell.

Mintz, S. W. (1996), *Tasting Food, Tasting Freedom: Excursions in Eating, Culture and the Past,* Boston: Beacon Press.

Mohanty, C. (1997), 'Under Western Eyes: Feminist Scholarship and Colonial Discourses', in N. Visvanathan, L. Duggan, L. Nisonoff and N. Wiegersma (eds.), *The Women, Gender and Development Reader,* Newark: Zed Books.

Muppidi, H. (2004), *The Politics of the Global,* Minneapolis: University of Minnesota Press.

Narayan, U. (1997), *Dislocating Cultures,* New York: Routledge.

Parkhurst Ferguson, P. (2004), *Accounting for Taste: The Triumph of French Cuisine,* Chicago: University of Chicago Press.

Parry, B. (1991), 'The Contradictions of Cultural Studies', *Transition,* 53: 37–45.

Penfold, S. (2002), ' "Eddie Shack was no Tim Horton": Donuts and the Folklore of Mass Culture in Canada', in W. Belasco and S. Scranton (eds.), *Food Nations: Selling Taste in Consumer Society,* New York: Routledge.

Pilcher, J. (1998), *Que Vivan los Tamales!: Food and the Making of Mexican Identity,* Albuquerque: University of New Mexico Press.

Pillsbury, R. (1998), *No Foreign Food: The American Diet in Time and Place,* Boulder: Westview Press.

Portes, A., Guarnizo, L., and Landlolt, P. (1999), 'The Study of Transnationalism: Pitfalls and Promise of an Emergent Field', *Ethnic and Racial Studies,* 22/1: 217–37.

Rabinow, P. (1996), *Essays on the Anthropology of Reason,* Princeton: Princeton University Press.

Renan, E. (1882), *Qu'est-ce Que la Nation?* Paris: Calmann-Levy.

Robbins, B. (1998), 'Introduction Part I: Actually Existing Cosmopolitanism', in P. Cheah and B. Robbins (eds.), *Cosmopolitics: Thinking and Feeling Beyond the Nation,* Minneapolis: University of Minnesota Press.

Said, E. (1978), *Orientalism,* New York: Vintage Books.

Smith, A. (1998), *Nationalism and Modernism: A Critical Survey of Recent Theories of Nations and Nationalism,* New York: Routledge.

Smith, A. D. (2005), 'The Myth of National Decline', *Axess Magazine* [online], 6, *The Persistent Nation,* <http://www.axess.se/english/index.htm> accessed 29 August 2008.

Snow, D. A., and Benford, R. D. (1992), 'Master Frames and Cycles of Protest', in A. Morriss and C. McClurg Mueller (eds.), *Frontiers in Social Movement Theory,* New Haven: Yale University Press.

Soysal, Y. (2000), 'Citizenship and Identity', *Ethnic and Racial Studies,* 23/1: 1–15.

Tuchman, G. (1978), 'Introduction: The Symbolic Annihilation of Women by the Mass Media', in G. Tuchman, A. K. Daniels and J. Benet (eds.), *Hearth and Home: Images of Women in the Mass Media,* Oxford: Oxford University Press.

Walby, R. (2005), 'How Closed-Circuit Television Surveillance Organizes the Social: An Institutional Ethnography', *Canadian Journal of Sociology,* 30/2: 189–209.

Wilk, R. (2002), 'Food and Nationalism: The Origins of "Belizean Food"', in W. Belasco and P. Scranton (eds.), *Food Nations: Selling Taste in Consumer Societies,* New York: Routledge.

Wodak, R., de Cillia, R., Reisigl, M., and Liebhart, K. (1999), *The Discursive Construction of National Identity,* translated by A. Hirsch and R. Mitten, Edinburgh: Edinburgh University Press.

–9–

Difference on the Menu: Neophilia, Neophobia and Globalization

Richard Wilk
Indiana University

In physical terms a hamburger is a relatively simple object—a cooked patty of ground meat inserted into a round bun. But culturally and politically, the hamburger has proven to be as complex and powerful as any of the electronic devices like cell phones which are transforming our world. What could give such a simple foodstuff an allure which attracts millions every day to eat something which has never before been part of their cuisine or way of life? And what could make the same hamburger so dangerous that politicians give impassioned speeches against it, and people go out to demonstrate in the streets to stop it being served?

The hamburger is just one of the many objects, symbols and people set in motion by the forces of globalization, which are capable of arousing strong passions, provoking new kinds of conflict. But food and cuisine are an exceptionally fertile way to understand and trace the way that globalization works, both as an objective cultural and economic phenomenon, and as a rhetorical field where a number of interests converge. This is because food is always both a physical substance which can be traced from origin to consumption and at the same time an object of intense emotional concern that is full of cultural meaning, so it is always a matter of public debate. Food is always *embodied* material culture—it enters our bodies and becomes part of us in an intimate way beyond any other thing we consume. This means that food is always deeply connected to our conceptions of health and well-being, and it therefore unavoidably connects meaningful symbols with practicalities and the hard facts of existence. From the standpoint of a social scientist, food also has the great advantage of being a universal topic, something almost everyone is willing to talk about, and sharing meals is always an entry point to wider social understanding.

The literature on food in the social sciences has tended to concentrate on the positive ways that meals and sharing food brings people together in social collectivities. Food binds and integrates, and a cuisine cements social identity. But food also expresses (and sometimes causes) cultural conflict, rebellion and disunity, and meals can also be events which cause pain and alienation—topics which have all been relatively neglected by scholars. The negative potential of food as an element in social conflict is especially apparent in modern globalizing industrial food systems where the sources and quality of food are increasingly invisible to consumers (see Lien and Nerlich, 2004). We are all familiar with many recent cases where real or imagined adulteration or contamination has led to widespread fear about the safety of food. Anxiety about science and technological change is often expressed through protests and arguments about the genetic, chemical or radiation content of foodstuffs. And hostility towards immigrants or foreign cultural influence may also focus on particular kinds of cuisine or chains of restaurants. Throughout the world, for example, first Coca-cola and then McDonalds became symbols of American cultural imperialism and attracted hostility and protest ranging from Charles De Gaul's withdrawal from NATO (Kuisel, 1993) to mass demonstrations against the opening of a McDonalds outlet in Oaxaca, Mexico (Pilcher, 2006; Weiner, 2002). Two centuries prior, American colonists were dumping British tea into Boston harbour and switching to coffee at home in protest of an earlier sort of colonialism.

In the Central American/Caribbean country of Belize, where I have been doing research for thirty-five years now, one of the consequences of recent trends in global migration has been a large influx of immigrants from Hong Kong and mainland China. Some have been quite prosperous and have built large housing estates and businesses, while others have scratched out a living in small shops and restaurants.[1] At the peak of the migration in the late 1990s, as the country was going through other wrenching economic and social changes, many local people, particularly those in business and government, complained that the Chinese were buying all the valuable real estate in the country. Few noted that locally born Belizeans were making a lot of money *selling* their property to the Chinese; they accused those aliens (as the Chinese, along with other recent immigrants, were increasingly called) of taking over the place.

The popular side of hostility towards Chinese immigration was often expressed through complaints about their food. While Chinese restaurants have been popular in all Belizean towns for well over a century, the new wave of immigrants opened take-away stands offering small portions of fried chicken and other familiar foods at very low prices. The low price of 'dolla fry chiken' made it immensely popular and extremely controversial. Public health officials blamed the Chinese for rising rates of high blood pressure and diabetes. Newspaper articles decried the way cheap Chinese fried chicken was debasing traditional cuisine and driving Belizean restaurants out of business.

In 1996 I listened to a morning radio call-in show, a very popular form of entertainment in Belize, during which several callers in a row complained that children were growing up eating too much Chinese fried chicken. Callers gave graphic accounts of greasy and disgusting servings of chicken they had been served and passed along stories they had heard about how some pieces were not chicken at all, but cats, rats and other animals. Callers talked freely of how 'those Chinee people' were getting rich and building big houses by selling unhealthy food to Belizean children.

The Chinese were killing off all the black people, who were already declining as a proportion of the population. One of the programme's hosts pointed out that Belize was a nation of immigrants and many of the Chinese were not aliens, but Belizean citizens. This changed the nature of the conversation for a while, as people tried to distinguish the 'good Chinese' from the 'bad'.

I heard this same kind of ugly discourse about Chinese chicken from friends and acquaintances in public and private during the 1990s while I was working in Belize. People who did not seem at all nationalistic on other issues would suddenly get angry, sometimes furious, when I mentioned Chinese fried chicken, and it would spark a diatribe against immigrants and their impact on Belize. Other immigrant groups did not get the same kind of reaction. On the contrary, the German-speaking Mennonites were often complimented or spoken of favourably because they were seen as hard-working farmers who produced a great deal of the country's food (including, ironically, all of those cheap chickens which the Chinese cook). And there are other kinds of foreign food which have been instantly accepted by Belizeans, who have a long history of culinary syncretism and creolization (Wilk, 2006). Indeed, Belize is a highly diverse, multi-ethnic country which has traditions of accepting immigrants, but clearly there are limits to what people there are willing to tolerate. While scholars of globalization have been praising creolization, hybridity and cosmopolitan mixing of cultures, a very large number of people around the world have reacted to globalization with xenophobia, rejection and a search for historical purity and authenticity.

Neophobia and Neophilia

Why and when does the flow of people and cuisine produce hostility, fear and disgust, as opposed to openness towards the exotic, or even fascination, faddism and interest? Mintz (1996) has suggested that there is something of a paradox when it comes to public attitudes of like and dislike towards local and foreign foods, for at times foodways and diet appear deeply rooted in longstanding and rigid cultural patterns and at other times they seem completely and suddenly changeable. So, for example, Ohnuki-Tierney (1993) tells us that rice eating is fundamentally connected to being Japanese, to the point where there is a spiritual identity between rice and personhood. But, then, what are we to make of a recent generation of Japanese teenagers who hardly eat rice at all? Have they stopped being Japanese? And Mintz (1996) points out that Americans who once thought of raw fish as inedible and disgusting, and Japanese food as tasteless and laughable, switched in a relatively short period of time into the largest sushi-consuming country in the world.

It is clear therefore that sometimes, and for some people, protecting food traditions and keeping them the same, rooted in time and place, can mean a great deal. McDonalds as a symbol of Americanization threatens French cultural identity, and drinking cola instead of wine erodes the distinctiveness of what it means to be French rather than just European. Even recently invented food traditions can be a vehicle for national discovery, as Appadurai (1988) documents in his study of the way the Indian nation was mapped and solidified by the writing of regional cookbooks in the postcolonial period. My own work in Belize shows how the country has discovered and reinvented itself partially through the medium of discovering its own distinctive cuisine (Wilk, 2006). A hundred ethnographies and thousands of novels, films, songs and even dances celebrate the close ties between a people and their favourite dishes.

The focus on local cuisine is often bolstered by local food historians and efforts to protect traditional sources of ingredients or preserve particular bakeries, mills or farms. Government subsidies may be turned to maintaining traditional varieties of crops, banking seeds or granting protection by recognizing local trademarks, names or appellations. In the United States, activists make highly publicized efforts to live for extended periods eating nothing produced outside their own home region (e.g. Nabhan, 2002). The explosive growth of local-food initiatives in the United States so far seems to be free of any overt political hostility to foreign cuisine or immigrants, but it seems hardly coincidental that it is taking place at the same time that anti-immigration activism is also a growing political movement, including for the first time an attempt to build a massive physical barrier along the Mexican border. A careful reading of some of the founding texts of the local food movement reveals more than a trace of xenophobia, including a statement that no country can be truly independent if it depends on other countries for food (Berry, 1999).

But food is also entertainment, and cooking and eating a particular cuisine does not necessarily have anything to do with identity at all. When I ask my undergraduate students if eating in a Chinese restaurant makes them feel Chinese, they laugh. Eating out in an ethnic restaurant can be no more than entertainment or a source of variety, completely superficial. Foreign food can be kept at a safe distance, so that eating pizza, sushi and Argentine steak has no more cultural significance than the fact that coffee and bananas come from South America or chocolate from Africa. Clearly, this is much easier if you belong to a rich and powerful country, a place which can pick and choose, rather than one where foreign influence is forced down your throat by a dominating or colonial power.

At the other end of the scale, there are many people who actively seek foreign food, who find it exciting, interesting, exotic and enticing. For hundreds (perhaps thousands) of years familiarity and comfort with foreign food has been part of the repertoire of sophistication in most civilizations, one of the essentials which distinguishes the educated and experienced and gives them cultural capital. French cuisine has been the dominant international standard for so long that elements of French technique have been absorbed and indigenized into most national traditions. Like French ideas of diplomacy and etiquette, French cuisine is also the basis for the modern *international* standards found all over the world embedded in state institutions, tourism and business.

Cuisine is of course part of an important business, and promoting a variety of cuisines is a major way of growing the size of the consuming public. The 'foodie' industry and press are well established in Europe and the United States, and are rapidly growing in Asia, Eastern Europe and Latin America. A large part of the population in North American cities reads the daily food press, tries out new restaurants and searches for new cuisines and taste sensations. They create add-on markets for ingredients, implements and cooking classes, and feed the rapid growth of the food-tourism industry, which takes diners out into the world to experience exotic food first hand. This is an important economic force promoting food *neophilia*, the desire to experience new taste sensations.

Globalization and the Status of Local Culture

When we talk about globalization, modernization, rapid cultural change, an influx of people, ideas, media or culture, the silent assumption which always lies beneath the surface is that the *opposite* of these terms is somehow *normal*. In other words, when we say that globalization is the exception, we are silently affirming that a normal world is a local one, a place where people and things stay in one place, where ideas are stable and relatively static. This is a commonplace assumption in food studies, where scholars generally begin with the idea that every place has its own local culinary customs, established through immemorial custom and steeped in time. The 'indigenous' is the natural pre-existing state, which makes the 'foreign' into something eternally new, always anomalous and dangerous. Anthropologists working in Africa and Latin America have been attacking these ideas over the last few decades, arguing that both local and foreign are equally constructed, historically contingent and always changing. But from the vantage point of Europe and Asia with their long literate traditions, the idea that each place has its own *terroir,* its folk culture, rooted in the historical past, is still accepted as self-evident by most people, even if they strongly disagree over just what that local culture really is.

This is why recent historical research on the European origins of the concept of the 'indigenous' is particularly exciting; it shows how earlier periods of globalization were responsible for the very *invention* of our ideas of local culture, local nature, *terroir* and all the cultural superstructures like cuisines which have been erected around them. Buried deep in European history, an early struggle between neophobics and neophilics created a shower of ideas and concepts which became the taken-for-granted bedrock of the ideology through which their descendents see the world, as well as the way today's social scientists analyse it.

In the 1520s, Paracelsus, a German-speaking itinerant preacher and medical entrepreneur living in what is now part of Switzerland, wrote a book titled *Herbarius, or a treatise Concerning the Powers of the Herbs, Roots, Seeds, Etc., of the Native Land and Realm of Germany.* As the historian Alix Cooper explains in her recent book, *Inventing the Indigenous* (2007), Paracelsus was partially motivated to write this work by his anger with the prevailing scholarly tradition of his time, a mishmash of recycled and disorganized classical and medieval medical sources, many of which came from Catholic southern Europe, particularly Italy. But a major impetus that sparked Paracelsus, and his followers who invented a robust tradition of herbalism and local natural history, was the deeply unsettling emotions raised by an influx of foreign medicine—the consequence of overseas exploration and international trade (in short, early forms of globalization). Cooper (2007: 27) quotes Paracelsus (as translated by Moran, 1993: 104):

> Moreover, there are in Germany so many more and better medicines than are to be found in Arabia, Chaldaea, Persia, and Greece that it would be more reasonable for the peoples of such places to get their medicines from us Germans, than for us to receive medicines from them. Indeed, these medicines are so good, that neither Italy, France, nor any other realm can boast of better ones. That this has not come to light for such a long time is the fault of Italy, the mother of ignorance and inexperience.

Later writers in this tradition went on to elaborate the doctrine that because Germans were the product of German climate, food and nature, only *German* herbs and medicines could effectively cure them of their ills. While Cooper (2007) does not stretch this point in her book, it is not hard to see the historical connection forward to notions of *Geist* and *Volk* which romantically identified a unique spirit of a people with their place of origin. It is also not too hard to see a pecuniary interest on the part of local herbalists and healers, whose livelihoods were threatened by an influx of exotic medicines imported and sold by urban merchants. Why should we be consuming stale, possibly contaminated, mysteriously foreign goods which have passed through the hands of strangers, and sold by rich urban merchants, when we could be using the products of our own soil, our own people, sold by honest country folk? The eye of suspicion is cast at those oversophisticated urban people who follow fashion, use the latest imported goods and in the process may be weakening the German essence within themselves, or perhaps even within society at large.

Cooper is concerned with tracing how this nativist herbal tradition fed the nascent science of natural history and its establishment within European universities at a crucial time. She makes a convincing argument that the impetus to invent the local and indigenous as a counterpoint to the foreign was a key foundation in the origin of Western natural science, particularly the classifications of plants and animals which were later codified by Linnaeus.

As far as I know, nobody has traced the connection of early herbalism to the development of cooking or to nascent ideas about German culinary identity. But that is not really important for my broader point—even in Europe the cultural definition of the local and national was historically *part of the process of globalization itself.* When people are exposed to foreign goods, especially novel ones which challenge culturally important consumption practices, some will always react by inventing tradition.[2] This means they will choose some subset of existing practice and codify it, grace it with a title and establish it as a standard. As I argued more generally in a study of Mayan ethnohistory, tradition often crystallizes and takes a 'timeless' form in periods of cultural crisis when people perceive their way of life to be under attack (Wilk, 1991).

The unique contribution of the herbalists of sixteenth century Germany was to establish nature, geography and classificatory natural science as the legitimizing principles of their concept of local tradition. Later in the eighteenth century, European antiquarians, historians, folklorists, archaeologists and ethnologists developed sciences which used *time* as a legitimizing trope, usually connected to notions of lineage and kinship.[3] Time and nature, kinship and geography, remain the intellectual foundations on which most ideas of tradition and locality are built, though today they are so firmly embedded in daily habits of thought that they largely go unchallenged and can be used unreflectively and without justification. It is only possible to say that "Parmesan cheese is a part of the identity of the city of Parma because it has been made there by the same line of cheese makers from unique local ingredients since time immemorial," because of the centuries of intellectual work which makes statements like this *seem* quite natural and reasonable. But they are not.

Instead, as Paracelsus's example demonstrates, an awareness of the value of the local grows only in the presence of an alternative, and not just *any* alternative. If nobody was attracted by the allure of the foreign, the local would be in no danger and there would be no need to protect it. The only reason one would have to make noise about the normal daily bread on the table is if it appears about to be replaced by rice, noodles or corn flakes. The important spice which makes that daily bread suddenly worthy of an ideology is fear that something is going to be lost, and this is exactly the same spice which makes exotic food seem dangerous and unhealthy. But why should the same taste appear so enticing in some settings and repellent in others?

Winners, Losers and Social Competition

Anthropologists, ancient historians and archaeologists have long been interested in the impetus which drives people to want foreign goods. Looking back into prehistory, it is sometimes possible to find justifications based on 'simple' utilitarian arguments. For example, ancient civilizations in flood plain areas sometimes lacked hard stone for making tools, while other areas suffered shortages of salt or other critical minerals and this served as an impetus to trade (Rathje, 1972). But early civilizations traded much more than utilitarian stone and salt. Ancient trade routes moved huge quantities of products which cannot be seen as immediately 'useful': sea shells, brightly coloured stones, decorated pottery, sculpture, cosmetics, beads, decorative metal, hides, ivory, fine cloth, worked bone, incense, spices, saps or gums, oils and wine. What made these materials and objects so desirable that people were willing to work hard to make things to trade for them, to engage with strangers in what might be dangerous transactions or to travel long distances?

Kent Flannery (1968) was the first archaeologist to notice that growth in early trade was always closely correlated with the rise of social hierarchy, in other words, with the origins of inherited class differentiation among societies which had previously been homogeneous farming villages with no status differences. He argued that when social inequality was emerging in small-scale societies, those who were seeking to establish their power sought exotic goods, especially the kinds of goods which had symbolic power, particularly if they had already been adopted by a more powerful distant civilization. In local small-scale struggles over land, water, kinship, labour and other resources, foreign objects can have tremendous symbolic power.

This, Flannery said, is why early art styles spread so rapidly over large areas, a point amplified by Mary Helms (1988) in an encyclopaedic study of the symbolic power of imported goods in chiefly societies in the ethnohistorical record of the Americas. Simply put, foreign goods become the tokens of power and sophistication. A local status system emerges where styles and fashions 'trickle down' from an elite which controls their importation. There may even be sumptuary laws that restrict the consumption of the highest valued goods to nobility. One can point to many historic examples: the way the Japanese elite imported Chinese writing, religion and court culture at the peak of their power struggles for hegemony over the island in the sixth century AD, or the popularity of Greek art among aspiring elites throughout the eastern Mediterranean in the Hellenistic period.[4]

While in its barest form Flannery's argument is simplistic, it is a powerful tool for understanding one of the forces which drives neophilia, the thirst for the foreign. In any sociopolitical system, established power rests to some extent on control of property and knowledge, rooted in history, family and place, a source which is inherently conservative and self-perpetuating. At the same time, within any system there are also factions, divisions and subordinate groups which seek advancement and advantage, particularly during times of instability and transition. This is all we need to create opportunities for the interplay between neophobia and neophilia: people whose status and position is threatened by imported goods, trends and fashions which they do not control, and those who stand to benefit from the same.

Of course the reality is more complex. Perhaps in the early stages of the development of civilization there was a real potential for foreign objects and ideologies to really cause revolutionary change. We can certainly point to the spread of the world's 'great religions' like Buddhism, Christianity and Islam as events in which foreign ideas prompted such sweeping social transformations. But most political regimes quickly learned to gain tight control over trade and contact across their borders, so the play between localists and globalists was largely carried out among factions within existing powerful classes, taking away its potential for causing social revolution. By the sixteenth century, most European elites had found ways to control and accommodate consumer culture that were hardly threatening to the established order of things. The rich and parts of the new middle classes became 'fashion leaders' who pioneered new consumption trends for items like coffee, sugar, magazines, novels, musical instruments, appliances, toys and cosmetics, which gradually diffused downward through the social scale as they became cheaper. The intellectual classes became the main arbiters for the entry of foreign music, art, ideology and decorative crafts.

In this way, over time some kinds of foreign products and styles become 'legitimate' and familiar (under control), like French cuisine and Italian opera for example, while other kinds are dangerous and threaten the established order. Subordinate groups may seize on these 'illegitimate' foreign fashions and goods as symbols of rebellion—though because these are real goods with real economic value, a change in fashion may truly have a destabilizing economic impact by changing mass consumption patterns. When middle-class Austrian youth in the early 1950s began to buy American clothes and music, as their passion for American pop iconography developed, they did more than outrage the taste of the established elite; they also created new economic niches and industries and developed new forms of consumer culture (Wagnleitner, 1994).

Concluding Thoughts

When Belize was still a British colony, the European styles of cuisine favoured by the local elite were considered the only legitimate form of cooking for public events, weddings and other festivities. The rituals of European dining were performed at formal dinners at the governor's residence, in the homes of diplomats and other members of the upper crust, in clubs and in one or two restaurants in the hotels deemed fit for foreign visitors. Even if the actual food that was served could rarely meet European standards, because so much of it came from tins and stale packages, it was served 'correctly' and eaten with the proper ceremony. The same standards were displayed and taught to the public in diverse settings, including church events like ice cream socials and tea parties and the balls and dances held by fraternal and Masonic lodges.

The firm cultural hegemony of British high culture was policed by the thorough censorship of foreign films and press and tight import controls which were aimed particularly at keeping out American popular culture. These controls all began to crumble during the 1970s as more and more Belizeans began to migrate to the United States and colonial control of local government gave way to self-rule by a nationalist party. The advent of satellite television in the early 1980s completely changed the balance of cultural power, giving the vast majority of Belizeans access to many new kinds of popular culture, sparking a dramatic increase in the consumption of foreign music, fashion, food and consumer goods. Many different groups in the country found this influx dangerous and frightening, and there was a great deal of agitation by church, state and the educational establishment to restrict television programming. The stage was set for a continuing interplay between neophilia and neophobia. But it is important to note two key aspects of this counterpoint, as different groups coalesce around positions of loyalty to the indigenous and enthusiasm for the imported in different cultural arenas.

First, the coalitions and positions, and indeed the kinds of objects and goods which arouse strong emotions and political discourse, are constantly changing. Baseball, seen in the early 1980s by many working-class Belizeans as an alien sport, whose popularity was endangering the traditional sports of cricket and soccer, has receded into the background and achieved a loyal but limited following mainly as a spectator sport to be watched on television. American hip hop and rap music provoked a similar reaction amongst different groups later in the decade; a strong revival of Belizean musical traditions in the 1990s, which even saw Belizean artists achieve success in international venues, seems to have set many of these anxieties to rest.

Second, new technologies and means of communication constantly seem to threaten to undercut and destroy the social order through which fashion and taste are controlled, yet social order persists. The opening of borders, the arrival of new immigrants, a flush of new prosperity, satellite television and the Internet all seem to promise completely new avenues for people to find new tastes, new styles of consumption, which do not 'trickle down' through a status hierarchy from above, or flow through the taste-making channels of a local artistic or cultural elite. Why bother with the local provincial elites if you can watch MTV and see what people in New York and Hollywood are wearing, eating, drinking and dancing to? The Internet offers access to every cuisine in the world for the aspiring food neophiliac. Could this be the end of any organized fashion system, a world of free lifestyle choices where each individual crafts their own consumption from a global smorgasbord of options?

Nothing of the sort is about to happen, for the basic reasons that consumption is always *embodied* and *socialized*. Consumption is more than simply a matter of choice; as Bourdieu effectively argued, it is embodied through what he called *hexis,* the daily habitus which tells us what tastes and feels right. This is why we feel ridiculous wearing the wrong colours and uncomfortable eating a food at the wrong time of day. It does not prevent us from changing our behaviour, but it provides a kind of friction, a drag on choice and change which means we cannot simply decide to switch diets or transform our mode of dress overnight without paying a substantial cost. No matter how weary we may be of familiar routines, following them is usually a lot easier than changing them, unless of course everyone else in your circle is also changing at the same time. And this is the crux of the socialized, communal aspect of all consumption, that we do it as much for and with others as for ourselves. Though everyone in a consumer society seeks a sort of individuality, in daily practice they seek to fit in with familiar groups, to do what is socially acceptable. Your curiosity may lead you to try eating Laotian vegetarian food, but unless you find others who share your passion, it is unlikely that you will continue for long. The vast spaces of choice opened up by new media and the Internet have really opened up new niches for professional tastemakers, critics and fashion leaders, who broker, translate and channel consumption trends in ways which often appear strikingly traditional rather than transformative.

This has not been a complete answer to my starting question—why should a hamburger arouse such strong passions? But it does suggest that by the time one has finished making a detailed study of the political and social meaning of the hamburger in any particular time and place, public attention will have already moved onward to some other significant object of both desire and fear.

Notes

1. At various times in the late 1980s and 1990s, the Belize government had a program which offered citizenship to immigrants who paid $50,000 US and agreed to invest in the country, which was a major incentive for those seeking to flee the impending Chinese takeover of Hong Kong. It is also much easier to get a tourist visa or green card to enter the United States from Belize than from China, so Belize became a stopover for prospective emigrants to the United States. Political controversy within Belize over the 'sale of citizenship' contributed to some hostility to Chinese immigrants, but it is important to remember that many Chinese families have been established in Belize since the nineteenth century.
2. Hobsbawm and Ranger (1983) suggest that this is one of the reasons why traditions are invented in their introduction to their book of the same name.
3. It is ironic that as archaeology and prehistory advanced as sciences, they proved that nothing about human culture in Europe could be seen as truly 'indigenous'. Agriculture came from the east, civilization from the south, and repeated migration and population movements obscure any attempt to read modern nations back into the past, despite the efforts of nationalists to manipulate the facts. Everything about origins and locality depends on the size of the time frame, and ultimately all humans are Africans.
4. I discuss some further contemporary parallels in Wilk (2004).

References

Appadurai, A. (1988), 'How to Make a National Cuisine: Cookbooks in Contemporary India', *Comparative Studies in Society and History,* 30/1: 3–24.

Berry, W. (1999), 'The Pleasures of Eating', in L. Glickman (ed.), *Consumer Society in American History: A Reader,* Ithaca: Cornell University Press.

Cooper, A. (2007), *Inventing the Indigenous,* Cambridge: Cambridge University Press.

Flannery, K. V. (1968), 'The Olmec and the Valley of Oaxaca: A Model for Inter-Regional Interaction in Formative Times', in E. Benson (ed.), *Dumbarton Oaks Conference on the Olmec,* Washington, DC: Dumbarton Oaks.

Helms, M. (1988), *Ulysses' Sail: An Ethnographic Odyssey of Power, Knowledge, and Geographical Distance,* Princeton: Princeton University Press.

Hobsbawm, E., and Ranger, T. (eds.) (1983), *The Invention of Tradition,* Cambridge, MA: Cambridge University Press.

Kuisel, R. (1993), *Seducing the French: The Dilemma of Americanization,* Berkeley: University of California Press.

Lien, M., and Nerlich, B. (eds.) (2004), *The Politics of Food,* Oxford: Berg Publishers.

Mintz, S. (1996), *Tasting Food, Tasting Freedom,* Boston: Beacon Press.

Moran, B. T. (1993), 'The Herbarius of Paracelsus', *Pharmacy in History,* 35: 99–127.

Nabhan, G. (2002). *Coming Home to Eat: The Pleasures and Politics of Local Foods,* New York: W. W. Norton.

Ohnuki-Tierney, E. (1993), *Rice as Self,* Princeton: Princeton University Press.

Pilcher, J. M. (2006), *Taco Bell, Maseca, and Slow Food: A Postmodern Apocalypse for Mexico's Peasant Cuisine?,* in R. Wilk (ed.), *Fast Food/Slow Food,* Walnut Creek: Altamira Press.

Rathje, W. L. (1972), 'Praise the Gods and Pass the Metates: An Hypothesis of the Development of Lowland Rainforest Civilizations in Mesoamerica', in M. P. Leone (ed.), *Contemporary Archaeology: An Introduction to Theory and Contributions,* Carbondale: Southern Illinois University Press.

Wagnleitner, R. (1994), *Coca-Colonization and the Cold War,* Chapel Hill: University of North Carolina Press.

Weiner, T. (2002), 'Mexicans Resisting McDonald's Fast Food Invasion', *New York Times* (24 August).

Wilk, R. (1991), *Household Ecology: Economic Change and Domestic Life among the Kekchi Maya of Belize,* Tucson: University of Arizona Press.

Wilk, R. (2004), 'Miss Universe, the Olmec, and the Valley of Oaxaca', *Journal of Social Archaeology,* 4/1: 81–98.

Wilk, R. (2006), *Home Cooking in the Global Village,* Belize City: Angelus Press and Berg Publishers.

–10–

Eating Your Way to Global Citizenship
Danielle Gallegos
Queensland University of Technology

The global food trade is not a new phenomenon. Since at least Columbus foods as commodities and cultural objects have been making an impact on the world stage (Sokolov, 1991). While it has been acknowledged that globalization in this context is not new, what is unprecedented is the intensity and speed at which foods are moved globally and appropriated locally (Caraher and Coveney, 2004). Food as a marker for globalization has in many instances been simplified as 'McDonaldization', 'Coco-colonization' or 'homogenization' of the food supply, but there is growing recognition of more complex relationships (James, 1996; Pollan, 2006; Ritzer, 1998). It is now acknowledged that food and food systems provide links across a broad spectrum of environmental, economic, cultural and social issues that are played out across the quadripartite matrix connecting global, local, public and private (Walter-Toews and Lang, 2000). In such an environment, food choice—from what appears to be an endless array of offerings—is more complex than ever before. This generates a level of anxiety requiring individuals to work through the plethora of expert systems and other technologies at their disposal in order to build identities (Giddens, 1990; Melucci, 1996).

While exhortations to watch what we eat pervade our everyday lives, this call for caution occurs amidst a surfeit of food. Disciplining the body through food is hardly a novel concept—dietetics as the practice of nutrition has its foundations in ancient Greece (see Coveney, 1999, 2000a; Foucault, 1990). It has been for the majority, however, a family affair, a localized response concerned with individual health. In its more recent construction, nutrition has moved from asceticism to *treat* disease to consumption to reduce risk of or to *prevent* disease. It still remains an individual response but the focus of its effect has now moved beyond the body. Practicing 'good' nutrition is now linked with environmental and social sustainability (Baum, 1999; Coveney, 2000b; Gussow, 2000) where the sphere of influence moves beyond the boundaries of the body to encompass the local and increasingly the global. Nutrition is one technology available to the self which can be used in an effort to become a 'good' global citizen.

The anxiety generated in the search for stable institutions and a 'place' within local and global spaces arises alongside the failure of more traditional governance provided by religious and political authority as well as family, custom and nature. There is a requirement, therefore, to search for and use a variety of novel signposts to attenuate risk in order to enhance predictability. This ontological anxiety inherent in a 'risk society' should not necessarily be considered counterproductive. Instead, ontological anxiety may be read positively as a generator of the self as a reflexive project. Without anxiety there would be no impetus to continue attempting to build identity. This is Foucault's (1984: 343) point when he indicates, 'not everything is bad but everything is dangerous ... if everything is dangerous, then we always have something to do. So my position leads not to apathy but to a hyper- and pessimistic activism'.

In order to minimize the health risk associated with either consuming or not consuming certain foods, food becomes a bridge linking time and space, and providing the means by which risk and other problems can be ameliorated but never actually solved. Nutrition as a form of pessimistic activism is part science, part spirituality, part taste and part consumption. As such it can work as a technique by which food as a bridge can be problematized. It is one technology with universal applicability and high visibility; everyone has the potential to take into consideration the foods that are eaten and their impact on health. In this chapter, the Mediterranean diet and genetically modified foods will be used to explore nutrition as a technology for risk minimization in order to build identity as a global citizen.

Nutrition as Risk Ethic

Nutrition as a discourse is as fragmented and complex as most other discourses; it has multiple expert knowledges that feed into it and a range of fashionable and commercial contributions with vested interests in its circulation. What results is nutrition as a form of governance in which 'individuals will *want* to be healthy, experts will instruct them on how to be so, and entrepreneurs will exploit and enhance this market for health. Health will be ensured through a combination of the market, expertise and a regulated autonomy' (Rose, 1992: 155, emphasis in original). As a form of governmentality and ethics, nutrition is based on the notion of risk and its effective reduction. It is deployed pre- and post-swallowing to guide and validate food choice. In the process, it simultaneously defines and either ameliorates or exacerbates health risk.[1] In other words, nutrition is a socially constructed 'hazard' that is 'invoked discursively to support estimations of risk, risky behaviour and of people who take the risks' (Fox, 1998: 19).

Food and nutrition are ubiquitous; everybody has to eat. Therefore, as a self-reflexive project, food consumption is one form of risk-taking that everybody indulges in. Eating is risky for a number of reasons. At a pragmatic level there is a risk of choking with every mouthful; there are also risks associated with microbiological and chemical safety, social mores, health and identity. Ultimately, however, the risk of eating (and therefore food choice) lies in the fact that eating is one of the few activities where the external is made internal. Food is a separate entity that, after being internalized is eventually incorporated into the body itself. In other words, food choice not only defines identity esoterically but also physically. It inscribes both body and soul.

Nutrition and medicine have high positivity. Any change in thinking or theory has an almost immediate impact on the wider community. This effect means that: '[T]he conditions of truth within these knowledges are much less stable and far more difficult to control. Yet somewhat disturbingly perhaps, these are also the knowledges most quick to pronounce truths about human nature, human potential, human endeavour and the future of the human condition in general' (McHoul and Grace, 1993: 58). This effect, in part, explains the complaint that nutritionists keep changing their minds about what is 'healthy' and 'good'. This variability only serves to emphasize nutrition as a reflexive project of the self that cannot be ideally completed. Bauman (2000: 79) reminds us of this point when he remarks that 'the concepts of "healthy diet" change more quickly than it takes for any of the successively or simultaneously recommended diets to run its course'. Consequently, 'almost every cure is strewn with risks, and more cures are needed to heal the consequences of past risk-taking' (Bauman, 2000: 79). It also means that nutrition risk has extended beyond the individual and the family unit. It now has links with the global via nutrition discourses that rely on not only physiological and psycho-social scientific precepts but also environmental, scientific tenets. In this context, risk becomes not just attributable to an individual but also to a social body, not just to a single national body but also to the world. These links to the global have always existed; being told to think of the starving children in Africa every time you considered leaving anything on your plate after a meal is testament to this connection. However, while solving world hunger has always been a problem for bureaucracies, the 'new' nutrition risk is a problem for the self. Not only do individuals need to concern themselves with their own bodies and those of their family members, they now have to shoulder the responsibility for the societies they live in—local, national and global. In this context, 'sustainability' becomes a part of risk terminology.

Like risk, sustainability in not a new concept; the rotation of crops is, at its most basic, an understanding that a food supply needs to be sustainable. In late modernity, however, this notion of sustainability has been amplified. To be responsible nutritionally is to be so at all levels: global, local, public and private. Foods need to be chosen not only on the basis of health but also for their economic and social sustainability. In countries where the food supply is assured, questions are now turning to 'eco-friendly' food systems, where the primary principle is the consumption of local fresh and seasonal foods (see Coveney, 2000b; Gussow, 2000). However, in addition to the economic and environmental sustainability of these systems, they are also heralded as being friendly to social environments, 'as they are often structured to promote cooperation, trust and social cohesion' (Coveney, 2000b: S99).

The introduction of sustainability as a viable question results in the need to authenticate the answer on an individual, local level with potential ramifications for the collective on a global scale. These questions of sustainability make us look at both the past and future and try to project the self into that future. Davison (2001: 202) argues that commodities, as part of the commerce of consumption, have caused disorientation. Consequently, 'commodities do not engage us with the stories of the past' and 'regardless of their eco-efficiency, distract and disorientate us from the world around us'. Food as a commodity, however, does perform this task; it provides a bridge between the irreversible past and an unknowable future. It is, in other words, an integral part of what it is to be human, attempting to bridge these two human conditions (Arendt, 1958). The sustainability of food globally, locally and in the private and public domains is one way in which the past can be acknowledged and the future opened up as potentiality. Food provides the opportunity to both focus attention on the world around us and distract us from that same world.

Nutrition as risk ethic is a form of 'unfreedom', built into which are varying degrees of agency. Bauman (1999: 79) describes 'unfreedom' as 'heteronomy', or:

> the state in which one follows rules and commands of someone else's; an agentic state, that is a state in which the acting person is an agent of somebody else's will. Persons may resent that alien will and watch for the occasion to deceive or rebel; they may accept—grudgingly—the uselessness of all resistance; they may be glad that someone else took the responsibility for their actions and freed them from the noxious need to choose and decide; they may even fail to notice that what they do and go on doing is done under compulsion, and never imagine a different way of going about their daily business.

Bauman (1999: 79) also argues that unfreedom, 'far from being perceived as tyrannical, underlies the feelings of safety and homeliness which on the whole are deeply gratifying'. Nutrition as risk, therefore, can be seen to act as a safety net and, in late modernity, the quests for safety and homeliness are built into nutrition science, which is fundamentally a product associated with the industrial. The facts and figures of science are infused with the 'cooperation, trust and social cohesion' of the local (Bauman, 1999: 79).

Nutrition, as a technology of practical subject formation, 'inscribes ethical incompleteness onto subjects in a process of two-way shifts between the subject as singular private person and the subject as collective, public citizen' (Miller, 1993: ix). The telos (or end goal for a life) that emerges is a tempered purity allowing subjects to be 'good' *global* citizens. The nutrition ethic has, therefore, been broadened beyond personal responsibility for an individual's own health. The ethic now encompasses personal responsibility for community health and personal responsibility for *global* health. These responsibilities are impossible to completely fulfil and so serve to reinforce the incompleteness of the self as a project. In order to undertake such a project consumers are required to become 'experts of themselves' and to 'adopt an educated and knowledgeable relation of self-care in respect to their bodies, their minds, their forms of conduct and that of the members of their own families' (Rose, 1996: 59). This process of self-realization involves decision making and the weighing up of risk in order to construct the self as 'responsible citizen' (Petersen, 1996: 55). The process also involves entering into partnerships not only with public authorities and 'experts' but also with 'lay actors' (Lupton, 1999: 122).

The sharing of food, therefore, requires trust between consumers, producers and all the food handlers in between (Mintz, 1996). As the agri-food business extends its global networks, the number of experts and actors increases, and it becomes increasingly difficult to form a partnership that can be trusted. The Mediterranean diet and the reaction to genetically modified foods provide two examples of the complex connections that form as individuals negotiate the quadripartite matrix in order to work on becoming good global citizens.

The Mediterranean Diet

The Mediterranean diet emerged into global consciousness in the late 1970s via the *Seven Countries Study* (Keys, 1995). Its essential components include the following: a high monounsaturated fatty acid/saturated fatty acid ratio obtained via the use of olive oil; moderate alcohol consumption; high legume consumption; high consumption of grains and cereals, including bread; high consumption of fruits and vegetables; low consumption of meat and meat products and moderate consumption of milk and dairy products (Trichopoulou and Lagiou, 1997). Since the Keys study there has been an ongoing scientific programme of research supporting the efficacy of such diet components in promoting longevity and in treating and reducing the risk of coronary heart disease, cancer, diabetes, obesity and a wealth of other afflictions including erectile dysfunction and Alzheimer's disease (see, for example, Bondia-Pons et al., 2007; de Longeril and Salen, 1998; Esposito et al., 2006; James and Phillip, 1995; Masana et al., 1991; Mendez et al., 2006; Paniagua et al., 2007; Sacks, 1998; Trichopoulou et al., 2005; Trichopoulou et al., 2006; Wahlqvist et al., 2005; Weih et al., 2007).

The science was, however, not enough. The debate that erupted was not over the components of the diet but rather whether it could be called *the* Mediterranean diet rather than *a* Mediterranean diet and indeed whether such an entity still existed or was instead a historical artefact. What is evident is that, with the pressures of late modernity, the advent of fast food, improved agricultural techniques and increased availability of certain food items, the diet of the Mediterranean has altered. In northern Italy, some areas of southern Italy (Alberti-Fidanza et al., 1994) and in parts of Greece (Trichopoulou et al., 1995), there are increasing numbers of inhabitants who no longer follow a so-called traditional Mediterranean style of eating, placing them at increased risk of dying from all causes (Giacco and Riccardi, 1991). The Mediterranean diet was eventually described as 'the dietary pattern found in the olive-growing areas of the Mediterranean region in the late 1950s and early 1960s, when the consequences of World War II were overcome but the fast-food culture had not yet *invaded* the area' (Trichopoulou and Lagiou, 1997: 383, my emphasis).

The use of the word 'invaded' is interesting in this context. It conveys the idea that the seemingly objective researchers of the 'science' of the Mediterranean diet have made value judgements. They have simultaneously distanced the Mediterranean diet from its origins in scarcity and constructed a binary. On one side of the binary, the 'bad end', is 'fast food' or 'industrial food' and on the other, the 'good end', is the Mediterranean diet. The 'science' is rearranging the Mediterranean diet so that it includes the cultural, incorporating social ritual, local relationships and commensality, resulting in this diet being overtly proclaimed as the antidote to globalization and the other dangers inherent in modern life. In reality the Mediterranean diet was a diet borne out of poverty and is unlikely to remain the same if living standards improve. For those in the Mediterranean, there were always aspirations for a 'better' way of living. In the Rockefeller study, undertaken in 1948 on Crete, only one in six families thought the typical diet was satisfactory. The foods they felt were needed to improve their diets, in order of priority, were meat, fish, pasta, butter and cheese (Nestle, 1995). These foods were associated with abundance, strength and health and were linked to being healthily fat.

The Mediterranean diet, therefore, as scientifically defined, is a myth. Following Barthes (1972), a myth is a cultural truth, in that it provides a fundamental narrative. As Barthes (1972: 142) indicates, 'what the world supplies to myth is an historical reality, defined, even if this goes back a while, by the way in which men have produced or used it; and what myth gives in return is a natural image of this reality'. The mythical Mediterranean diet in becoming a global diet is increasingly marketed as a cultural package where 'the nicest one' is chosen for promotion (Crotty, 1998: 230). The attractive parts are singled out, while the more difficult components to market, such as legumes, are ignored (O'Dea, 1994). Symons (1994: 27) also comments that 'the Mediterranean diet has nutritionists' approval; it carries glamorous connotations; it reeks of tradition; and it tastes good too'.[2] While some proponents of the diet have taken exception to the criticism, being a myth potentially works in the Mediterranean diet's favour, and its efficacy improves when it equates symbolically to 'health food'. In this way, as Coward (1989: 124) intimates, good nutrition, in this case encapsulated as the Mediterranean diet

is seen not just as opening up new possibilities for the individual but also as a way of solving major social problems. The symbolism surrounding health foods encapsulates far more than a concern with nutrition or a critique of the social organisation of food production. Instead, the symbolism links to a new sense of the inner geography of the body and the significance of this body for society in general. Nowhere are new attitudes towards health and the body clearer than in these beliefs in the power of healthy eating as a solution to all individual and social ills.

In other words, the Mediterranean diet operates as an antidote to the problems associated with late modernity. As a myth, it is a part of the technologies of the self that provide some semblance of reassurance in the face of risk and unpredictability and, as such, look paradoxical. The Mediterranean diet as encapsulated in recommended dietary intakes, dietary guidelines and commercial interests of the Mediterranean diet are the industrial edicts that encapsulate risk and the industrialized nature of eating in late modernity but simultaneously give rise to their own anti-industrial antidote. Consequently, underlying the industrial, and fundamental to its success, is the Mediterranean diet as a more intimate understanding of nutrition. This understanding recognizes that 'food is there to be enjoyed—a perfect blend of science and art' (Tapsell et al., 1998: S31).

What has developed is a nutrition practice that has been validated by science and history but that also enables the consumer to connect with a pastoral idyll which ignores the origins in frugality and instead encourages consumption as pleasure. This brings us to a dichotomy, a bifurcation in the concept of the Mediterranean diet. While this diet, within the nutrition discourse, brings hope of salvation from the scourge of lifestyle diseases, in its original form, it remains a diet of frugality. There can be pleasure in denial and prudence, but the pleasure of the Mediterranean diet stems from measured abundance. The diet is not a product of the industrial kitchen but rather encapsulates all that is 'good', 'natural' and 'wholesome'. The Mediterranean diet successfully negotiates sustainability in a global context. As has already been indicated, the risks that need to be addressed in late modernity, for any diet, apply not only to the self but also to the population.

The sustainability of the Mediterranean diet again brings into juxtaposition the dichotomy between abundance and scarcity. The consumption of fish advocated by this diet has health benefits but, because of the fragility of international fish stocks, any global increase in fish consumption would be unsustainable, and so the call for a wholesale increase in fish consumption has been moderated (Gussow, 1995, 2000). Gussow (1995) argues that the Mediterranean diet has the potential to improve the sustainability of farming globally by supporting local farmers and the maintenance of local farmland, with the inclusion of locally available fruit and vegetables in season. The Mediterranean diet is extended further, as the obscure producers of commodities become people with whom face-to-face relationships can be formed. Not only is the environment enriched on a global scale, but the local community is also enhanced and a sense of cooperation, trust and social cohesion is generated; that is, there is a positive solution to the ethical anxiety of eaters.

The Mediterranean diet is an example of a proactive technique based on hyper- and pessimistic activism. That is, individuals actively consume the components of their diets, in their measured abundance, in order to prevent death for as long as possible. In so doing they form partnerships and build trust. Conversely, the response to 'food fright', of which genetically modified food is the most recent on a list that includes irradiation, 'mad cow' disease, pesticide residues and the addition of preservatives and colourings, is a reaction. The result, however, is still a pessimistic activism that requires the recognition of a loss of trust and the subsequent formation of new alliances using food as the bridge for action.

Genetically Modified Foods

Genetically enhancing the quality of our food supply is not a new practice. The process was first described by the monk Mendel between 1856 and 1863 when he explained the genetic selection of subsequent crops of peas. This type of enhancement relies on growing a crop and then selecting those plants that did not succumb to a disease or that produced a better end result—for example, bigger, tastier fruit—and then breeding from those plants (a comparable practice has long been used in animal husbandry). It is a lengthy process, and any aberrant strains simply fail to survive. Genetic modification in its current usage relies on techniques at the molecular level. It allows scientists to insert specific genes into organisms and, therefore, bypass the trial-and-error process. It also enables cross-species insertion of genes. For example, genes can be moved from bacteria into crops to increase their resistance to disease (Commonwealth Scientific and Industrial Research Organisation [CSIRO], 2004).

Since their first commercial outing in 1994, genetically modified (GM) or genetically engineered (GE) foods have polarized opinion. Supporters claim that GM foods will result in increased yields, lowered pesticide and herbicide use, faster ripening and maturing processes, control of growth and decay and increased profits ([Economic and Social Research Council] ESRC Global Environmental Change Programme, 1999). The technology is seen by proponents as vital for alleviating world food insecurity and delivering cheaper food. Its use, therefore, 'must not be rejected through ignorance and irrational fears fuelled by the anti-technology lobby' (Wilson et al., 1999: 76). Those not in favour of GM foods argue about the unknown long-term effects on health of introducing antibiotic-resistant bacteria, toxins and allergens. Detractors also claim that the technology creates genetically uniform crops, thereby reducing biodiversity and making crops more vulnerable to disease. World food shortages, they argue, are not due to an inadequate supply of food but to political and economic problems, so increases in yield will have little effect.

The public discourse around GM foods and the polarization into a pro and anti dichotomy has generated discussions around the relationship between biotechnology and trust. The technophiles have argued that the 'ignorant public' simply requires education on the benefits of GM foods in order to accept the 'correct' view. This approach has been criticized as being too simplistic and failing to take into consideration that individual risk perception is not linear but multidimensional. It also fails to acknowledge that there is generally a good public grasp of the technical issues but what is lacking is a convincing argument of universal benefit on health, environmental and social grounds (Costa-Font & Mossialos, 2007; ESCR, 1999; Hansen et al., 2003). The issue for GM foods is not one of information but rather of the perceived lack of control over the consumption of certain foods and trust in the agents and institutions that can affect that control (Biotechnology Australia, 2005; ESCR, 1999; Eureka Strategic Research, 2007). The numerous studies investigating the opposition to GM foods highlight the changes that have occurred with time in both the dynamics of the agri-food networks and the relationship between 'expert' and 'lay' knowledge. The Mediterranean diet essentially took a diet that was already available, tried and tested, and used science to explain its benefits. The connection between the 'industrial' and the 'natural' reinforces its usefulness in both local and global contexts. GM food, on the other hand, is the industrial trying to find a connection with the natural.

Food choice, as Fischler (1980) has argued, is an activity that now engenders 'gastro-anomy'. This anomic state referred to the individualization of choice resulting in few clear sociocultural cues to guide choice. Individual 'choice' remains but is now combined with the rapid expansion of new foods or the alteration of once familiar foods through biotechnology, generating new levels of anxiety and increasing the imperative to search for and find adequate signposts to assist in guiding that choice. While globalization has increased exposure to new foods it has also created spaces for new collective action as well as the creation of new imagined communities that are able to generate a sense of belonging and shared identity (Melucci, 1989; Warde, 1997). These imagined communities generally centre on collective actions that focus on anti-neoliberal activism, often deploying a rhetoric of anti- or responsible consumerism. In this context as a pessimist action against GM foods, the tenets of anti-globalization and environmental organizations provide signposts or cues to temper food choice in terms of social, environmental and nutritional sustainability.

Greenpeace is one of the organizations in Australia leading the campaign against GM food through their 'true food' movement. Now in its fourth edition, the *True Food Guide* provides consumers with information about food manufacturers that produce items known to be free of GM ingredients versus those who cannot guarantee GM-free status. The link between Greenpeace's anti-GM campaign and notions of sustainability and the global are very much evident both on the organization's Web site and in previous editions of its *True Food Guide: How to Shop GE-free,* which states:

> All over the world, a growing movement of people is cooking up a new vision of food. In this vision, food is an integral thread in the fabric of the community, connecting people to each other and to the earth itself. In this vision, food is also plentiful, sustainable and nourishing. This groundswell of people wants food that is pure, tasty and authentic. We want food that is true. (Greenpeace Australia Pacific, 2003: 27)

The problem for GM foods is that their basis in the industrial leaves very few opportunities to incorporate trust and social cohesion. Consuming organic food, on the other hand, reverses that trend and brings nostalgia as a key strategy to ameliorate the impact of the industrial. This nostalgia is for a time when there was a direct relationship with growing food or at the very least with the people who grew the food. In so doing, nostalgia is created not as a negative going back but as a bridge between past, present and future (Hage, 1997). Nostalgia, however, is one way to develop such an ethos by harnessing it to create a bridge between historical epochs, between 'spheres of living'; to create a self that can use an ethic of food choice, one part of which is nutrition, 'for living a life that is both pleasurable and respectable, both personally unique and socially normal' (Rose, 1999: 86).

Organic Food

GM foods have crossed the boundary that separates 'good' from 'bad', 'normal' from 'deviant'. However, these distinctions are difficult to maintain absolutely; they are like the problem Douglas (1966) identifies with respect to dirt. As she says, 'there is no such thing as absolute dirt: it exists in the eye of the beholder' (Douglas, 1966: 2). Soil becomes dirt when it crosses a predetermined boundary and, in the process, becomes a potential pollutant. Likewise, food is neither absolutely 'good' nor 'bad'. The dichotomy only emerges when it crosses the boundary into either the body or the extracorporeal space. GM foods have been described as 'genetic pollutants' and as 'tampering with nature' (Ho, 2002: 81). What emerges then is a binary where, on the one hand, GM foods are described as unnatural, dangerous and industrial, while on the other, organic food is characterized as natural, safe, wholesome and local (Pence, 2002).

Organic food consumption relies on what Giddens (1990) describes as trust in persons or 'face work commitment', as opposed to GM food, which requires trust in institutions or 'faceless commitment'. The form of trust associated with organic products was built on the development of reciprocal relationships between consumers and small producers, hence Greenpeace's mantra 'eat GE-free, eat organic, eat local' (Greenpeace Australia Pacific, 2007). While organic food still has associations with trust and face-to-face relationships, it is nonetheless undergoing transition. Worldwide, the organic food market has grown markedly; in Australia, production has increased from less than 500 producers with an estimated value of $28 million to over 1,600 producers with an estimated value of $400 million (Biological Farmers of Australia, 2006). Organic food production is no longer a local industry but has been co-opted by big business and as such it has now moved from the periphery to the core. It is no longer the domain of the 'hippie' and radical 'greenie', but is now consumed by a broad cross-section of Australians (Lyons et al., 2001). Furthermore, its shift out of a wholly local domain characterized by face-to-face contact has required the creation of new vehicles for trust, including legal specifications for the word 'organic' and branding in order to be able to identify certified organic products.

Organic foods act as 'islands of predictability' and 'islands of certainty' (Arendt, 1958: 244). In this regard, these technologies simultaneously acknowledge anxiety and resolutely incorporate pleasure to be exploited for the self by the self by encapsulating the ascetic/aesthetic, anxiety/pleasure dilemmas. As a bundle of techniques, their primary function is to resolve the ontological condition of action. That is, they serve to establish predictability through a combination of nature and science and via a number of acts of undoing or forgiveness, as cures, remedies and treatments. They are perfect foils for GM foods.

Conclusion

The self oscillates between private person and local collective, and between public and global citizen, or, as Hunter (1994: 177) intimates, 'government negotiates between spheres of living that give rise to quite different ethical personae'. As forms of nutrition, the Mediterranean diet and GM foods are proactive and reactive pathways to illuminate the self as simultaneously different and participatory. They provide a bridge that connects the self as private with the self as public citizen and connects the local with the global. In providing this bridge, nutrition offers a number of opportunities for constructing an ethic of food choice based on what is historically, culturally and nutritionally relevant and for using food to reinvent the self in order to become a part of a sustainable food system, albeit by proxy. For the middle classes, the active pessimistic activism of the Mediterranean diet and the antidotes against GM foods provide a way to become a 'good' global citizen.

The Mediterranean diet and the antidotes to GM foods demonstrate how, in late modernity, the project that is the self and the management of risk remains ongoing. However, they also highlight that the project of the self is increasingly complex; there are no clear delineations of risk or the opportunities for ameliorating that risk. This increasing complexity requires an ever-increasing number of subtle techniques. The Mediterranean diet and antidotes to GM food provide these techniques to train the self to be morally pure using exercises in freedom and unfreedom that still remain within the frameworks that constitute the government of nutrition. The outcome of this training is a tempered self that can take its place as a citizen of the world. Nutrition, in late modernity, becomes another bridge connecting the public with the private, the global with the local, risk with pleasure and the universal with the particular. In so doing, it enables an ethic of food choice that is a local, occasioned practice based on what is historically, culturally and nutritionally relevant at that time.

Notes

1. Pre-swallowing nutrition culture refers to interests that 'centre on socio-cultural issues and food, food distribution patterns and habits, values and beliefs' (Coveney and Santich, 1997: 274). Postswallowing, on the other hand, refers to an interest in the nutrient–disease interface where the interest in nutrition is solely focussed on disease causation and prevention (Crotty, 1995).

2. In Australia during the 1990s, olive oil companies and the International Olive Oil Council (IOOC) made concerted efforts to woo the public to become olive oil consumers. You could be a member of the Bertolli Club, be a Friend of Tertullia or attend a number of events staged by the IOOC. Australians no longer need to be convinced. Olive oil production has risen from 500 tonnes in 1998–1999 to a predicted yield of 13,000 tonnes in 2008–2009 (IOOC, 2008).

References

Alberti-Fidanza, A., Alunni Paolacci, C., Chiuchiù, M.P., Coli, R., Fruttini, D., Verducci, G., and Fidanza, F. (1994), 'Dietary Studies on Two Rural Italian Population Groups of the Seven Countries Study 1: Food and Nutrient Intake at the Thirty-first Year Follow-up in 1991', *European Journal of Clinical Nutrition,* 48: 85–91.

Arendt, H. (1958), *The Human Condition.* Chicago: University of Chicago Press.

Barthes, R. (1972), *Mythologies,* trans. Annette Lavers, London: Vintage.

Baum, F. (1999), 'Food, Social Capital and Public Health: Exploring the Links', *Eating into the Future: The First Australian Conference on Food, Health and the Environment, Adelaide 1999,* 10 Nov. 2000, <http://www.chdf.org.au/eatwellsa/conference>.

Bauman, Z. (1999), *In Search of Politics,* Cambridge: Polity Press.

Bauman, Z. (2000), *Liquid Modernity,* Cambridge: Polity Press.

Biological Farmers of Australia (2006), *Organic Annual 2006,* <http://www.bfa.com.au/_files/BFA_FINALREPORT_WEB.pdf> accessed 16 September 2009.

Biotechnology Australia (2005), 'What You Really Need to Know about What the Public Really Thinks about GM Foods', Canberra: Biotechnology Australia.

Bondia-Pons, I., Schroder, H., Covas, M., Castellote, A.I., Kaakkonen, J., Poulsen, H.E., Gaddi, A.V., Machowetz, A., Kiesewetter, H., and López-Sabater, M.C. (2007), 'Moderate Consumption of Olive Oil by Healthy European Men Reduces Systolic Blood Pressure in Non-Mediterranean Participants 1', *The Journal of Nutrition,* 137/1: 84–8.

Caraher, M., and Coveney, J. (2004), 'Public Health Nutrition and Food Policy', *Public Health Nutrition,* 7/5: 591–8.

Costa-Font, J., and Mossialos, E. (2007) 'Are Perceptions of "Risks" and "Benefits" of Genetically Modified Food (In)dependent?', *Food Quality and Preference,* 18: 173–82.

Coveney, J. (1999), 'The Science and Spirituality of Nutrition'. *Critical Public Health* 9/1: 23–37.

Coveney, J. (2000a), *Food, Morals and Meaning: The Pleasure and Anxiety of Eating,* London: Routledge.

Coveney, J. (2000b) 'Food Security and Sustainability', *Asia Pacific Journal of Clinical Nutrition,* 9(Suppl.): S97–S100.

Coveney, J., and Santich, B. (1997), 'A Question of Balance: Nutrition, Health and Gastronomy', *Appetite,* 28: 267–77.

Coward, R. (1989), *The Whole Truth: The Myth of Alternative Health,* London: Faber & Faber.

Crotty, P. (1995), *Good Nutrition: Fact and Fashion in Dietary Advice,* Sydney: Allen & Unwin.

Crotty, P. (1998), 'The Mediterranean Diet as a Food Guide: The Problem of Culture and History', *Nutrition Today* 33/6: 227–31.

Commonwealth Scientific and Industrial Research Organisation (CSIRO). (2004), *GM food safety, questions and answers,* <http://www.csiro.au/pubgenesite/food safe_faqs.htm> accessed November 2007.

Davison, A. (2001), *Technology and the Contested Meanings of Sustainability,* Albany: State University of New York Press.

de Longeril, M, and Salen, P. (1998), 'Mediterranean Diet in Secondary Prevention of Coronary Heart Disease', *Australian Journal of Nutrition and Dietetics. Profiles in Nutrition: The Mediterranean Diet for the New Millennium,* 55/4(Suppl.): S16–S20.

Douglas, M. (1966), *Purity and Danger: An Analysis of Concepts of Pollution and Taboo,* London: Routledge & Kegan Paul.

ESRC Global Environmental Change Programme (1999), *The Politics of GM Food: Risk, Science and Public Trust,* Special Briefing Paper #5, <http:www.sussex.ac.uk/units/gec/gecko/gec-gm-f.pdf> accessed 12 November 2003.

Esposito, K., Ciotola, M., Guigliano, F., and De Sio, M. (2006), 'Mediterranean Diet Improves Erectile Function in Subjects with the Metabolic Syndrome', *International Journal of Impotence Research,* 18/4: 405–10.

Eureka Strategic Research (2007), *Community Attitudes to Biotechnology: Report on Food and Agriculture Applications,* Canberra: Biotechnology Australia.

Fischler, C. (1980), 'Food Habits, Social Change and the Nature/Culture Dilemma', *Social Science Information,* 19/6: 937–53.

Foucault, M. (1984), 'On the Genealogy of Ethics: An Overview of Work in Progress', in P. Rabinow (ed.), *The Foucault Reader,* London: Penguin.

Foucault, M. (1990), *The Care of the Self: The History of Sexuality Volume 3,* translated by Robert Hurley, London: Penguin.

Fox, N.J. (1998), 'Postmodernism and "Health"', in A. Petersen and C. Waddell (eds.), *Health Matters: A Sociology of Illness, Prevention and Care,* Sydney: Allen & Unwin.

Giacco, R., and Riccardi, G. (1991), 'Comparison of Current Eating Habits in Various Mediterranean Countries', in G.A. Spiller (ed.), *The Mediterranean Diets in Health and Disease,* New York: Van Nostrand Reinhold.

Giddens, A. (1990), *Consequences of Modernity,* Stanford: Stanford University Press.

Greenpeace Australia Pacific (2003), *True Food Guide: How to Shop GE-free,* third edition, Sydney: Greenpeace.

Greenpeace Australia Pacific (2007), *True Food Network,* <http://www.truefood.org.au/ index2.html> accessed November 2007.

Gussow, J.D. (1995), 'Mediterranean Diets: Are They Environmentally Responsible', *American Journal of Clinical Nutrition,* 61(Suppl.): S1383–S9.

Gussow, J.D. (2000), 'Is Local vs. Global the Next Environmental Imperative?', *Nutrition Today,* 1/1: 29–34.

Hage, G. (1997), 'At Home in the Entrails of the West: Multiculturalism, Ethnic Food and Migrant Home-Building', in H. Grace, G. Hage, L. Johnson, J. Langsworth and M. Symonds (eds.), *Home/World. Space, Community and Marginality in Sydney's West,* Sydney: Pluto Press.

Hansen, J., Holm, L., Frewer, L., Robinson, P., and Sandøe, P. (2003), 'Beyond the Knowledge Deficit: Recent Research into Lay and Expert Attitudes to Food Risks', *Appetite,* 41: 111–21.

Ho, M. (2002), 'The Unholy Alliance', in G.E. Pence (ed.), *The Ethics of Food: A Reader for the Twenty First Century,* Lanham: Rowman & Littlefield Publishers.

Hunter, I. (1994), *Rethinking the School: Subjectivity, Bureaucracy, Criticism,* Sydney: Allen & Unwin.

International Olive Oil Council (IOOC) (2008), *World Olive Oil Figures.* <http://www.internationaloliveoil.org/downloads/production1_ang.PDF> accessed 16 September 2009.

James, A. (1996), 'Cooking the Books: Global or Local Identities in Contemporary British Food Cultures', in D. Howes (ed.), *Cross Cultural Consumption: Global Markets Local Realities,* London: Routledge.

James, W., and Philip, T. (1995), 'Nutrition Science and Policy Research: Implications for Mediterranean Diets', *American Journal of Clinical Nutrition,* 61(Suppl.): S1324–S8.

Keys, A. (1995), 'Mediterranean Diet and Public Health: Personal Reflections', *American Journal of Clinical Nutrition,* 61(Suppl.): S1321–S3.

Lupton, D. (1999), *Risk,* London: Routledge.

Lyons, K., Lockie, S., and Lawrence, G. (2001), 'Consuming "Green": the Symbolic Construction of Organic Foods', *Rural Society,* 11/3: 197–211.

Masana, L., Camprubi, M., Sarda, P., Sola, R., Joven, J. and Turner, P.R. (1991), 'The Mediterranean-Type Diet: Is There a Need for Further Modification', *American Journal of Clinical Nutrition,* 53: 886–9.

McHoul, A., and Grace, W. (1993), *A Foucault Primer: Discourse, Power and the Subject,* Melbourne: Melbourne University Press.

Melucci, Λ. (1989), *Challenging Codes: Collective Action in the Information Age,* New York: Cambridge University Press.

Melucci, A. (1996), *The Playing Self: Person and Meaning in the Planetary Society,* New York: Cambridge University Press

Mendez, M., Popkin, B., Jaksyn, P., and Berenguer, A. (2006), 'Adherence to a Mediterranean Diet Is Associated with Reduced 3-Year Incidence of Obesity', *The Journal of Nutrition,* 136/11: 2934–9.

Miller, Toby. (1993), *The Well-Tempered Self: Citizenship, Culture and the Postmodern Subject,* Baltimore: Johns Hopkins University Press.

Mintz, S. (1996), *Tasting Food, Tasting Freedom: Excursions into Eating, Power and the Past,* Boston: Beacon Press.

Nestle, M. (1995), 'Mediterranean Diets: Historical and Research Overview', *American Journal of Clinical Nutrition,* 61(Suppl.): S1313–S20.

O'Dea, K. (1994), 'The Australian Approach to the Mediterranean Diet', *Food Chain: Newsletter of Deakin University's Food and Nutrition Program,* 11: 1–3.

Paniagua, J.A., Gallego de la Sacristana, A., Romero, I., Vidal-Puig, A., Latre, J.M., Sanchez, E., Perez-Martinez, P., Lopez-Miranda, J., and Perez-Jiminez, F. (2007), 'Monounsaturated Fat-Rich Diet Prevents Central Body Fat Distribution and Decreases Postprandial Adiponectin Expression Induced by a Carbohydrate Rich Diet in Insulin-Resistant Subjects', *Diabetes Care,* 30/7: 1717–23.

Pence, G.E. (2002), 'Organic or Genetically Modified Food: Which is Better?', in G.E. Pence (ed.), *The Ethics of Food: A Reader for the Twenty First Century,* Lanham: Rowman & Littlefield Publishers.

Petersen, A.R. (1996), 'Risk and the Regulated Self: The Discourse of Health Promotion as Politics of Uncertainty', *Australia and New Zealand Journal of Sociology,* 32/1: 44–57.

Pollan, M. (2006), *The Omnivore's Dilemma: The Search for the Perfect Meal in a Fast-Food World,* London: Bloomsbury.

Ritzer, G. (1998), *The McDonaldization Thesis: Explorations and Extensions,* London: Sage.

Rose, N. (1992), 'Governing the Enterprising Self', in P. Heelas and P. Morris (eds.), *The Values of the Enterprise Culture: The Moral Debate,* London: Routledge.

Rose, N. (1996), 'Governing "Advanced" Liberal Democracies', in A. Barry, T. Osborne and N. Rose (eds.), *Foucault and Political Reason: Liberalism, Neo-liberalism and Rationalities of Government,* London: University College of London Press.

Rose, N. (1999), *Powers of Freedom: Reframing Political Thought,* Cambridge: Cambridge University Press.

Sacks, F.M. (1998), 'Scientific Basis of the Healthy Mediterranean Diet', *Australian Journal of Nutrition and Dietetics. Profiles in Nutrition: The Mediterranean Diet for the New Millennium,* 55/4 (Suppl.): S4–S7.

Sokolov, R. (1991), *Why We Eat What We Eat: How the Encounter between the New World and the Old Changed the Way Everyone on the Planet Eats,* New York: Summit.

Symons, M. (1994), 'Olive Oil and Air-conditioned Culture', *Westerly,* 4: 27–36.

Tapsell, L.C., Calvert, G.D., Meyer, B.J., and Storlien, L.H. (1998), 'Energy Balance: Fats and Fallacies', *Australian Journal of Nutrition and Dietetics. Profiles in Nutrition: The Mediterranean Diet for the New Millennium,* 55/4 (Suppl.): S29–S32.

Trichopoulou, A., Bamia, C., and Trichopoulos, D. (2005), 'Mediterranean Diet and Survival Among Patients with Coronary Heart Disease in Greece', *Archives of Internal Medicine,* 165/8: 929–36.

Trichopoulou, A., Corella, D., Martinez-Gonzalez, M.A., Soriguer, F., and Ordovas, J.M. (2006), 'The Mediterranean Diet and Cardiovascular Epidemiology', *Nutrition Reviews,* 64/10: S13–S19.

Trichopoulou, A., Kouris-Blazos, A., Vassilakou, T., Gnardellis, C., Polychronopoulos, E., Venizelos, M., Lagiou, P., Wahlqvist, M.L., and Trichopoulos, D. (1995), 'Diet and Survival of Elderly Greeks: A Link to the Past', *American Journal of Clinical Nutrition,* 61 (Suppl.): S1346–S1350.

Trichopoulou, A., and Lagiou, P. (1997), 'Healthy Traditional Mediterranean Diet: An Expression of Culture, History, and Lifestyle', *Nutrition Reviews,* 55/11: 383–9.

Wahlqvist, M., Darmadi-Blackberry, I., Kouris-Blazos, A., Jolley, D., Steen, B., Lukito, W., Horie, Y. (2005), 'Does Diet Matter for Survival in Long-Lived Cultures?', *Asia Pacific Journal of Clinical Nutrition,* 14/1: 2–6.

Walter-Toews, D., and Lang, T. (2000), 'The New Conceptual Base for Food and Agricultural Policy: The Emerging Model of Links between Agriculture, Food, Health, Environment and Society', *Global Change and Human Health,* 1/2: 116–30.

Warde, A. (1997), *Consumption, Food and Taste: Culinary Antinomies and Commodity Culture,* London: Routledge.

Weih, M., Wiltfang, J., and Kornhuber, J. (2007), 'Non-Pharmacologic Prevention of Alzheimer's Disease: Nutritional and Life-Style Risk Factors', *Journal of Neural Transmission,* 114: 1187–97.

Wilson, M.A., Hillman, J.R., and Robinson, D.J. (1999), 'Genetic Modification in Context and Perspective', In J. Morris and R. Bate (eds.), *Fearing Food: Risk, Health and Environment,* Oxford: Butterworth-Heinemann.

–11–

Exotic Restaurants and Expatriate Home Cooking: Indian Food in Manhattan

Krishnendu Ray

New York University

On 2 November 2005, Julia Moskin, a food critic for *The New York Times* (NYT) wrote, 'New Yorkers have learned to tread fearlessly in the world of real Indian food. They know pakoras from samosas and dabble in idlis and utthappams' (2005: F1). Frank Bruni, arguably the most influential restaurant critic in the United States, reviewed the restaurant Mint and found it wanting (2005: E2, 43). But he found the *chole bhature* at Tandoori Hut exquisite. In 1998, Danny Meyer, one of New York's elite restaurateurs, accelerated this trend by recruiting the Goan chef Floyd Cardoz to open the most expensive Indo-French restaurant, calling it Tabla. That was right in the middle of the rising tide of talk on Indian food in Manhattan. The fact that the NYT has carried about a dozen different stories on fine-dining Indian restaurants over the last few years tells us something about how trendy Indian food has become among Manhattan taste-makers.

The Indian Restaurant in Manhattan

Indian food is fashionable but it does not reach the heights of other cuisines. The 2006 *Zagat,* which is a survey of fine-dining restaurants, listed 43 Indian restaurants, after Italian at 389, American 270, French 202, Japanese 101 and Chinese at 63. *MenuPages,* a more exhaustive listing, identified 163 Indian restaurants out of a total of 8,561 eateries. To get a perspective on these numbers, it is important to remember that there are more than 23,000 eating and drinking establishments in New York City.

In terms of check averages in *Zagat* 2006—which is good shorthand for the hierarchy of taste—Indian restaurants came in at $33.85, after French at $47.81, Japanese at $46.72, American at $42.83, Italian at $42.27, Greek at $38.71 and Spanish (as separate from Latino) at $37.73. In general there is an inverse relationship between the demographic weight of a group and the check average. For example, out of about eight million people in the five boroughs of New York City, only 52,907 claim

French ancestry, yet French restaurants are among the most popular destinations for the fine-dining clientele, with 202 French eateries evaluated by *Zagat* 2006. In addition, the most high-priced restaurants classify themselves as Continental, French, Japanese or American. The two most expensive restaurants in Manhattan in 2007 were Masa and Per Se. In contrast, almost two million New Yorkers claim an African American heritage, and another two million claim Latino ancestry, but fine-dining restaurants even remotely associated with their identities are among the fewest (11 and 10 respectively out of a total of over 2,000 restaurants evaluated by *Zagat* in 2006) and by far the cheapest ($24.50 for Soul and $22.00 for TexMex).

Just as there is a social clustering of Indian restaurants in the middle—along with Chinese, Thai, Vietnamese and Korean eateries—there is some degree of spatial clustering in three geographic areas: the stretch of East 6th Street between First and Second Avenues that houses almost fifteen Indian restaurants run mostly by Bangladeshi migrants; the area between 26th and 29th Streets on Lexington Avenue, which houses about twenty restaurants; and Jackson Heights in Queens, which is popular among expatriate Indian men and hipster American students with adventurous palates.[1] By the end of the 1990s, the city and its suburbs were also peppered by Indian and Pakistani grocery stores and bodegas that sell cooked food—such as *samosas, dals* and vegetable curries—on the side. But such eateries have rarely entered the rarefied realm of restaurant criticism.

Indian Food Enters the Discourse on Fine-Dining Restaurants

Understandably, Indian food was covered sparingly in the NYT during the first hundred years of its publication (from 1853 to 1953). The first proper discussion of it appeared in 1876 under the title 'An Essay on Curry', which was really a diatribe against serving Chablis with curry. It ended with the judgement that 'For, though curry is a good thing in its place and time ... it hardly deserves to win its way, into the higher domain of the gastronomic art. It still rather deserves the epithet of "barbaric" than that of "marvellous"' (Anonymous, 1876: 2).

If Indian food was mentioned in passing and mostly in disdain, it is no surprise that Indian *restaurants* in the United States were equally rare, first showing up in the 1920s but disappearing quickly thereafter until the 1960s. On 3 April 1921 Helen Lowry identified the first Indian restaurant in the NYT in an article titled 'The Old World in New York' (1921: 37). She did not give its name but wrote, 'Six short weeks ago an Indian restaurant was discovered on Eighth Avenue near 42nd Street. Grave Indian gentlemen, with American clothes but with great turbans on their heads, used to come in for their curry and rice' (1921: 37). There was one other reference to an Indian restaurant in New York before that, on 7 August 1912, but it is unclear from the report whether the restaurant was real or just rumoured:

Ranji Smile, who said he was a Prince, the fifth son of the late Ameer of Baluchistan ... was married yesterday at the City Hall to Miss Violet Ethel Rochlitz, daughter of Julian W. Rochlitz of this city ... In May, 1910, he [had] obtained a license to wed Miss Anna Maria W. Davieson, but no return was ever made to the License Bureau to indicate that a wedding had been performed. At that time the Prince said he had formerly run an Indian restaurant on Fifth Avenue, between Thirty-third and Thirty fourth Streets. About thirteen years ago Mr. Smile was a curry cook at Sherry's. (Anonymous, 1912: 11)

The first named restaurant advertising itself as a 'Magnificent New Indian Restaurant' was Longchamps on Madison Avenue at 59th Street, which was a chain of nine restaurants that also served Hungarian beef goulash (4 October 1935).

Indian *food* in America has been covered over a longer duration and in much greater detail, starting with a reference to make-believe Delhi at Luna Park, in Coney Island in 1904, where there was a passing discussion of Bombay duck and other peculiarities of the Indian diet (Anonymous, 1904). The next ripple came just ahead of the 1933 World Fair at Chicago, which included an India pavilion financed by the Indian cricketing prince Ranji, who promised, to the great delight of Americans, it would appear from the article, that 'Indian food, such as rice and curry, will be featured in the restaurant and served in typical Indian fashion by Indian waiters and waitresses in native costumes' (Anonymous, 1932: 17).

One of the earliest discussions of curry in the context of gourmandise appeared on 12 March 1939. Charlotte Hughes (1939: 53) asserted that 'Curry has come to be a lot more popular in New York in the last few years, with curry restaurants springing up here and there and with hotels putting curry dishes on their menus'. Unfortunately, she did not list either those restaurants or the menu items. She conceded that 'Men, it seems, are more likely to be curry fans than women'. She went on to assert that 'Curry powder is a blend of fifteen or twenty spices' that needs proper blending, as explained by 'Darmadasa, of the East India Curry Shop, for Ceylon curry of oysters'.

Jane Holt, working in conjunction with the Civilian Defense Volunteer Office (with an interest in civilian nutrition, especially vitamin deficiency) and trade organizations such as the Spice Trader's Association, wrote a number of articles on curry in the 1940s. Where Holt left off, Jane Nickerson continued in her 'News of Food' column, announcing the 'first direct shipment of curry powder since the war' to arrive from Madras on 7 September 1976. She informed us that 'Chutney, by definition, is a relish that is equally sour and sweet, according to the proprietor of the East India Curry Shop, a restaurant that probably serves the most "authentic" curries in town' (Nickerson, 1946: 12). By 1948 India Prince was opened on 47th Street by C. B. Deva. The new restaurant, 'neat but unpretentious in appearance, provides an opportunity for savouring some excellent Indian food, at prices ranging from $1.50 to $5 for a complete luncheon or dinner' (Anonymous, 1948: 10).

The Hungarian-born chef Ernest Koves at Hotel Sulgrave in New York had to explain through June Owen of the NYT that 'Indian or Bengali curry is a very refined dish. You get just a faint taste of the spices', and curry anyway is a mixture of 'sixteen or seventeen different spices, with red pepper, saffron, ginger, cayenne and black pepper predominating. In India, one "rolls one's own curry," that is, you place the whole spices on a stone slab and work over with a rolling pin until they are completely powderized'. He concluded, 'To taste a truly fine curry, one must go to India' (in Owen, 1955: 24). Similarly, Nickerson noted that there was hardly 'a hint of curry' in the cuisine of Dharamjit Singh, a 'crimson-turbaned Sikh' who cooked an Indian meal for some food-minded New Yorkers in 1955 (Nickerson, 1955: 20). He said, 'the authentic cooking of his country had a diversity that included many mild dishes. Mr. Singh observed that curries he had eaten in east Indian restaurants in New York were hotter than anything he ever had tasted in Delhi' (Nickerson, 1955: 20).

Until about 1961 an authoritative native interlocutor was always invoked in talking about Indian food. The informant was often a spice trader, a restaurateur, a housewife but rarely a cook. Craig Claiborne, who changed the shape of restaurant reviews and culinary reporting by acquiring an increasingly authoritative posture towards the food and the audience, initially also depended on the exotic housewife to vindicate him. On 25 February 1960, perhaps in his first piece on Indian food in the NYT, Claiborne depended on Manorama Phillips (Claiborne, 1960: 22): 'Miss Phillips is a diminutive, dark-haired young woman with a mercurial smile who has lived in the United States for nearly four years'. Phillips worked for the Government of India Trade Center and roomed with an American woman. Her three-room apartment was 'handsomely furnished with Indian accessories'. The article was accompanied by a six-by-six inch photograph of Phillips in her apartment, clad in a sari and framed by exquisite Indian hand-crafted textiles.

In 1960 Nan Ickeringill advertised another kind of authority: the Conservative English knight Sir William Steward—owner of the famous Veeraswammy's in London—who was credited with launching a 'one-man crusade to discover the secret of good curries' (Ickeringill, 1960: 41). 'It was really hard work', recalled the tenacious Englishman. Knowledge of curry had to be wrested from the hands of the inscrutable native. The tenacious knight forced his way into kitchens; none 'would tell him how curry was made, but the kitchen staff let him watch. They did not think he would be able to solve the puzzle that way. However they sadly underestimated both Sir William's diligence and intelligence'. As late as 11 May 1961, Claiborne depended on the figure of the sahib gone native to flavour his curry. He called on William Clifford, 'the young editor with Simon & Schuster' who 'is an excellent and enthusiastic cook who lived in India several years ago' (Claiborne, 1961b: 44).

Only by 9 July 1961 did Claiborne let go of such aides as the adventurous knight, the housewife or the spice trader to give five recipes for chutney (Claiborne, 1961a: SM35). By mid-1962 Claiborne's self-confidence about ethnic food peaked, and he ranged widely through hot tamale, chilli con carne, Senegalese soup, lamb curry and chicken curry (Claiborne, 1962a: 148). 'An enthusiasm for curried dishes', he said, 'seems to be national and curries are as welcome in Wichita as in Westchester' (Claiborne, 1962b: 32). Then there was the long explanation of what the curry is not, which we have seen before: 'It is almost easier to define a curry by what it is not than by what it is. It is not made from the single spice of a tree, vine or bush. In the western hemisphere, at least, curry powder is a combination of a dozen or more spices, the prominent one being turmeric' (Claiborne, 1962b: 32). This appears to be an enduring trope of culinary journalism on curry and other ethnic and foreign things—it is not what you think—asserting an early kind of expertise that came to bloom slowly among this cohort of cultural experts. This was the beginning of the process of sacralization of the restaurant critic in American society that had emerged in full force by the end of the twentieth century.

Claiborne eventually launched an explanation of the authentic thing: 'In India and Pakistan, a curry is not a single dish made from a classic formula but is more or less any spiced sauce made with various meats, fish or fowl. Within the course of a single meal at an Indian table there may be several curries, none of which will taste the same because the spices are varied with considerable care and discrimination'. How does he know all this? We are not told any more. No native is paraded out nor any claims made about travels in India. Perhaps by now Claiborne is expected to be an expert by his increasingly cosmopolitan audience and he is therefore supposed to know such things. As a result he launches into three remarkable recipes that are curries precisely and only because curry powder is added, presumably the very thing curries in India do not have, but the recipes are of the universe of sweet and spicy meat sauces with added fruits, perhaps a curry only in name (Claiborne, 1962b: 32).

Subsequently, he appeared as jaded as the title of the next restaurant review, 'A Rare Thing: Indian Restaurant with Food to Get Excited About'. In it he was full of praise for the Gaylord restaurant housed in the Blackstone Hotel, at 50 East 58th Street, for being the 'only Indian restaurant in the city with genuine tandoors or tandoori, the authentic Indian hot-fired clay ovens. We find these ovens an enormous plus, for without them an authentic "tandoori chicken"—and that of the Gaylord is equal to the best we've eaten in New Delhi or London—cannot really be made' (Claiborne, 1974: 34).

He had recently strengthened his credentials by travelling in northern India (in 1970), in particular Delhi and Agra, and by dining at Moti Mahal, the Moghul Room (at the Oberoi Intercontinental Hotel), the Tandoor (at the President Hotel) and at the Flora across from Jama Masjid, all in Delhi. He also visited the Clarks Shiraz in Agra. On his travels, connoting an expanding budget for the coverage of food, Claiborne momentarily lost his capacity to be critical, and was giddy about hotel cuisine, where it seemed it was impossible to 'find a bad native dish' (Claiborne, 1970: 56). In this case, the friendly exoticism returned, such that it became impossible to distinguish the good from the bad. But just because he could not discriminate between various hotel cuisines, Claiborne did not give up on creating a hierarchy. He maintained his distance from common Americans, by scolding them: 'how odd it is that so many Americans go to foreign countries and ignore the native food of whatever place they happen to be' (Claiborne, 1970: 56). How does he know that? We are not told.

The 1974 article is also the first where Claiborne named the chefs—Ram Dass and Daulat Ram Sharma—neither of whom became celebrities. Claiborne was the first major restaurant critic in the United States to save the cook from anonymity, which turned out to be an important step in the making of a self-conscious cuisine. That trend took another two decades to bloom, and it happened rarely for an ethnic cook. The next time an Indian chef was named was by Florence Fabricant on 7 May 1978.[2] In 1979, when Mimi Sheraton reviewed Tandoor and Tre Scalini on the same page, the Indian chef was ignored, but we learn that the Italian chef was Vittorio Guarini (1979: C16). In 1985, even when Patricia Brooks credited improvements in an Indian restaurant to a new chef she did not find out who it was (1985: CN17). In 1986, when Bryan Miller reviewed Akbar and Meridies on the same page, only chef Susan Sugarman of the latter was named (1986: C24).

In 1984 when Marian Burros wrote that 'America is flexing its gastronomic muscles, and no where is this more obvious as in California. Here, where chefs are as glamorous as movie stars ...' (1984, C1) she was referring to named chefs. It is instructive to see who got named in a December 1985 roundup of notable suburban restaurants in Westchester County by M.H. Reed, who evaluated thirty eateries by name (1985: WC13). Almost every owner and chef of French and Continental restaurants—eleven total—was named. Exclusively Italian chefs were *not* named, although if they cooked French *and* northern Italian food they came out of the shadows. Spanish entrepreneurs were named but not the chef (*contra* Chithelen, 1986: LI5). Indian chefs were unknown. Japanese chefs were anonymous, and still are. This was a stark confirmation of the hierarchy of taste in terms of its relationship to the ethnicity of the cook in 1985.

Over the next decade some things changed as Italian and Japanese chefs got their say, but rarely did a Mexican, Korean or an Indian chef. Ethnic cooks generally remained invisible. 'It's a rare Indian restaurant', Eric Asimov noted as late as 2002, 'that acknowledges the existence of its chef, unless it's a star consultant like Madhur Jaffrey or Raji Jallepalli-Reiss' (2002: F10). Note the sleight of hand by which he assigned blame, apparently on Indian restaurateurs, but not restaurant critics for their complicity in the problem. By the 1990s coverage of Indian restaurants reached new heights, with 300 articles in the NYT in that decade, at a respectable distance behind Italian restaurants (1,264), Chinese (840), French (594), Japanese (368), American (347) and Mexican (316). The coverage of Indian restaurants was up from 182 in the 1980s, 100 in the 1970s, 13 in the 1960s and 2 in the 1950s. As coverage intensified, the associated commentary appropriated a more objective language of critique rather than just factual information, exotic fascination, or even sneering Orientalism.

For instance, on 13 September 1963 in reviewing the Kashmir Restaurant, an unnamed correspondent noted the mere facts of its location, price and décor, ending with a quick judgment—'it is one of the best Pakistani and Indian restaurants in town' (Anonymous, 1963: 51). By the 1964 World Fair the critical load was increased when Claiborne (the critic was named by then) noted that 'The food is admirably spiced but without the overpowering hotness that is frequently and often mistakenly ascribed to Indian cuisine … [although] the salad was ordinary and uninspired' (1964: 16). A touch of the exotic was maintained by reference to 'the most incredibly beautiful women, hostesses with delicate faces wearing saris and sandals'. In a 1969 review of Shalimar, Claiborne explained a new cuisine when he wrote, 'There's a very good appetizer called samosas, a pastry filled with well-spiced meat or vegetable', and sharpened his critical focus with 'There are two faults that seem basic to the Shalimar: The various curries are bland and have a sameness of flavor; and some of the dishes seem woefully over-cooked, particularly the shrimp' (Claiborne, 1969a: 42). Claiborne had come a long way from 1960 when he had to depend on Manorama Phillips to help him understand Indian food. He returned to the native informant once more in 1985 but this time to fathom a regional Indian cuisine— Gujarati (Claiborne, 1985: C1). By 1969 he was able to assert with confidence, all on his own, that 'There is not a restaurant in New York that prepares food equal to that in a well-staffed Indian or Pakistani home' (1969b: 12).

I do not want to insinuate that Claiborne was being pretentious. He was merely developing a script that distinguished a restaurant critic from others—as every new profession must—and that developed credibility with the public who had to be willing to pay for it. Practitioners in 'communities of practice are engaged in the generative process of producing their own future' (Lave and Wenger, 1991: 57–58). Claiborne in fact hit the perfect note. He came across as someone who knew his stuff but who could also display humility with a sense of humour. He was even willing to be corrected about Indian food.

It also appears that for the last 100 years everyone began their coverage of Indian food with a comment about heat. For instance, an anonymous 1897 piece titled 'Indian Curries' noted that the curry offered in the West 'consists principally of turmeric and cayenne pepper that sacrifices the roof of your mouth and tongue and gives no pleasure in eating' (Anonymous, 1897: BR7). Almost 100 years later, on 26 November 1982, Mimi Sheraton writing about an Indian restaurant noted,

> Dynamite is merely hot, but double [dynamite] is promised as the real thing, so insist on it if your tolerance is high. Having had a problem with customers who ask for food very spicy, then return it because it is too spicy, the owner has become reluctant to add the full share of chili and pepper, until he is sure of his customer. (1982, C18)

One thing had changed in 100 years: the complaint had been turned on its head. Sheraton, David Canady and Raymond Sokolov repeatedly insisted on the real thing, real heat, like connoisseurs. In the process they also incessantly berated the American public for forcing these ethnic folks to tone down the real thing. Why bother to have Indian food if it did not cauterize your throat, they wondered? Burros composed a whole piece titled 'A Quest for the Hottest of the Hot' (Burros, 1986: 52). Her complaint was typical: 'if you can convince the staff at the Indian restaurant *Darbar* that you mean business when you say hot, they may make the *ghost vindaloo* hot enough to call for a fire extinguisher. Now if there were some way to convince the local Thai restaurants to believe customers when they say they want the food authentically hot' (Burros, 1986: 52). Heat became shorthand for difference, and tolerating it, nay appreciating it, appeared to be an important way for critics to distinguish themselves from the run of the mill American.

That act of distinction from the common American was particularly difficult to pull off until the 1980s because the critics in their reviews did not typically include any material on the entrepreneurial or production conditions of the cuisine they were covering. That was a surprise to me, that critics did not take advantage of their access to the backstage, which is where they could have a clear and easy advantage over the consumer. Perhaps this was because their public was not interested in the production of cuisine, only in its consumption. Attention to craftsmanship and artistry came later, mostly in the 1990s, by way of display kitchens and celebrity entrepreneurs. Instead, in the 1980s, heat became the carrier of a double difference, of ethnic food from nonethnic, and the taste of the critic from that of the standard American consumer, so much so that claims of inauthentic mildness of ethnic food were often repeated, in the exact same words, in reviews of distinctly different cuisines—for example, Indian, Thai, Mexican, Vietnamese and so on. Thankfully, Claiborne was never enamoured by heat per se.

What Claiborne set out to do in the 1960s and 1970s became a norm by the new millennium. Mark Bittman's 2003 piece on upscale Asian restaurants in London can be used to mark the apogee of promotion of Indian food and also underline the international circuit of global cities on which such things get played out. He wrote:

> The excitement generated by Tamarind's opening eight years ago [1995] cannot be overstated. Here was an Indian restaurant on a chic Mayfair street charging upscale prices and serving Indian food in glamorous style. It quickly became not only the talk of the town but, with Zaika … among the first Indian restaurants in Europe to receive a Michelin star. Now, the phenomenon is almost commonplace: most major cities in Britain, the United States, India and elsewhere have similar restaurants (Bittman, 2003: 57).

Many of the ancient formulas have by now been abandoned: (1) the incessant focus on heat is gone, (2) the endless explaining of what is curry and what it is not is done with, (3) outsider descriptions of *samosas, pakoras, idlis* and *utthappam* are passé and (4) the backstage is no longer effaced, making the entrepreneur and the chef visible. The first three transformations are possible because by now the critic and the public have tightly constituted each other, with less and less that needs to be explained, hence there is room to delve into design, décor and the making of the backstage. As less and less needs to be said, an entire ensemble of assumptions is re-inscribed in the body of the field of restaurant criticism. Furthermore, it is precisely the invisible networks of affiliation between entrepreneur, chef and menu—invisible to the mere customer—which become the locus of the critic's new expertise. It is the access to the back that now distinguishes the critic. In addition, new expertise is indicated in having familiarity both with upscale temples of cuisine such as Devi and cheap, quirky joints at the bottom of the market that might include the Dosa Cart at Washington Square, which is what others have characterized as cultural omnivorousness (Johnston and Baumann, 2007).

Today food has entered the fashion cycle, at least in Manhattan, and Indian food is playing its part in it. The process began in the 1960s and 1970s when we witnessed the birth of a new discourse through the pen of a new kind of expert, the restaurant critic, that hastened the circulation of cultural capital through the sinews of an urban, public space, already invigorated by discussion of fashion, movies and music, in the burgeoning magazine and newspaper trade. But all this is from the perspective of the connoisseur and critic. What of the Indian immigrant? Unfortunately we know next to nothing about the Indian immigrant restaurateur or cook or server.[3] I am just beginning the process of interviewing about eighty restaurateurs and conducting a census of their labour force. Although we will have to wait for the results of that study, what we do know is that just as Indian-born New Yorkers are overrepresented as physicians, professors and yellow cab drivers, they are underrepresented as chefs, bartenders, dishwashers and hostesses. We know very little about them. But we do know what middle-class Indian professionals eat, especially at home.

Expatriate Home Cooking

To say something about expatriate domestic cookery I have to abandon the category 'Indian' and look more closely at any of the linguistic subsets such as Punjabi-American, Gujarati-American, Bengali-American and so on. Since Bengali-Americans have been most closely studied, I will use their case to illustrate my points about Indian-American domestic cookery. There are about 100,000 Bengalis in the United States. For most of the approximately 30,000 Bengali-American households, breakfast eaten at home consists of milk and cereal or toast. The exception is that tea is served instead of the ubiquitous American coffee. Lunch, consumed at or near the workplace, is a salad or a slice of pizza, sometimes a sandwich, or a packed lunch from home of *roti* and *subgi*. It is dinner that remains the realm of 'tradition', where there is still a literal truth to the question asked by a Bengali: 'Have you eaten rice?' Rice, *dal,* and fish cooked in a sauce with *panch phoron* (a Bengali five-spice mix of fenugreek, onion seed, fennel, cumin and mustard seed), is eaten for dinner, *more often* in the United States than in Kolkata (for details on methodology, sample size, etc. see Ray, 2004).

It is of course an exaggeration to say that dinner remains wholly 'traditional' in any meaningful sense. For instance, the appetizer for one of the households I observed for a Sunday dinner was turkey *pakora* cooked with chopped garlic, ginger, onion and fresh cilantro. Turkey is hardly a traditional Bengali ingredient. Yet it is cooked in a typically Bengali form, with ground turkey replacing ground goat meat. Any meat in Bengali cuisine is usually cooked with the trinity of wet spices—onion, ginger and garlic. It is so in the case of the *pakoras*. Then there is the more explicit intermingling of what are self-consciously defined as American and Bengali cuisines on Monday night when the menu was roast chicken, steamed rice, American style salad, sautéed bittermelon, grapes and apple juice. On Tuesday it was a typically Bengali repertoire, albeit with the exception of strawberry shortcake for dessert and grape juice as an accompaniment. On Wednesday, dinner was at Red Lobster—hardly a classical Bengali option.

Nonetheless, there is a pervasive Bengaliness in all this mixing up. Rice continues to be the core of the evening meal. The animal protein is important but remains a fringe item in terms of the calorie contribution to the meal. It is usually two small pieces of fish or a few bite-sized portions of meat. The complex carbohydrate core and the animal-protein fringe is paired with the third defining element—*dal*. *Dal* is sparsely spiced, which is often a few roasted cumin seeds. The animal protein fringe, in contrast, is highly spiced, as is typical in Bengali cuisine. The spices and herbs are drawn mostly from the Bengali repertoire, and the cooking processes are typically limited to sautéing, stewing and braising—basic Bengali notions of cooking.

Further, we see the greatest change in the elements that are peripheral to the Bengali conception of the 'meal', that is, turkey replacing goat meat in the appetizer, juices and soda replacing water and strawberry shortcake simulating Bengali desserts. It is because the most radical changes are confined to the accompaniments—the drinks, the dessert and the appetizer—that the 'meal' as such can still be defined as Bengali. Hence, in spite of rampant creolization of ingredients, dinner is perceived as the realm of traditional Bengali cuisine. What might encourage the perception of the Bengaliness of dinner is that it is truly so, almost in an exaggerated manner. Middle-class Bengalis consider rice and fish to be the most distinctive ethnic ingredients of their meal. About 60 per cent of Bengali-American households serve rice for dinner almost every day. An equally dramatic sign of change is the rate of consumption of fish. Almost one-half of Bengali-American households eat fish at dinner on an average day in a week, while only a third or fewer comparable households in Kolkata serve fish for dinner on a typical day. Thus expatriate families have become even more Bengali in their food habits in exile!

In addition, rice and fish have migrated from lunch to dinner, and dinner has become more important in defining a Bengali culinary identity in the United States. The heightened valorization of dinner is in itself a product of modern work schedules, which de-valorize other meals in the enactment of the self, although, in this case, the same modern transformation is being used to strengthen a tradition—a dinner of rice and fish. Further, the portion size of fish has almost doubled from about four ounces on the outside in Kolkata to about six to eight ounces in the United States, which is also a development that can be seen either as Westerniza-tion (because of the valorization of the protein component of the meal) or as a traditional carryover (because of the stress on fish—a self-conscious marker of Bengaliness). Perhaps a Bengali would not be a Bengali without consuming rice and fish in one of the main meals of the day. As dinner has come to be the only cooked meal, Bengali-Americans feel compelled to partake of ingredients that an-chor their Bengaliness—that is, rice and fish. Thus dinner has changed in two direc-tions: new ingredients, such as turkey, are absorbed into old culinary paradigms, and the use of old constituents, such as rice and fish, are insisted upon. One absorbs change and the other accentuates tradition.

Middle-class Bengali men are particularly insistent on a Bengali dinner and that may be for a number of reasons: (1) their limited social interaction with other Ameri-cans outside the context of work, hence their unfamiliarity with American food other than the hotdog, hamburger and salad; (2) as a respite from the American world that they confront each day; (3) their culinary incompetence as men—only one man in 126 households cooks regularly—which makes their nostalgia particularly acute and takes the form of a desperate longing for their mother's cooking; and (4) the smell of Bengali food cooking at the hearth confirms their very nature as Bengali men and is proof of both patriarchal control and containment of polluting American cultural influences.

With breakfast and dinner, it is as if middle-class Bengali migrants have divided up the day into what they characterize as moments of 'modernity' and moments of 'tradition', both perceived as good and necessary in their separate places. This complementary duality towards the 'modern' and the 'traditional'—the former imag-ined as embodied in something as mundane as industrialized breakfast cereal and the latter with traditional rice and fish—is central to the identity of the Bengali *bhad-rasamaj*. The Indian middle-class has long been *both* threatened and seduced by the promise of modernization, and they have acted on those concerns in organizing their food practices in the United States.

Reprise

There are at least two configurations in which Indian food is served in Manhattan, one in exotic restaurants to the imaginary voyager, and the other in familiar settings to the travel-weary expatriate. They are opposite but complementary approaches to home and heritage. The migrant's search for stringency in home cooking and the tourist's quest for authentic ethnic food—where one can distinguish between a *samosa* and a *pakora* or maybe even a *singara* with the help of the critic—are congruent strategies to still the turbulence of time, one projected on another people, and the other projected on another place. The cool metropolitan *flaneur* and the awkward immigrant are caught in their corresponding quest for authenticity. Both are complementary considerations about home and heritage, which is nothing more than our relationship to a place and a past.

Notes

An earlier version of this chapter was published as 'Feeding Modern Desires' in *Seminar,* 566 (October): 30–4, Delhi, India.
1. There are more eateries in Queens than in the other boroughs (perhaps with the exception of Manhattan), and that is related to the demand for Indian food, which is partially related to residency of the Indian immigrant population. According to the 2005–2007 American Community Survey of the Census Bureau of the United States, a total of about 247,292 Indian Americans (alone or in combination) lived in New York City, of which 65 per cent lived in Queens, 15 per cent in Brooklyn, 10 per cent in Manhattan, 7 per cent in the Bronx, and 4 per cent in Staten Island (Asian American Federation Census Information Center, 2009).
2. The chefs at Sitar were Ranjit Kundu and Mohan Singh, listed by Fabricant (1978: L18). Julie Sahni is probably New York's first Indian celebrity chef, named and venerated by Burros (1984: C20).
3. For aggregate data and some interview material, see Fiscal Policy Institute (2007) and Restaurant Opportunities Center of New York (2005).

References

Anonymous (1876), 'An Essay on Curry', *New York Times* (19 January): 2.

Anonymous (1897), 'Indian Curries', *New York Times* (27 February): BR7.

Anonymous (1904), 'A New Coney Island Rises from the Ashes of the Old', *New York Times* (8 May): SM5.

Anonymous (1912), '"Prince" Ranji Smile Weds', *New York Times* (7 August): 11.

Anonymous (1932), 'Building for India at 33 Fair Assured', *New York Times* (13 August): 17.

Anonymous (1948), 'News of Food', *New York Times* (21 February): 10.

Anonymous (1963), 'Directory to Dining', *New York Times* (13 September): 51.

Asian American Federation Census Information Center (2009), *Profile of New York City's Indian Americans: 2005–2007,* <http://www.aafny.org/cic/briefs/indian2009.pdf>, accessed on 31 August 2009.

Asimov, E. (2002), 'From an Indian Chef, Tandoori Fare and Wild Cards', *New York Times* (30 October): F10.

Bittman, M. (2003), 'In London, Four Asian Stars', *New York Times* (14 September): F7

Brooks, P. (1985), 'New Haven's Bit of India Improves', *New York Times* (22 December): CN17.

Bruni, F. (2005), 'Diner's Journal', *New York Times* (25 March): E2, 33.

Burros, M. (1984), 'California Cuisine: Fresh and Fadish', *New York Times* (20 June): C1.

Burros, M. (1986), 'A Quest for the Hottest of the Hot', *New York Times* (11 October): 52.

Chithelen, I. (1986), 'Bringing the Flavors of India to L.I.', *New York Times* (June 29): LI5.

Claiborne, C. (1960), 'Native of New Delhi Prepares Indian Dishes Here', *New York Times* (25 February): 22.

Claiborne, C. (1961a), 'Chutney Cupboard', *New York Times* (9 July): SM35.

Claiborne, C. (1961b), 'Flavor of India has Regional Traits. Foods Vary Greatly with Diversity of Cooking Fats', *New York Times* (11 May): 44.

Claiborne, C. (1962a), 'Article 7—Making It Hot—for Summer', *New York Times* (15 July): 148

Claiborne, C. (1962b), 'Seasonal Fresh Fruits Complement Many Curry Dishes', *New York Times* (23 August): 32.

Claiborne, C. (1964), 'Dining at the Fair', *New York Times* (27 June): 16.

Claiborne, C. (1969a), 'Dining Out on Greek or Indian Cooking', *New York Times* (25 April): 42.

Claiborne, C. (1969b), 'Dining Out on Mexican, Indian or Pakistani Fare', *New York Times* (4 July): 12.

Claiborne, C. (1970), 'In Delhi, It's Difficult to Find Bad Native Dish', *New York Times* (14 April): 56.

Claiborne, C. (1974), 'A Rare Thing: Indian Restaurant with Food to Get Excited About', *New York Times* (26 September): 34.

Claiborne, C. (1985), 'Exotic Vegetarian Discover: The Cuisine of an Indian State', *New York Times* (21 August): C1.

Fabricant, F. (1978), 'Temple Carvings to Dine Beside', *New York Times* (7 May): L18.

Fiscal Policy Institute (FPI) (2007), *Working for a Better Life,* New York, FPI.

Hughes, C. (1939), 'For Gourmets and Others: Curry Comes to the Table', *New York Times* (12 March): 53.

Ickeringill, N. (1960), 'Food: "King of Curry". British Knight Recalls His Journeys In Pursuit of Perfect Indian Sauces', *New York Times* (26 September): 41.

Johnston, J., and Baumann, S. (2007), 'Democracy versus Distinction: A Study of Omnivorousness in Gourmet Food Writing', *American Journal of Sociology,* 113/1: 165–204.

Lave, J., and Wenger, E. (1991), *Situated Learning: Legitimate Peripheral Participation,* Cambridge: Cambridge University Press.

Lowry, H. B. (1921), 'The Old World In New York', *New York Times* (3 April): 37.

Miller, B. (1986), 'Restaurants. Midtown Indian, Downtown Eclectic', *New York Times* (27 June): C24.

Moskin, J. (2005), 'Festival of Lights, Parade of Sweets', *New York Times* (2 November): F1.

Nickerson, J. (1946), 'News of Food', *New York Times* (7 September): 12.

Nickerson, J. (1955), 'Food: A Touch of India in New York', *New York Times* (19 September): 20.

Owen, J. (1955), 'News of Food: Indian Curry', *New York Times* (19 June): 24.

Ray, K. (2004), *The Migrant's Table. Meals and Memories in Bengali-American Households,* Philadelphia: Temple University Press.

Reed, M. H. (1985), 'A Critic's Choice: The Best of 1985', *New York Times* (29 December): WC13.

Restaurant Opportunities Center of New York (ROC-NY) (2005), *Behind the Kitchen Door,* New York: ROC-NY.

Sheraton, M. (1979), 'Restaurants: Indian and Italian Cuisines Revisited', *New York Times* (3 August): C16.

Sheraton, M. (1982), 'A Taste of India on the East Side', *New York Times* (26 November): C18.

–12–

Globalization and the Challenge of Variety: A Comparison of Eating in Britain and France

Alan Warde
University of Manchester

Variety in the Global Context

Mintz (2008) notes that the transportation of foodstuffs across state boundaries, including specifically into Europe, has occurred continuously over hundreds of years, from the transporting of new plants, to the trading of spices, through the extraction of staples from colonies overseas, to the integrated transnational regime of the industrialized food corporations of today. As Nutzenadel and Trentmann (2008: 4) observe, this makes putting a date on the beginning of globalization controversial and suggests a multiple, rather than a singular, process. In this chapter, following Appadurai (1990, 1996), I take globalization in its *current* phase to mean that more social entities (people, money, messages, ideas and commands) are moving more frequently, farther and faster than before, with consequences for networks of interaction and social relations in different places across the world.

The consequence of accelerated flows is also contentious. As Lizardo (2008) notes, one school of thought, following the 'media imperialism' approach, predicts homogeneity and uniformity on a global scale. Another, based on local ethnographies, shows that empirically this is not the case and that national cultural diversity persists. Indeed there is probably an emerging consensus that at present the global inflects the local, such that Lizardo is probably right to aspire to a better theoretical explication of the process that has sometimes been called 'glocalization' (Robertson, 1992).

In the field of food many different entities flow. Ingredients, recipes, dishes, meals and cuisines circulate, not to mention cooks, capital and broadcast images. Surely one of the most interesting questions about food in the current period of globalization is the diffusion of knowledge and appreciation of different cuisines across the world. By cuisine I mean not just cooking, but all that the composition of meals entails for a social collectivity—tools, recipes, condiments, typical ingredients and organization of eating.[1] Such cuisines are typically accorded spatial delimiters and are most frequently identified as national—French, Italian, Greek, Thai and so forth. They may also appear (in cookbooks and in restaurant reviews) under regional designations, for example Provencal, Tuscan or Cantonese. The circulation and reception of different cuisines means that some have come to be recognized by many people as 'foreign', arguably the most appropriate term to capture the idea that while people mostly could not describe the defining principles of their 'native' cuisine, they operate with a general sense that such a cuisine exists and that they can identify deviations from it (Ashley et al., 2004).

The situation is, then, one where 'instruments of homogenization' (Appadurai, 1990: 306) exist, but without achieving dominance. At least for the moment it seems, globalization produces variety. For the populations of the rich countries of the world, geographical distance between site of production and site of consumption is no barrier to the availability of any foodstuff or cuisine. Those with most resources have the opportunity to import diversity and transcend dependence on local production. The brute forces of globalization appear to outstrip the capacity of discourses to incorporate ideas and products into universal hierarchies or to establish authoritative judgments about qualities.

However, the resultant variety might be a threat or an opportunity, since it demands procedures of selection. It might accelerate the condition of gastro-anomie, identified by Fischler (1980) as a condition where rules of eating cease to be identifiable or binding and people become uncertain about what they should eat. On the other hand, it creates many new interesting possibilities for valued culinary experience. If homo sapiens is incurably omnivorous, then a much greater range of options could be a positive boon. Arguably the latter has been the dominant mode of reception in Britain, especially with respect to incorporation of foreign foods. In France, where there existed previously a more highly respected national tradition of cuisine, the situation is somewhat different. This chapter tells a speculative story about some differences in the processes of diffusion of culinary variety in postwar Britain and France.

Britain and the Discovery of National Cuisine

It is generally agreed that the consolidation of national cuisine, as represented by cookery books, is something that accompanies nation-building (Appadurai, 1988). This means that it occurs in the nineteenth century mostly in European societies. However, regarding Germany, Mohring (2008) notes that for much of the twentieth century little attention was paid to the symbolic associations between food and nation. She suggests that the German cookbook in the nineteenth century comprised recipes of regional and international origin but that there was no recognition or representation of a cuisine of German ethnic provenance until the 1990s, when familiarity with the cuisines of other countries finally brought to self-consciousness the issue of what is specifically German. Something very similar happened in the UK. Panayi, in *Spicing Up Britain* (2008: 191), noted 'the durability of what we can describe as the British diet. This meant fried breakfast in the morning, meat and two veg at other times and roast on Sunday. This pattern would not begin to disintegrate until the end of the twentieth century.' However, such habits were not referred to or marked as British per se. There might have been a British diet but there was no self-conscious British cuisine. Panayi, using a very extensive survey of cookery books published in England since the mid-nineteenth century, problematizes the notion of 'British' food, arguing that while a few authors sought to capture explicitly the specificity of British or English cookery, most took little notice of the national associations of recipes. It was not until the 1950s that cookbooks presenting the cuisines of other nations become commonplace. Only then did 'foods develop nationalities' (2008: 36).

Nevertheless, for most people thereafter, it was probably greater contact with *prepared* foreign cuisine—that sold through catering outlets of various sorts—rather than their use of recipe books to cook foreign dishes at home, that the British population learned a familiarity with the exotic and distinctive tastes and flavours of the global kitchen. Eating out was not in itself a new phenomenon in Britain. Long a primarily urbanized society, many people took meals away from home, particularly during working hours. However, as Burnett (2004: 288) pointed out, eating out for pleasure or entertainment is, for most of the population, a relatively recent development. It was only in the 1970s that restaurants became part of popular experience. According to a national random sample survey in 2004, 62 per cent of Britons ate a main meal out for pleasure at least once a month and only 4 per cent claimed never to eat out, eating out now being one of the most popular of contemporary leisure activities, increasingly common to all strata of the population (Bennett et al., 2009).

As Panayi said about cookbooks, neither restaurateurs nor their customers seemed to find the culinary origins of the dishes a matter of concern in the mid-twentieth century. This is evident from early editions of the British *Good Food Guide,* the most influential of guides to fine dining in Britain after World War II. Begun in 1951 as a campaign to improve British dining out, it was a small social movement. It berated restaurateurs for their many failings and rewarded those it deemed to be providing the best service by inclusion in the independently published *Guide.* The *Guide* was compiled from the reports of volunteers, honorary members of the Good Food Club and by Raymond Postgate, founder and editor from 1951 to 1969. Initially, restaurants were not described by cuisine type and menus appeared to contain dishes of diverse origin. Consider the example of the four entries for Manchester in the 1955/6 edition (Table 1).

Restaurants clearly offer a promiscuous spread of dishes, occasionally attributed to particular cuisines, but without any attempt at unification or coherence. The *Good Food Guide* only embarked on systematic classification in the edition of 2001, although a listing of London restaurants by cuisine was introduced in 1963. Until then,

Table 12.1.

Restaurant	Comments from the Good Food Guide
Bombay Restaurant	'Mr. Nazir Uddlin's curries are certified to be the real thing' ... 'it is open Sundays; it is clear; it is not cluttered up with brass pots and nonesense. The menu is extensive, as there ar 74 dishes on it, ranging from vegetable curry (3/3 to chicken Danchack 6/6). Picking out the best would be a tough job; Bhuna lamb with white rice and chapathies (6/3), prawn pilaw (5/9) and mushroom curry with Pilaw rice and poppadoms are candidates; there is also the chicken Biryani at 8/6. No licence; drinks will be fetched.'
Finnigan's Normandie Restaurant	'An overdue attempt to introduce some French gastronomic life to Manchester business men, whose chief preoccupation is shown by the fact that they can make long-distance calls from their tables, while their mouths are actually full of vol-au-vent de sole Normandie. Table-d'hote lunch from 8/6; tea 3/6, high tea, 7/6; dinner, from 12/6. Larger and interesting a la carte selection: very good omelettes 4/6 to 8/6, mixed grill 10/6, Dover sole 8/6, Poulet poele Vallee d'Auge (10/6—give half an hour's notice), filet mignon 8/6. The helpings are ample ... About 40 wines, from 15/6 upwards, nearly all vintage wines.'
New Elizabethan	'Manchester is bleakly unsupplied with good restaurants. It has a comprehensive menu, including Greek and Continental dishes, which recalls an ambitious Soho restaurant. There were also grills—rump steak with mushrooms was very good. Table d'hote in 1954: lunch 5/6 and 7/6, dinner 8/6 and 12/6, both filling. Coffee also very good. Large a la carte menu. A visiting member took a very good half bottle of Ch. Neuf du Pape '49 at 8/– and Cordial Medoc (unusual, and about the only liqueur worth drinking by an adult) at 3/6.'
Prince's Restaurant	'This is the place patronized by Mancunians who take their eating seriously, and wish to be assured that they can sit down to a meal which has been properly considered, ... Members have praised particularly the roast turkey, fruit pie, and the grills ... Main dishes from 3/6 to 7/6 ... Fully licensed: wine list of about 50 wines, mostly 18/– or more.'

and for some time after, cooking in British restaurants was still largely in thrall to a French-influenced international array of dishes.

In the second half of his book, titled 'The Culinary Revolution after 1945,' Panayi (2008) argues that many more migrants, from more diverse origins, going to live in more parts of Britain had a great impact on everyone's habits. He observes that in the catering trade 'the most significant changes occurred from the 1960s when Chinese, Italian and Indian restaurants and takeaways began to proliferate in high streets throughout Britain. US multinationals followed from the 1970s. Foreign staffing essentially continued pre-war patterns whereas changes in menus involved more mainstream restaurants aping the food served in establishments opened by migrants and US firms' (2008: 154). The 1960s, as Panayi suggests, saw a period of extensive growth of interest and availability of foreign cuisine in restaurants and takeaway outlets. Arguably it was the latter which have had greatest impetus for the establishment of the idea that there might be national cuisines and that multicultural food might be acceptable in the UK. Perhaps it is then unsurprising that British recognition of the names of foreign dishes in 1970s was, according to Burnett (1989: 312), growing fast but remained limited and clearly skewed:

> In a Gallup survey in 1976 into people's knowledge of foreign dishes, chow mein and sweet and sour pork were known by seven out of ten, pizza by eight out of ten, and ravioli by nearly as many; chilli con carne was familiar to four out of ten, while moussaka, sole meuniere, and wienerschnitzel had reached only one in three.

These shifts occurred a little sooner than would be suggested by accounts attributing change to a postmodern or aestheticized reaction to an industrialized food system. The search for the local, now almost an obsession, was stimulated more recently by reaction to bovine spongiform encephalopathy (BSE) and crises of food safety, by environmental concerns about 'food miles', and a perception of the superior quality of locally produced foods, symbolized in the UK by movements like Slow Food. While the current period of globalization vociferously fosters the local, the earlier period paid more attention to the national. To echo Panayi (2008), restaurants developed nationalities from the 1960s.

By the beginning of the twenty-first century very many commercial outlets were selling various types of meal with attributions to cuisines from most parts of the globe, the exceptions being Africa and South America. The national provenance of cuisine had been generally well learned. In a recent study of cultural consumption in the UK, no one who claimed to eat out baulked at being asked questions about preferences among restaurants defined by cuisine type (Bennett et al., 2009). Survey responses indicated that, when presented with a list of a dozen types, almost half nominated one of three foreign restaurants as their favourite (46 per cent said Italian, Indian or Chinese). Conversely, very few selected these as their least favourite (4 per cent). The overwhelmingly least popular category, however, was American fast food and burgers (38 per cent). Supplementary qualitative data suggested that foreign cuisine was highly relevant to experiences and choices when eating out. Almost every individual interviewed was aware of the availability of foreign cuisine, though importantly few appeared to be acquainted with a complete range (Warde, 2004). There was a significant statistical association between social class position and extent of experience. As focus group discussions indicated, the range of restaurant types had a hierarchy, with French ones still considered the most exclusive. For the working class groups, Indian and Chinese food were widely appreciated, while the middle class was likely to include these and to add Italian and French in addition (see also Warde et al., 1999). The implication is that Britain has left behind the situation where national identities of food were unimportant, even if in actuality there had been implicit symbolic domination by French cuisine. Instead there is recognition of the positive value of a plurality of foreign cuisines.

Now a central and normal market device, the symbolic association of restaurants in Britain with foreign cuisines is an instance where globalization has reinforced national identification, creating a knowledge and commitment to particular cuisines. For many, initial exposure was primarily to takeaway outlets, whose effect was heavily reinforced by the supermarkets offering extensive ranges of pre-prepared, frozen and cook-chilled foreign dishes for convenient reheating at home. Consequently, many Britons eat regularly from a global menu without having to cook themselves.

Panayi's explanation of this transformation focuses on the role that immigrants played in the making of contemporary British food habits. Panayi emphasizes the movement of people, rather than of foodstuffs, in changing eating habits. He says (2008: 67), 'The idea of the foreign restaurant does not refer to the food served ... Instead it primarily refers to the ownership and staffing of places where both members of the ethnic majority and the ethnic minorities dined.' While in part true, the case is somewhat overstated, espousing a hypothesis probably more applicable to the United States (see Gabaccia, 1998). In Britain, in fact, the arrival of the most influential cuisine, French, operated with a different logic, offering a counter-example. Trubek (2000) estimates that by the 1960s there were 5,000 French chefs in Britain, serving the royal family, the aristocracy, the big hotels and the clubs. Unlike the groups described by Panayi, the chefs' presence was not associated with the creation of a community of expatriates, for these men were temporary migrants who remained French nationals and often would return home (rather than merely intend to do so). The dominance of professional haute cuisine by French chefs was an international feature—they dominated elite establishments in the United States, Canada and Australia too—and were responsible for the establishment of an international standard. Second, the migration hypothesis says little about the growth of a readiness on the part of customers to buy foreign foods. The presence of foreign chefs and foodstuffs alone is not enough. It requires a climate of receptivity to novelty and variety and an apparatus to recommend the adoption of new possibilities. In this respect, the role of cultural intermediation is crucial, for foods sold on a global scale are always filtered through the symbolic codes of particular national cultural markets.

Since the 1970s there has been a swelling stream of media output which 'educates' people about foreign foods and which has had the effect of increasing their acceptability and palatability for a vast swathe of European populations. One, admittedly specialized, source of awareness of the exotic, especially Chinese, Indian and Italian cuisine, was the *Guide,* which in the late 1970s included informative glossaries of terms used in various foreign cuisines (e.g. *Guide,* 1974, 1978). In the process, food has increasingly been subjected to aesthetic judgment. Whereas it is still probably the case that Britons, as Mennell (1985) pointed out, pay more attention to economy and hygiene, the idea that food can be a matter of style or lifestyle circulates freely. In this register, tasting the 'other' is the height of fashion and perhaps for some, sophistication. Many purposes lie behind the decision to eat out and various satisfactions are sought, but one goal has certainly been a search for social distinction (Warde et al., 1999; Warde and Martens, 2000). Since acknowledgement of status claims requires recognition of a set of symbolic indicators of refinement, commercial intermediation has a key role to play in establishing meanings, through advertisements, recommendations and marketing devices.

Greater contact with prepared foreign cuisine—sold through catering outlets of various sorts—rather than use of recipe books to cook foreign dishes at home probably gave most of the British population their familiarity with the exotic and distinctive tastes and flavours of the global kitchen. Indeed, most households have few cookery books, and those that do are said not to use them very much as practical resources for the purpose of preparing meals (Humble, 2005: 4). Meanwhile, other forms of media coverage have increased, though only recently; food columns in newspapers were rare before the 1980s, and the growth of television programmes that did more than teach basic techniques was a phenomenon of the 1990s.

A distinction can be made between rejection, naturalization, improvisation and authentication as ways in which populations deal with exotic or foreign foods (see Warde, 2000). These occurred almost sequentially in the UK. Considering Asian food, initially there was a considerable degree of hostility and rejection, expressed sometimes in racist fashion among some sections of the population who associated unwelcome migrants with distinctive and undesirable eating habits (Hardyment, 1995: 129–31). Generally, however, the population increasingly frequented Indian and Chinese restaurants and takeaway establishments, if we are to judge from the rapid growth of such businesses in the 1970s and especially 1980s (for estimates of growth see Burnett, 2004; Hardyment, 1995; Oddy, 2003). In the years between 1965 and 1980, Asian restaurants and takeaways both created dishes that were particularly palatable to British tastes, modifications which made them fit locally to British tastes; restaurants included popular European dishes on their menus.[2] In the course of time, with greater sophistication among those dining out, a space became available in the market for more 'authentic' Asian cuisine, a reaction which might be interpreted as conscious resistance to the potential of globalization as imposing uniformity. However, a much greater impact was had in the interim by improvisation, as British chefs increasingly incorporated the ingredients, combinations and flavours of exotic cuisines into their menus. Many of the most celebrated restaurants of the 1990s typically constructed menus which can best be described as eclectic in relation to culinary pedigrees. For example, the *Guide,* which was much in favour of such styles of cooking in the 1990s, said:

> The restaurant scene has never been so exciting. Many restaurants, as ever, specialise in a particular style of cooking or a national cuisine ... But just look at what else is happening. Hundreds of dishes, in scores of restaurants, do not fit easily into any single national framework. Tagliolini with ceps and creme fraiche, steamed mussels with curry spices and coriander, roast quail with wild mushrooms and polenta, and lambs steaks with parsley pesto and Spanish butter-beans. Those are all from just one menu in one restaurant. What a glorious mix.
>
> And this particular brew could only happen here. No other country has quite the same blend of British, French, Italian, Spanish, Indian, Chinese, Thai and other cultures to call on. In that sense, diverse as it all is, it is very British, full of real invention and the sheer exuberance of let's-have-a-go cookery ... It is British in the sense that Britain is the melting pot. British cooking is no longer defined by just what we grow here, or by traditional recipes and techniques. It is the sum of what we cook here.
>
> British restaurants, and their customers, have been receptive to all this, perhaps, because Britain's food culture is less sharply drawn than some others—a state of affairs seen as something of a handicap until now—and it provides a gap waiting to be filled with whatever ideas can be pinched from elsewhere (*Guide,* 1995: 21).

In addition, there was even an attempt to claim eclecticism as the persistent and defining attribute of British cuisine (*Guide,* 1998: 24; see also Spencer, 2004: 339–41). For one of the consequences of entanglement with foreign cuisines was a greater concern for the essential characteristics of the native species. Alongside what Smart (1994) dubbed 'gastro-global eclecticism', then, came a familiarization with many exotic cuisines—a familiarization that was wider within some sections of the population than others—as people developed tastes for new foods for which they would have had no vocabulary, expectations or standards for judgment two decades earlier. Hence Britons learned alternatives in the 1970s and fostered an eclectic appreciation of foreign cuisine. Eclecticism entails fragmentation, and taste remains differentiated by class and generation, but its effect was to subject food to aesthetic standards and establish an appreciation of cuisines which now extends to include a category which is specifically British. The rapid attribution to restaurants of labels to indicate cuisine type, including the invention of several versions of 'British' cuisine in, for example, the *Guide* (see Warde, 2009), is a consequence of a general search to add meaning to commodities in competitive markets. The implication is that initially described by Panayi, of attributing nationality to menus in a new manner. In Britain, omnivorousness has become a solution to meaninglessness, at least for the middle class; though as we have seen, some 'foreign' cuisines are widely accepted and appreciated by a broad spectrum of the population. Omnivorousness is an orientation supportive of drawing on multicultural culinary resources. Britain has grasped eclecticism in several of its senses. France resists. France, however, already had an internal regional differentiation upon which to draw.

France

Many of the same global forces that affect the UK also affect France. Although both were founding members of the European Common Market, these countries' different immigration policies and different holiday patterns may partially explain some of the differences in their reception and adaptation of foreign foods. However, features interior to the culinary field of Britain and France are probably in themselves sufficient to explain their different trajectories. The presence of a thoroughly established French cuisine (indeed some promoters of *nouvelle cuisine* said too well established) by the mid-twentieth century was one key differentiating factor.

The restaurant trade had a very different impact in France than in Britain. Arguably, the restaurant also transformed French eating habits, but at a much earlier date than in the UK. Its development was based primarily on the work of professional chefs and the critical gastronomic literature, from which the self-image of French cuisine arose in the early nineteenth century (Ferguson, 1998; Spang, 2001; Trubek, 2000). One consequence was a profound impact on domestic cookery. Aspirations imputed to readers of cookery books were very different than in Britain. In France cookbooks were mostly written by professional chefs, men for whom culinary values were central, whereas in Britain they arose from a concern with household management, a concern later to become formalized in educational institutions as 'home economics', which meant mostly women writers advising about economy and efficiency. So while the audience for cookery books in both countries was until very recently almost exclusively the housewife, the values and the practices recommended were significantly different. Hence the formation of culinary value in France, which Ferguson (2004) demonstrated, was achieved in a copious literary mode, part gastronomic, part didactic. A shared sense of culinary tradition derived from the practice of the restaurant rather than the household. According to Trubek (2000), the French organizations of professional chefs established and maintained a powerful hold over the definition of good cooking and good food and exported their techniques throughout the Western world such that restaurant provision took French standards as hegemonic, refracting adversely on pretensions to invent a British cuisine.

Ferguson (2004: 109) in a neat (if perhaps slightly exaggerated) account of how French cuisine was invented, emphasized the 'culinary imagination that has impelled the French to tell stories about their cuisine for two centuries or more'. She noted the importance of the gastronomic field in France, characterizing its features thus:

> The gastronomic field works off the split between the material product—the foodstuff, the dish, or the meal—and the critical, intellectual, and aesthetic by-products that discuss,

review, and debate the original product. The relentless intellectuality so characteristic of culinary discourse in France is as necessary to the gastronomic field as the insistent materiality. In a paradigm of what cooking is all about, culinary discourse transforms the material into the intellectual, the imaginative, the symbolic, and the aesthetic. The cultural construct that we know today as French cuisine is largely the accomplishment of this discourse. (Ferguson, 2004: 105)

The same discourse was simply not current in Britain. Burnett (2004) charts a faltering course for gastronomy in Britain, with some vitality in the nineteenth century, but more or less snuffed out during the World War I. Thereafter, it was not until the late twentieth century that aesthetic discourses about food came into common circulation, though there were minor exceptions in the inter-war period (see Mennell, 1985), and from the 1950s women writers like Elizabeth David and Jane Grigson began to bridge the gulf between recipe books deriving from the home economics tradition and gastronomic commentary with literary pretension (Ashley et al., 2004: 165–9).

Gastronomy, according to Poulain (2002: 205), cultivated a sense of the coherence, refinement and excellence of the national cuisine of France. The authoritative stance of the *Michelin Red Guide,* when passing judgment on restaurant provision, for example, depended upon the acceptance of shared standards of what constitutes good cooking. The mutual reinforcement of a developed gastronomy and ambitious chefs sustained a form of cultural institutionalization which is only just beginning to take hold in Britain. The UK phenomenon of the celebrity chef has meant that the status of cooking has risen to some degree in that country. Moreover, these chefs now write a significant proportion of the most widely sold cookery books. A discourse favourable to professional cooking is thus beginning—but only beginning—to emerge in Britain.

France is a country where the character, and the survival, of regional food habits is a public preoccupation. It is not unusual to see special displays of products from particular regions in a market, or at some special promotion in a railway station or an office foyer. The symbolic importance of the origin of things is also reflected in, and often accomplished by, the developed system of product accreditation. At present, the French have many more items registered with the European Union and World Trade Organization than does Britain.[3] For the French consumer the identification of source is a matter of assurance of quality—the authenticity attributed to *terroir,* that distinctive cultural category which permeates French discussion of wine and, to a lesser extent, food—framing perceptions and justifications of taste (see Trubek, 2005).

Geographical determinism provides a key resource for French culinary culture. Ferguson (2004: 130) insists that there is no tension between national and regional identities; instead, there exists 'a culinary symbiosis of provincial part and national whole'. While it is clear that 'regional cuisines owed their existence to Paris' (Ferguson, 2004: 126), the happy outcome that was French cuisine could be seen as the sum of its regional cuisines was a consequence of intellectual and aesthetic underpinnings which validated those regional resources. She is mindful that these are, and have always been, a nostalgic construction of the imagination. 'National identity emerged from a complex interaction of centre and periphery, a negotiation between Paris as the centre of a culture and the provinces as repository of that culture' (Ferguson, 2004: 123). The regions of the mind have a long gestation: 'The regional cuisines that we know today, with their special dishes tied to local produce, evolved out of an extended confrontation of those products with the codes and practices imposed by Paris, the norm diffused by the culinary journals that flourished at the end of the [nineteenth] century' (Ferguson, 2004: 128).

The notion that Paris imposed an understanding suggests that antagonisms are perhaps being ignored; Csergo (1996) suggests that the provinces asserted their distinctiveness as a form of resistance to the metropolis. Nevertheless, the idea of French gastronomy as founded upon appreciations of a nonconflictual combination of regional traditions, imagined and real, were regularly reinforced, not least through the circulation of regional recipe books. Culinary-geographical maps had existed since the early nineteenth century. By the twentieth century, with the spread of motor travel, a series of influential commentaries and guidebooks were published identifying unique particularities of different places in terms of their local produce (Karpik, 2000). Today tourist guides are likely to refer first to local foods, producing tourist routes that are justified by the culinary experiences available from place to place (e.g. Ratcliffe, 1995; Whiteman, 2008; see also chapter 8 in this volume). Nothing remotely similar exists in Britain. No doubt this is partly because there is such limited regional variation in eating habits in the UK, as differences in consumption between regions within the UK are comparatively minor and clearly in decline over the long term (Mennell, 1985; Warde, 1997).

Confronting nationality in relation to cuisine in France involves an imperative to conserve and consolidate. It is possible to combine this with an interest in diversity because of the existence of regional differentiation. One of the most obvious differences between Britain and France has been the role of the state in shaping understandings of diet and cuisine, keeping taste a public and political concern. In Britain, as Mennell (1985) observed, nutrition and economy have dominated the agenda. Food is a matter for the ministries of agriculture and heath, not the ministry of culture. It is no coincidence that whereas the British government issued its first nutrition guidelines in the early 1980s, French food policy failed to make any such recommendations until a report of 2005 and even then the issue of nutrition was subordinated to that of national culinary quality or excellence.

The French government has been consistently concerned to promote eating and taste, as for instance with sponsoring a national tasting week in primary schools with the objective of ensuring that children learn to recognize the flavours of fresh and local foods. The degree to which food is central to public culture is neatly demonstrated by Leynse (2006), whose ethnographic observation in the Loire Valley included a school field trip for ten-year-old pupils, lasting four days. Organized around an integrated study package including science, agriculture, ecology, geography and food, the children are taken to talk to farmers, to pick strawberries and to smell wild mint in the hedgerows. They record these activities in the log of the trip, reporting appreciatively on experiences of tasting. Such an activity would be inconceivable in Britain. However, in the Loire, children are inculcated into a particular identity, learning the shared attributes required to be a member of an informal collectivity. They acquire a loose but tangible sense of belonging, in this case a result of exposure to and identification with food products which are said to be, and treated as if they are, defining properties of a locale. They, like their parents, come to think of France as a patchwork of local and distinctive food areas, of which they want to have knowledge and experience, starting with their own. Where food has already a central place in national culture, opportunities are taken to reinforce the sense that food matters. In important part, state agencies help both to preserve and to celebrate French cuisine.

Conclusions

The French have long assumed the superiority of their own cuisine, largely because elites in other countries confirmed its excellence by adopting it themselves, or more specifically, by employing French chefs. The object of this reputation, recognizable on an international basis, was a consequence of the particular mode of construction of the idea of French cuisine. This idea flourished on the strength of at least three distinctive forces: an attachment to a notion of *terroir* which sustained and validated a regime of regional diversity, a literary tradition of gastronomy and state investment in the symbolic value of French food. These forces have served to perpetuate eating habits in France. While the country has been exposed to many of the same forces from the global economy—the expansion of supermarkets, international migration, urbanization—it has changed rather less quickly than has Britain. Remarkably in comparative context, time spent eating at home has remained more or less constant in France (Warde et al., 2007), and despite the aesthetic controversies surrounding *nouvelle cuisine* and much-vaunted worries about the corrosive impact of American fast food, the pattern of eating out has changed more slowly. Notwithstanding panics about declining standards of food provision, culinary disruption, disordering of meal patterns and the like, French habits are unusually stable.

In contrast, eating habits have changed more quickly in Britain during the last thirty years. This might indicate a providential evolutionary process, given the reputation of British food. Britain has proved highly adaptive in recent years, and certainly not all developments are for the worse. In a comparative survey of six Western European countries conducted in 2003, Britons were more likely than any other population to say that their food had improved in quality in the previous twenty years (Kjaernes et al., 2007: 66). From their experiences of eating out, Britons have certainly been exposed to more varied and probably more interesting food, including some of high quality and considerable ingenuity, producing a more knowledgeable and interested population. Gault-Millau's *Guide Londres* (1994) suggests that the best of British restaurant food has improved enormously:

> The city has become a high place of gastronomy. It had a reputation earlier only for foreign restaurants, Indian and Chinese principally. In the last few years everything has changed with the arrival of talented young chefs, imposing little by little a new and seductive cuisine which has been called 'modern British' ('nouvelle cuisine anglaise'). Those who believe that British cuisine is limited to boiled meat flanked by over cooked vegetable ought to take a trip to Bibendum ... or Alastair Little's.

But the *Guide Londres* did not fail to add the rider that still the best food in London is cooked by the French school, with Pierre Koffman of Tante Claire top of the class and Marco Pierre White at The Restaurant, Hyde Park Hotel just behind.

Eating out has thus been a particular, though often underestimated, force for change. In fact, writers about food and diet typically concentrate on the home, which is in some ways unsurprising given that the home still makes by far the most substantial contribution to human nutrition. However, when considering change it is not accidental that more attention is paid to eating out (e.g. Panayi, 2008; see also Mennell, 1985, on chefs, restaurant guides, etc.). Britons have emerged only recently from the kitchen into the public dining room. Restaurants, and I suggest perhaps even more importantly takeaway businesses, have been key to the revolution in Britain. In contrast, the more restricted change in the French catering trade is perhaps the reason for comparatively more limited change in eating habits in that country. A hypothesis might be that a nation with an expanding trade in eating out for pleasure is more receptive to foreign or novel food formats than ones where main external influences are via domestic cookery. For example, one might predict that in the Netherlands, where very little time is spent eating out (Warde et al., 2007), the impact of foreign cuisines would be more limited in both domestic and commercial settings.

Economic globalization does not necessarily entail cultural homogenization: its consequence is not mass uniformity. Rather the opposite, it offers greater opportunity for distinctive and differentiated behaviour. Global trade brings most manufactured commodities within range for all rich countries, a process which produces opportunities for much more varied taste cultures. Hence, in the realm of cuisine, we see more access to specialised quasi-'authentic' foreign cuisines (one can eat Mexican or Lebanese in Manchester), more eclectic mixing of ingredients (global, fusion and other forms of experimentalism), and availability of more specialized commercial diets (Atkins, Cambridge, South Bay, etc.). The consequence is unlikely to be mass conformity. Globalization, from one perspective, amounts to the diffusion of diversity. The 'same' items do become available in many more places, but the number of items is great, and their permutations enormous. When they impinge upon contexts which are already very different, the impact is far from uniform. Globalization multiplies the circulation of identities, though arguably those identities may come to matter less as they proliferate and multiply. The real issue is how diversity is constructed, conceptualized, presented and represented, appropriated and appreciated.

The British and the French have created quite different meanings for their current diversity. In Britain, distinction arises from being an omnivore of principle; people of higher status eat at the widest range of restaurants (Warde et al., 1999). In the absence of a tradition of gastronomy to provide rules and recommendations with appropriate aesthetic justifications, and in a world where style matters, adopting the guise of a cultural omnivore may be the optimal solution to the problem of eating meaningfully. Dishes or menus may be eclectic, or it may be a matter of eating from one cuisine on Thursdays and another on Fridays. No authority disciplines taste. The situation is different in France, where distinction still comes from command of the dominant national cultural repertoire of food, where the meaning of good food is equated with France, and the good citizen eats for France. Foreign cuisines are thus more of a threat. However, a culturally omnivorous option is at hand based upon the positive view of internal differentiation, of region and *terroir,* in a country which is a patchwork of nonantagonistic differences adding up to a national unity. Variety plays a different role, and one not determined by the global supply chain.

Notes

1. This would be the orthodox understanding in the contemporary literature on gastronomy (see, for instance, Gault, 2001).
2. Mechanisms of naturalization are described in detail by Wilk (2006: 112–21) regarding the formation of the cuisine of Belize, showing how creolization works to merge foreign and local culinary practices through blending, submersion, substitution, wrapping and stuffing, compression and alternation and promotion.
3. In 2007, France had registered 148 products as Protected Designation of Origin (PDO) or Protected Geographical Indication (PGI), compared with 36 for the UK.

References

Appadurai, A. (1988), 'How to Make a National Cuisine: Cookbooks in Contemporary India,' *Comparative Studies of Society & History,* 30/1: 3–24.
Appadurai, A. (1990), 'Disjuncture and Difference in the Global Cultural Economy', *Theory Culture & Society,* 18/5: 97–122.

Appadurai, A. (1996), *Modernity at Large,* Minneapolis: University of Minnesota Press.

Ashley, B., Hollows, J., Jones, S., and Taylor, B. (2004), *Food and Cultural Studies,* London: Routledge.

Bennett, T., Savage, M., Silva, E., Warde, A., Gayo-Cal, M., and Wright, D. (2009), *Culture, Class, Distinction,* London: Routledge.

Burnett, J. (1989), *Plenty and Want: A Social History of Food from 1815 to the Present Day,* London: Routledge.

Burnett, J. (2004), *England Eats Out: A Social History of Eating Out in England from 1830 to the Present,* Harlow: Longman.

Csergo, J. (1996), 'L'Emergence Des Cuisines Regionales', in J.L. Flandrin and M. Montanari (eds.), *Historie de l'Alimentation,* Paris: Fayard.

Ferguson, P. (1998), 'A Cultural Field in the Making: Gastronomy in Nineteenth-Century France,' *American Journal of Sociology,* 104/3: 597–641.

Ferguson, P. (2004), *Accounting for Taste: The Triumph of French Cuisine,* Chicago: Chicago University Press.

Fischler, C. (1980), 'Food Habits, Social Change and the Nature/Culture Dilemma', *Social Science Information,* 19: 937–53.

Gabaccia, D. (1998), *We Are What We Eat: Ethnic Food and the Making of Americans,* Cambridge, MA: Harvard University Press.

Gault, H. (2001), *Restaurants de Paris*, Paris: Éditions Nouveaux Loisirs.

Guides Londres, (1994), Paris: Gault-Millau.

The *Good Food Guide,* various years, various publishers.

Hardyment, C. (1995), *Slice of Life: The British Way of Eating Since 1945,* London: BBC Books.

Humble, N. (2005), *Culinary Pleasures: Cookbooks and the Transformation of British Food,* London: Faber and Faber.

Karpik, L. (2000), 'Le Guide Rouge Michelin', *Sociologie du Travail,* 42: 369–89.

Kjaernes, U., Harvey, M., and Warde, A. (2007), *Trust in Food: An Institutional and Comparative Analysis,* Basingstoke: Palgrave.

Leynse, W. (2006), 'Journeys through "Ingestible Topography": Socializing the "Situated Eater" in France', *European Studies,* 22: 129–58.

Lizardo, O. (2008), 'Understanding the Flow of Symbolic Goods in the Global Cultural Economy', *International Journal of Contemporary Sociology,* 45/1: 13–34.

Mennell, S. (1985), *All Manners of Food: Eating and Taste in England and France from the Middle Ages to the Present,* Oxford: Blackwell.

Mintz, S. (2008), 'Food, Culture and Energy', in A. Nutzenadel and F. Trentmann (eds.), *Food and Globalization: Consumption, Markets and Politics in the Modern World,* Oxford: Berg.

Mohring, M. (2008), 'Transnational Food Migration an the Internalization of Food Consumption: Ethnic Cuisine in West Germany', in A. Nutzenadel and F. Trentmann (eds.), *Food and Globalization: Consumption, Markets and Politics in the Modern World,* Oxford: Berg.

Nutzenadel, A. and Trentmann, F. (eds.) (2008), *Food and Globalization: Consumption, Markets and Politics in the Modern World,* Oxford: Berg.

Oddy, D. (2003), *From Plain Fare to Fusion Food: British Diet from the 1890s to the 1990s,* Woodbridge: Boydell Press.

Panayi, P. (2008), *Spicing Up Britain: London: The Multicultural History of British Food,* London: Reaktion Books.

Poulain J. P. (2002), *Sociologies de l'Alimentation: Les Mangeurs et L'Espace Social Alimentaire,* Paris: PUF.

Ratcliffe, K. (1995), *A Culinary Journey in Gascony: Recipes and Stories from My French Canal Boat,* New York: Ten Speed Press.

Robertson, R. (1992), *Globalization: Social Theory and Global Culture,* London: Sage.

Smart, B. (1994), 'Digesting the Modern Diet: Gastro-Porn, Fast Food and Panic Eating', in K. Tester (ed.), *The Flaneur,* London: Routledge.

Spang, R. (2001), *The Invention of the Restaurant: Paris and Modern Gastronomic Culture.* Harvard Historical Studies, Cambridge, MA: Harvard University Press.

Spencer, C. (2004), *British Food: An Extraordinary Thousand Years of History,* London: Grub Street.

Trubek, A. (2000), *Haute Cuisine: How the French Invented the Culinary Profession,* Philadelphia: University of Pennsylvania Press.

Trubek, A. (2005), *The Taste of Place: A Cultural Journey into Terroir,* Berkeley: University of California Press.

Warde, A. (1997), *Consumption, Food and Taste: Culinary Antinomies and Commodity Culture,* London: Sage.

Warde, A. (2000), 'Eating Globally: Cultural Flows and the Spread of Ethnic Restaurants', in D. Kalb, M. van der Land, R. Staring, B. van Steenbergen and N. Wilterdink (eds.), *The Ends of Globalization: Bringing Society Back In,* Boulder: Rowman and Littlefield.

Warde, A. (2004), 'La normalita del mangiare fuori' ['The Normality of Eating Out'], *Rassegna Italiana di Sociologia* (special issue on 'Sociology of Food', editor R. Sassatelli), 45/4: 493–518.

Warde, A. (2009), 'Inventing British Cuisine: Representations of Culinary Identity in the *Good Food Guide,* 1951–2007', *Food, Culture and Society,* 12/2: 151–72.

Warde, A., Cheng, S. L, Olsen, W., and Southerton, D. (2007), 'Changes in the Practice of Eating: A Comparative Analysis', *Acta Sociologica,* 50/4: 365–85.

Warde, A., and Martens, L. (2000), *Eating Out: Social Differentiation, Consumption and Pleasure,* Cambridge: Cambridge University Press.

Warde, A., Olsen, W., and Martens, L. (1999), 'Consumption and the Problem of Variety: Cultural Omnivorousness, Social Distinction and Dining Out', *Sociology,* 33/1: 105–27.

Whiteman, K. (2008), *The Food Lover's Guide to the Gourmet Secrets of Paris,* Riverside: Universe.

Wilk, R. (2006), *Home Cooking in the Global Village: Caribbean Food from Buccaneers to Ecotourists,* Oxford: Berg.

Hispanic Foodways in the San Luis Valley of Colorado: The Local, Global, Hybrid and Processed Fourth of July Feast

Carole Counihan
Millersville University

During ten summers of ethnographic fieldwork on changing foodways in the small Hispanic town of Antonito in Colorado's San Luis Valley, I have attended many Fourth of July celebrations. In this predominantly Hispanic community, the Fourth of July is an important holiday, which is always marked by a big outdoor meal, usually centred on a barbecue, as it is in so many communities and homes around the nation.[1]

The Fourth of July is an important holiday in Antonito and across the United States because it symbolizes independence, freedom, nationalism and patriotism—key elements in the country's mythos. By participating in this holiday, people act out their belonging to the culture and their ideals of U.S. national identity. This chapter uses the methods of ethnography—the in-depth study of people and culture through long-term participant observation and interview—to examine the Fourth of July feast as an exemplar of contemporary foodways in Antonito. It examines what people eat and why and how through food they define their place in U.S. society. It is grounded in the understanding that U.S. foodways are composed of a multiplicity of national and ethnic cuisines that have met, mingled and evolved in the legendary U.S. melting pot.[2] The chapter examines the many culinary strains composing the Fourth of July feast in Antonito, links them to the broader diet, and suggests their grounding in diverse cultural, economic and ecological realities.

I have been studying changing food habits in Antonito since 1996 using what I call a food-centred life history methodology. This methodology consists of conducting multiple semistructured interviews with willing participants on their foodways, which I define as their beliefs and behaviours about food production, distribution, preparation and consumption. Interviews cover diverse topics including gardening, farming, food preservation, shopping, daily and festive meals, infant and child feeding, food sharing and so on. I have conducted fifty-five interviews with twenty-five residents of the town to document and understand their changing diet and culture.[3]

Antonito lies on the northern edge of what anthropologists have called 'greater Mexico'[4]—that region in the south-western United States that was part of Mexico until the end of the Mexican American war in 1848 when the Treaty of Guadalupe

Hidalgo ceded this region (almost half of Mexico's territory) to the United States. In the mid-nineteenth century, settlers from the Upper Rio Grande villages of northern New Mexico's Rio Arriba and Taos counties moved north into Colorado and settled along the relatively fertile and well-watered Conejos, San Antonio and Los Pinos rivers in an area that today consists of Conejos and Costilla Counties. These two counties are part of what Martínez calls the *'siete condados del norte'*—the seven rural counties spanning southern Colorado and northern New Mexico that have Chicano demographic majorities and an enduring *Mexicano* culture.[5] Ninety per cent of the population of Antonito self-identified as 'Hispanic' in the 2000 census, while sixty per cent of its surrounding Conejos County did, making Antonito one of the most 'Hispanic' towns in Colorado and indeed in the United States.

Antonito was founded six miles north of the Colorado–New Mexico border in 1881 by the Denver and Rio Grande Railroad in the southern end of the San Luis Valley, a cold desert valley that lies between 7,500 and 8,000 feet (2,300–2,400 metres), between the Sangre de Cristo and San Juan mountains, in a rural area with a very low population density.[6] Antonito was the railroad depot, market town and commercial centre of a predominantly Hispanic region that had been settled by people who variously called themselves Spanish-Americans, *Hispanos, Mexicanos, raza* and, more recently, Chicanos. The earliest settlers practised a subsistence farming and ranching economy in the river valleys, and today there is some irrigated commercial farming of barley, potatoes, carrots and alfalfa, but little horticulture.[7] According to the 2002 census of agriculture, there were 494 farms in Conejos County with an average size of 542 acres and an average market value of production per farm of $46,259, down 18 per cent from 1997. The dominant crop item in terms of acreage was forage for livestock (43,700 acres), followed by barley (5,600), potatoes (1,200), wheat (900) and oats (450). In terms of livestock, cattle dominated with 25,000 units, followed by sheep (11,000), bee colonies (2,000), horses and ponies (1,500) and laying hens (750).[8] According to the 2000 U.S. Census, only 14.6 per cent of the population worked in 'agriculture, forestry, fishing and hunting, and mining'.[9] Rather than supporting a local food-centred economy, Conejos County's agriculture produced cash crops for external markets.

The Fourth of July Meal

On the Fourth of July in 2000, we were invited to a gathering at our friend José Inez (Joe) Taylor's house. His 'Anglo' name notwithstanding, Joe considered himself 100 per cent 'Chicano', and he discussed his ethnic identity at length in his book co-authored with my husband, anthropologist Jim Taggart (Taylor and Taggart, 2003). We spent many holidays with Joe's extended family, including Christmas, New Year's, Fourth of July and several birthday parties. For the Fourth of July gathering in 2000, I baked a big batch of chocolate chip cookies, using the classic recipe on the back of the chocolate chip package, and my husband Jim made a big fruit salad out of watermelon, cantaloupe and honeydew melon. We arrived at Joe's and found his two daughters and son with their partners and children. Joe's oldest sister, Cordi, was present, and she brought *chicharrones*—fried crunchy pork skins. Several friends and in-laws came and went. Joe's son-in-law manned the barbecue and grilled hamburgers, hotdogs, sausages, bratwurst, steaks and ribs. Joe made red chilli, green chilli, a pot of pinto bean and an enchilada casserole. Red chilli, green chilli and pinto beans were the most emblematic *Mexicano* foods and accompanied many meals. But of enchilada casserole, on the other hand, Joe said, 'With all due respect, it's gringo food'. He made it by building several layers of store-bought corn tortillas, canned refried beans and grated orange cheese, and then sprinkling over the top red chilli made with ground beef. Joe said it should have had lettuce and tomato on the top but he didn't have any. It was 'gringo food' because it was not part of the traditional San Luis Valley *Mexicano* diet—the corn tortillas, canned beans and cheddar cheese marked it as a recent import.

Joe's son, Joe Jr, contributed two traditional *Mexicano* dishes: home-made *menudo* (a stew made of tripe, hominy [lime-soaked dried corn], onion and chilli) and *posole* (a stew made of hominy, pork, oregano, onion, garlic and chilli). Joe's girlfriend, Martha, made guacamole out of mashed avocado, some diced jalapeño peppers and sour cream with salt and paprika. A coworker of Joe Jr's brought potato salad made of cold boiled potatoes, celery, pickles and mayonnaise dressing—without onions because Joe hates them. Another coworker brought potato chips and carbonated sodas—some sugared and others artificially sweetened. Joe's daughter Shanda brought a big supermarket vegetable tray containing carrots, celery and cauliflower pieces with a ranch dressing dip. Joe's daughter Monica brought pasta salad. There were packages of store-bought flour tortillas and buns for the hamburgers and hot-dogs. As people arrived, Joe made *sopaipillas* by mixing flour, water, salt and baking powder, rolling the dough out in small thin circles and frying them in vegetable oil until they puffed up and turned golden brown.

After thirty or so adults and children arrived, Joe urged us to eat. We formed a ragged line that snaked around the kitchen, and we filled our plates from the many dishes. Then we sat outside in Joe's back yard, under a tarp to protect us from the hot San Luis Valley sun, enjoying the slight breeze and delicious air, crisp and clean at 7,880 feet above sea level. The dusty yard reminded us of the ongoing drought, and we welcomed the distant clouds and lightning flashes but were disappointed that no rain fell on Antonito, especially because July Fourth was the traditional start of the summer monsoon season and its intermittent rain showers. Because the San Luis Valley is essentially a desert, with less than eight inches average rainfall per year, every drop of rain and flake of snow is valued, especially in terribly dry years. We passed a leisurely afternoon working our way through the food and chatting about how the drought had forced many local ranchers to sell their cattle and had depleted the wild food plants that were so important in the old days.

The Complex Origins of the Antonito Diet

The Fourth of July foods, like the Antonito diet in general, showed influences of *Mexicano* culinary traditions, local farming and ranching, generic 'American' food and products of the global food economy. As they consumed a diet with diverse culinary strands, the people of Antonito defined various dimensions of their Hispanic and American selves. Many elements in the Antonito diet derived from Mexican American culinary traditions, which were a fusion of Spanish and Native American cuisines, adapted to the local ecology, high altitude and cold climate.[10] Older people described the dietary staples of the first two-thirds of the twentieth century as potatoes, beans and chilli supplemented by meat, vegetables, wheat tortillas and bread. The renowned Native American 'three sisters'—corn, beans and squash—were present in modest degrees in Antonito. Beans have always been and still are a staple, boiled with salt and possibly onion, garlic or lard and eaten with many meals, including Joe Taylor's Fourth of July feast. Before World War II many people grew the native *bolita* beans, but after the war, pinto beans brought by traders from New Mexico increasingly prevailed, and in recent times most people purchased pintos at supermarkets although some sought out *bolitas* at specialty stores.

Traditionally, rural Hispanic women grew summer gardens with a wide variety of vegetables and fruits that they either ate fresh or dried and canned. Some of these foods were native to the Americas including corn, *bolita* beans, potatoes, pumpkins (especially the small round tender *calabacitas*), squashes, potatoes, strawberries and raspberries. They also grew diverse plant foods that were not native to the Americas including radishes, lettuce, turnips, carrots, onions, rutabagas, wax beans, string beans, *habas* beans, peas, cabbage, cauliflower, crab apples and apricots.[11] From Native Americans, *Mexicanos* learned about wild foods: *quelites* (lambs quarters), *verdolagas* (purslane), *capulines* (chokecherries), *champes* (rosehips) and *piñon* (pine nuts). Old people spoke about how they used to consume and dry vast quantities of these plants, but few ate them regularly anymore, and they have become nostalgic icons of times past. By 2006, hardly anyone in Antonito tended gardens, and many ate plant foods grown all over the globe like the carrots, celery and cauliflower in the supermarket vegetable tray brought by his daughter to Joe's Fourth of July party. Whether purchased at Antonito's locally owned Hometown Market or at big chain supermarkets in Alamosa thirty miles north, fruits and vegetables came from factory farms all over the globe—California, Florida, Mexico and South America.

The only locally grown vegetables regularly available in Antonito were potatoes, which are a major cash crop in the San Luis Valley, whose cold climate was ideally suited for irrigated potato production. Originating in the Andes, potatoes were carried to Europe by the explorers and then back to the southwest with the Spanish (Messer, 2004). Inexpensive and highly nutritious, potatoes have always made a key contribution to the Antonito diet. Several older people spoke about working in the potato fields to earn extra money as well as about gleaning potatoes from the commercial fields after the harvest. In their culinary versatility, potatoes reflected multicultural influences on the local cuisine. In the *Mexicano* tradition people ate them fried—in lard in the old days, but in olive or vegetable oil in recent times. In the American tradition, Antonito folks ate potatoes mashed with roasts or boiled in potato salad. In the industrialized food tradition, people ate lots of fast food fried potatoes and high-fat potato crisps.

In addition to the staple foods of potatoes and beans, people in Antonito ate diverse grain products. Rather than eating the corn tortillas typical of warmer climates, they consumed wheat tortillas and bread, rolls or *sopaipillas*—a version of the fry bread so popular with south-western Native Americans. They also ate wheat in the form of pasta—whether spaghetti with meat sauce, macaroni and cheese or the pasta salad present at Joe's and many other Fourth of July parties. These pasta products had their origins in Italian cuisine brought to America by Sicilian and southern Italian immigrants in the late nineteenth and early twentieth centuries.[12] But pasta as well as pizza had penetrated so deeply into U.S. foodways that people in Antonito defined them not as 'Italian' but as 'American'.[13]

In addition to consuming diverse kinds of wheat products that spanned *Mexicano/* American, homemade/processed and local/global foodways, people in Antonito ate lots of corn. They ate it fresh on the cob or dried and cooked into various dishes with Mexican origins like the *menudo* and *posole* Joe's son made for the Fourth of July party, as well as *chicos* (dried tender corn), *atole* (blue corn meal made into a sweet or savoury cereal or drink) and *tamales*. Red and green chilli dishes were omnipresent in Antonito. These were sauces or soups made with lard or oil, a touch of flour, garlic, water and either dried and ground red chilli or fresh or frozen peeled green chilli. Red chilli was sometimes made with ground beef and green was made with diced pork. The Spanish brought Central American chillies north into the Southwest, where they became integrated into Pueblo Indian and Mexican American cuisine and evolved with the addition of Spanish-introduced beef, mutton or pork (Ross, 2004).

Meat was always a key item in the Fourth of July meal in Antonito and across the nation. Typically men barbecued meat—usually beef and pork, especially in the ubiquitous hamburgers and hotdogs. These two quintessentially 'American' foods originated in Germany. The hamburger first appeared in the United States in the early nineteenth century and was on the menu at Delmonico's fancy New York restaurant by 1834 (Hogan, 2004). Today it is one of the most widely consumed American foods, particularly through its place on restaurant menus, especially fast food ones. At Joe's Fourth of July feast there were also steaks, sausages, ribs and even bratwurst, another hint of German Americans' influence on foodways in Colorado, where they formed a significant ethnic group. At some parties there were even burgers made from the meat of native buffalos raised by a local rancher. Many Hispanics in Antonito named meat as an important dietary staple, past and present, some serving it at every meal. Many still ate local meat—beef from relatives' cattle, venison or elk hunted by male family members and rarely locally raised mutton, pork or chicken. Meat crossed categories of *Mexicano*-Spanish and Anglo-American foods depending on where it came from, how it was cooked and where and with whom it was eaten.

On the Fourth of July, *Mexicanos* in Antonito highlighted not only certain foods but also the social and physical context of the meal. Extended families came together from far and wide for the Fourth of July and many groups camped in the nearby San Juan Mountains for the long weekend. Others went for the day to one of many beautiful picnic spots or at least ate outside in their backyards, reaffirming their ties to the land which have severely thinned as fewer and fewer people practised ranching and farming.

Seventy-six-year-old Asuncionita described her family's Fourth of July celebrations in the 1940s. She said,

> We always went to the mountains ... Generally speaking there was always somebody that we went with or they went with us ... It wasn't like it is now. Anybody could camp ... In those days there were hardly any tourists up there. It was mostly people from here, from the valley ... We'd go early in the morning and spend the day, coming down there at the hairpin curves, my dad used to cook again, fried potatoes and meat and grandpa used to make coffee. We'd have dinner up there before we'd get home ... We had pop and then you didn't drink pop every day the way they buy it now ... Oh it was very special.

Already in the late 1940s Asuncionita and her family were drinking 'pop' or sweetened, flavoured, carbonated drinks that today are consumed in staggering amounts in Antonito and across the United States—more than fifty-five gallons per capita in 1999 (Putnam, 2000). Pop was present not only at special occasions like Joe's Fourth of July party, but also on a daily basis in many homes and all restaurants. Pop epitomized the processed foods consumed in increasing amounts in Antonito and across the nation, foods that often were high in calories and low in nutritional value. By drinking pop, people in Antonito participated in national cuisine and culture but also increased their risk of diabetes, the rates of which were skyrocketing among Hispanics and Native Americans (Gladwell, 1998) and were a growing problem among *Mexicanos* in the San Luis Valley.[14]

Discussion

Antonito foodways reflected a place, culture and history and were influenced by diverse culinary forces. Antonito cuisine spanned four continua: (1) Spanish/*Mexicano* versus American/Anglo cooking, (2) homemade versus processed food, (3) native versus imported species and (4) local versus global products. Different families ate at different points on these four continua and consumed foods ranging from the age-old staples of beans, chilli and potatoes, through stews, roast meats, hamburgers, macaroni, hot dogs, pasta, frozen pizza, pop, fast food, processed dishes and myriad other foods.

My ethnographic research in Antonito revealed several important forces that affected where people ate along the four continua. One was accessibility. People ate foods that were available whether by purchase, exchange or production. Over the past sixty years, local horticulture and gathering have declined to almost zero in Antonito, and people purchased almost all of their food like most Americans.[15] I knew only one person who had a vegetable garden in Antonito. The reasons people gave for no longer gardening were that water was too expensive and gardening was too much work. Perhaps there was also a negative association of gardening with poverty. People did, however, continue to produce and consume local meat. Many men still hunted for elk and deer, and families welcomed the important contribution of game to the diet. Hunting was an important male-bonding activity, and a significant milestone for an adolescent boy was killing his first deer or elk. People spoke of purchasing or raising their own local beef or mutton and were enthusiastic about the superior quality and taste as well as cheaper cost of meat from local range-fed cattle and sheep. By and large, however, most of what people ate came from the global food industry.

In spite of the decline in subsistence gardening and meat production, however, many people in Antonito still preferred local foods and purchased them when possible. In the late summer, Antonito's Hometown Market sold and roasted green chillies from New Mexico, which many locals bought, peeled and froze to use all year long in sauces and stews. Occasional vendors from northern New Mexico sold door-to-door local honey, *piñon* nuts, *chicos,* peaches, melons, green chilli, ground red chilli or the dramatic *ristras*—braided wreaths of the small bright red peppers. The recently opened Salazar Trading Post in Antonito sold some local foods: potatoes, tamales, meat, *atole, panocha* (sprouted wheat flour), *bolita* beans, beef and buffalo meat. From July through early October, the Saturday Farmers' Market in Alamosa sold a variety of local fruits, vegetables and herbs. Several people I interviewed in Antonito willingly made the sixty-mile round trip to Alamosa to purchase these foods that they deemed better tasting, more nutritious and culturally significant.

A second force that affected food consumption along the four continua was how it fit habits of time, space and division of labour. The extent to which Antonito families ate homemade or processed foods depended on many factors, especially who was cooking, how much time they had, whether they defined cooking as oppressive or satisfying and what their economic resources were. Processed foods shortened cooking time, although they were more expensive and almost always nutritionally inferior to fresh food. Eating processed products involved the consumer in a standardized national cuisine and culture, whereas eating *Mexicano* foods renewed ethnic affiliation, family roots, individual creativity and ties to the land. Some people—especially older ones—appreciated the culture and values associated with *Mexicano* cuisine, whereas others—especially younger people—embraced the modern American world typified by fast, processed and globalized food.

A third force affecting Antonito consumption was the intertwining of food and meaning. For public consumption at a party, cooks often made a special or signature dish that signified something important. Sometimes they made 'traditional' dishes to reveal their mastery of and adherence to traditional culture, like Joe Jr making *menudo* and *posole* for the Fourth of July party. Sometimes people made brand new dishes to signify their creativity. For example, Janice said,

> When we have holidays, when I make a lot of different things and we have many courses, I get a lot of satisfaction then … because I'm creating, it has to be something I thought up. Something I didn't get from anybody else. I'm trying this out. Then we unveil and then see the reaction. So I do see it as an artist; I'm an artist then and that's when I get a lot of satisfaction and happiness from creating.

Other people made dishes that reinforced family identity, like Bernadette, who recalled,

> Whenever we get together, the Vigil clan, it seems like all we eat is devilled eggs! For whatever occasion—bring the devilled eggs! I was thinking maybe it's a comfort food. It's associated with the warmness of a family. Devilled eggs themselves means we're all getting together, as a family, as a unit and that's one of our good foods that we're going to share.

People embraced foods that held meaning and tasted good, but taste was learned and based on habits of eating. Joe Taylor and all his male descendents hated onions yet ate without protest soups or stews in which onions were disguised by being finely chopped and disintegrated in the broth. Yet eschewing onions was a clearly important emblem of their masculine Taylor identity. Taste was related to meaning, for through taste people experienced food and through experience they created meaning and identity.

One woman I interviewed, fifty-two-year-old Bernadette, made clear how she defined her identity through her food consumption: 'We're all *Mexicanos*. And where in the heck do we get the *frijoles* and the tortillas and all that if it wasn't from the *Mexicanos?* We all eat the same tortillas. We all eat in the same way'. Yet at the same time as she defined herself as *Mexicana* because she ate culturally distinct Mexican foods, she also proclaimed her 'American' identity in the many multicultural foods she described, including Puerto Rican rice, macaroni, lasagne, sweet-potato-corn-flake-marshmallow-croquettes, Chinese chicken and fast food. Eating the foods of multiple ethnic groups and of the global food economy gave Bernadette and others a legitimate place in the American melting pot.

But the consumption of these diverse foods threatened *Mexicanos*' distinct cultural identity. Food industrialization has altered taste and affected the associations embedded in diverse foods, and most young people would not eat the *posole* and *menudo* that Joe made for the Fourth of July Feast, finding them 'gross' and not caring about their cultural distinctiveness. The reliance on foods produced all over the globe has gone hand in hand with and legitimized *Mexicanos'* loss of land and water and the decline of local production that were integral to the long-standing *Mexicano* culture of the *siete condados*. In the analysis of the Antonito Fourth of July feast, we can see how food globalization has affected not only what people in Antonito ate but also how their changing foodways reflected the decline of *Mexicano* culture and economic autonomy.

Notes

An earlier version of this chapter appeared in *Scienze Gastronomiche/Gastronomic Sciences*, 0/6: 74–83.

1. See Stevens (2005), who estimates that there are sixty million barbecues in the United States on the Fourth of July each year.
2. On the regional and ethnic diversity of U.S. cuisine, see Counihan (2002), Diner (2001), Gabaccia (1998), Gray and Counihan (2004), Levenstein (1985), Pillsbury (1998), Shortridge and Shortridge (1998) and Spivey (1999).
3. See Counihan (2005, 2006, 2008, 2009).
4. Paredes (1976: xiv) defined greater Mexico as "all the areas inhabited by people of a Mexican culture" in the United States and Mexico. See also Limón (1998).
5. The *siete condados del norte* are Costilla and Conejos Counties in Colorado, and Taos, Río Arriba, San Miguel, Mora and Guadalupe Counties in New Mexico (Martínez, 1998: 70).
6. In 2006 the estimated population density of Conejos County was 6.5 people/ square mile, and of Colorado was 45.9 people/square mile (U.S. Census Bureau Population Division, 2006).
7. On the history, economy and culture of the region see Bean (1975), Deutsch (1987), García (1998), Gutierrez and Eckert (1991), Peña (1998), Simmons (1979), Swadesh (1974), Taylor and Taggart (2003), Tushar (1992) and Weigle (1975).
8. Data on agriculture come from the National Agricultural Statistics Service (NASS, 2002).
9. Data come from U.S. Census Bureau (2000).
10. The diet of Antonito resembles what Pilcher (2004: 81) calls *norteño* cuisine characterized by wheat instead of corn tortillas, lots of meat and limited vegetables. On Mexican American foodways, see Abarca (2006), Bentley (1998), Cabeza de Baca Gilbert (1970), Counihan (2005), and Jaramillo (1981).
11. See Ross (2004) on native and imported North American plants.
12. On Italian American cuisine, see Diner (2001) and Levenstein (1985).
13. Average annual U.S. pizza consumption was twenty-three pounds per capita in the late 1990s (Pillsbury, 1998: 179).
14. See Hamman et al. (1989), who found in their San Luis Valley diabetes study that the age-adjusted prevalence of confirmed non-insulin-dependent diabetes

mellitus was 21 per 1,000 in Anglo males and 44 per 1,000 in Hispanic males, accounting for nonresponse. For Anglo females, the prevalence was 13 per 1,000 compared with 62 per 1,000 for Hispanic females, accounting for nonresponse. See also Marshall et al. (1991), whose San Luis Valley diabetes study concluded that high-fat, low-carbohydrate diets are associated with the onset of non-insulin-dependent diabetes mellitus in humans.

15. Until World War I, Americans ate roughly equal amounts of purchased and produced food, but by the late 1990s, 98 per cent of the food consumed in the United States was purchased (Pillsbury, 1998: 107).

References

Abarca, M. (2006), *Voices in the Kitchen: Views of Food and the World from Working-Class Mexican and Mexican American Women,* College Station: Texas A & M University Press.

Bean, L. E. (1975), *Land of the Blue Sky People,* Alamosa: Ye Olde Print Shoppe.

Bentley, A. (1998), 'From Culinary Other to Mainstream America: Meanings and Uses of Southwestern Cuisine'. *Southern Folklore,* 55/3: 238–52.

Cabeza de Baca Gilbert, F. (1970), *Historic Cookery,* Santa Fe: Ancient City.

Counihan, C. (ed.) (2002), *Food in the USA: A Reader,* New York: Routledge.

Counihan, C. (2005), 'The Border as Barrier and Bridge: Food, Gender and Ethnicity in the San Luis Valley of Colorado', In A. Avakian and B. Haber (eds.), *From Betty Crocker to Feminist Food Studies,* Amherst: University of Massachusetts Press.

Counihan, C. (2006), 'Food as Mediating Voice and Oppositional Consciousness for Chicanas in Colorado's San Luis Valley', In S. Baugh (ed.), *Mediating Chicana/o Culture: Multicultural American Vernacular,* Cambridge, MA: Cambridge Scholars Press.

Counihan, C. (2008), '*Mexicanas*' Food Voice and Differential Consciousness in the San Luis Valley of Colorado'. In C. Counihan and P. Van Esterik (eds.), *Food and Culture: A Reader,* 2nd edition, New York: Routledge.

Counihan, C. (2009), *A Tortilla Is Like Life: Food and Culture in the San Luis Valley of Colorado,* Austin: University of Texas Press.

Deutsch, S. (1987), *No Separate Refuge: Culture, Class and Gender on an Anglo-Hispanic Frontier in the American Southwest, 1880–1940,* Oxford: Oxford University Press.

Diner, H. R. (2001), *Hungering for America: Italian, Irish and Jewish Foodways in the Age of Migration,* Cambridge, MA: Harvard University Press.

Gabaccia, D. (1998), *We Are What We Eat: Ethnic Foods and the Making of Americans,* Cambridge, MA: Harvard University Press.

García, R. (1998), 'Notes on (Home)Land Ethics: Ideas, Values and the Land', In D. Peña (ed.), *Chicano Culture, Ecology, Politics: Subversive Kin,* Tucson: University of Arizona Press.

Gladwell, M. (1998), 'The Pima Paradox', *The New Yorker* (2 February): 44–57.

Gray, R. R., and Counihan, C. M. (2004), 'Stati Uniti d'America e Melting Pot', in M. Montanari and F. Sabban (eds.), *Atlante dell'Alimentazione e della Gastronomia*, vol. 2, Torino: UTET.

Gutierrez, P., and Eckert, J. (1991), 'Contrasts and Commonalities: Hispanic and Anglo Farming in Concjos County, Colorado', *Rural Sociology*, 562: 247–63.

Hamman R. F., Marshall, J.A., Baxter, J., Kahn, L.B., Mayer, E.J., Orleans, M, Murphy, J. R., and Lezotte, D. C. (1989), 'Methods and Prevalence of Non-insulin-dependent Diabetes Mellitus in a Biethnic Colorado Population: The San Luis Valley Diabetes Study', *American Journal of Epidemiology*, 129: 295–311.

Hogan, D. G. (2004), 'Hamburger', in A. F. Smith (ed.), *The Oxford Encyclopedia of Food and Drink in America*, vol. 2, Oxford: Oxford University Press.

Jaramillo, C. (1981), *The Genuine New Mexico Tasty Recipes*, Santa Fe: Ancient City.

Levenstein, H. (1985), 'The American Response to Italian Food, 1880–1931', *Food and Foodways*, 1/1: 1–24.

Limón, J. E. (1998), *American Encounters: Greater Mexico, the United States and Erotics of Culture*, Boston: Beacon Press.

Marshall, J. A., Hamman, R. F., and Baxter, J. (1991), 'High-fat, Low-carbohydrate Diet and the Etiology of Non-insulin-dependent Diabetes Mellitus: the San Luis Valley Diabetes Study', *American Journal of Epidemiology*, 134/6: 590–603.

Martínez, R. O. (1998), 'Social Action Research, Bioregionalism and the Upper Rio Grande', in D. Peña (ed.), *Chicano Culture, Ecology, Politics: Subversive Kin*, Tucson: University of Arizona Press.

Messer, E. (2004), 'Potatoes', in A. F. Smith (ed.), *The Oxford Encyclopedia of Food and Drink in America*, vol. 2, Oxford: Oxford University Press.

National Agricultural Statistics Service (2002), '2002 Census of Agriculture, County Profile, Conejos, Colorado', Washington, DC: Fact Finders for Agriculture, USDA, <http://www.nass.usda.gov/census/census02/profiles/co/cp08021.PDF> accessed 22 February 2008.

Paredes, A. (1976), *A Texas-Mexican Cancionero*, Urbana: University of Illinois Press.

Peña, D. (ed.) (1998), *Chicano Culture, Ecology, Politics: Subversive Kin*, Tucson: University of Arizona Press.

Pilcher, J. M. (2004), 'Mexican American Food', in A. F. Smith (ed.), *The Oxford Encyclopedia of Food and Drink in America*, vol. 2, Oxford: Oxford University Press.

Pillsbury, R. (1998), *No Foreign Food: The American Diet in Time and Place*, Boulder: Westview Press.

Putnam, J. (2000), 'Major Trends in U.S. Food Supply, 1909–1999', *Food Review*, 23/1: 8–15.

Ross, A. (2004), 'Native American Foods: Technology and Sources', in A. F. Smith (ed.), *The Oxford Encyclopedia of Food and Drink in America*, vol. 2, Oxford: Oxford University Press.

Shortridge, B. G., and Shortridge, J. R. (eds.) (1998), *The Taste of American Place: A Reader on Regional and Ethnic Foods,* Lanham: Rowman and Littlefield.

Simmons, V. M. (1979), *The San Luis Valley: Land of the Six-Armed Cross,* Boulder: Pruett.

Spivey, D. M. (1999), *The Peppers, Cracklings and Knots of Wool Cookbook: The Global Migration of African Cuisine,* Albany: SUNY Press.

Stevens, S. (2005), 'P's and Q's of BBQ', *Sierra,* 90/4: 20.

Swadesh, F. L. (1974), *Los Primeros Pobladores: Hispanic Americans of the Ute Frontier,* Notre Dame: University of Notre Dame Press.

Taylor, J. I., and Taggart, J. M. (2003), *Alex and the Hobo: A Chicano Life and Story,* Austin: University of Texas Press.

Tushar, O. L. (1992), *The People of El Valle: A History of the Spanish Colonials in the San Luis Valley,* Pueblo: Escritorio.

U.S. Census Bureau (2000), 'Census 2000 Summary File 3', <http://factfinder.census.gov/> accessed 30 August 2009.

U.S. Census Bureau Population Division (2006), 'Cumulative Estimates of Population Change for the United States, States and Counties, and Puerto Rico, April 1, 2000 to July 1, 2006', <http://www.census.gov/popest/gallery/maps/Maps_StCty2006.xls> accessed 30 August 2009.

Weigle, M. (ed.) (1975), *Hispanic Villages of Northern New Mexico,* Santa Fe: The Lightning Tree Press.

–14–

Globalization and Obesity

Jeffery Sobal

Cornell University

Wm. Alex McIntosh

Texas A&M University

The concept of globalization is widely used in a multitude of often incongruent ways to characterize a great variety of phenomena (Guillen, 2001; McMichael, 2008; Sklair, 2002). We interpret globalization as a structural phenomenon where globalization represents 'the process of worldwide integration and unification of previously local, national and regional phenomena into global units' (Sobal, 2001a). Globalization involves a process of movement towards globality, where global institutions dominate human life rather than smaller institutions representing smaller-scale spatial units such as regions, nations or communities (Sobal, 1999a). Global institutions occur in many sectors, including business/economics, government/policy, civil society/publics and others. Consequences of global institutions include high rates of trade growth and foreign direct investment on the order of 300 per cent from the 1980s to 2000, although this has resulted in lower governmental spending for social welfare and healthcare (Brune and Garrett, 2005). Many consider globalization the path to increased income inequalities and increased disparities in healthcare expenditures and health (Bornschier et al., 1978; Bornschier and Chase-Dunn, 1985; McIntosh and Thomas, 2004). Using a globalization perspective, we will examine how obesity is increasing with globalization, the global mechanisms involved in the worldwide rise in obesity and how global institutions are beginning to address obesity.

Obesity is the presence of high levels of stored body fat (World Health Organization [WHO], 1995; 2001). Scientists have developed a general agreement about measurement of body fatness in populations, and global health institutions have established anthropometric levels of fatness that indicate underweight, normal weight, overweight and obesity that are widely used in research and policy (WHO, 1995). However, measurement and criteria for assessing weight norms, ideals and designations of cut-offs for the population as a whole and for subpopulations remain debated and contested (e.g. Jebb and Prentice, 2001).

High levels of body fat are associated with a variety of chronic diseases including heart disease, hypertension, diabetes and some cancers and also with higher death rates (Allison et al., 1999; Kushner, 1993), although there is scientific debate about the levels and patterns of health consequences of body weight (Troiano et al., 1996; Wildman et al., 2008). These types of obesity-related chronic degenerative diseases are sometimes labelled 'diseases of affluence' in contrast to the starvation-related diseases of stunting and wasting sometimes labelled 'diseases of poverty' (e.g. Ezzati et al., 2005), with the use and usefulness of these labels also deliberated and disputed as conflations with Westernization (Pollard, 2008) and globalization (McMurray and Smith, 2001).

It is useful to distinguish analyses of the globalization *of* obesity from the examination of globalization *and* obesity. Analysing globalization of obesity considers the prevalence and patterns of obesity and is largely an epidemiological exercise in establishing how much, when, where and who has become obese in the world. Understanding globalization of obesity is important and will be the focus of the next section in this chapter. In contrast, examining globalization and obesity considers social science perspectives about how the structural processes involved in globalization both influence and are influenced by obesity; this will be the focus of a subsequent section in this chapter.

Globalization of Obesity

Worldwide levels of body weight and obesity differ geographically and fluctuate historically. Some societies have fatter populations and a higher prevalence of obese citizens. Over the course of human history, particularly in the late twentieth and early twenty-first century, body weights have risen in most societies, with some variations, fluctuations and reversals in broader trends towards higher body weights. Societies and the subgroups they contain vary widely in body weights. Some societies are largely composed of people who are very thin, while other societies include primarily fatter individuals (Pelletier and Rahn, 1998). Historically, body weights have increased considerably since the industrial revolution (Stearns, 1997). Additionally, there has been a particularly large increase in obesity in Western postindustrial societies beginning in the late twentieth century (Ogden et al., 2006). Rising body weight levels within a developing nation over historical time may be labelled a 'body weight transition' (Lee and Sobal, 2003).

Western increases in obesity are often labelled an 'obesity epidemic' in developed societies (Contaldo and Pasanisi, 2005) and an 'obesity pandemic' as obesity became more prevalent in an increasing number of societies (Roth et al., 2004). However, no official criteria exist for delineation of an 'epidemic' or 'pandemic' (Boero, 2007; Rosenberg, 1992), and this characterization is problematic (Gard and Wright, 2005; Mitchell and McTigue, 2007). Others have framed the worldwide spreading of higher body fatness using the term 'globesity' (WHO Consultation on Obesity, 1999). Data about global patterns of obesity are drawn from many sources. Nutritional surveillance projects collect data about nutrition problems and have traditionally focused on undernutrition, with obesity only recently receiving attention. Some global health analysts have drawn attention to overweight in reports that worldwide obesity is surpassing undernutrition in prevalence (Gardner and Halweil, 2000; Patel, 2007).

A number of researchers have collected cross-sectional and historical data about obesity in segments of nations (e.g. Pelletier and Rahn, 1998). Comparisons of obesity levels have been done for sets of developing countries (Prentice, 2006) and other collections of nations (e.g. Lissau et al., 2004; Molarius et al., 2000). Some reviews focus on segments of populations, such as women (e.g. Martorell et al., 2000) or children (e.g. Wang, 2001). For at least the past two decades, attempts have been made to compile worldwide obesity data (Gurney and Gorsteen, 1988). In a world of over six billion inhabitants, the prevalence of people who are overweight has been estimated to be over one billion, and the prevalence of obesity is estimated at over 300 million individuals (WHO, 2001). A recent compilation of worldwide obesity data found the greatest penetration of high body weight in the northern hemisphere in postindustrial nations (WHO Global Infobase Team, 2005). The incidence of obesity, measured as the number of new cases per year, is more difficult to calculate than prevalence and varies more by time and place. One estimate of the incidence of obesity in the United States suggests that about 2 per cent of adult men and women become obese each year (Parikh et al., 2007).

It is essential to carefully evaluate research designs of global obesity studies (Sobal, 1998). Cross-sectional comparisons of nations with different levels of economic development should not be assumed to represent a historical trend because it may lead to incorrect conclusions by conflating spatial differences with historical differences. Avoiding this fallacy of 'reading history sideways' (Thornton, 2005) requires actual historical data over a substantial amount of time. Historical data about body weight and obesity in many nations over many years is rarely available. Overall, it appears that obesity has shifted from epidemic to endemic and from prevalent to prevailing. While it is essential to document and describe worldwide levels and patterns of obesity, it is even more important to examine how global structures and globalization processes influence world body weights.

Globalization and Obesity

Many analysts have described rising levels of obesity as a worldwide phenomenon (e.g. Popkin and Doak, 1998). Others have labelled rising weights of the world as a global pattern (e.g. Caballero, 2007). However, most existing analyses use the term 'global' only as a descriptor of the international prevalence of obesity across many nations and do not consider globalization as a structural change that includes new global institutional forms that are crucial to obesity (Sobal, 2001b). We interpret global obesity as a consequence of the goal-seeking activities of global organizations and institutions. Many forms of global institutions seek economic, political, cultural and other goals that are not directly oriented towards or cognizant of their influence upon body weights but do influence body weights as unintended or secondary consequences of their primary goals (Tillotson, 2004a). For example, transnational corporations (TNCs) seek profits by maximizing food and beverage sales, worldwide governmental institutions seek efficiency by facilitating transportation and communication, and global cultural organizations seek audiences by providing sedentary entertainment (Witkowski, 2007). In the process of pursuing such goals, many global actors have created conditions that have increased the fatness of the world population by raising collective caloric intake and lowering collective energy expenditure.

It is important to note that TNCs are key players in globalization in different structural ways than national companies. Such corporations conduct the majority of international trade (United Nations Conference on Trade and Development, 2007). Sklair (2001: 5) argues that a 'trans-national class' operates TNCs and can 'more or less controls the process of globalization'. This has led to the globalism of capitalism, which is 'reproduced' by a 'cultural ideology of consumerism' (Sklair, 2001: 6). Corporate structure is based on investors who focus on economic rates of return over other considerations. This creates an obligation of TNCs to maximize the profit of stockholders above other matters. Thus corporations consider effects on nutrition and obesity only to the extent that they do not preclude, compromise or diminish profits. Also, the drive for profit pushes corporations to seek growth in space (entering new nations and territories) and in market (gaining a larger market share than other corporations). Thus corporations seek to sell the most profitable foods (which often involves selling the greatest number of calories) everywhere to everyone, creating worldwide obesity as one consequence of these corporate profit-maximization activities.

Globalization of Food and Drink

The United States and other developed nations have proposed a project of 'global development', which involves the reconstitution of national agricultural sectors into a single global economy with agriculture serving as a 'world economic sector' (McMichael, 2005: 265). While national governments discuss this plan, TNCs are putting it into practice. Transnational food corporations (TFCs) are corporate entities that span the boundaries of nations and operate at a global level (Hawkes, 2006). As trade liberalization and other policies remove barriers to the import and export of agricultural commodities and manufactured food products, cheap, high-calorie foods become increasingly available on a global scale and lead to higher collective levels of body fat. This is particularly seen in the globalization of manufacturing foods high in oils and other fats, sugars and other sweeteners, refined grain and tuber carbohydrates and animal flesh and milk (Popkin and Gordon-Larson, 2004).

Global food and beverage companies claim that their success is due to not only global marketing but also expanding processing and bottling facilities in over 100 countries (Goizueta, 2000). Others point to the development of globalized marketing and advertising techniques (Witkowski, 2007). Globalization of advertising agencies occurs through concentration and then localization of their operations in 'global' cities like New York, Tokyo and London (Leslie, 1995: 410). Along with the globalization of food advertising has come the 'push towards standardized campaigns, global research studies, global media buying and international accounts' (Leslie, 1995: 402). Furthermore, Handy (1990) argues that production within a country in which a food corporation expects to sell its product makes it easier to deal with local regulatory bodies.

Fast food has not spread as rapidly as soft drinks, and thus the full potential for its contribution to global obesity has yet to be fully realized. However, this is changing as the number of fast food purveyor outlets grew from 900 in the early 1970s to over 7,000 in 1989 (Handy, 1990). Since the late 1980s, expansion of the fast food outlet McDonald's has largely taken place outside the Western hemisphere (Allen, 1994). More recently McDonalds' sales increased by 11 per cent in Asian/Pacific, Middle Eastern and African stores, compared with only 5 per cent in U.S.-based stores (Sarkar, 2007; Workman, 2006). Processed or high-value food (e.g. bakery and grain mill products, meat, preserved fruits) represents another source of globalized food, expanding sales in both rich and poor countries. Sales have grown from $160.8 billion US worldwide to $3 trillion US in 2004 (Neff et al., 1997; Regmi and Gehlhar, 2005). With the diffusion of Western-style meals, particularly those from fast food establishments, has come the globalization of the frozen potato industry (Plummer and Makki, 2002: 8) and the spread of a global fast food chicken industry (Dixon, 2002). This institutionalized worldwide provision of high energy intake leads to storage of energy as body fat and the consequent globalization of obesity.

Globalization of communications has important implications for the spread of new global food consumption patterns too. This process is abetted by the rise of a global communications industry that includes international news agencies such as VISNEWS and UPITN (Inkeles, 1998: 200) and international business communications systems such as the International Business Service (IBS) launched by INTELSAT. The latter itself is a product of globalization as it was set up by the United Nations as the International Telecommunications Satellite Organization (Inkeles, 1998: 198). Companies have long struck arrangements for their products (including branded food items and beverages) to visibly appear in American movies (a practice known as product placement) (Cassady et al., 2006). These movies are available to a vast, international audience. Others report the successful marketing strategy of stocking global hotel chains with brand name cola beverage products (Yip, 2000).

Beverage globalization has been at the forefront of TNC activities. For example, soft drink corporations promote global brands of beverages that contain many calories and few other nutrients. Global soft drink corporations have penetrated virtually all nations of the world in what has been labelled 'coca-colonization' (Leatherman and Goodman, 2005; Zimmet, 2000). The empty calories from these drinks contribute to rising body weights in many populations (Popkin and Nielsen, 2003). Processed foods have led the penetration of the global food marketplace (Handy, 1990) and have become a major source of foreign direct investment (FDI). Many researchers consider FDI a primary tool in the exploitation of low-income countries (Bornschier et al., 1978; Bornschier and Chase-Dunn, 1985). As a consequence, the value of these assets rose from nearly $100 billion US in 1990 to $240 billion in 2001 (Hawkes, 2005: 359). The globalization of the food and nutrition system has produced unprecedented supplies of energy-dense foods that are distributed worldwide, require minimum energy and effort to prepare, are easy and acceptable to consume at almost all times and places and produce high levels of caloric intake when ingested. This provision of highly available, tasty and cheap foods has contributed to greater levels of worldwide obesity.

Societies with a tradition of famines and food insecurity may welcome the additional calories that come with marketization and globalization (Tillotson, 2004b). Such caloric overload may lead to development of overweight and obesity that may initially be accepted by individuals and groups. However, as cultural values emphasizing thinness rise, obesity then becomes stigmatized and solutions are sought to redress the fattening of individuals and groups (Sobal, 1999b). There is often a lag between access to many calories and access to the means of weight reduction (Sobal, 1991), which leads to a rise in obesity with initial globalization and penetration of globality into traditional settings.

Globalization of Efficient and Sedentary Physical Activity

While some authors report that caloric intake through foods is more important to worldwide increases in obesity than energy expenditure through physical activity (e.g. Bleich et al., 2008; Kumanyika, 2008), caloric expenditure remains an important part of the energy balance equation involved in obesity. The globalization of technologically sophisticated built environments provides widespread ergonomic efficiencies and economies of energy in performing activities at home, work and leisure. These enhance convenience and minimize effort, producing low levels of energy expenditure by minimizing involuntary physical activity and making exercise into a voluntary leisure pursuit (Sobal and Wansink, 2008). Obesogenic environments (Swinburn et al., 1999) create ergonomic efficiencies that lessen energy expenditure through human movements. For example, shifting occupational activity from physical labour to sedentary service provision has lessened human energy output considerably (Monda et al., 2007). Also, the ubiquitous and normative global shift to automobile-based transportation has been a major influence upon rising body weights across the world (Hinde, 2007).

The expansion of global mass media networks controlled by TNCs decreases physical activity and energy expenditure, leading to higher body weights. A global shift from spending leisure time as active participants to engaging in leisure as passive spectators has decreased caloric expenditure in people's lives. Entertainment that requires little activity, such as viewing television, film, computer screens or other passive media consumption provides little energy expenditure and leads to weight gain (Sobal, 2001b). Additionally, global sport organizations encourage a shift from personal participation in active recreation to passive spectatorship of a few active players, also facilitating body weight gain and obesity (Dixon and Winter, 2007). Overall, the globalization of culture in sport, music, art, film, television, reading, the Internet and other areas has led to less caloric expenditure and higher body weights.

Global Interventions for Obesity

Most public attempts to decrease body weight and obesity draw upon cultural values about the aesthetics of slimness and have largely been co-opted into corporate, political and cultural institutions. Concern about obesity and health consequences led to oppositional efforts to counter the effects of global structures and processes on obesity, but those attempts have had low exposure and minimal success due in part to their grounding in individualistic biological/psychological thinking and lack of consideration of macro-level economic, political and cultural processes generating and maintaining the globality of too much food and too little activity that led to the globalization of obesity (James, 2008).

At the global level, much like with the problem of tobacco and attempts at 'tobacco control' (Chopra and Darnton-Hill, 2004), collaborative efforts between WHO and international nongovernmental organizations (INGOs) have been proposed as a mechanism for 'obesity control' (World Health Organization Consultation on Obesity, 1999). As the rising global prevalence of obesity is recognized as a result of global influences, an increasing call for global interventions has been made by many health professionals (e.g. Rigby et al., 2004). Collin et al. (2002) argue that global solutions are needed when confronting global companies. Tobacco control is useful as an example, in so far as the procedures are applicable to TFCs. Some globalization of public health efforts to deal with obesity have been undertaken by the international governmental organization (IGO) the WHO, operating in conjunction with INGOs such as the American Heart Society (AHS). Particular elements of global culture involve IGOs and INGOs. Lechner and Boli (2005) describe the interactions between these two kinds of groups, such as efforts by the WHO with INGOs to deal with health issues. Calls for this kind of structural effort seek to stem the flow of unhealthy foods to various populations. Lechner and Boli (2005) suggest that the 'authority' that an IGO like the WHO brings to other health issues like smoking and HIV/AIDS can have the same impact for obesity as the WHO begins to tackle that issue (Yach et al., 2004).

Global solutions to food-related problems represent a change in how world food dilemmas are approached. In the past, when undernutrition was considered a major concern, individual NGOs such as the Rockefeller Foundation or Bread for the World led the charge to combat hunger. This approach differed from current efforts because it did not consist of a collection of various national and international NGOs, working together to form a global response under the shared assumption that malnutrition was a globally produced problem. Instead, NGOs worked alone, spending their time reacting to undernutrition crises in specific countries or communities. Others, such as the Rockefeller Foundation's international agricultural research stations, attempted to solve regional food shortages with regionally specific, modified food crops such as the miracle rice, IR-8, developed by the International Rice Research Institute (Los Banos, Philippines) (Tribe, 1994).

An obesity crisis is perceived to be partly a product of globalization and thus in need of a global response. Certainly in the case of undernutrition, TNCs were not implicated as a contributing factor. The WHO has promulgated the WHO Global Strategy on Diet, Physical Activity and Health. One hundred ninety-two countries have endorsed this proposal. The International Association for the Study of Obesity formed the International Obesity Taskforce, which, in turn, has developed a partnership with the WHO, the World Heart Association (WHA), International Diabetes Federation (IFD) and the International Union of Nutritional Sciences (IUNS) and the International Association for the Study of Obesity identified as the Global Alliance for the Prevention of Obesity and Related Chronic Disease. The organization's goals include coordinating NGO actions to assist in implementing the WHO Global Strategy (Global Alliance for the Prevention of Obesity and Related Chronic Disease, 2007). A similar global alliance has developed around the issue of tobacco consumption, with the WHO's Tobacco Control Framework Convention. Transnational tobacco companies (TNTCs) have attempted to undermine tobacco controls such as those suggested by this convention in various countries. TNTCs have had some success in co-opting antismoking efforts by feigning cooperation and then slowing down the momentum towards action while making minimal concessions (Knight and Chapman, 2004; McDaniel et al., 2006). Somewhat similarly, the 2001–2009 Bush administration in the United States objected to those aspects of the WHO Global Strategy that might negatively affect particular agricultural products. Apparently this objection was raised on behalf of the U.S. sugar industry. Another means available to TFCs is co-optation, following the example of Coca-Cola and Pepsico joining the National Institutes of Heart, Lung and Blood Institute's Heart Truth campaign (National Heart, Lung and Blood Institute, 2008). Coca-Cola argues that its diet soda is an appropriate means of providing heart health information, given that 'about 51% of Diet Coke consumers are women' (McKay, 2008).

The role of the state remains important in an increasingly globalized world. Some states are strong enough to resist TNCs when it is perceived that their populations are at risk. A case in point is the temporary banning of Coca-Cola sales in three European countries, after unsanitary practices in bottling plants were linked to illnesses (Ignatius, 1999). At other times, the state supports TNCs, often because of economic benefits received from such companies. For example, the High Court of Kerela (India) recently threw out a ban on Coca-Cola and Pepsi sales (Surendran, 2006).

Another sort of globalization is taking place with regard to liberalizing trade, including the trade of food. The World Trade Organization (WTO) has attempted to eliminate trade barriers under the justification of liberalization. Alongside this is a shift (that can be seen as global) from import substitution to outward policies, meaning that nations are now switching to export-oriented policies, including policies about food. Lock and McKee (2005: 188), for example, note that while some European countries like Poland abolished food subsidies for animal fats, 'Wider availability and lower prices for unsaturated fats and fruits caused rapid dietary changes'. The Polish government has also attempted to minimize the trans-fat content of margarine. These policies and prices are threatened by the European Union's (EU's) Common Agricultural Policy (CAP), which has an impact on diet. However, this policy is not aimed at a healthy diet but rather a healthy agriculture sector and does not directly focus on obesity.

The interpenetration of global and local has received increasing attention as a macro–micro dynamic where local embeddedness in the global is negotiated (Kearney, 1995). The concept of globalization has been characterized as a deterministic structural force, and the concept of 'globesity' sometimes invokes this model of inevitability (WHO Consultation on Obesity, 1999). In contrast, resistance to globalization is often characterized as localization (Kearney, 1995), where global forces are opposed in particular places and local repulsion of globesity can be seen as 'lobesity'. A middle ground where global and local interact is labelled glocalization (Matejowsky, 2007) and this can be considered in cases where 'glocalobesity' occurs only partially or only selectively influences the body weights of particular parts of the population.

While global corporate structures influence the foods available in markets, potential consumers are autonomous agents who can resist consumption of these foods both individually and collectively. Much has been made of the need for individual 'will power' to eat less to prevent and treat obesity (Oliver, 2006; Saguy and Riley, 2005), although this is difficult in the face of cheap, tasty food that is available virtually everywhere at anytime and increasingly to anyone. Some motivated consumers advocate eaters of the world to unite to resist global caloric overload. These healthy food movements have emerged but generally pale in response to the size and scope of global food corporations. Local resistance to global institutions occurs through counter-globalization and de-globalization. Counter-globalization can be seen in resistance to global influences on eating, such as the Slow Food Movement, which has an oppositional stance towards global fast foods and mass foods. Members of these movements perceive globalization as simply another mechanism for TNCs to gain greater market entry. The spread of McDonalds, for example, is credited with the rise of the Slow Food Movement, which has organizational bases in several countries and a membership of over 100,000 persons (Petrini et al., 2001). In addition to countering global food culture, local communities are rebuilding environments by constructing parks, recreation facilities, sidewalks, trails and other structures to enhance physical activity by resisting automotive culture and encouraging active leisure and human powered transportation.

De-globalization often occurs in revitalization movements (Kandel and Pelto, 1980) that reject global manufactured foods from TNCs in favour of indigenous foods that are cultivated, cooked and consumed locally. Resistance and opposition to globalization has occurred in indigenous food movements that seek to re-establish previous local food independence, where traditional food culture (and often other traditional components of culture) are re-adopted (e.g. Conti, 2006; Shintani et al., 1991). These traditional foodways expend more calories in food production and provide fewer calories in food consumption, decreasing obesity. In a number of wealthy countries, some have attempted to return to what might be seen as more traditional diets via community supported agriculture (CSA). CSA, in which residents formulate contracts with local farmers, involves the distribution of foods produced by these farmers and community gardens, which at times may be a communal plot and, at other times, individually managed garden plots (Allen, 2004). These efforts are undertaken by local consumers for health, environmental and ideological reasons and as such have the potential to lessen the risk of obesity.

The Internet is credited with allowing NGOs such as the 'International Forum on Globalization, the Third World Network, the Hemispheric Social Alliance … [to share] information and critical perspectives' (Ayres, 2005: 17). Smith (2005) found that the number of transnational social movement organizations has increased from less than 200 in 1973 to nearly 900 in 2000. This suggests that the future will include the rise of additional social movements, including those which seek to reduce or eliminate obesity, opposed by movements that respect and celebrate fatness (Sobal, 1999c). As these opposed movements clash, debates over individual and human rights are likely to appear, as has been the case in disagreements over the basis for tobacco control (Fox and Katz, 2005).

Further parallels between global tobacco and global food are instructive. Globalization of tobacco consumption through the efforts of TNTCs has occurred in order to expand profits despite an increasingly hostile political climate. Many wealthy countries have a series of tobacco controls, which limit or eliminate certain kinds of advertising, places where smoking is allowed and promotion of sporting and other events. Countries where smoking rates are lower and governmental tobacco controls are limited have become attractive to TNTCs, leading to entry by these companies into such markets. This entry is associated with increased smoking rates among females, both adolescent and adult, and appears only slightly deterred by tobacco control policies (McIntosh, 2008). In one sense, the rates of tobacco-related chronic illnesses will undergo a shift from their concentration in wealthy countries to their concentration in poor ones (Ezzati et al., 2005). As similar efforts to control the consumption of foods associated with obesity (e.g. limiting advertising aimed at children; removing select foods from school menus) become more widespread, food companies, like those selling tobacco, may concentrate efforts to increase sales in poorer countries, where such food controls are currently lacking. As wealthy countries have learned, TNTCs work to overcome limits placed on the advertising and promotion of their products.

Conclusion

People of the world have become fatter and more obese, although considerable heterogeneity occurs in the patterns and timing of increases in body weights of individuals, institutions and settings. Framing obesity in terms of globalization offers important insights and understandings. Globalization has influenced body weight throughout the world as a side effect of the actions of global institutions. However, now that these global entities have become aware of the secondary consequences of their actions on body weight, counter movements, opposition by other global institutions and policy interventions are being used to oppose, prevent and treat the influences of globalization on body weight. How efforts to lessen the effects of globalization on body weight will be challenged by those whose profits are tied to more rather than less food consumption will fare is unknown. If the global tobacco industry and worldwide smoking rates have some parallels with the global food industry and obesity rates, the world will likely experience significant increases in obesity before rates begin to fall. However, food and tobacco are not entirely the same in the sense that human beings must consume food in order to survive but do not need to consume tobacco to do so. Obesity control efforts may thus be more difficult to put in place and enforce than tobacco control measures. It is currently not clear how the emergence and development of globality will play out for obesity in the future, but analysis, understanding and action based on the concept of globalization will provide crucial insights about the future course of world obesity.

References

Allen, P. (2004), *Together at the Table: Sustainability and Sustenance in the American Agrifood System,* 14, University Park: Penn State University Press.

Allen, R.L. (1994), 'International Sales, Value Pricing Boost McDonald's Net', *National Restaurant News* (7 Nov.).

Allison, D.B., Fontaine, K.B., Manson, J.E., Stevens, J., and Van Itallie, T.B. (1999), 'Annual Deaths Attributable to Obesity in the United States', *Journal of the American Medical Association,* 282/16: 1530–8.

Ayres, J. M. (2005), 'From "Anti-Globalization" to Global Justice Movement: Framing Collective Action against Neoliberalism', in B. Podobnik and T. Reifer (eds.), *Transforming Globalization: Challenges and Opportunities in the Post 9/11 Era,* Boston: Brill.

Bleich, S., Cutler, D., Murray, C., and Adams, A. (2008), 'Why Is the Developed World Obese?', *Annual Review of Public Health,* 29: 273–95.

Boero, N. (2007), 'All the News That's Fat to Print: The American "Obesity Epidemic" and the Media', *Qualitative Sociology,* 30/1: 41–60.

Bornschier, V., and Chase-Dunn, C. (1985), *Trans-National Corporations and Underdevelopment,* New York: Praeger.

Bornschier, V., Chase-Dunn, C., and Rubinson, R. (1978), 'Cross-National Evidence of the Effects of Foreign Investment and Aid on the Economic Growth and Inequality: A Survey of Findings and a Reanalysis', *American Journal of Sociology,* 84: 651–83.

Brune, N., and Garrett, G. (2005), 'The Globalization Rorschach Test: International Economic Integration, Inequality and the Role of Government', *Annual Review of Political Science,* 8: 399–423.

Caballero, B. (2007), 'The Global Epidemic of Obesity: An Overview', *Epidemiologic Reviews,* 29: 1–5.

Cassady, D., Townsend, M., Bell, R. A., and Watnik, M. (2006), 'Portrayals of Branded Soft-Drinks in Popular American Movies: A Content Analysis', *International Journal of Behavioral Nutrition and Physical Activity* [online journal], 3: <http://www.ijbnpa.org/content/3/1/4> (accessed 5 January 2008).

Chopra, M., and Darnton-Hill, I. (2004), 'Tobacco and Obesity Epidemics: Not So Different After All?', *British Medical Journal,* 328: 1558–60.

Collin, J., Lee, K., and Bissell, K. (2002), 'The Framework Convention on Tobacco Control: The Politics of Global Governance', *Third World Quarterly,* 23/2: 265–82.

Contaldo, F., and Pasanisi, F. (2005), 'Obesity Epidemics: Simple or Simplistic Answers?', *Clinical Nutrition,* 24/1: 1–4.

Conti, K. M. (2006), 'Diabetes Prevention in Indian Country: Developing Nutrition Models to Tell the Story of Food-System Change', *Journal of Transcultural Nursing,* 17/3: 234–45.

Dixon, J. (2002), *The Changing Chicken: Chooks, Cooks and Culinary Culture,* Sydney: University of New South Wales Press.

Dixon, J., and Winter, C. (2007), 'The Environment of Competing Authorities', in J. Dixon and D. H. Broom (eds.), *The 7 Deadly Sins of Obesity: How the Modern World Is Making Us Fat,* Sydney: University of New South Wales Press.

Ezzati, M, VanderHoorn, S., Lawes, C.M.M., Leach, R., James, W.P.T., Lopez, A. D., Rodgers, A., and Murray, C.J.L. (2005), 'Rethinking the "Diseases of Affluence" Paradigm: Global Patterns of Nutritional Risks in Relation to Economic Development', *PLoS Medicine,* 2: e133.

Fox, B. J., and Katz, J. E. (2005), 'Individual and Human Rights in Tobacco Control: Help or Hindrance?', *Tobacco Control,* 14: 1–2.

Gard, M., and Wright, J. (2005), *The Obesity Epidemic: Science, Morality and Ideology,* New York: Routledge.

Gardner, G., and Halweil, B. (2000), *Underfed and Overfed: The Global Epidemic of Malnutrition* (Worldwatch Paper 150), Washington, DC: Worldwatch Institute.

Goizueta, R. C. (2000), 'Globalization: A Soft Drink Perspective', In P. Kras (ed.), *The Book of Management Wisdom: Classic Writings by Legendary Managers,* New York: John Wiley and Sons.

Guillen, M. F. (2001), 'Is Globalizing Civilizing, Destructive or Feeble? A Critique of Five Key Debates in the Social Science Literature', *Annual Review of Sociology,* 27: 213–34.

Gurney, M., and Gorstein, J. (1988), 'The Global Prevalence of Obesity—an Initial Overview of Available Data', *World Health Statistics Quarterly,* 41: 251–4.

Handy, C. R. (1990), 'The Globalization of Food Marketing', *National Food Review,* 13 (Oct.–Dec.): 1–5.

Hawkes, C. (2005), 'The Role of Foreign Direct Investment in the Nutrition Transition', *Public Health Nutrition,* 8/4: 357–65.

Hawkes, C. (2006), 'Uneven Dietary Development: Linking the Policies and Processes of Globalization with the Nutrition Transition, Obesity and Diet-Related Chronic Diseases', *Globalization and Health,* 2: 4.

Hinde, S. (2007), 'The Car-Related Environment: The Vehicle That Drives Obesity', in J. Dixon and D. H. Broom (eds.), *The 7 Deadly Sins of Obesity: How the Modern World is Making Us Fat,* Sydney: University of New South Wales Press.

Ignatius, D. (1999), 'A Global Marketplace Means Global Vulnerability', *Washington Post* (22 June): A19.

Inkeles, A. (1998), 'Communication: Linking the Whole Human Race', in A. Inkeles (ed.), *One World Emerging: Convergence and Divergence in Industrial Societies,* Boulder: Westview Press.

James, W. P. (2008), 'The Fundamental Drivers of the Obesity Epidemic', *Obesity Reviews,* 9(Supplement 1): 6–13.

Jebb, S. A., and Prentice, A. M. (2001), 'Single Definition of Overweight and Obesity Should Be Used', *British Medical Journal,* 323/7319: 999.

Kandel, R. F., and Pelto, G. H. (1980), 'The Health Food Movement: Social Revitalization or Alternative Health Maintenance System?', in N. W. Jerome, R. F. Kandel and G. H. Pelto (eds.), *Nutritional Anthropology: Contemporary Approaches to Diet & Culture,* Pleasantville: Redgrave Publishing.

Kearney, M. (1995), 'The Local and the Global: The Anthropology of Globalization and Trans-Nationalism', *Annual Review of Anthropology,* 24: 547–65.

Knight, J., and Chapman, S. (2004), 'A Phony Way to Show Sincerity, as We All Know: Tobacco Industry Lobbying against Tobacco Control in Hong Kong', *Tobacco Control,* 13: 13–21.

Kumanyika, S.K. (2008), 'Global Calorie Counting: A Fitting Exercise for Obese Societies', *Annual Review of Public Health,* 29: 297–302.

Kushner, R.F. (1993), 'Body Weight and Mortality', *Nutrition Reviews,* 51/5: 127–36.

Leatherman, T.L., and Goodman, A. (2005), 'Coca-Colonization of Diets in the Yucatan', *Social Science & Medicine,* 61/4: 833–46.

Lechner, F.J., and Boli, J. (2005), *World Culture: Origins and Consequences,* Malden: Blackwell.

Lee, S., and Sobal, J. (2003), 'Socio-Economic, Dietary, Activity, Nutrition and Body Weight Transitions in South Korea', *Public Health Nutrition,* 6/7: 665–74.

Leslie, D.A. (1995), 'Global Scan: The Globalization of Advertising Agencies, Concepts and Campaigns', *Economic Geography,* 71/4: 402–26.

Lissau, I., Overpeck, M.D., Ruan, W.J., Due, P., Holstein, B.E., Hediger, M.L., and the Health Behavior in School-aged Children Obesity Working Group (2004), 'Body Mass Index and Overweight in Adolescents in 13 European Countries, Israel and the United States', *Archives of Pediatrics and Adolescent Medicine,* 158: 27–33.

Lock, K., and McKee, M. (2005), 'Commentary: Will Europe's Agriculture Policy Damage Progress on Cardiovascular Disease?', *British Journal of Medicine,* 331: 188–9.

Martorell, R., Khan, L.K., Hughes, M.L., and Grummer-Strawn, L.M. (2000), 'Obesity in Women from Developing Countries', *European Journal of Clinical Nutrition,* 54/3: 247–52.

Matejowsky, T. (2007), 'SPAM and Fast-Food 'Glocalization' in the Philippines', *Food, Culture & Society,* 10/1: 23–41.

McDaniel, P.A., Smith, E.A., and Malone, R.E. (2006), 'Philip Morris's Project Sunrise: Weakening Tobacco Control by Working with It', *Tobacco Control,* 15: 215–23.

McIntosh, W.A. (2008), 'Trans-National Tobacco Companies, the Tobacco Political Economy and Rates of Smoking: A Global Assessment', *Rural Sociology,* unpublished manuscript.

McIntosh, W.A., and Thomas, J.K. (2004), 'Economic and Other Societal Determinants of the Prevalence of HIV: A Test of Competing Hypotheses', *Sociological Quarterly,* 45/2: 303–24.

McKay, B. (2008), Heart Health Goes Better with Diet Coke? *The Wall Street Journal,* Heart Blog, <http://blogs.wsj.com/health/2008/01/08/heart-health-goes-better-with-coke/trackback/> (accessed 11 January 2008).

McMichael, P. (2005), 'Global Development and the Corporate Food Regime', *Research in Rural Development,* 11: 265–99.

McMichael, P. (2008), *Development and Social Change: A Global Perspective*, fourth edition, Thousand Oaks: Pine Forge Press.

McMurray, C., and Smith, R. (2001), *Diseases of Globalization: Socioeconomic Transitions and Health*, Sterling: Earthscan.

Mitchell, G.R., and McTigue, K.M. (2007), 'The US Obesity "Epidemic": Metaphor, Method or Madness?', *Social Epistemology*, 21/4: 391–423.

Molarius, A., Seidell, J.C., Sans, S., Tuomilehto, J., and Kuulasmaa, K. (2000), 'Education Level, Relative Body Weight and Changes in Their Association over 10 Years: An International Perspective from the WHO MONICA Project', *American Journal of Public Health*, 90/8: 1260–8.

Monda, K.L., Gordon-Larsen, P., Stevens, J. and Popkin, B.M. (2007), 'China's Transition: The Effect of Rapid Urbanization on Adult Occupational Physical Activity', *Social Science & Medicine*, 64/4: 858–70.

National Heart, Lung and Blood Institute (2008), *What Is Heart Truth?* <http://www.nhlbi. nih.gov/ health/hearttruth/whatis/index.htm> (accessed 11 January 2008).

Neff, S., Harris, M., Malanoski, M., and Ruppel, F. (1997), 'US Trade in Processed Foods', in D. Henderson, C.C. Handy and S.A. Neff (eds.), *Globalization of Processed Foods* (Agriculture Economic Report no. 742), Washington, DC: Food and Consumer Division, United States Department of Agriculture.

Ogden, C., Carroll, M., Curtin, L., McDowell, M.A., Tabak, C.J., and Flegal, K.M. (2006), 'Prevalence of Overweight and Obesity in the United States, 1999–2004', *Journal of the American Medical Association*, 295: 1549–55.

Oliver, J.E. (2006), *Fat Politics: The Real Story Behind America's Obesity Epidemic*, New York: Oxford University Press.

Parikh, N.I., Pencina, M.J., Wang, T.J., Lanier, K.J., Fox, C.S., D'Agostino, R.B., and Vasan, R.S. (2007), 'Increasing Trends in Incidence of Overweight and Obesity over 5 Decades', *American Journal of Medicine*, 120/3: 242–50.

Patel, R.C. (2007), *Stuffed and Starved: The Hidden Battle for the World Food System*, Brooklyn: Melville House.

Pelletier, D.L., and Rahn, M. (1998), 'Trends in Body Mass Index in Developing Countries', *Food and Nutrition Bulletin*, 19/3: 223–38.

Petrini, C., McCuaig, W., and Waters, A. (2001), *Slow Food: The Case for Taste*, New York: Columbia University Press.

Plummer, C., and Makki, S. (2002), 'French Fries Driving Globalization of Frozen Potato Industry', *Agriculture Outlook*, AGO-295: 8–11.

Pollard, T.M. (2008), *Western Diseases: An Evolutionary Perspective*, Cambridge: Cambridge University Press.

Popkin, B.M., and Doak, C.M. (1998), 'The Obesity Epidemic as a Worldwide Phenomenon', *Nutrition Reviews*, 56/4: 106–14.

Popkin, B.M., and Gordon-Larson, P. (2004), 'The Nutrition Transition: Worldwide Obesity Dynamics and Their Determinants', *International Journal of Obesity*, 28: 52–9.

Popkin, B. M., and Nielsen, S. J. (2003), 'The Sweetening of the World's Diet', *Obesity Research,* 11/11: 1325–32.

Prentice, A. M. (2006), 'The Emerging Epidemic of Obesity in Developing Countries', *International Journal of Epidemiology,* 35/1: 93–9.

Regmi, A., and Gehlhar, M. (2005), 'Processed Food Trade Pressured by Evolving Global Supply Chains', *Amber Waves,* 3/1: 12–19.

Rigby, N., and Baillie, K. (2006), 'Challenging the Future: The Global Prevention Alliance', *Lancet,* 368: 1629–31.

Rigby, N. J., Kumanyika, S., and James, W. P. (2004), 'Confronting the Epidemic: The Need for Global Solutions', *Journal of Public Health Policy,* 25/3–4: 418–34.

Rosenberg, C. (1992), *Explaining Epidemics and Other Studies in the History of Medicine,* Cambridge: Cambridge University Press.

Roth, J., Qiang, X., Marban, S. L., Redelt, H., and Lowell, B. C. (2004), 'The Obesity Pandemic: Where Have We Been and Where Are We Going?', *Obesity Research,* 12(Suppl. 2): S88–S101.

Saguy, A. C., and Riley, K. W. (2005), 'Weighing Both Sides: Morality, Mortality and Framing Contests over Obesity', *Journal of Health Politics, Policy and Law,* 30/5: 869–921.

Sarkar, P. (2007), Battered Retailers Have Harbor Overseas', The Street.com, <http://www. thestreet.com/newsanalysis/retail/10389531.html> (accessed 9 January 2008).

Shintani, T. T., Hughes, C. K., Beckham, S., and O'Connor, H. K. (1991), 'Obesity and Cardiovascular Risk Intervention through the Ad Libitum Feeding of Traditional Hawaiian Diet', *American Journal of Clinical Nutrition,* 53: 1647S–1651S.

Sklair, L. (2001), *The Trans-National Capitalist Class,* Malden: Blackwell.

Sklair, L. (2002), *Globalization: Capitalism and Its Alternatives,* Oxford: Oxford University Press.

Smith, J. (2005), 'Exploring Connections between Global Integration and Political Mobilization', in B. Podobnki and T. Reifer (eds.), *Transforming Globalization: Challenges and Opportunities in the Post 9/11 Era,* Boston: Brill.

Sobal, J. (1991), 'Obesity and Socioeconomic Status: A Framework for Examining Relationships between Physical and Social Variables', *Medical Anthropology,* 13/3: 231–47.

Sobal, J. (1998), 'Cultural Comparison Research Designs in Food, Eating and Nutrition', *Food Quality and Preference,* 9/6: 385–92.

Sobal, J. (1999a), 'Food System Globalization, Eating Transformations and Nutrition Transitions', in R. Grew (ed.), *Food in Global History,* Boulder: Westview Press.

Sobal, J. (1999b), 'Sociological Analysis of the Stigmatisation of Obesity', in J. Germov and L. Williams (eds.), *A Sociology of Food and Nutrition: Introducing the Social Appetite,* Melbourne: Oxford University Press.

Sobal, J. (1999c), 'The Size Acceptance Movement and the Social Construction of Body Weight', in J. Sobal and D. Maurer (eds.), *Weighty Issues: Fatness and Thinness as Social Problems,* Hawthorne: Aldine de Gruyter.

Sobal, J. (2001a), 'Commentary: Globalization and the Epidemiology of Obesity', *International Journal of Epidemiology,* 30: 1136–37.

Sobal, J. (2001b), 'Social and Cultural Influences on Obesity', in P. Bjorntorp (ed.), *International Textbook of Obesity,* New York: John Wiley and Sons.

Sobal, J., and Wansink, B. (2008), 'Built Environments and Obesity', in E. Blass (ed.), *Obesity: Causes, Mechanisms, Prevention and Treatment,* Sunderland: Sinauer Associates.

Stearns, P. (1997), *Fat History: Bodies and Beauty in the Modern West,* New York: New York University Press.

Surendran, P.K. (2006), 'Kerala Cans Coca-Cola', *The Times of India* (10 August), <http://timesofindia.indiatimes.com/articleshow/msid-18793300> (accessed 22 August 2008).

Swinburn, B., Egger, G., and Raza, F. (1999), 'Dissecting Obesogenic Environments: The Development and Application of a Framework for Identifying and Prioritizing Environmental Interventions for Obesity', *Preventive Medicine,* 29: 563–70.

Thornton, A. (2005), *Reading History Sideways: The Fallacy and Enduring Impact of the Developmental Paradigm on Family Life,* Chicago: University of Chicago Press.

Tillotson, J.E. (2004a), 'America's Obesity: Conflicting Public Policies, Industrial Economic Development and Unintended Human Consequences', *Annual Review of Nutrition,* 29: 617–43.

Tillotson, J.E. (2004b), 'Global Food Companies in the Developing World: Benefactors, Malefactors or Inevitable Change Agents?', *Nutrition Today,* 39/3: 118–21.

Tribe, D. (1994), *Feeding and Greening the World: The Role of International Agricultural Research,* Oxford: CAB Press.

Troiano, R.P., Frongillo, E.A., Sobal, J., and Levitsky, D. (1996), The Relationship between Body Weight and Mortality: A Quantitative Analysis of Combined Information from Existing Studies', *International Journal of Obesity,* 20: 63–75.

United Nations Conference on Trade and Development (2007), *World Investment Report,* New York: United Nations.

Wang, Y. (2001), 'Cross-National Comparison of Childhood Obesity: The Epidemic and the Relationship between Obesity and Socioeconomic Status', *International Journal of Epidemiology,* 30: 1143–50.

World Health Organization. (1995), *Physical Status: The Use and Interpretation of Anthropometry,* Technical Report Series 854. Geneva: World Health Organization.

World Health Organization (2001), *Obesity: Preventing and Managing the Global Epidemic* (Technical Report Series, No. 894), Geneva: World Health Organization.

World Health Organization Consultation on Obesity (1999), *Preventing and Managing the Global Epidemic,* Geneva: World Health Organization.

World Health Organization Global InfoBase Team (2005), *The SuRF Report 2. Surveillance of Chronic Disease: Risk Factors, Country-Level Data and Comparable Estimates*, Geneva: World Health Organization.

Wildman, R. P., Munter, P., Reynolds, K., McGinn, A. P., Rajpathak, S., Wylie-Rosett, J., and Sowers, M. R. (2008), 'The Obese without Cardiometabolic Risk Factor Clustering and the Normal Weight with Cardiometabolic Risk Factor Clustering: Prevalence and Correlates of 2 Phenotypes among the US Population', *Archives of Internal Medicine,* 168/15: 1617–24.

Witkowski, T. H. (2007), 'Food Marketing and Obesity in Developing Countries: Analysis, Ethics and Public Policy', *Journal of Macromarketing,* 27/2: 126–37.

Workman, D. (2006), 'McDonalds Global Sales', Suite101.com, <http://international trade.suite101.com> (accessed 9 January 2008).

Yach, D., Hawkes, C., Epping-Jordan, J. E., and Galbraith, S. (2004), 'The World Health Organization's Convention on Tobacco Control: Implications for Global Epidemics of Food-related Deaths and Diseases', *Journal of Public Health Policy,* 24/34: 274–90.

Yip, G. S. (2000), *Asia Advantage: Key Strategies in the Asian-Pacific Region,* New York: Basic Books.

Zimmet, P. (2000), 'Globalization, Coca-Colonization and the Chronic Disease Epidemic: Can the Doomsday Scenario Be Averted?', *Journal of Internal Medicine,* 247: 301–10.

'Is It Real Food?': Who Benefits from Globalization in Tanzania and India?

Pat Caplan
Goldsmiths College, London

The old order changeth, yielding place to new.

—Tennyson, 'The Passing of Arthur: The Idylls of the King', 1856

In this chapter, I consider the implications of what is usually glossed as 'globalization' on two very different societies: a rural, coastal part of Tanzania, where I have been carrying out fieldwork among peasant farmers and fisher-folk since 1965,[1] and a suburb of Chennai/Madras City in south India, where research was conducted between the 1970s and 1990s among middle-class, highly educated professionals.[2]

Anthropologists have approached the subject of globalization in a variety of ways. What they tend to have in common is their belief that anthropology is distinguished from the other social sciences by its 'long-standing and defiant pre-occupation with the mundane, the ordinary and the intimate' (Watson and Caldwell, 2005: 2). However, the contexts in which studies of such issues take place are often now multi-sited, considering global flows of persons and things (e.g. Eriksen, 2003). In other respects, however, their work in this field, as indeed in others, is diverse, both in its subject matter and its fundamental premises.

In a recent book on the anthropology of globalization, the editors Inda and Rosaldo (2002: 9) argue that anthropologists are mainly interested in meaning and culture, and thus what is of concern to them is the cultural dynamics of globalization and in particular cultures' resultant deterritorialization. In the process of discussing these concepts, they attack the notion of 'cultural imperialism' which suggests that the processes of globalization involve the domination of certain cultures over others: 'the picture the discourse of cultural imperialism draws of the world fails to adequately capture its complexities … it constructs Third World subjects as passive consumers of imported cultural goods' (Inda and Rosaldo, 2002: 15). Instead, they argue for a more detailed and nuanced consideration of what happens when goods move from one location and culture to another by considering 'their complex reception and appropriation' (Inda and Rosaldo, 2002: 17).

Inda and Rosaldo also reject the notion that the consumers of foreign cultural products internalize the values allegedly contained in them, arguing instead that people 'do not necessarily absorb the ideologies, values, and life-style position of the texts they consume ... subjects always bring their own cultural dispositions to bear' (Inda and Rosaldo, 2002: 17).[3] They further argue that the traffic in goods such as food is two-way, with many Westerners now eating not only food sourced from places such as Asia but also enjoying its cuisines. Such examples reveal what they term a 'process of mutual imbrication'. In short, their view of globalization appears to suggest that it is a rather benign and reciprocal process.

The approach of Inda and Rosaldo contrasts interestingly with the recent work on the cultural politics of food and eating by Watson and Caldwell (2005). While also investigating issues of culture, they stress, in contrast to Inda and Rosaldo, that it is important to concentrate on food as a window on the *political,* since the process of paying attention to matters such as how people relate to food allows us to find ways of understanding the 'big issues' of the day, including global flows.

In this chapter, I will be following the second, rather than the first approach to the topic of food. An anthropological approach, with its fine-grained and often long-term ethnography, can indeed reveal the enormous complexities of the processes under consideration, particularly their local effects, in a way that few other disciplines can do. It can also reveal the important roles played by culture. However, I will argue here that it is also important to consider how power is deployed in the process of globalization, that it is essential to consider globalization as an economic and political, as well as a cultural process, and one that can be far from benign.

A second set of concepts which will be used are those of order and disorder. Baumann (2002: 252) has recently argued that globalization is actually a form of 'new world disorder', pointing out that in earlier times, the immense task of order-making was largely undertaken by the state, but that this has now been expropriated by the mega-companies and 'the market'. Further, unlike the situation in the nineteenth century captured by Tennyson in the quote which begins this chapter, the new situation is not necessarily one of order. As a result, globalization is 'not about what we all ... wish or hope to do. It is about what is happening to us all' (Baumann, 2002: 253). Of course order-making is not undertaken only at the macro-level such as the state; it is also carried out by people who have to make sense of the world in which they live. Food is a good example of the way in which 'order-making' occurs on an everyday level. As Fischler pointed out over two decades ago, 'to identify a food, one has to "think" it, to understand its place in the world and therefore understand the world' (1988: 284). This is what he means by the 'culinary order'. In this respect, he is building on the work of earlier anthropologists such as Mary Douglas who have shown that food can powerfully express the 'order of things', of things and people being in their place, but they have also suggested that food can be suggestive of disorder as well, sometimes conceptualized as pollution (Douglas, 1970).

In both of the regions under consideration, the 'order of things' is changing rapidly, not least because of one important manifestation of globalization: the neoliberal 'free market' policies adopted by their respective governments under pressure from multilateral financial institutions. As a result of liberalizing policies, new foods have entered both geographical areas. In what follows, I consider how local people have responded in terms of accepting new foods, whether they do so reluctantly or enthusiastically and the reasons for their reactions. One way of conceptualizing this issue is whether the changes in eating patterns which I will be describing have meant a change from order to disorder—what some anthropologists have described as 'gastro-anomie' (Fischler, 1980) or 'alienation' (Mintz, 1985)—or whether new forms of order/pattern are emerging. There will be a discussion of such topics in the second part of this chapter, but I begin by giving a brief history of food in each of these two contrasting areas.

Part Historical Background

Mafia Island, Tanzania, 1965–2004

Mafia Island lies off the southern coast of Tanzania, near to the Rufiji Delta (see Figure 15.1).[4] It was first colonized by Arabs during the Omani Sultanate of Zanzibar in the nineteenth century, and its southern half became largely a plantation economy growing coconuts with slave labour. Indigenous people were left mainly with the northern half of the island, which was less suitable for coconuts, and grew subsistence crops such as millet, as well as keeping cattle. When Germany took over Tanganyika at the end of the nineteenth century, Mafia was exchanged for another parcel of land close to Uganda, and so became a part of German East Africa or Tanganyika. The Germans pushed the cultivation of coconuts into the northern areas of the island, and there was a big change in the settlement patterns of the northern villages, as their inhabitants moved nearer to the coast to take advantage of the sandy soil to plant the coconut trees required by the colonial power (fifty trees for each able-bodied male on pain of beating for failure to comply).

In the north of the island, people lived in nucleated villages, each of which was and still is surrounded by a large belt of bush land, cultivated on a shifting system in which rights were obtained by descent (see Caplan, 1975, see also Figure 15.2). Such cultivation was typical of large areas of sub-Saharan Africa, as Richards's (1939) classic work on the Bemba of (what is now) Zambia demonstrates, but this has become difficult to sustain, both on Mafia and elsewhere in sub-Saharan Africa, in the light of population growth and the increasing use of land for cash crops, as well as greater commoditization of land. In the south of the island, there was much less land available for food crops, and people have long relied mainly on income from labour or cash crops to purchase food. Even in the north, where there was more cultivable land, people were not completely self-sufficient in food and needed to rely on imports to the island. Indeed, the Mafia district book shows that the island has been a food-deficient area since German times.[5]

Successive governments, both colonial and postcolonial, have nonetheless sought to improve the ratio of grown to bought food. When I first carried out research in the 1960s, there were campaigns to plant cassava, which is drought resistant but nutritionally inferior, and by the 1990s, there was strong encouragement to grow plantains. Such campaigns have had only limited success, not least because the most valued food remains rice, which was always the food of choice of the elites on the coast.

Interviews I conducted in the 1980s and 1990s with older people revealed that during German and British colonial periods, the main staple food crop grown in

Figure 15.1 Map of East Africa.

the north of the island was millet. It was still being grown to a lesser extent when I first did fieldwork in the 1960s but has now largely been replaced by cassava grown locally, shop-bought maize flour (*dona*) and, to a lesser extent, wheat flour, which began to be imported both from abroad (mainly Kenya, but even occasionally from the United States) and from further afield in Tanganyika during the British colonial period. Rice is also grown in both dry and wet fields, but the amount produced is insufficient for demand, and it has long been supplemented by rice brought in from the nearby Rufiji Delta, a surplus area.

During the post-independence period of the 1960s and 1970s, marked by 'African socialism' (*ujamaa*) under the leadership of President Julius Nyerere, the food industry, along with many others, was nationalized. Staples grown commercially were

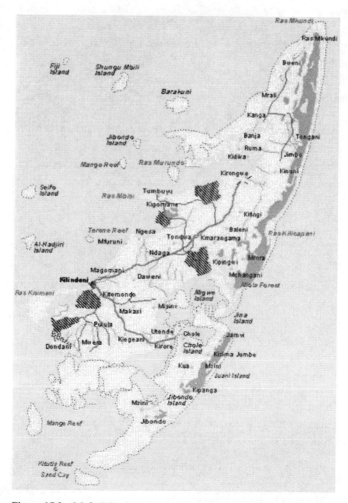

Figure 15.2 Mafia Island.

placed under the control of the parastatal National Milling Corporation. Food prices were controlled by the government. In the 1980s, however, as a result of extreme economic pressures, the Tanzanian government, at the urging of the International Monetary Fund, began a process of liberalization of the economy and of structural adjustment. Parastatals were sold off to private investors, controlled prices were lifted on food, and imports, including food products, increased dramatically. By the 1990s, even food such as rice which could be produced locally began to be imported into Tanzania from as far away as Pakistan and Thailand.

In this rural area, there are no processed or ready-made foods, except perhaps the odd tin of tomato puree in some of the small shops. Many people purchase food items on a daily basis: a little sugar, tea, maize flour, dried beans and spices from the shops and, if they are lucky, a bit of fish from a local fisherman. Women cook twice daily, a laborious task involving fetching firewood and water often over long distances and pounding paddy into rice or peeling a substitute, such as plantains, sweet potatoes or cassava. This is performed on top of their major responsibility of agricultural labour.

On Mafia Island, then, people have long relied on a mixture of home-grown and bought food, and the latter has tied them to wider trading networks. In order to obtain cash to purchase food, people had to sell their coconuts locally to traders who made the difficult journey to Dar es Salaam to sell them in the main market. For both local producers and traders, margins were always fairly small, since the costs of transport consumed much of the profit. However, the Mafians' reliance on cash crops such as coconuts to generate income to purchase food also made them vulnerable to world commodity prices. The Germans and British wanted coconuts grown because at that time, they were useful in such processes as making soap and producing coir. However, as more and more trees were planted, both on the east coast and elsewhere in the tropics, a situation of overproduction arose, exacerbated by changes in manufacturing processes and the consequent slackening of world demand for coconuts in the last few decades. Thus many people are trying to sustain their households at a time of rising prices for food and falling prices for their cash crops. On top of this difficult scenario, drought has been a serious factor over the last few years, possibly a harbinger of worse to come if climate change accelerates.

From this account, I would like to stress the following points. First of all, even in a remote area such as Mafia, where many people still practice a largely subsistence economy, food has a history and diets change. This is partly because of changes of regime[6]—including the policies of both colonial powers and independent governments—but it is also because Mafia has long been tied by its maritime history into much wider trading networks with mainland Tanganyika/Tanzania, the rest of the east coast, the Gulf and the wider Indian Ocean littoral. Like the rest of the east coast, it has long been part of a mercantile economy (Middleton, 1992).

Second, it is important to note that the local diet is viewed as a part of Swahili cuisine, marked by the use of coconut rice and Zanzibari spices (cloves, cinnamon, ginger, turmeric, pepper, and cumin). While this is inevitably hybrid, with African, Arab and Indian influences, on Mafia Island it is not as elaborate as it might be in wealthier areas such as Zanzibar. Nonetheless Mafians are strongly attached to particular foods and ways of preparing them. Coconut rice (*wali kwa nazi*) with spicy fish or chicken stew or meat *pilau* are the foods of choice, just as they have been for a longer period in the Swahili towns, and such foods also symbolize Swahili identity.

Middle-Class Households in Chennai (Madras), South India

Let me turn now to my other case study, a southern suburb of Chennai-Madras, in Tamil Nadu state in south India. The residents of this area are middle class and highly educated, with salaried posts in government, medicine, engineering, law and other professions. Many of their sons and daughters are resident in the Untied States, which most have visited. When I first began to carry out research here in 1974, India, following both Gandhian *swadeshi* ideas and Nehruvian socialism, still operated an import substitution policy.[7] The only food imported came in as aid, especially the American wheat brought in under PL480.[8] Both for this reason and because the so-called Green Revolution happened first in the wheat-growing areas of the Punjab, there was plenty of wheat in the country. Rice-eating southerners were encouraged to learn to like *chapatis*. I remember vividly in the 1970s how some restaurants in south India would first serve only *chapatis* with *sambar* (curry) or *dahl* long before the rice appeared! Sometimes it seemed that one had to eat enough *chapatis* before being allowed rice. At this time too, staples were available from government-run shops, which sold items such as rice, sugar and lentils for low and controlled prices to those who had the requisite ration cards.

In the suburb where I worked, most households had a 'vegetable man' who brought a selection daily to the door or who would move his stall around a neighbourhood, calling out his wares. Food such as rice and lentils, the main staples, was purchased in its raw state, often from wholesalers. Some households still owned family land in their 'native place' (*sonda ur*) in the countryside and obtained their paddy from there.[9] Shops carried little in the way of packaged food; it was mostly stored in sacks and weighed out into paper bags as required. Tamil cooking was elaborate and time-consuming, and carried out mainly by women except in households wealthy enough to employ a (usually male) cook; in the time budgets I did in the 1970s, women daily spent between four and six hours cooking. Housewives not fortunate enough to have cooks would call on their maidservants to do such time-consuming jobs as cleaning rice and lentil grains, or grinding them to make such dishes as *dosai* (rice pancakes) and *idly* (steamed rice cakes). Many men and children would take food prepared at home with them to work or school, or have it sent with a *tiffin-wallah* (man who carried tiffin boxes). There was relatively little eating out.

Meals, eaten twice daily by the middle classes, followed a clear pattern, consisting of rice, *dahl* and some form of curry, while snacks or 'tiffin' such as *vadai* (fried rice and lentil cakes), *dosai* (rice pancakes) or *idly* (steamed rice cakes) were taken in the early morning and late afternoon. Although there is a distinctive and elaborate Tamil cuisine, there would be variations depending on caste and subcaste. Considerations of caste and purity were extremely important. Brahmins and members of some other sub-castes were strict vegetarians, and households who employed cooks, or whose members occasionally ate out, would make sure that those who prepared food for them were from the highest caste. Here, then, we find a highly elaborated grammar or lexicon of food in which the order of things—caste, gender, class—was clearly reflected.

Even at that time, however, changes were happening and often commented on by informants. Some women went along with the demands of their offspring that they buy bread and have toast for breakfast, rather than *iddlies*. Mothers were concerned that their children obtain sufficient vitamins, especially if they were vegetarians, and advertising played upon and probably contributed to such concern. At the same time, many of these women wanted to be 'modern' and some joined in a cookery class held at the local women's club, where they learned to make cakes.

There were gender differences in reaction to such innovation. Men would some-times admit to eating rather unorthodox food, even meat, in the course of their work-related activities, but would state proudly that their wives were *pure* vegetarians. In some households, women would be willing to cook food which they would not eat themselves, such as meat for their husbands or eggs for their children. In this way, then, a single household could be both orthodox and unorthodox, with differences of inside/outside the house, male/female, adult/child (see Caplan, 1985).

By the late 1980s, India had begun to liberalize its economy and supermarkets were beginning to appear, as well as consumer goods such as freezers. Small amounts of 'foreign' food such as packaged Maggi soups, made in India under licence, were promoted and sold. Increasingly, Indian soft drinks brands such as Thums Up were replaced by Pepsi and Coke. By the 1990s this change had gathered speed, with a wide variety of supermarkets springing up and carrying a range of foods such as fruit and vegetables, some frozen foods like meat (chicken and lamb; rarely beef or pork), convenience foods such as *dosai* mixes and spice pastes, and even imported items. In the area where I worked, covering only a few square miles, I counted no fewer than a dozen supermarkets in the late 1990s (Caplan, 2001).

There has also been a proliferation of restaurants in the last decade or so, and eat-ing out has become much more common among the middle classes.[10] Here we see an interesting mix of globalization and localization. Chennai now boasts its share of Tex-Mex restaurants and pizza parlours (or 'joints' as they are referred to locally), and the latter are particularly popular with children and young people, including the Americanized grandchildren who visit from time to time. However, the city also has many Indian regional restaurants; one such restaurant serves dishes from Chettinad, a particular area of Tamilnadu, while north Indian foods, notably *chaat* (a Punjabi snack) and *tandoori* (food cooked in a clay oven), have become extremely popular.

There has been a very visible entry of large multinational food and drink companies, such as Kellogg's, Nestle, Coca Cola and Pepsico, into India. Even food companies which are entirely Indian-owned now market in a more sophisticated way. Packaging has become much more elaborate, and brand names, which are heavily advertised in the mass media, have become more significant. These companies have been astute in taking account of local sensibilities when marketing their foods.[11] One brand of Kellogg's cornflakes, for example, which is fortified with iron, not only claims that 'dieticians have shown that teenagers are mostly anaemic' but also calls their product *Shakti*, a term which means 'spiritual power/energy' in Hindu thought. Vegetarians' refusal to eat eggs is catered for by Baskin-Robbins advertising that its ice cream is made 'without egg'. Aside from the avoidance of forbidden foods (such as beef and ham), they have targeted certain segments of the population very successfully:

1. Young people—foods such as pizzas are presented as 'modern' and pizza parlours as places where teenagers can gather to meet their friends.
2. Mothers—certain foods are 'good for children' and will increase their growth or their intelligence because they are fortified with iron and/or vitamins.
3. The middle classes in general—these foods are well packaged and therefore deemed 'hygienic', unlike unpackaged and unprocessed food which may be 'dirty' or 'adulterated'.

The changes I have witnessed over the last three decades in relation to the kinds of foods available have been dramatic, and the complex patterns which I observed in the 1970s have become even more complex three decades later. This raises questions about why people are willing at particular points in time to make changes in their diet, to accommodate new foods, to create new orders, a question which I will be addressing for both regions in the next part of this chapter. But it also raises the question about for whom, where and why important existing patterns are retained and certain new forms are resisted (see Caplan in press).

Conceptions of Order and Disorder: The Local Response to Changes in Food

Mafia Island

I returned to Mafia Island in 2002 and again in 2004 to research local concepts of modernity, particularly through understandings of food and food security (Caplan, 2003). When asked what they saw as the major risks in their lives, most people replied that it was food security, placing it higher than endemic diseases such as malaria or HIV/AIDS. It was clear that people were struggling, some more than others, primarily because of the lack of work and cash in the local economy. Households without income-earners and with little capital found it difficult to manage; indeed, in 2004 I found some which had cut meals to one per day, otherwise subsisting on sweetened tea, usually drunk without milk, just as had the Victorian working classes (Bennett, 1982).

Whom did they blame for this situation? Primarily the government, with its free-market policies. They looked back nostalgically to the period of the 1980s when, in spite of the extreme economic hardship in Tanzania caused by a dearth of foreign exchange, or rather perhaps because of it, Mafians were able to sell their coconuts for good prices to city dwellers who could not obtain imported cooking oil and so used coconut oil instead. But they also bemoaned the quality of the newly imported food, especially rice which they were forced to buy because it was cheaper. Rice grown locally was termed 'heavy', in other words, satisfying (it 'stayed in the stomach'), whereas the rice imported from abroad had 'travelled a long way', 'sat around for years' and thus, like drugs which had passed their due date, was not good to eat.

Extract 1: Interview with MJ, a Middle-Aged Man, Mafia Island

People today don't have enough strength because they don't eat as well [as they used to do]. The food they eat comes from all over the place, some of it's alright, but some of it isn't …

Q. So is the food which is grown here better?

A. Yes, first of all it's heavy (*kizito*), the other [kind of food] is very light (*kinyepesi*). A person has to fill their stomach, but these days people don't feel satisfied! You need two kilos of rice for five children and one and a half kilos of flour daily. Furthermore often people don't eat from their morning tea until night time.

Q. So what constitutes good food?

A. I eat cassava just to fill my stomach. But the food that you really need is rice and beans. Bananas don't stay in the stomach (*hazikai tumboni*) and [just] to fill my stomach I eat porridge made of maize flour (*unga/ugali*).

Extract 2: Interview with SA, a Middle-Aged Man, Mafia Island

Q. What about the food people eat nowadays?

A. The [imported] food has its problems—it's been around for years before it gets sold. It like medicine—you shouldn't use it after its due date [has expired]. So can it be real food?

In short, imported food is not *real* food and in many respects; it symbolizes the disorder which many people on Mafia perceive to have been brought about in Tanzania by the liberalization process (*ruksa*—literally 'permission') and free market (*soko huria*). It is scarcely surprising then that, in response to my question, one man summed up the future by saying 'We will eat grass'. So for Mafians good food is above all sufficient, locally produced and fresh. For them, as for the Japanese described in the study by Ohnuki-Tierney (1993), 'rice is self'—it is the most important, ritually pure food, required for all major rituals, and used symbolically on a number of occasions. But such rice has to be produced locally, if not on Mafia, then at least nearby—Indian or Thai rice is just not the same and is still not used for rituals even if people are forced by poverty to buy it for everyday use. Thus Mafians have not accommodated the new food situation with pleasure—they eat what they deem inferior because they must.

Chennai/Madras City

When I asked people in Chennai in 1998 what they thought constituted good food, vegetables and fruit were mentioned most frequently, regardless of caste or religious background, whereas 'bad foods' mentioned by various informants included aerated drinks, frozen, fried or oily food, and food served at roadside stalls and in some restaurants.[12] In addition, many people identified two main qualities: that food should be 'modern', which for many meant 'foreign' (i.e. imported) and that it should be 'hygienic', which essentially meant packaged, as the following quotations from interviews shows:

From a Group Discussion on Food Changes Held at a Neighbourhood Women's Club, Shastri Nagar, Madras, Concerning Food That Is Imported

Q. How do people feel about so many foreign companies and multinationals coming in?

Housewife: It is no big deal. No one goes to a shop and wonders whether something is Indian-made or foreign-made. You just pick it up [and buy it]. It doesn't matter …

Teenage Boy: People here want what people in Europe have. Previously they didn't have information about what was being sold in the U.S. and Europe. Now they do. So why shouldn't we have a part of it? Why shouldn't we have a taste of it? That's the main thing.

From an Interview with a Middle-Aged Couple, 1 March 1999, Kottivakkam, Chennai

Q. Are there any food issues which worry you?

Wife: No, only that we eat good and clean food.

Q. What about foreign foods which have come in—is that a good thing?

Wife: Yes, if I see it is foreign I always buy it! It must be good, [since] the standards [there] are high.

Husband: (Jokingly) The other side of the river is always greener!

From an Interview with Supermarket Manager 1, Adayar, Madras, Concerning Food That Is Hygienic

Everything in the store is packaged—nothing should appear to be touched by the fingers. We even do some of our own packaging.

Perhaps inevitably, the search for hygiene had extended to water and bottled water, which was by this time heavily promoted and widely available.

From an Interview with Supermarket Manager 2 and Deputy Manager, Adayar, Madras

Q. Do you sell bottled water?

A. Yes, lots of it, the usage is increasing, because as soon as someone has an upset stomach that is what the doctors recommend.

Q. But I understand that bottled water is very expensive. It costs more than milk, doesn't it?

A. (They look at each other). It's true, it is very expensive and actually it isn't always purer than any other.

But many, especially older people, also regretted the innovations: 'Nothing tastes like fresh home cooking'; 'Aerated drinks are bad for health'.

From an Interview with a Housewife

Q. What foods are bad?

A. Pepsi, Coke, I don't like those aerated drinks—and they have something in them, what is it? Caffeine? Yes that's right. But they insist on buying them, just yesterday I had a fight with him [son] about it. So I do buy the large bottles for the house.

There were clearly often tensions between the generations in this regard, and in many three-generation families, considerable differences in taste had to be catered for. Most children and young people now eat cereals (cornflakes, 'chocos', etc.) for breakfast, but older people continue to prefer their *iddlies*. A few informants extrapolated from the kinds of food changes they observed to make observations on the changes in lifestyle of which they were symptomatic. Older women bemoaned the tendency of younger ones to take short cuts with their cooking but recognized that, given the pressures on their time and the relative dearth of servants (compared with the old days), such a trend was inevitable.

From an Interview with the Same Housewife

I don't know if my son is going to find a girl [wife] who will be willing to cook for him in the way that I did. All the girls [women] these days are working and want convenience foods.

Others stated that they were unsure how much India's economy was benefiting from the use of imported foods, or foods produced in India under foreign licences or collaborative arrangements.

From a Discussion with Two Neighbours Who Are Housewives

Q. What do you think about all these new Western foods coming in?

A.   It is both good and bad: good that we have new things, bad that we are being exploited. Collaboration [with foreign companies] is good if we Indians hold a majority of the shares.

However, few of the people I interviewed were aware of the kinds of protests which were taking place in other parts of India against McDonalds, and, more recently, against Coca-Cola, which is accused of divesting huge areas of their water supply because of the needs of their bottling plants.[13] Rather, middle-class people in southern Chennai saw the changes in food policies which allowed for a much wider variety of food, at least some of which is imported, as a sign that India was now part of the modern world.

Yet things are not quite so simple. Much depends on context. It is fine to eat a pizza in a restaurant, but none would (yet) dream of serving a pizza on a ritual occasion such as a wedding. Further, the increase in eating out as a family has meant that differences between 'inside' and 'outside' food have become greater. The following interview excerpt is with a non-Brahmin women's club member describing her family's preferences at home and outside.

From an interview with a Women's Club Member

Q. Do you eat out?

A.   Yes, we are members of the [mixed-sex residents'] club in the neighbouring suburb [which has a restaurant] and go there frequently. One of the reasons is that my husband and children like to eat chicken or fish occasionally, whereas in the house they are pure vegetarians. Also they like to have a change—different kinds of food such as Chinese ('not cooked by Chinese, but Indian Chinese') which are served there.

Furthermore, while older people tend to stick to what they know, rather than experimenting like younger ones do, paradoxically, most 'ready-meals' delivered to the house are ordered by those same older people whose children are now resident in the United States and who lack the kind of care they might have expected in a joint family household.[14] The status of the cooks of such meals may be flagged up in the adverts which appear regularly in the local *Adayar Times* newspaper such as the following:

> We will arrange [a] Brahmin cook on [a] monthly basis and [deliver] order[ed] meals also Iyangar's catering … tasty, homely north and south Indian meals, home delivery, party functions orders taken.

In the latter case, the very name of the enterprise, Iyangar, which is one of the two kinds of Tamil Brahmins, signals its caste status, although its clients might well come from other caste backgrounds.

In a group discussion at the local women's club, I asked for more information about this new practice:

Club member A: I know a woman who uses this daily. She is a doctor and so is her husband, the children eat at her mother's house every day, but her food comes in a tiffin-carrier at 2 p.m. so she comes back for lunch, which is ready, and whatever is left over she takes for dinner.

Q. So what is that system called?

A. It's just catering, house catering.

Club member B: When we did not have a servant for two or three months we used that system. They will come and deliver; in some places you have to go and fetch it.

The changes which I have described here have thus resulted in various forms of accommodation, and we find new orders of food emerging alongside the existing ones. While middle-class people have, with varying degrees of enthusiasm, adopted new foods, this has been facilitated by food manufacturers and retailers taking care not to step over the line. Ice cream is advertised as 'eggless', as are many cakes, while most restaurants are either vegetarian or do not sell either beef or pork dishes. What appeared, however, to be the most significant factor for my informants was that they could now eat, if they chose to do so, like the rest of the world: 'These days, you can get *anything* in Madras,' I was often told. This powerfully signified that India, which had once banned Coke and Pepsi, had taken its rightful place in the global community.

Conclusion—So Who Benefits?

Although I have not carried out research on peasant farmers in India, there is a large literature which suggests that they have not benefited greatly from the changes of recent decades, and indeed, it is from their ranks that most recent protest movements centred on food rights have come.[15] Conversely, had I carried out research on the middle classes in Dar es Salaam, I suspect there might well have been a different set of responses to those obtained on Mafia. From my own observations in the city, as well as the comments of Tanzanian friends and colleagues, it is clear that in the last decade, not only have Coke and Pepsi become ubiquitous in Tanzania, but in the commercial capital Dar es Salaam, there has been an enormous proliferation of supermarkets, stocked with every conceivable food, mostly from South Africa. Such stores are patronized not only by foreigners such as tourists and expatriates, but also by the new middle class of Tanzanians. In short, then, class, as well as location and culture, plays an important part in determining how new foods will be received.

So to what extent do people in the two areas discussed in this chapter feel that their diets have benefited from processes stemming from globalization, such as economic liberalization? Clearly for most Mafians, the answer is that they have not, and they see their diets as having worsened both in quality and quantity. Perhaps what is more important is that there is little they can do about it, given the constraints on their lives. Whether they like rice from abroad or not, their poverty dictates that they buy the cheapest available. They see their current predicament as evidence that the government is not looking after them as they believe it should, that they are not in control of their lives—in short, that there is a situation of disorder. They do not accept this passively, since they constantly analyse the reasons for it and attempt to mitigate its effects by, for example, ensuring that locally grown, not imported, rice is consumed at rituals such as weddings, but their poverty precludes total resistance to cheaper imported rice.

For middle-class residents of Madras-Chennai, on the other hand, economic liberalization has meant a huge increase in the variety of foods they can eat, both inside and outside the home, including many more convenience foods to different kinds. Most argued that this was an unmitigated blessing. But then they are in the fortunate position of being able to choose whether or not to adopt new foods, to eat traditional foods, or even to eat both kinds in different contexts. Members of the professional middle classes in Chennai consider themselves to be both Tamil/Indian and also part of a global system in which they want to occupy a prominent place. They are less likely to challenge the free market economy or to question the import of food than are, for example, farmers who have lost livelihoods, as many have in India, just as they have on Mafia.

In short, awareness of the consequences of globalization stems, unsurprisingly, from people's personal experience, which is largely determined by their positions in the local, regional, national and global socioeconomic orders. While it would be wrong to deny people agency in either location, it would be equally wrong to assume that people always have a choice in what they eat. We may perhaps see food systems as in constant tension between order and disorder, with people attempting to resist disorder and seeking greater order by making sense of changes and attempting to incorporate them into local systems of meaning and values. What I have tried to show in this chapter is that, perhaps unsurprisingly, wealth, class and power are crucial determinants in their ability to do this.

Notes

An earlier version of this chapter was published in *Sociological Research Online,* 11/4, <http://www.socresonline.org.uk/11/4/caplan.html>.

1. Fieldwork in Tanzania has been funded by a variety of sources: the Economic and Social Research Council (ESRC), the Worshipful Company of Gold-smiths, the University of London, the Nuffield Foundation and the Lever-hulme Trust.

2. Fieldwork in Madras-Chennai has been funded by the ESRC and the Lever-hulme and Nuffield Foundations.

3. In this respect, their argument is not new. In the introduction to his book on the effects of the entry of McDonalds into south-east Asia, Watson (1997) argues that people do not accept changes in food habits passively—they 'domesticate' new foods like those sold by McDonalds.

4. In this section I consider only the situation on Mafia; for an account of Tanzania more generally, see Bryceson (1990).

5. Under both the German and British colonial regimes, district officers were re-sponsible for keeping the district book, which had information on population, customs, flora, fauna, agriculture and many other topics. The district books are now housed in the National Archives in Dar es Salaam.

6. See Bryceson (1980, 1990) for Tanzania as a whole.

7. *Swadeshi*—literally 'own country'—promulgated the view that Indians could and should be self-sufficient and should fulfil their own needs rather than rely-ing on imports.

8. PL (Public Law) 480 in the United States allowed for the export of American wheat (of which there was a considerable surplus) to selected recipients in re-turn for payment in rupees, instead of dollars. The ensuing rupee money was used to support much research by U.S. scholars in India.

9. Even if they do not own land, all Tamilians have a 'native place', where their ancestors came from and where their family deity's temple is still located. Tamilian notions of the body include the idea that substance is derived at least in part from food and water ingested (Daniel, 1984). One couple whom I in-terviewed in 1998 stated that they recently bought some land outside Madras in order to get rice from it, telling me 'It is rain-fed [in Tamil 'sky dependent'] land, but there is a good well for irrigation'.

10. The work of Finkelstein (1989) and Martens and Warde (1987) offers a com-parison with the growth in eating out in the West.

11. A similar situation is discussed in Watson's (1997) collection on the impact of the entry of McDonalds into south-east Asia.

12. Compare Mukhopadhyay (2004) for a similar view from Calcutta.

13. There have been regular reports in the British press. See, for example, Brown (2003), Vidal (2003), Paul (2006) or Mathiason (2006).

14. Although they may be unhappy at being left alone by their children, they admit that they themselves encouraged their migration in the first place, as they wished to see them doing well in the world.
15. Notably in the writing of Vandana Shiva (e.g. 1989), Akhil Gupta (1998) and J. Scott (1985). See also the recent special edition of the *Economic and Political Weekly* on suicides among Indian farmers (e.g. Vaiyanathan, 2006).

References

Bauman, Z. (2002), 'After the Nation-State—What?', in J. Beynon and D. Dunkerley (eds.), *Globalization: The Reader,* London: The Athlone Press.

Bennett, J. (1982), *Plenty and Want: A Social History of Diet in England from 1815 to the Present Day,* London: Methuen.

Brown, P. (2003), 'Coca-Cola in India Accused of Leaving Farms Parched and Land Poisoned', *Guardian* (25 July), <http://www.guardian.co.uk/environment/2003/jul/25/water.india>.

Bryceson, D. (1980), 'Changes in Peasant Food Production and Food Supply in Relation to the Historical Development of Commodity Production in Pre-colonial and Colonial Tanganyika', *Journal of Peasant Studies,* 7/3: 281–309.

Bryceson, D. (1990), *Food Insecurity and the Social Division of Labour in Tanzania, 1919–85,* Basingstoke, Hants: Macmillan.

Caplan, P. (1975), *Choice and Constraint in a Swahili Community,* Oxford: Oxford University Press for the International African Institute.

Caplan, P. (1985), *Class and Gender in India: Women and Their Organisations in a South Indian City,* London: Tavistock Publications.

Caplan, P. (2001), 'Food in Middle-Class Households in Madras, 1974–94', in B.C.A. Walraven and K. Cwiertka (eds.), *Food in Asia: the Global and the Local,* Richmond: Curzon Press.

Caplan, P. (2003), *Local Understandings of Modernity: Food and Food Security on Mafia Island, Tanzania,* (Report Presented to the Tanzania Commission for Science and Technology), <http://www.goldsmiths.ac.uk/department/anthropology/staff/pat-caplan/project-Tanzania-modernity.pdf>.

Caplan, P. (2008), 'Crossing the Veg/Non-Veg Divide: Practising Commensality Among Middle Class Women in Chennai', *South Asia: Journal of South Asian Studies,* 31/1: 118–42.

Caplan, P. (in press). 'Welcome to the Way the World Lives': Constructions of Cosmopolitan Identities Through Food in Urban South India' to appear in Rai, Krishnendu and Tulasi Srinivas, (eds.) 'Curried Cultures', University of California Press.

Daniel, E. V. (1984), *Fluid Signs: Being a Person the Tamil Way,* Berkeley: University of California Press.

Douglas, M. (1970), *Purity and Danger,* Harmondsworth: Penguin Books

Eriksen, T. H. (2003), *Globalization: Studies in Anthropology,* London: Pluto Press.

Finkelstein, J. (1989), *Dining Out: A Sociology of Modern Manners,* New York: New York University Press.

Fischler, C. (1980), 'Food Habits, Social Change and the Nature-Culture Debate', *Social Science Information,* 19/6: 937–53.

Fischler, C. (1988), 'Food, Self and Identity', *Social Science Information,* 27/2: 275–92.

Gupta, A. (1998), *Postcolonial Developments: Agriculture in the Making of Modern India,* Durham: Duke University Press.

Inda, J. X., and Rosaldo, R. (2002), 'Introduction: A World in Motion', in J. X. Inda and R. Rosaldo (eds.), *The Anthropology of Globalization: A Reader,* Oxford: Blackwell Publishing.

Martens, L., and Warde, A. (1997), 'Urban Pleasure: On the Meaning of Eating Out in a Northern City', in P. Caplan, ed., *Food, Health and Identity,* London: Routledge.

Mathiason, N. (2006) 'Coke "Drinks India Dry" ', *The Observer* (19 March), <http://www.guardian.co.uk/money/2006/mar/19/business.india1>.

Middleton, J. (1992), *The World of the Swahili: An African Mercantile Civilization,* New Haven: Yale University Press.

Mintz, S. (1985), *Sweetness and Power: The Place of Sugar in Modern Industry,* New York: Viking Press.

Mukhopadhyay, B. (2004), 'Between Elite Hysteria and Subaltern Carnivalesque: The Politics of Street-Food in the City of Calcutta', *South Asia Research,* 24/1: 37–50.

Ohnuki-Tierney, E. (1993), *Rice as Self: Japanese Identities Through Time,* Princeton: Princeton University Press.

Paul, A. (2006) 'Drawing a Line with Coke', *Red Pepper* (March): 7.

Richards, A. (1939), *Land, Labour and Diet in Northern Rhodesia,* London: Routledge and Kegan Paul.

Scott, J. C. (1985), *Weapons of the Weak: Everyday Forms of Peasant Resistance,* New Haven: Yale University Press.

Shiva, V. (1989), *The Violence of the Green Revolution,* London: Zed Press.

Vaiyanathan, A. (2006), 'Farmers' Suicides and Agrarian Crisis', *Economic and Political Weekly,* 41/38: 4009–13.

Vidal, J. (2003), 'Coke on Trial as Indian Villagers Accuse Plant of Sucking Them Dry', *Guardian* (19 November), <http://www.guardian.co.uk/world/2003/nov/19/india.johnvidal>.

Watson, J. L. (1997), *Golden Arches East: McDonald's in East Asia,* Stanford: Stanford University Press.

Watson, J. L., and Caldwell, M. L. (eds.) (2005), *The Cultural Politics of Food and Eating: A Reader,* Maldon: Blackwell.

Index

agribusiness, 4–5
  exploitation, 15
  factory-farming, 14, 22
  food-chain crises, 20
  globalization, 6, 13–14
  innovations, 14
  labor, 15
  organic food, 83
  public opinion, 20
  TNCs, 14
  urbanization and, 13–14
agriculture history, 10–11
AHS. *see* American Heart Society
ALOP. *see* appropriate level of protection
alternative food, emerging markets, 81–2
alternative food movements, 124–5
Alternative Trade Organization (ATO), 143
American gourmet culture
  American classics, 170–3
  banal nationalism, 164–6
  cosmopolitanism, 165–7, 177–9
  culinary discourse, 162
  discursive mappings, 172
  ethnic cuisine, 175–7
  exotic cuisine, 166
  food magazines, 163
  gourmet food writing, 167–79
  holiday food, 168–70
  July 4th, 168
  national cuisine, 163–4
  national imagery, 168–71, 173–5
  nationalism and, 163–5
  rural America, 173–7
  shared culinary experience, 168–9
  social constructions, 164, 166
  Thanksgiving, 168–70
American Heart Society (AHS), 261
animal rights groups, 22

Animal, Vegetable, Miracle: A Year of Food Life
  (Kingsolver), 85
Antonito, 243
  diet, 246–8
  food meanings, 249–51
  Fourth of July foods, 244–8
  gardening, meat production, 248–9
  homemade foods, 249
Appellation d'Origine Controlée (AOC), 84, 91
appropriate level of protection (ALOP), 72, 75
AQIS. *see* Australian Quarantine and Inspection
  Service
aquaculture, 65
ARCI Gola, 47–9
Ark of Taste, 53
Atlantic salmon
  Australia, 70–7
  economies *vs.* ecologies, 77
  genetic modification, 66–7
  globalization, 65–6
  global production, 65–6
  locality variations, 68
  Tasmania, 67–72, 74–7
  transnational flows, 67
ATO. *see* Alternative Trade Organization
Australia
  Atlantic salmon, 70–7
  IRA, 70–2
  organic food market, 206
  WTO *vs.*, 70–2
Australian Quarantine and Inspection Service
  (AQIS), 70–3, 75
avian flu, 19

Belize, 193–4
blue revolution, 65–6
Boltanski Thévenot framework, GVC, 100–1
Bon Appétit, 51, 163

Bové, Jose, 25, 59–60
bovine spongiform encephalopathy (BSE),
    51, 86–7, 231
Bread for the World, 262
Bruni, Frank, 213
BSE. *see* bovine spongiform encephalopathy

Cafédirect, 143–52
Chernobyl disaster, 48
Clairborne, Craig, 216–20
class issues, 57–8
Codex Alimentarius, 19
The Communist Manifesto (Marx), 6
community supported agriculture (CSA), 264
Compassion in World Farming, 19
Confédération Paysanne (CP), 58–60, 87
consumer brands, 7
Cooper, Alice, 189–90
Corn Laws, 10
crises and critiques, 17–23
CSA. *see* community supported agriculture
The Culinary Revolution after 1945 (Panayi), 230

Decanter, 106

Edible Schoolyard, 125–6
Equal Exchange, 132
ethnographic studies, 26
European Peasant Coordination, 58
European Union (EU), 16, 49, 52
expatriate home cooking, 221–3

Fairtrade food
    ATOs, 143
    Cafédirect, 143–52
    certification, 140
    coffee, 143–52
    conventional trade *vs.,* 142
    cultural connections, 151–2
    defined, 140
    economics, 150–1
    ethics, 147–8
    FLO International, 140, 149–50
    growth, 142–4
    history, 139
    marketing, 146, 148
    NGOs, 142, 144, 149
    politics, 148–9

        practices, 15
        principles, 140
        producers *vs.* consumers, 144–53
        products, 139
        social connections, 146–7
        supermarket distribution, 143–4
        trade organizations, 143
        UK sector, 139
Fairtrade Foundation, 140, 145
famines, 17
FAO. *see* Food and Agriculture Organization
farmers' markets, 85
Faucheurs Volontaires, 87
fish consumption, 21, 23–4
FLO International, 140, 149–50
FNSEA. *see* National Federated Union of
    Agricultural Enterprises
food
    choice, 197, 205
    critics, 167–79, 213–21
    expatriate home cooking, 221–3
    fast food, 4, 25–6, 259
    food-chain crises, 20
    food miles, 85, 131–2
    global regimes, 14
    global systems, 13–17
    order, disorder, 281–2
    politics, 274
    prohibitions, 22
    recalls, 86
    riots, 17
    safety, 284
    security, 17, 86, 140–1, 281–2
Food and Agriculture Organization (FAO),
    19, 62, 65, 141
food globalization
    academic inquiries, 5–9
    early *vs.* late modern, 12–13
    Fairtrade food and, 141–2
    historical, 10–14
    pluralities, contradictions, 4–5
The FoodRoutes Network, 91
food traditions
    class differentiation, 192–3, 240
    European, 189–90
    immigration and, 186–7, 192–4
    indigenous *vs.* foreign, 189–90
    national identity and, 188

neophilia, 189, 192–4
neophobia, 186–8, 192–4
social competition, 190–1
social science and, 185–6
Food & Wine, 172
Foundation for Diversity, 53
France
agricultural biotechnology, 58–9
diet, 90
food labels, 89, 91
gastronomic tourism, 88–9
GM foods, 27
GMO laws, 87
local food, 83–5, 91, 93
McDonald's, 26–7
national cuisine, 235–40
patrimoine, 91
terroir, 90, 240
fusion cuisines, 12

Gambero Rosso, 45
gastronomic tourism, 88–9
General Agreement on Tariffs and Trade
(GATT), 19
genetically engineered (GE) foods, 204–7
genetically modified (MON810) corn seed, 87
genetically modified (GM) foods, 20–1, 27,
204–7
genetically modified organisms (GMOs)
European activism, 87
France, 58–9, 87
unwanted crop dissemination, 87
globalization
agribusiness, 6, 13–14
anthropology of, 273
communications, 259
complexities, 6–9
cultural responses, 8
defined, 6–9, 227, 255
economic liberalization *vs.,* 275, 287
food, drink, 258–60
history, 10–13
national identification *vs.,* 231–2
obesity, 256–8
physical activity, 260–1
political dimensions, 6–7
virtuous, 45
Global Value Chain (GVC) analysis

Boltanski Thévenot framework, 100–1
convention theory and quality, 99–102
justification systems, 99–100
lead firms, 98–9
power/reward distribution, governance, 98–9
quality convention framework, 100–2
value chains *vs.* markets, 98
wine trade, 102–11
global warming, 18
GM. *see* genetically modified foods
GMOs. *see* genetically modified organisms
Good Food Club, 229
Gourmet and *Food & Wine,* 163
gourmet food writing, 167–79
grain cultivation, 10–11
Greenpeace, 87, 205
Green Revolution, India, 279
Grupo Maseca, 57
Guide, 228–9, 233–4
Guide Londres, 239

Hall of Tastes, 53
Herbarius (Paracelsus), 189
homogenization *vs.* heterogenization
culture, 7–8, 23, 27–8, 228, 239–40
wine trade, 24, 110–11

IBS. *see* International Business Service
Il Manifesto, 45
import risk analysis (IRA), 70–5
India
Chennai, 279–81, 283–6
food safety, 284
foreign, multinational food companies,
280–1, 283
generational differences, 284–6
Green Revolution, 279
house catering system, 286
population segments, 281
supermarkets, 280
Tamil cooking, 279–80
Indian food
Bengali-American, 221–3
Clairborne reviews, 216–20
cost, 213
demographics, 213–14
fine-dining and, 214–21
Manhattan restaurants, 213–21

INTELSAT, 259
International Business Service (IBS), 259
International Obesity Taskforce, 262
International Rice Research Institute, 262
International Telecommunications Satellite
    Organization, 259
Inventing the Indigenous (Cooper), 190
IR-8, 262
IRA. *see* import risk analysis
Italian Communist Party, 46
Italy Daily, 46

July 4th, 168, 243–8

Kentucky Fried Chicken, 7, 24
Kenya, 15
Kingsolver, Barbara, 85

labor, 15, 58–9
Lafargue, Paul, 56
La Gola, 57
lardo di Colonnata, 49–53
La Republica, 51
Linnaeus, 190
local food, 30–1
    agri-global marketplace and, 90–1
    authenticity, 87–9
    boundaries, 92–3
    consumer education, 90–1
    cultural packaging, 88–9
    defined, 82–3
    food miles, 85, 131–2
    global context, 93
    global food problems and, 85–7
    institutional challenges, 92
    institutional classification, 84
    market exchange spaces, 84–5
    marketing, 85–7, 126–8
    national certification programs, 90–1
    safety, risks, 86–7
    social change and, 85–6
    social, environmental value, 82, 91–2
    sustainable agriculture and, 83
    U.S. *vs.* France, 83–5, 90
local food, scale theory
    capitalization, 123–5
    ecological sustainability, 126, 129
    empirical findings, 118–19

exchange systems, 130
    fluid *vs.* fixed scale, 120–2
    food quality, human health, 130–2
    food systems activism, 124–33
    geopolitics, 121
    localization arguments, 126, 129–33
    local trap, 118–20, 123–6
    national strategies, 130
    overview, 117–18
    relationships among scales, 122–3
    scale as strategy, 120–1
    scale research, geography, 120–3
    scale structure, 120–2
    Slow Food and, 125
    social construction, 120–1
    social, ecological outcomes, 119
    social, economic justice, 129–30

Maastricht Accord (1992), 49
mad-cow disease. *see* bovine spongiform
    encephalopathy
Marfia Island, 275–8, 281–3
Martins, Patrick, 132
Marx, Karl, 6
McDonald's, 7, 23, 264
    French, 26
    global icon, 24–6
    Spanish Steps, 46
media, 7
    crisis portrayal, 17–18
    imperialism, 227
    obesity and, 261
    Slow Food, 54
Mediterranean diet, 29, 201–4
Mexico
    culinary modernism, 57
    Grupo Maseca, 57
    Slow Food, 57–8
    tortilla production, 57
Meyer, Danny, 213
MON810. *see* genetically modified
    corn seed
Moskin, Julia, 213

National Federated Union of Agricultural
    Enterprises (FNSEA), 58
National Milling Corporation, 278
Newman, Penny, 146

The New York Times, 51, 86, 132, 213
nutrition
  GE, GM foods, 204–7
  global citizenship and, 197, 200–1
  global health and, 200–1
  as governance, 198
  historical foundations, 197
  Mediterranean diet, 201–4
  organic foods, 206–7
  risk ethic, 198–201, 207–8
  sustainability and, 199–200
  UN criteria, 17
Nyerere, Julius, 277

obesity, 22–3
  chronic disease and, 256
  fast food and, 259
  global interventions, 261–5
  globalization of, 256–7
  historical, 256–7
  incidence *vs.* prevalence, 257
  measurements, 255–6
  population segments, 257
  scientific studies, 256–7
Office International des Epitoozes (OIE),
  72, 74
OIE Animal Health Code, 74
The Omnivores Dilemma (Pollan), 85
organic food, 21, 83, 132

Pacific fishing industry, 17
Panayi, Panikos, 229–32
Paracelsus, 189–90
Parker, Robert, 16, 106–7
patrimonialization, 91
Pavese, Cesare, 47
Petrini, Carlo, 46–7, 52–3, 60
Pizza Hut, 7
Pollan, Michael, 85
Postgate, Raymond, 229
Presidia initiative, 53

Radio Bra Onde Rosse, 47
Red Brigades, 46
Red Tomato, 132
Reisal, Rene, 59
Revelli, Nuto, 47
The Right to Be Lazy (Lafargue), 56

Rockefeller Foundation, 262
Roman Empire, 11

Salone del Gusto, 53
Sanitary and Phytosanitary Agreement (SPS),
  71–3, 75
Saveur, 163
seed banks, 20
Seven Countries Study, 201
Slow Food, 4, 30, 132
  Australia, 56
  class issues, 57–8
  critics, 55–8
  endangered foods campaign, 49–53
  generational politics, 61
  goals, 45–6
  lardo di Colonnata, 49–53
  local trap and, 125
  media, 54
  membership, 54
  Mexico, 57–8
  national associates, 54
  olive oil marketing, 57
  origins, 45–9
  politics, 55–6
  projects, initiatives, 52–4
  Slow Cities campaign, 56
  success, 54
  TNCs *vs.,* 263–4
Slow Guide to Sydney, 56
Slow Life, 55–6
South America, 12–13
Spanish empire, 12
Spicing Up Britain (Panayi), 229
SPS. *see* Sanitary and Phytosanitary Agreement
standards, defined, 72–3
Starbucks, 7, 26
sustainability
  agriculture, 83
  local food, scale theory, 126, 129
  Mediterranean diet, 203
  nutrition, 199–200

Tanzania
  food imports, 278
  local diets, 279
  Marfia Island, 275–8, 281–3
  National Milling Corporation, 278

Tasmania, 67–72, 74–7
Tassal, 69
Terre Madre: World Meeting of Food
    Communities, 53–4
terroir, 90, 107
Tim Hortons, 165
transnational corporations (TNCs), 14, 258–64
transnational tobacco companies (TNTCs), 262,
    264–5
True Food Guide (Greenpeace), 205

United Kingdom (UK), 228–35, 238–40
United Nations (UN), nutrition criteria, 17
United States (U.S.)
    farmers' markets, 85
    food certification, 90–1
    institutional challenges, 92
    local food, 83–5
    trade wars, 16
UPITN, 259
Urban Organic, 132

Veronelli, Luigi, 47
Via Campesina, 58
VISNEWS, 259

Waters, Alice, 125
WHO Global Strategy on Diet, Physical
    Activity and Health, 262
Wine Spectator, 106
wine trade, 15

AOC system, 84
basic quality wines, 109–10
best-selling brands, 103–4
branding, 108
competition, 108
France, 90–1
general trends, 97
GVC analysis, 98–111
history, 97
homogenization *vs.* heterogenization,
    24, 110–11
industry concentration, 97, 102–3
international, 97
mid-range wines, 107–9
Parker, 106–7
product flow, GVC model,
    102–4
production, consumption, 97
quality verification systems, 108
terroir, 107
top quality wines, 106–7
world's top 10 wine marketers, 104
World Bank, 6
World Trade Organization (WTO),
    5, 19
    ALOP, 72, 75
    Australia *vs.,* 70–2
    quarantine standards, 72–3

Zagat, 213
Zuni Cafe, 177